EDITED BY
Nat Wright,
Clare Gerada and
Laura Sheard

RCGP Guide to The Management of Substance Misuse in Primary Care

Second Edition

Royal College of General Practitioners

The Royal College of General Practitioners was founded in 1952 with this object:

'To encourage, foster and maintain the highest possible standards in general practice and for that purpose to take or join with others in taking steps consistent with the charitable nature of that object which may assist towards the same.'

Among its responsibilities under its Royal Charter the College is entitled to:

'Diffuse information on all matters affecting general practice and issue such publications as may assist the object of the College.'

British Library Cataloguing-in-Publication Data
A catalogue record for this book is available from the British Library

© Royal College of General Practitioners, 2013
Published by the Royal College of General Practitioners, 2013
30 Euston Square, London NW1 2FB

DISCLAIMER
This publication is intended for the use of medical practitioners in the UK and not for patients. The authors, editors and publisher have taken care to ensure that the information contained in this book is correct to the best of their knowledge, at the time of publication. Whilst efforts have been made to ensure the accuracy of the information presented, particularly that related to the prescription of drugs, the authors, editors and publisher cannot accept liability for information that is subsequently shown to be wrong. Readers are advised to check that the information, especially that related to drug usage, complies with information contained in the *British National Formulary*, or equivalent, or manufacturers' datasheets, and that it complies with the latest legislation and standards of practice.

Designed and typeset by Typographic Design Unit

Printed by Hobbs

Indexed by Susan Leech

ISBN: 978-0-85084-345-3

Contents

Editors

Dr Nat Wright FRCGP PhD is the Clinical Director for Vulnerable Groups at NHS Leeds. He has worked with drug users for almost 20 years in both community primary care and secure-environment settings. Between 2003 and 2010 he held various positions as a government GP adviser with a remit to support GPs working in both mainstream primary care and secure environments. He is a regular contributor to the development of national and international guidelines pertaining to the care of drug users. He is currently a member of the RCGP Substance Misuse Unit Executive Committee and also the RCGP Secure Environments Group. He is also the clinical lead for the RCGP Certificate in Substance Misuse Part 2 course. From 2003–8 he was the Chair of the RCGP Health Inequalities Standing Group. He has published extensively on issues relating to the care of drug users.

Prof. Clare Gerada MBE FRCP (Hon) FICS FRCGP (Hon) FRCPsych has held a number of local and national leadership positions, including Director of Primary Care for the National Clinical Governance Team and Senior Medical Adviser to the Department of Health. She is Medical Director of the Practitioner Health Programme and has published a number of academic papers, articles, books and chapters. Clare has been a GP since 1992, when she became a partner for the Hurley Clinic in South London. The practice started life in 1969, and remains on its original site, located on the ground floor of a 19-storey housing estate in Lambeth. Clare has a long involvement with the RCGP and established its groundbreaking Substance Misuse Unit. She became Chair of Council in November 2010, having previously been Vice Chair of College Council and a former Chair of the Ethics Committee. Prior to general practice, she worked in psychiatry at the Maudsley Hospital in South London, specialising in substance misuse. She has been awarded an MBE for services to medicine and the treatment of substance misuse.

Laura Sheard PhD is a sociologist and a health services researcher. She spent the first six years of her career conducting research with injecting drug users and prisoners. This entailed in-depth qualitative research and several randomised controlled trials comparing opiate detoxification agents. Laura undertook her doctoral research at the University of Leeds and was awarded her PhD (sociology) in 2010. Since then, she has worked on varied health research projects concerning: cancer-associated thrombosis; open surgical wounds; and patient safety on hospital wards. She has published 23 articles to date on a wide variety of topics.

Preface

Almost every day in our surgeries, GPs and practice teams witness the destructive effect that drug and alcohol dependence have on individuals, families and wider society.

This new resource will provide invaluable support to health professionals working with and caring for those patients with drug problems within primary care. The comprehensive text has been written by experts in the field who have struggled with the issues presented by people using uncontrolled drugs. What is evident is that they continued to engage with drug users, determined to find practical and pragmatic ways of improving the quality of life for those using their services.

Having worked with drug users for over 20 years, I know how far primary care has progressed in the management of drug dependence. Gone are the days when the primary care response to issues posed by illicit drug use was limited to a handful of enthusiasts working with an extremely limited evidence base.

This guide brings together the wealth of knowledge and experience that is now found in the 'family' of primary care practitioners working with drug users. I recommend it to those starting out in their careers working with drug users, and to those who have been working with drug users for many years and are seeking an update on current policy, practice and evidence.

I hope that the learning presented here will translate into improved primary care provision for drug users, as well as addressing health inequalities in their localities.

Clare Gerada

Acknowledgements

Nat would like to thank Ruth Fleming for her tenacity, persistence and organisational skills in keeping the editors to task in what proved to be a huge and demanding editorial undertaking. Without Ruth's input this edition would not have been published within the tight timescales.

CHAPTER 1

Overview of dependence, treatment and outcome

Clare Gerada and Nat Wright

IN THIS CHAPTER

Introduction || Terminology || Classification of substance misuse and dependence || Natural history of drug use || Principles of treatment || Practical aspects of prescribing || Improving the outcome of treatment || Conclusion

Introduction

Because drug users are a heterogeneous group of people there is no one-fits-all method of treatment. Treatment needs to be flexible enough to cater for the differences within this group while ensuring that any intervention is evidence based and effective. The treatment for drug use goes beyond the prescription of medication, although prescribing remains a powerful and effective intervention. The primary care team is well placed to deal with many of the physical, psychological and social needs of the drug user.

Terminology

In the field of addiction there are a number of terms currently in use to describe the taking of both illicit and licit drugs; the terminology changes over time, often dictated by the prevailing mood of political correctness. For example, the term 'addict' was a medical term used to distinguish those who used drugs owing to a medically defined dependence as opposed to the criminal context of drug use. Since then, the term addict has developed derogatory connotations and has been replaced by various differing terms such as user, misuser, abuser, problem drug user, dependent user and so on, each meant to distinguish different consequences of use – from non-problematic 'use' through to problematic 'misuse' or dependence.

Throughout this book the authors have tried to be consistent: using the word 'substance' to describe licit (legal) or illicit (illegal) products, including alcohol and nicotine; using the term 'drug' to describe mainly illicit products such as opioids, cannabis and stimulants, though also included are benzodiazepines that are not prescribed; and using the term 'medicines' to describe any prescribed products.

Opioid vs. opiate

The term opioid indicates not only the naturally occurring opiates, which are derived from the opium poppy, but also their synthetic analogues such as methadone and pethidine.

Patient, client, substance user

As with the terminology describing the behaviour of taking drugs, there has also been confusing and conflicting terminology describing the person entering drug and/or alcohol treatment services.

A study undertaken in a large treatment centre asked service users which name they preferred between 'client', 'patient' or 'service user'. The majority preferred the term 'patient'. They were also asked if they considered themselves to have mental health problems. The majority (59%) felt that 'substance misuse' was in the category of mental health problems, though paradoxically most did not consider themselves to have a mental health problem. Broadly similar results were found for those attending alcohol services, but not tobacco cessation services.[1]

Classification of substance misuse and dependence

As there is a variety of terms to describe substance use so there is a spectrum of substance use behaviours, and over time clinicians and researchers have taken different approaches to understanding and describing them. The dependence syndrome was first proposed for alcohol use and is now incorporated in both the World Health Organization (WHO) tenth revision of the International Classification of Diseases (ICD)[2] and the US fourth edition of the Diagnostic and Statistical Manual (DSM)[3] classification systems (the eleventh revision of the ICD is due for publication in 2015 and the fifth edition of the DSM is due for publication in 2013).

The latest versions of both these systems (ICD-10 and DSM-IV) use the same approach to both alcohol and drugs of use (including nicotine), and both systems make a distinction between the dependence syndrome and other harmful patterns of substance use (see below for definitions and diagnostic criteria). The criteria for the dependence syndrome are similar in the two systems (though this has not always been the case). The criteria for the categories 'harmful use' (ICD-

10) and 'substance abuse' (DSM-IV) differ, with the emphasis on negative social consequences of substance use in the DSM classification, and on the physical and mental health consequences in the ICD-10 classification (see Box 1.1).

Box 1.1 **Drugs recognised by ICD-10**

✓ Alcohol.

✓ Opioids (including naturally occurring opiates, synthetic or semisynthetic opiates, and opiate agonist-antagonists).

✓ Cannabinoids.

✓ Sedative hypnotics.

✓ Cocaine.

✓ Other stimulants (including amphetamines, anorectic drugs, khat).

✓ Hallucinogens.

✓ Tobacco.

✓ Volatile solvents.

✓ Multiple drug use and other psychoactive drugs.

Dependence, neuroadaptation, tolerance

The terms 'addiction' and 'dependence' are often used interchangeably to describe a constellation of behavioural, physical and psychological factors associated with drug/alcohol use. Strictly speaking, the term dependence, when used alone, is a state of bodily adaptation to the presence of a particular psychoactive substance (tolerance) and manifests itself in physical disturbances or withdrawal symptoms when the drug is withdrawn. The term 'neuroadaptation' has been used to describe this phenomenon. Many, but not all, medicines cause neuroadaptation and, of those that do, not all are subject to misuse. Many people are treated for painful conditions with opioids; often they will exhibit tolerance and even experience withdrawal symptoms when stopping the drug. However, only a small proportion will become 'addicted' to the drug.

By 'addiction', or 'dependence syndrome', we mean a specific psychological state in which the drug takes up an overriding importance in the person's life. When they do not have the drug, they crave it. They plan their days around ensuring a regular supply, sometimes spending many hours obtaining their drug of desire. Other personal goals and interests no longer seem important when the supply is threatened. If they manage to stop using the drug for any length of time, relapse is followed by a rapid return of the habit at the same intensity as before the period of abstinence (reinstatement).

A dependence syndrome can occur with activities other than drugs, for example gambling, playing computer games, or even shopping. The potential of a drug to create addiction or dependence is determined by a number of factors: its potency (especially the strength of the hedonistic or pleasurable effects), the immediacy of the onset of its effect (not exclusively the property of the drug but also related to its route of use), the predictability of the effects of the drug, and its elimination half-life.

Of the illicit drugs, heroin is deemed to score highest in its addictive potential, with its most potent of opioid effects, its short elimination half-life of only a few hours and its rapid onset of action, especially after smoking or intravenous use. In comparison, methadone has a lower addictive potential, being less potent in its effect and having a slower onset of effect, particularly when taken by mouth. Not only does methadone have a lower addictive potential but it also directly reduces dependence on heroin, in so far as heroin use is often driven by the fear of, or experience of, withdrawal. Methadone reduces this fear and therefore removes the need for drug seeking.

Tolerance

Tolerance is a behavioural state: the way the body usually adapts to the repeated presence of a drug. Higher doses of the psychoactive substance are required to reproduce the original or similar effects. Tolerance may develop rapidly (to LSD, for example) or slowly (to alcohol or cannabis). The drug must be taken on a regular basis and in adequate quantities for tolerance to occur.

Tolerance can occur to different effects of the same drug. For example, a high degree of tolerance develops to the actions of opioids that cause analgesia and respiratory depression. Thus, the effects of opioids are not apparent even when the individual is consuming high daily amounts if that dose level has been reached gradually. Little or no tolerance develops to the action of opioids on the pupil size or bowel activity, however, so that the same individual usually displays a typically constricted pupil and suffers from constipation – the latter a troublesome and common complaint in patients on methadone maintenance programmes.

After a relatively short period of abstinence (for example around two weeks in the case of opioids) tolerance is lost and the dose that was taken before this period of abstinence can now prove to be a fatal overdose. Tolerance is usually a feature of a dependence syndrome.

The clinical diagnostic criteria for dependence syndrome adopted by the WHO and contained in the ICD-10 and the DSM-IV emphasise both the physical factors (such as tolerance) and psychological aspects (subjective awareness of compulsion to use, diminished capacity to control drug use and salience of drug-seeking behaviour) as important aspects of a dependence syndrome.

Validity of diagnostic categories

The concept of the dependence syndrome was originally the description given to the pattern of cognitive, behavioural and physiological symptoms seen in those who consumed alcohol over long periods of time and in large amounts. The applicability of this description when used to describe the effects of other drugs of abuse has been questioned. There is relatively little controversy regarding its use for opioid and benzodiazepine drugs, as both can produce a clear increase in tolerance and characteristic withdrawal syndromes. However, its use has been less certain for drugs such as cannabis, nicotine, cocaine and amphetamines (in 2004 the British Approved Name (BAN) for amphetamines was modified to accord with the Recommended International Non-proprietary Name (rINN), amfetamines). A large study of alcohol, opioid, cocaine and cannabis users conducted by the WHO in 12 countries found the 'dependence' and 'abuse' constructs to be broadly general across alcohol, opioids, cocaine and cannabis, but the use of this two-dimensional model was found to fit cocaine use less well than that of the other three substances.[4]

For tobacco addiction, it may be more sensible to use the terms 'dependence' and 'failed cessation' in that there is no equivalent to 'misuse' in nicotine usage (though if nicotine is ever made an illicit substance this of course could result in the user engaging in acquisitive crime to obtain it!). Recent research on cannabis use has supported the validity of the dependence syndrome, though the definition of a withdrawal syndrome remains unclear.

ICD-10 (International Classification of Diseases)

Harmful substance use

Actual damage should have been caused to the mental or physical health of the user in the absence of diagnosis of dependence syndrome.

Substance dependence (three or more in the past year)

▶ A strong desire or sense of compulsion to use.

▶ Difficulties in controlling substance-taking behaviour in terms of its onset, termination or levels of use.

▶ A physiological withdrawal state when use has ceased or been reduced, as evidenced by the characteristic withdrawal syndrome, or use with the intention of relieving or avoiding withdrawal symptoms.

▶ Evidence of tolerance, such that increased doses are required in order to achieve effects originally produced by lower doses (clear examples of this are found in alcohol-dependent individuals who may take daily doses sufficient to incapacitate or kill non-tolerant users).

▶ Progressive neglect of other pleasures or interests because of substance use, increased amount of time necessary to obtain or take substance, or to recover from its effects.

▶ Persisting with use despite clear evidence of overtly harmful consequences.

DSM-IV

Substance abuse (one or more criteria for over one year) and never met criteria for dependence

▶ Substance abuse (one or more criteria for over one year) and never met criteria for dependence.

▶ Recurrent substance use resulting in a failure to fulfil major role obligations at work, school or home.

▶ Recurrent substance use in situations in which it is physically hazardous.

▶ Recurrent substance-related legal problems.

▶ Continued substance use despite having persistent or recurrent social or interpersonal problems caused or exacerbated by the effects of the substance.

Substance dependence (three criteria or more over one year)

▶ Tolerance: a need for markedly increased amounts of the substance to achieve intoxication or desired effect or markedly diminished effect with continued use of the same amount of the substance.

▶ Withdrawal: the characteristic withdrawal syndrome for the substance or the same (or closely related) substance is taken to relieve or avoid withdrawal symptoms.

▶ The substance is often taken in larger amounts or over a longer period than was intended.

▶ There is a persistent desire or unsuccessful effort to cut down or control substance use.

▶ A great deal of time is spent in activities necessary to obtain the substance, use of the substance, or recovering from its effects.

▶ Important social, occupational or recreational activities are given up or reduced because of substance use.

▶ The substance use is continued despite knowledge of having a persistent or recurrent physical or psychological problem that is likely to have been caused or exacerbated by the substance.

Natural history of drug use

Getting started

The different definitions described in ICD and DSM classifications are designed to distinguish problematic from non-problematic use, as not everyone who uses drugs or alcohol goes on to develop problems, and even of those who do develop dependent problematic use many may not have lifelong problems. Drug use, especially in adolescence, is in the main experimental and transient, seen by many as a 'rite of passage' between childhood and adulthood.

What factors therefore influence experimental use becoming problematic use? A prospective US study conducted a series of interviews on a sample of young people aged between 15 and 16 years. These adolescents were asked to describe patterns of initiation, persistence and cessation in drug use, and were then followed up over a period of time spanning 19 years, from adolescence to adulthood. A school survey was administered at age 15–16 and further interviews with participants and school absentees were conducted at ages 24–5, 28–9 and 34–5. Retrospective continuous histories of 12 drug classes were obtained at each follow-up.

The results showed that there was no initiation into alcohol and cigarettes, and hardly any initiation into illicit drugs after the age of 29, the age at which most use ceased. The largest proportion of new users after this age was observed for prescribed psychoactive drugs, such as benzodiazepines. Among daily users, the proportion of heavy users of alcohol and cannabis declined but not of cigarettes. Cigarettes were the most persistent of any drug used.[5]

Factors that predicted cessation of use in adulthood paralleled those that predicted lack of initiation in adolescence: conventionality in social role (e.g. job, family responsibilities), social context unfavourable to the use of drugs (e.g. employment, communities where alcohol use was banned) and good health.

Peer influences were found to be the major predictor of experimental drug use and also likely to influence the evolution into more regular drug use (see Table 1.1, overleaf). Initiation of use before the age of 15 is associated with more developmental disruption.[6]

Table 1.1   **Predictors of drug initiation in adolescence**

Individual factors	Prior delinquent behaviour
	Peer group influences
	Risk-taking behaviours
Parental factors	Poor quality of relationship
	Inconsistent parenting
Lack of participation in conventional activities	Such as employment, education and relationships

Continued use

Since cessation of drug use typically takes place at a different phase in the life cycle from initiation, that is in early adulthood rather than adolescence, factors important for persistence at a later phase of the life cycle may be equivalent to factors important for explaining initiation at a younger age. Whereas conformity to social roles in adolescence involves satisfactory academic performance, in adulthood the new social roles include being married or in a stable relationship and working. It is highly likely that adults' roles such as marriage and stable employment are not compatible with illicit drug use.

The level of drug use is also a predictor of future drug use; the more used, the more likely problematic use is to develop. Once an individual is dependent, drug use is generally a chronic condition, interspersed by periods of relapse and remission; it takes many attempts to achieve permanent abstinence.

Just as there is no one path towards successful abstinence, so there is no single risk factor for problematic drug use. There are a number of complex social factors, including the influence of intimate partners, parents and friends, and work and other activities, that can significantly affect the pattern of drug use. The severely dependent long-term heroin or cocaine user is likely after five to ten years of continuous use to be less amenable to change and have less access to social support networks necessary to support changes in use. Repeated involvement with the criminal justice system, long-term unemployment and increasing social isolation further entrench their drug-using behaviour. Strategies needed for this group are likely to involve significant social, physical and psychological interventions. If abstinence is going to occur it is more likely to happen earlier than later in a drug user's career.

Principles of treatment

Treatment aims

There are many possible aims of treatment. For those patients who meet criteria for harmful use (ICD-10) or misuse (DSM-IV), but who do not meet criteria for a dependence syndrome, psychosocial approaches are the mainstay of treatment.

Pharmacological interventions currently have limited application, except in treating coexisting conditions such as depression or anxiety, which may be inhibiting progress towards less harmful use. Pharmacological interventions aimed at treating the substance use disorder itself, many of which will be discussed in detail in this book, are of most value in patients who have developed the features of the dependence syndrome, and are targeted at the following areas of patient management:

▸ management of withdrawal symptoms

▸ reduction of physical, social and psychological harms to the individual and the public associated with illicit drug use by prescribing a substitute drug or drugs (for example methadone maintenance treatment in which aims may include cessation of injecting, reduction or cessation of illicit heroin use, and reduction or cessation of other high-risk behaviours)

▸ relapse prevention and maintenance of abstinence (for example oral naltrexone, cognitive behavioural therapy)

▸ prevention of complications of substance use (for example hepatitis B immunisation, the use of thiamine to prevent Wernicke's encephalopathy and Korsakoff's syndrome).

General principles of treatment

▸ No single treatment is appropriate for all individuals.

▸ Treatment needs to be readily available, and begin where the user presents.

▸ Treatment should over time address the multiple needs of the individual, physical, psychological, social and educational.

▸ Treatment modalities used will change over time and at different times during treatment.

▸ Retention in treatment is most predictive of a good outcome.

▸ Substitute medications, such as methadone and buprenorphine, are important elements of treatment for many patients, especially when combined with counselling and behavioural therapies.

▸ Patients with coexisting problems, such as mental health problems, should have these dealt with alongside their drug misuse problems. Treatment does not need to be voluntary to be successful.

▸ Recovery from drug addiction takes time, and addiction is a chronic relapsing condition often requiring multiple episodes of treatment.

▸ Trained and competent clinicians should provide treatment.

Models of behaviour change

Prochaska and DiClemente developed a model of behavioural change that has become influential in the field of addiction (see Figure 1.1).[7] The model hypothesis is that interventions are most effective when mapped to the state of readiness for change that the user is at. The model also helps to define the clinician's expectations and helps to foster a more realistic relationship between the clinician and the patient, and views change as a process rather than an event – the change process being characterised by a series of stages of change. It may be helpful to explain these stages of change to less informed members of the primary care team, in the hope that they too will see the potentials for intervention even if the patient does not want to stop drug use. By engaging in harm reduction strategies the clinician may be able to nudge the reluctant user gently into abstinence. The Prochaska and DiClemente model divides the individual state of readiness into the following states.

▸ *Precontemplators* do not want to stop and are not concerned enough about the associated risks to change their use. The interventions available are concentrated on harm reduction advice, information about needle exchange schemes, and provision of hepatitis B immunisation.

▸ *Contemplators* are concerned about their drug use and are considering change but have not yet decided to stop. These individuals would benefit from motivational interviewing and other behaviour therapies, nudging them gently into the action stage.

▸ The *action* stage is one in which people decide to stop and put their plan into action; substitution therapies are vital interventions during this phase.

▸ *Maintenance* of the behavioural change: addictive behaviour involves cycles of change with efforts to stop being punctuated by relapse. Maintaining the effects of the treatment needs to involve a range of psychosocial and pharmacological interventions. Marlatt and Gordon described the cognitive behavioural approach called relapse prevention, which aims to develop coping strategies that can help to maintain the phase of change.[8]

Figure 1.1 **Stages of change model**

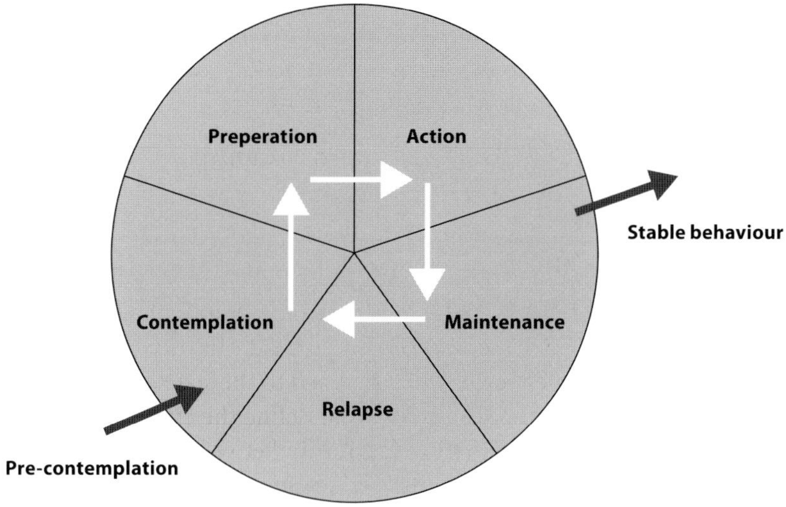

Source: Prochaska J O, DiClemente C C. Stages of change in the modification of problem behaviors.[7]

However, in utilising such a psychological model of behavioural change in consultations it should not be forgotten that an individual's state of readiness is influenced in part by his or her own internal motivating factors. Readiness can be influenced by wider socioeconomic determinants of ill health such as poor housing or unemployment and it could be that such factors need to be addressed before an individual is able to make sustained positive changes to illicit drug-using behaviour.

Harm reduction

The ultimate aim of treatment is to stop or reduce the use of illicit or harmful drugs and to prevent or reduce the harms resulting from drug use. The emphasis on harm reduction is a legacy of the response to the HIV problem: the establishment of needle exchange schemes, outreach clinics and methadone maintenance programmes. The theme of harm reduction has continued now for over two decades and has been the backbone of UK treatment policy. As early as 1996 a Department of Health Task Force[9] defined the outcomes of treatment into three main domains. These domains act as a guide to the harm minimisation steps that clinicians and commissioners can use when delivering or designing services (see Table 1.2, overleaf).[9] This will be discussed more fully in Chapter 15.

Table 1.2   **Treatment outcome domains**

Outcome domain	Measure
Drug use	Abstinence from drugs. Near abstinence from drugs. Reduction in the quantity of drugs consumed. Abstinence from street drugs. Reduced use of street drugs. Change in drug-taking behaviour from injecting to oral consumption. Reduction in the frequency of injecting
Physical and psychological health	Improvement in physical health. No deterioration in physical health. Improvement in psychological health. No deterioration in psychological health. Reduction in sharing injecting equipment. Reduction in sexual health risk taking
Social functioning and life context	Reduction in criminal activity. Improvement in employment status. Fewer working/school days missed. Improved family relationships. Improved personal relationships. Domiciliary stability/improvement

Source: Department of Health.[9]

From harm reduction to recovery

Over the last five years UK drug treatment and policy has shifted, and emphasis has shifted from 'harm reduction' to 'recovery'. This has at times been a contentious debate, with some stakeholders seeing a recovery agenda as synonymous with 'abstinence'. To many the concept of recovery has not been easy to define. In 2008 the UK Drug Policy Commission Recovery Consensus Group highlighted the key features of recovery from any problematic substance use as follows.[10]

▸ Recovery is about the accrual of positive benefits, not just reducing or removing harms caused by substance use.

▸ Recovery requires the building of aspirations and hope from the individual drug user, their families and those providing services and support.

▶ Recovery may be associated with a number of different types of support and interventions or may occur without any formal external help. No 'one size fits all'.

▶ Recovery is a process, not a single event, and may take time to achieve and effort to maintain. The process and the time required will vary between individuals.

▶ Recovery must be voluntarily sustained in order to be lasting, although it may sometimes be initiated or assisted by 'coerced' or 'mandated' interventions within the criminal justice system.

▶ Recovery requires control over substance use (although it is not sufficient on its own). This means a comfortable and sustained freedom from compulsion to use. This is not the same as controlled use, which may still be harmful. Having control over one's substance use means being able to make the choice to use a substance in a way that is not problematic for self, family or society. For many people this will require abstinence from the problem substance or all substances, but for others it may mean abstinence supported by prescribed medication or consistently moderate use of some substances (for example the occasional alcoholic drink).

▶ Recovery maximises health and wellbeing, encompassing both physical and mental good health as far as they may be attained for a person, as well as a satisfactory social environment. The term 'maximises' is used to reflect the need for high aspirations to ensure that users in treatment are enabled to move on and achieve lives that are as fulfilling as possible.

▶ Recovery is about building a satisfying and meaningful life, as defined by the patient him or herself, and involves participation in the rights, roles and responsibilities of society. The word 'rights' is included in recognition of the stigma that is often associated with problematic substance use and the discrimination that users may experience and which may inhibit recovery. Recovery embraces inclusion, or a re-entry into society and the improved self-identity that comes with a productive and meaningful role. For many people this is likely to include being able to participate fully in family life and be able to undertake work in a paid or voluntary capacity.

Moving from the 'British System' to a system underpinned by clinical governance

Historically the UK has been in the unique position of having minimal restrictions on how doctors manage drug users.[11] Doctors had the freedom to prescribe almost any drug and restrictions apply only to the prescription of heroin, cocaine and Diconal, which require a Home Office licence when used for the purpose of treating addiction.

This relative freedom has been referred to as the 'British System', the origins of which arose with the Rolleston Report in 1926, which argued that addicts were patients and not criminals, and should receive drugs on prescription, contrasting sharply with the situation in the USA. The British System allowed practitioners the freedom to take account of possible social and criminal justice gains as part of their prescribing decisions. It hence gives doctors the flexibility to respond to the changing nature of drug problems. However, this flexibility does not negate the duty of care for the individual or the need to adhere to good-practice guidance and safe prescribing. This is highlighted further below in the 2007 clinical guidelines section.[12] Essentially the increasing emphasis in the 2007 clinical guidelines on the importance of practising within safe parameters of clinical governance has curtailed many of the historic prescribing freedoms of the British System.

Practical aspects of prescribing

The British National Formulary (BNF), issued free to all GPs, contains a wealth of information concerning the overall management of addiction as well as laying out guiding principles when prescribing any medication in the UK. These principles are:

1. To avoid creating dependence caused by introducing drugs to patients without sufficient reason

2. To see that the patient does not gradually increase the dose for a drug given for good medical reasons to the point where dependence becomes likely. The prescriber should keep a close eye on the amount prescribed to prevent patients from accumulating stocks that would enable them to arrange their own dosage or even supply their families and friends

3. To avoid being used as an unwitting source of supply to addicts. Methods include visiting more than one doctor, fabricating stories and forging prescriptions.

The 2007 clinical guidelines

The Department of Health's *Drug Misuse and Dependence: UK guidelines on clinical management* (2007)[13] is the authoritative publication for primary care practitioners on the treatment of substance misusers. It is used as a reference source throughout this book. It is likely that the health professional reading this book is already familiar with the 2007 national clinical guidelines. These were written nearly a decade after the previous guidelines (1997), which had coincided with both a rapid increase in the number of drug users presenting for care and a predicted HIV crisis among injecting drug users.

In 1994, Gerada carried out a small local survey in South London and found that 50% of all drug users in the area were being treated by only 5% of GPs, most of whom were largely untrained and unsupported, a trend that was common in other parts of the country (Gerada, unpublished data). The guidelines provide a framework from which to work safely, and are relevant to any professional group working in the addiction field. They laid down the minimum responsibilities of clinicians, which are as follows:

- clinicians working with drug misusers must be appropriately competent, trained and supervised

- effective, safe and responsive services for drug misusers will usually involve clinicians working together and with others in teams in primary care, in secondary care or across both

- the setting in which health professionals work in treating drug misusers will affect the clinical governance mechanisms that need to be in place. Those working in relative isolation must ensure they have an opportunity to discuss and review their work with colleagues in the field, to maintain good and up-to-date practice

- services should be provided consistent with national guidance and principles, and in line with the evidence base

- policy and statutory frameworks for providing substance misuse treatment to those under 18 years of age are often different from adults and different approaches are required from clinicians

- the expansion of non-medical prescribing has implications for drug misuse treatment and care and clinical governance

- a timely and regular audit and review cycle should be in place

- information governance policies and practice are critical, including confidentiality and information sharing. They should specifically include guidance for clinicians working with drug-misusing parents

- patients must be involved in their own treatment and should be involved in planning, developing, designing and delivering local drug treatment services, as far as their competence and interests allow

- families and carers of drug misusers are both an important resource in treating drug misusers and often in need of support for themselves

- carers of adults can be involved in patients' treatment, usually with the patients' consent, although there may be an obligation to involve the carers of young people in their treatment.

Assessment

The guidelines emphasise that a good assessment is essential to the continuing care of the patient. Assessment skills are vital to all members of the primary care team. The diagnosis of drug use itself is of central importance. Before substitute treatment is initiated doctors should ensure that they have taken a history, carried out an examination, and undertaken relevant investigations. A good assessment should enable the practitioner to confirm the diagnosis of drug dependence through obtaining a history of drug misuse, examination of the signs of misuse, urine analysis, and other investigations where necessary.

All doctors must undertake assessment commensurate with the complexity of prescribing. Prescribing decisions (drug used, amount and duration of use) should, in most cases and as a tenet of good practice, be dependent on national clinical guidelines, the level of the doctor's training and experience, and discussion with others involved in the care of the patient.

The assessment of a patient is a continuous process carried out at every consultation over many years. The first assessment should not be prolonged and should not delay the initiation of effective treatment. Before prescribing it is important that the clinician remembers three golden rules:

1. Confirm the diagnosis of dependence, through history taking, urine analysis and, where appropriate, corroboration with previous health professionals

2. The responsibility for the prescription is always that of the prescribing doctor (or nurse or pharmacist) and this responsibility cannot be delegated

3. If using substitute medication, start low and increase the dose slowly.

Essentials of a good assessment

History taking should elicit, as accurately as possible, information about the past and current drug-taking behaviour. It should include the reason for presentation, past and current drug use, history of injecting, risk of HIV and other blood-borne diseases, medical history, and psychiatric, forensic and social history. The history should also determine previous contact with treatment services.

Examination should include an assessment of motivation, general and mental health, and family and social situation.

Urine analysis should be regarded as an adjunct to the history taking and examination in confirming drug use. It should be obtained before the onset of prescribing and randomly throughout treatment. Alternatively, some services will use oral fluid samples, or less commonly hair samples. Hair analysis uses a single strand of hair and can yield information spanning a period of several weeks or months.

The patient should be reviewed in detail at least every three months.

Prescribing issues

Prescribing substitute medication is a useful tool in changing the behaviour of some drug users towards abstinence or towards intermediate goals of reducing the harm to themselves or others. If opioids are prescribed, the 2007 clinical guidelines recommend liquid preparations such as methadone 1 mg/ml to avoid the risks associated with injecting crushed tablets or melted suppositories, for example, and to reduce the risk of potential sale on the black market. Drugs that are capable of being injected, such as tablets, carry a greater risk of being dangerously misused by the patient or sold on the black market. The clinical guidelines recommend that tablets should not be prescribed to drug users.

The most common source of problems when prescribing to drug users is the prescription of open-ended prescriptions of drugs without clearly defined and agreed goals. Prescribing too little leads to lies and manipulation, and too much can lead to drugs leaking onto the illicit market.

The prescribing doctor should, ideally, see the patient on each occasion that a prescription is issued. Other doctors, such as the patient's GP, should be informed of any prescription. This is important to avoid duplication.

Doctors in the private sector must ensure that their patients have sufficient legitimate sums to pay for the cost of treatment and the cost of the prescriptions. Doctors in this sector must be aware of the potential pitfalls of receiving payments for drug dependency treatment. A private prescription for controlled drugs must not be construed as a supply of drugs in exchange for money. There is a risk that patients may try to finance their consultations and prescriptions by selling higher-value controlled drugs on the black market. It is good practice for doctors in the private sector to communicate with the patient's NHS GP. The more the clinician deviates from established good practice the greater is the onus on the clinician to justify it.

Improving the outcome of treatment

Inherent to successful treatment is its ability to help people overcome drug problems. Despite the growth in treatment services in the 1980s and 1990s treatment provision remained patchy across the country. This led the Audit Commission to conclude in its 2002 report, *Changing Habits*,[14] that a significant number of drug users struggle to get the help they need. It identified that many treatment services had long waiting lists and limited treatment options that drove potential patients away. Care often failed to consider drug users' wider social problems and some treatment was delivered inconsistently and not in line with good practice. For example, some clinicians offered fixed short-term detoxification only. In the context of such barriers to the availability and accessibility to drug treatment the new Labour government oversaw the development of the National Treatment Agency, a special health authority tasked with increasing the numbers of drug users receiving effective drug treatment.

Factors associated with good outcome are multifactorial, relating to the service itself, such as minimising barriers to entry, having well-trained staff, and having a commitment to providing high-quality medical and psychosocial services. Other factors identified as fostering improved outcomes were related to the actual treatment provided, in particular providing optimal daily doses of substitute medication.

Whereas the Audit Commission report looked predominately at secondary care services, it is likely that many of the factors that promote good outcome in specialist settings will be similar for primary care settings. Flexible appointment systems, with a mixture of advanced access (appointments on the day) and booked appointments, will attract and maintain users in treatment. Informed staff, systems that allow for sharing of information about patients, the ability to discuss significant events, and reception and administrative staff who understand the ethos of care with drug users all smooth the sometimes turbulent early and relapse stages of the users' treatment. Continuity and consistent care will also retain the user in treatment. It is the authors' belief that a well-organised primary care practice should be able to accommodate even the most chaotic patients and provide for their primary healthcare needs.

Comparative rates for treatment compliance and relapse

It is perhaps surprising to many clinicians that the overall treatment of opioid addiction, as measured by compliance in treatment and rate of relapse, is as successful as treatment of other chronic diseases such as diabetes, hypertension and asthma. The outcome, in terms of abstinence at six months, is greater for opioid addiction than that for tobacco or alcohol addiction.[15]

Conclusion

Treating drug users is ripe with challenges, but it also provides clinical satisfaction. The very contact between a user and a health professional can bring about enormous changes. Treatment in its broadest sense can (and does) save many lives. There are many interventions available and a competent GP, primary care nurse or pharmacist can provide most of them. We hope that this book will ensure that the most effective treatment is given.

Further reading

Ghodse H. *Drugs and Addictive Behaviour: a guide to treatment* (2nd edn). Oxford: Blackwell Science, 1995.

Lingford-Hughes A R, Welch S, Nutt D J. BAP Guidelines. Evidence-based guidelines for the pharmacological management of substance misuse, addiction and comorbidity: recommendations from the British Association for Psychopharmacology. *Journal of Psychopharmacology* (Oxford) 2004; **18(3)**: 293–335.

References

1. Keaney F, Strang J, Martinez-Raga J, *et al*. Does anyone care about names? How attendees at substance misuse services like to be addressed by health professionals. *European Addiction Research* 2004; **10(2)**: 75–9.

2. World Health Organization. *The ICD-10 Classification of Mental and Behavioural Disorders: clinical descriptions and diagnostic guidelines, tenth revision*. Geneva: WHO, 1992.

3. American Psychiatric Association. *Diagnostic and Statistical Manual of Mental Disorders, Fourth Edition*. Washington, DC: APA, 1994.

4. World Health Organization. *WHO Expert Committee on Drug Dependence, thirtieth report* (WHO Technical Report Series, No. 873). Geneva: WHO, 1998.

5. Chen K, Kandel D B. The natural history of drug use from adolescence to the mid-thirties in a general population sample. *American Journal of Public Health* 1995; **85(1)**: 41–7.

6. Kandel D B, Raveis V H. Cessation of illicit drug use in young adulthood. *Archives of General Psychiatry* 1989; **46(2)**: 109–16.

7. Prochaska J O, DiClemente C C. Stages of change in the modification of problem behaviors. *Progress in Behavior Modification* 1992; **28**: 183–218.

8. Marlatt G A, Gordon J R (eds). *Relapse Prevention: maintenance strategies in the treatment of addictive behaviours*. New York: Guilford, 1985.

9. Department of Health. *The Task Force Review of Services for Drug Misusers: report of an independent review of drug treatment services in England*. London: HMSO, 1996.

10. UK Drug Policy Commission Recovery Consensus Group. *A Vision for Recovery*. London: UK Drug Policy Commission, 2008.

11. Strang J, Gossop M. The 'British System': visionary anticipation or masterly inactivity? In: J Strang, M Gossop (eds). *Heroin Addiction and Drug Policy*. Oxford: Oxford University Press, 1994, pp. 342–51.

12. Zador D. Injectable opiate maintenance in the UK: is it good clinical practice? *Addiction* 2001; **96**: 547–53.

13. Department of Health (England) and the devolved administrations. *Drug Misuse and Dependence: UK guidelines on clinical management*. London: Department of Health (England), the Scottish Government, Welsh Assembly Government and Northern Ireland Executive, 2007.

14. Audit Commission. *Changing Habits: the commissioning and management of community drug treatment services for adults*. London: Audit Commission, 2002.

15. O'Brien C P, McLellan A T. Myths about the treatment of addiction. *Lancet* 1996; **347**: 237–40.

CHAPTER 2

Drug policy in the UK

Steve Taylor

(based on original text by Clare Gerada and Alex Laffan)

IN THIS CHAPTER

Introduction ‖ UK drug policy today ‖ Law and enforcement ‖ Treatment ‖ Young people: interventions and education ‖ Changing landscape ‖ Conclusion

Introduction

The use of alcohol and psychoactive substances has been woven into every society since the beginnings of the human race. And governments, monarchs and religious leaders have had to decide whether and how to sanction or control their use.

Attempts to prevent importation of drugs and restrict their use have a long history. In 100 BC the Roman senate attempted to suppress alcoholic excesses and orgies connected with the worship of Bacchus. King James's dislike of tobacco led him to write one of the earliest anti-tobacco publications in 1604 and to levy taxes on tobacco importation. In 1796 the Chinese government made opium smoking punishable by death in response to decades of excess and problematic smoking of the drug by its population.

Attempts to deal with addiction through prevention and treatment have met with variable success. In the 1850s the hypodermic syringe was introduced in the belief that morphine injected by a syringe was non-addictive because it did not 'reach the stomach'. In 1878 cocaine was believed to be a treatment for morphine addiction, a belief that persisted for some decades. Cocaine became illegal in the USA in 1914, but not before many became addicted to it.

The past hundred years have seen, perhaps unsurprisingly in a modern world of greater government control, unprecedented levels of both national and international law-making regarding psychoactive substances. Since the Hague Convention of 1912, the international monitoring and control of the illicit drugs supply has been increasingly better resourced. In the latter part of the twentieth century, treatment for those dependent on illicit, and licit, drugs received greater funding and attention, both in the UK and worldwide.

This chapter explores the UK's current attitude to drugs regarding tackling supply and demand, providing treatment, and reducing harm to both individuals and communities. It will also analyse how these policies have developed over the twentieth and twenty-first centuries.

UK drug policy today

The 2010 drug strategy [1] sought to portray a departure from its predecessors by focusing on enabling more people to recover. But the previous government's 2008 strategy [2] had already promised 'to focus more upon treatment outcomes, with a greater proportion free from their dependence and being re-integrated into society, coming off benefits and getting back to work'. And this was just a logical extension of strategies going back to the first national drug strategy in 1985.

Although their priorities and wording have differed, all the strategies since have included:

▸ reducing demand for drugs by prohibition and education

▸ reducing the availability of drugs by tackling supply at home and abroad

▸ reducing drug-related crime, including advancing treatment within the criminal justice system

▸ reducing the risks of harm to those who take drugs through education, vaccination and needle and syringe provision

▸ treating those for whom drug use has become a problem by providing support that enables them to reduce or stop their use and begin their recovery.

It is difficult to see how a drug policy could operate without a combination of these building blocks. Without prohibition, the UK treatment system might face uncontainable demand and education would be undermined; without treatment and harm reduction, drug-related illness and deaths would rise; without education, young people might fail to associate drug use with danger.

Law and enforcement

Domestic enforcement of drug control and international supply reduction together account for a substantial proportion of the UK's budget for tackling drug misuse. While the previous lengthy sentencing of some drug users has been reduced with increasing diversion to treatment, drug trafficking into the UK and drug dealing once inside the UK remain areas of criminal behaviour that are treated with little tolerance. Reducing the supply of illegal drugs is expensive and often seemingly impossible. It is further complicated by the ability of illicit laboratories to synthesise and market new drugs that (at least temporarily) fall outside legal control.

The international nature of drug production and supply makes it difficult for a domestic government to control alone and the UK government is at the forefront of countries in the international community pushing for greater global cooperation.

The government has been criticised for its eagerness to take short-term credit for its efforts to crack down on illegal drug imports at the expense of the long-term trend. In 2011 the UK Border Agency (UKBA) publicised a large rise in the amount of Class A drugs seized at British ports and airports. The published figures,[3] though, show that the annual total number of seizures has been falling since 2008–9 (although it remains almost double what it was a decade ago). Quantities seized tell another story, with both police force and UKBA cocaine and heroin seizures plummeting over the last ten years, and being replaced by a massive increase in seizures of domestic cannabis plants by police forces.

Meanwhile the government continues to use the law as a deterrent, with those caught drug trafficking or dealing remaining subject to harsh penalties – a maximum of life imprisonment for Class A drugs and 14 years for Class B and C drugs.

Targeting suppliers as distinct from the actual drug users has been cemented in British drug policy since the 1971 Misuse of Drugs Act, which distinguished between the two for the first time.[4] Since then, sentences for dealers have been far more severe than for users.

Strategies for reducing production in foreign countries and tackling international supply are usually formed on the basis of international agreements and therefore Britain's ability to enact its own policies is often subject to the cooperation of the international community. The Hague Convention of 1912 was the starting point for a century of international regulation of drug production and transportation. The Geneva Conference on Opium in 1924/5 further raised the barriers on importing and exporting drugs. In 1946 international drugs policy fell under United Nations jurisdiction and continued apace, with an international opium protocol agreed in 1953, which severely restricted poppy and coca production.

Yet it is the 1961 Single Convention that forms the real basis of international drug policy today, limiting cultivation, manufacture, importation and possession of drugs as well as introducing strict record keeping and prescriptive measures. While the Single Convention is perhaps not as rigid as it might seem, it has ensured that the UK has little room for manoeuvre when dealing with drug trafficking. Yet when the UK is continually at the forefront of the United Nations in pushing for stricter international controls on drug production and supply, this has not been a contentious issue in the UK. By investing personnel resources into seizing drugs, using the force of the law to deter potential dealers, and targeting specific areas where dealers are known to operate, the UK strategy seems to encompass all the available avenues for reducing drug supply in the UK. When this is combined with continuing international cooperation and enforcement in reducing the production of illegal drugs at source, and work to block key international trafficking routes, reducing supply is clearly a massive operation. The continued availability of drugs measured against the extent to which the UK has worked, domestically and internationally, to reduce supply raises questions about the strategy's limited success.

Supply reduction efforts have not resulted in an increase in the price of drugs, in real terms, or deterred use. Contrary to some popular literature, a rise in price is more likely to result in a fall in use than in the widely expected rise in crime. Increases in the price of alcohol and tobacco have had a significant effect on consumption. A study conducted before the Second World War predicted similar results for other drugs. But, over 30 years, the price of heroin in the UK has remained relatively steady between around £90 and £60 per gram with no sustained reduction in purity. The same pattern is seen in the USA.

Without the serious deterrents in place to prohibit the production of drugs in source countries, and barriers to entry into consumer countries, drug supply would likely increase. However, in real terms, prices are still falling with these comprehensive measures in place and it is reasonable to ask whether large sums of money are being well spent, especially as production-reducing programmes such as crop substitution and crop destruction are unlikely to have any effect on consumer countries and their retail drug prices.

Interdiction can be effective only if it covers all smuggling routes. Such measures are surely beyond the UK's limited budget and will only eat into more cost-effective solutions such as treatment and rehabilitation.

If supply reduction is not working then what about the other side of the prohibition coin, namely reducing recreational drug use? There are several notable aspects of the UK's changing attitude towards the criminal status of the drug user, but the most important is the focus on Class A drugs. The police continue to focus on arresting, and referring to treatment, users of Class A drugs, which, as the government repeatedly stresses, cause most destruction to communities and individuals. Nevertheless the UK remains dedicated to the continuing prohibition of all illegal drugs as a deterrent to uptake and continued use.

Another aspect of domestic enforcement was the noticeable shift in drug policy during the twentieth century away from health issues and towards criminal justice issues, evident in the increased responsibility of the Home Office, as opposed to the Department of Health. We may now be witnessing another shift to policy based on notions of public health and social justice that recognises the need to redress inequalities but expects individuals to take personal responsibility and make a fair contribution to society.

Other domestic developments have often been in response to popular pressure. The 1964 Drugs Act was the first post-war piece of drug legislation and controlled amphetamine use. The 1971 Misuse of Drugs Act remains the centrepiece of British drug law, with its categorisation of controlled drugs into classes according to their perceived harm and consequent punishment, and schedules according to their legitimate uses (or lack of them). The 1961 Single Convention that has dictated British policy on trafficking has long been quoted by Home Secretaries as committing Britain to a policy of prohibition for drug possession as well. In fact, this has been obligatory only since 1988 and even then, as the Dutch have shown, there is plenty of room for manoeuvre.

While successive governments have made their priority on Class A drugs clear, some commentators are not satisfied. Some see the government's strategy as too focused on the criminal justice system, while others see the government as being 'soft' on drugs and encouraging – or at least turning a blind eye to – cannabis use.

Meanwhile, supply of and demand for so-called 'legal highs' has increased. Sold online and in 'head' shops, usually as products not for human consumption such as plant food and bath salts, and therefore ostensibly outside the controlled drugs (and medicines) legislation, some do contain substances already controlled. Others contain new psychoactive substances not covered by the Misuse of Drugs Act, and the increasing disparity between the time taken to impose full legal controls and the speed of suppliers to produce and market new chemicals brought new powers to rapidly and temporarily ban them. The use of 'Temporary Class Drug Orders' is in its infancy but a temporary control seems likely only ever to lead to permanent control. It is hard to imagine a government being seen to move from temporarily controlling a drug to saying, in effect, this one doesn't need controlling so is okay to take.

The number of young people taking these and more established drugs is a continuing problem and suggests that law enforcement alone is not having the desired effect.

Treatment

The evidence is good that treatment works, reducing damage to communities and individuals, including (and especially, as far as government is concerned) crime. Spending on drug treatment in England doubled from 2002 to 2010 and enabled a matching doubling of the numbers in treatment. Treatment services and the criminal justice system are designed to work alongside each other, one to deter and one to ensure that those who cannot stop using drugs are at least prevented from causing damage to themselves and communities.

The first specialist clinic was set up in 1964 by John Owens in Birmingham, dispensing heroin to addicts. This sparked off a considerable growth, throughout the 1960s and 1970s, of voluntary services and specialist drug and therapeutic residential communities. From 1968 to 1972 drug dependency units were established in major cities affected by drugs. Alongside the formation of these units was the implementation of the Second Brain Report recommendation of restricting prescribing rights of heroin to licensed doctors, in effect to doctors who worked within the units and hence only to psychiatrists.

Following the rapid increase of treatment services in the 1960s and 1970s, the 1980s saw central government funding for the development of a network of community services that defined the roles of specialist drug services and gave new responsibilities to GPs in treating drug misusers, an area that continues to develop.

The National Treatment Agency oversaw the expansion and improvement of drug treatment services in England from 2001 to 2013. Government set ambitious targets aimed at bringing more drug users into treatment, making them wait less time to access that treatment, and retaining them in it for longer. The target to double the number of drug users in treatment between 1998 and 2008 was achieved two years early.

Other goals included greater involvement of GPs, more referrals from the criminal justice system, and improving prison-based treatment.

HIV and harm reduction

The biggest influence on increasing treatment in the late 1980s and early 1990s, and in particular treatment provided by GPs, was HIV/AIDS, with the Advisory Council on the Misuse of Drugs stating in 1988:

> *HIV is a greater threat to public and individual health than drug misuse. The first goal of work with drug misusers must therefore be to prevent them acquiring or transmitting the virus. In some cases this will be achieved through abstinence. In others, abstinence will not be achievable for the time being and efforts will have to focus on risk reduction. Abstinence remains the ultimate goal but efforts to bring it about in individual cases must not jeopardise any reduction in HIV risk behaviour which has already been achieved.*[5]

This report led to the development of community-based and pharmacy needle and syringe exchange schemes all over Britain. The report articulated the policy of directing treatment towards abstinence by achieving intermediate goals such as:

▸ stopping injecting with unsterile equipment

▸ taking drugs by mouth or inhalation

▸ taking prescribed rather than illegal drugs.

The report advocated a comprehensive approach to the prevention of the spread of HIV, and the reversal of the then abstinence-oriented (detoxification) prescribing policy as it legitimised longer-term prescribing to enable users to stop injecting.

The arrival of HIV/AIDS meant that this harm reduction approach to treatment had taken on a new, arguably more important role. The essence of harm reduction has always been to protect the non-drug-taking community from the crimes committed by drug misusers, but for the first time, in the 1980s, the general public's health was seen to be at risk from drug users' injecting behaviour. With the spread of HIV from shared injecting equipment increasing rapidly across the world, it was suddenly demanded that British drug policy be changed. Drug users would be coaxed out of hiding and into needle exchange schemes where sterile equipment was available to be used only once and then discarded.

The creation of needle exchange schemes has been remarkably successful in containing HIV and reducing unsafe injecting, and as a public health intervention can be seen alongside the action of John Snow removing the Broad Street pump handle in the nineteenth century. For drug users who cannot stop injecting, the government is prepared to endorse more controversial treatments such as injectable methadone and heroin.

Harm reduction has been successful, reducing both crime and drug-related deaths, as well as diseases such as HIV and hepatitis contracted from sharing needles. But its success has not been enough to prevent sustained attacks on the policy and its practice from those who believe it is permissive of drug use and lacking in ambition for drug users' recovery. They argue too that it has demonstrated a lack of effectiveness in current treatment.

Evidence for treatment

The evidence that treatment works has been vital to stem the continued diversion of funding into reducing supply rather than reducing demand and providing treatment.

To 'prove' treatment works requires investment in long-term studies, such as the National Treatment Outcome Research Study (NTORS)[6] and Drug Treatment Outcomes Research Study (DTORS).[7] Both demonstrated that drug treatment reduced drug use and crime, and that for every £1 spent on treatment £2.50 or more was saved in criminal justice and other costs. Improvements were largely maintained after treatment.

The increasing comprehensiveness and sophistication of long-term data from national drug treatment monitoring systems across the UK have enabled more and better evidence to be put before governments that supports the effectiveness of treatment. Data for 2010–11 from England's National Drug Treatment Monitoring System show fewer people seeking treatment for heroin and crack use, and increasing numbers successfully completing treatment and not needing to return.[8]

Treatment therefore does work, though to work effectively it needs to be delivered by well-trained staff, delivering effective evidence-based interventions.

Whereas there is evidence of the effectiveness of treatment and adequate budgets devoted to treating patients, there is a lack of detailed clinical research into different treatment methods and their effectiveness.

High-quality research in the UK is lacking, and research using primary care patients or clinicians virtually non-existent. Much of the evidence cited in this book is from the USA and Australia, which, although useful, can sometimes not be easily transferable to a UK setting. Dedicated programmes of drug research, and the funding to support them, have been developed in recent years but UK spending on research is still dwarfed by that in the USA, which funds 85% of the world's research on drug use and dependence.

Recovery

After Labour had been in power for 13 years and before the 2010 election following which the coalition government was formed, the Conservatives were promising a new approach to tackling drug misuse. They had been driven by and were driving a policy championed by the Centre for Social Justice and future welfare minister Iain Duncan Smith. This proposed an even greater emphasis on abstinence as the end goal of treatment than had already been evident in the Labour government's 2008 drug strategy. The critique of the existing system was that treatment replaced drug misuse with 'methadone, wine and welfare' – a phrase coined in 1977.[9] The way to get people out of their dependence and back to work was to rely on benefits sanctions and the power of recovery, the latter a road down which Scotland was already travelling. The National Treatment Agency (NTA), which had championed the existing English treatment system, was to be abolished.

After the coalition was formed, and in the run-up to the 2010 drug strategy, the hard lines were moderated somewhat: recovery was still to be the focus of treatment but an insistence on abstinence as the only route to recovery was modified to allow that medically assisted recovery could and did happen. In addition, the functions of the NTA were to be transferred to the new Public Health England.

Government's fondness for recovery mirrored an already fast-growing grassroots recovery movement that has much in common with (and perhaps much to learn from) an earlier one in the field of mental health. Many drug treatment services and commissioners have enthusiastically adopted the principles and ambitions of recovery, and changed their programmes, service user involvement and support for recovery communities. Recovery communities have appeared or grown in many parts of the country and set their own agendas for how recovery can best be supported, and whether and how treatment should be involved.

The efforts of the NTA in its final years were focused on improvements that can support recovery while preventing an excessive swing towards abstinence that could lead to people being hurried out of treatment before they are ready, and risking relapse, infection, overdose and death.

But, for many people, the major obstacle to long-term recovery is a continuing lack of access to employment and housing, some of it perpetuated by stigma towards those who have used drugs and those still receiving treatment for their drug dependence.

Treatment models involving criminal justice

Long-term outcome studies like NTORS in the late 1990s and, more recently, DTORS (see above) confirmed the findings of arrest referral and Drug Treatment and Testing Order (DTTO) evaluations that showed significant reductions in offending when drug-misusing offenders were engaged in treatment. DTORS, a national, multi-site, longitudinal study with a cohort of 1796 adults in a range of structured treatment settings, showed a 50% reduction in self-reported offences for all clients between the start of treatment and first follow-up.

Doubts about the validity or accuracy of studies based on self-report data have been largely dispelled. Recent research matching drug treatment and police data-bases have provided an objective measure of offending by drug-misusing offend-ers before and after treatment. A study matching data from the Police National Computer to England's National Drug Treatment Monitoring System (NTDMS) database looked at a sample of opiate and crack users who had recently offended but had not been imprisoned, and had started drug treatment (prescribing) in the community. The study showed an overall reduction of 46% across all crime types and all drug use profiles.[10]

The realisation that drug treatment exerts such a positive impact on reducing crime, allied to the increased availability of community drug treatment, led to a concerted policy drive to ensure that drug-misusing offenders could access treat-ment at every point in the criminal justice system. Rather than offering separate criminal justice provision, the system that has been developed is based on offend-ers accessing mainstream treatment. In this respect, the substantial investment in creating a treatment sector that delivers effective, evidence-based services with low waiting times has probably reaped significant crime reduction dividends. The effectiveness of this approach is evidenced by a number of studies that consist-ently find that clients who are referred into treatment via the criminal justice system achieve the same positive outcomes as those who enter treatment via mainstream referral routes.

A range of initiatives has been developed and implemented:

▶ *Drug Interventions Programme* (DIP) – provides a national network of criminal justice intervention teams that operate in all police custody suites and courts to identify, assess and case-manage drug-misusing offenders, and where required facilitate their engagement in structured treatment

▶ *Drug Rehabilitation Requirements* (DRR) – community sentences that divert offenders out of crime by requiring drug treatment, drug testing and court reviews of progress

▶ *prison-based treatment* – each year, 75,000 opioid and/or crack users enter the prison system and, on average, 55% of prisoners are heroin and/or crack users (significantly more in some local prisons). The influential 2010 Patel Report recommended a more evidence-based, outcome-focused and locally com-missioned approach to prison-based substance misuse services.[11] Evidence-based clinical treatment is available across the adult prison estate – in England through the Integrated Drug Treatment System (IDTS). The transfer of respon-sibility to the Department of Health for all prison-based treatment in April 2011 brought together the commissioning of drug treatment for those in the community and in custody.

Young people: interventions and education

The final major aspect of drug policy in the UK is in relation to young people.

The propensity for young people to develop substance misuse problems is dependent on 'risk' and 'protection' factors in their life. These factors exist in both young people themselves (genetics, temperament, attitudes, social expectations, class and gender performance) and in their environment (family, socioeconomic status, neighbourhood and peer groups).

Risk and protection factors change and it is important to regularly review them to ensure that appropriate support continues to be provided.

Alongside other 'universal' services, GPs have a role in identifying and respond-ing to the substance misuse needs of children and young people, and in ensuring they can access specialist substance misuse interventions if needed.

They should offer early intervention to prevent young people developing risk factors that cause them harm. They can identify and address the underlying causes of issues and provide help early to prevent problems getting worse and to reduce future harm.

Specialist interventions for young people are very different from those for adults as, among the minority of young people for whom use of drugs and alcohol becomes a problem, few have been using long enough to become dependent in the way adults can. Drug and alcohol misuse among teenagers is usually a symp-tom of broader difficulties in their lives – family breakdown, inadequate housing, offending, truancy, antisocial behaviour, poor educational attainment and mental health concerns such as self-harm – so specialist drug and alcohol interventions are usually part of a package of support.

The 2010 drug strategy says that:

> *The aim of specialist substance misuse interventions is to stop young people's drug and alcohol use from escalating, to reduce harm to themselves or others and to prevent them becoming drug or alcohol-dependent adults. Specialist substance misuse interventions should be delivered according to a young per-son's age, their levels of vulnerability and the severity of their substance misuse problem, and should help young people become drug and alcohol-free.*[1]

The number of under-18s accessing specialist interventions for substance mis-use in England (the vast majority for alcohol and cannabis) and the number being treated primarily for Class A drugs, such as heroin and cocaine, have both been falling recently.[12]

Education is mainly done in schools and through public information cam-paigns. Public information is produced as part of the Talk to FRANK campaign, at the heart of which is a website and national drugs helpline driving home the risks of using drugs and encouraging young people and their parents to seek advice and help.

In the 1960s, school-based drug prevention programmes were focused on the provision of factual information to scare young people away from drugs and their risks. By the 1970s, with information dissemination arousing as much curiosity as fear, there was a shift towards personal development. This included a focus on decision making and values clarification. Instead of being drug specific, it was intended to be applied by the students themselves to decisions such as whether to take drugs.

Since then more drug-specific policies have been reintroduced, complemented by disturbing images and high-profile case studies, such as that of Leah Betts whose death in 1995 from ecstasy received a great deal of publicity in the hope of warning other young people of the dangers of this drug.

Evidence that education works does exist, but is very limited. Educational pro-grammes have been evaluated far less fully and rigorously than treatment pro-grammes, in part because of the complexities of carrying out longitudinal studies in this area and disentangling all the potential variables.

A long-awaited six-year, multi-million pound research project to determine the most effective approach to delivering drug education in England ended with the disappointing conclusion in 2009 that, 'The original design of the Blueprint evaluation was not sufficiently robust to allow an evaluation of impact and out-comes, and consequently the report cannot drawn any conclusions on the efficacy of Blueprint in comparison to existing drug education programmes.'[13]

The number of 11–15-year-olds smoking, drinking alcohol and taking illegal drugs has been decreasing so it might be argued that education is succeeding. But it is hard to disentangle the relative contributions of legislation, school education, public information campaigns and fashion. And the apparently increasing popu-larity of 'legal highs' may be displacing illicit drug and alcohol use.

Changing landscape

Changes to health and care services brought about by the long-disputed Health and Social Care Bill saw the responsibility for commissioning drug and alco-hol treatment move from local partnerships and NHS primary care trusts to new local authority public health teams in 2013. At the same time, government created police and crime commissioners, elected officials accountable for how crime is tackled in their police force areas. The funding available to them includes a proportion of what was the funding for the DIP.

Whether these changes will see continued investment in proven drug treatments, a shift to the increasingly high-profile problem of alcohol misuse, or treatment funding raided for other local priorities may be down to local electors and the people they elect. The potential for greater integration of health and social care, housing, employment and criminal justice to address local priorities has perhaps never been higher but so is the potential for fragmentation.

The introduction of payment by results (PBR) also promises changes in how services are commissioned and delivered. In PBR, each patient is allocated a payment tariff and services then paid only as they achieve specified outcomes for that patient. Although the PBR programme for drug treatment was initially restricted to a handful of pilot sites, it is already changing how many commissioners think about the outcomes they expect from the services they commission, and how service providers think about how and when they get paid.

Conclusion

The use of criminal justice to prevent drug use and treat drug users has made good use of the wide scope to rehabilitate drug users within the criminal justice system, and the number of patients coming into treatment through the system has grown rapidly.

More research is needed into methods of treatment to refine the services available, but the general efficacy of treatment is proven. Realistically, the prohibition of currently illicit drugs remains an obligation for any government when popular opinion and international agreements are taken into account. Enforcement and reducing supply are, however, expensive. Although in-country enforcement can funnel users into treatment, there are questions to be asked about the relative cost-effectiveness of tackling international production and supply. Even with the large budget available the problem cannot be solved without ever greater international funding.

The focus on recovery from drug and alcohol dependence is resulting in big shifts in thinking and practice. Local communities of recovery in many parts of the country are increasingly taking responsibility for their own recovery. The challenge for treatment services is to demonstrate how they can work with these communities and more effectively contribute to people's long-term recovery while continuing to deliver the proven and protective harm reduction benefits of treatment.

The difficulty of demonstrating the effectiveness of substantial government investment in prevention suggests that drugs education, too, should be subjected to serious scrutiny.

Drug use is not spiralling out of control in the UK. The use of the most problematic drugs, heroin and cocaine, is falling as are the number of young people taking drugs, drinking and smoking. But dependence on prescribed medicines and the availability and use of new, often untested, psychoactive substances that may, for a time, not be controlled by law, seem likely to present new challenges.

Further reading

Babor T, Caulkins J P, Edwards G. *Drug Policy and the Public Good*. Oxford: Oxford University Press, 2010.

References

1. HM Government. *Reducing Demand, Restricting Supply, Building Recovery: supporting people to live a drug free life* [Drug Strategy 2010]. London: HM Government, 2010.

2. HM Government. *Drugs: protecting families and communities* [Drug Strategy 2008]. London: HM Government, 2008.

3. Coleman K. Seizures of drugs in England and Wales, 2010/11. *Home Office Statistical Bulletin* 17/11, 2011

4. Davenport-Hines R. *The Pursuit of Oblivion: a global history of narcotics 1500–2000*. London: Weidenfeld & Nicolson, 2001.

5. Advisory Council on the Misuse of Drugs. *AIDS and Drug Misuse: part 1*. London: HMSO, 1988.

6. Gossop M, Marsden J, Stewart D. *NTORS after Five Years (National Treatment Outcome Research Study): changes in substance use, health and criminal behaviour in the five years after intake*. London: National Addiction Centre, 2001.

7. Donmall M, Jones A, Davies L, *et al. Summary of Key Findings from the Drug Treatment Outcomes Research Study (DTORS)*. London: Home Office, 2009.

8. Department of Health, National Treatment Agency. *Statistics from the National Drug Treatment Monitoring System (NDTMS) 1 April 2011–31 March 2012. Vol. 1: the numbers*. London: NTA, 2012.

9. Preble E, Miller T. Methadone, wine and welfare. In: RS Weppner (ed.). *Street Ethnography: selected studies of crime and drug use in natural settings*. Beverly Hills: Sage Publications, 1977, pp. 229–48.

10. Millar T, Jones A, Donmall M, *et al. Changes in Offending Following Prescribing Treatment for Drug Misuse*. London: NTA, 2011.

11. Patel K, Prison Drug Treatment Strategy Review Group. *Reducing Drug-Related Crime and Rehabilitating Offenders: recovery and rehabilitation for drug users in prison and on release: recommendations for action*. London: House of Lords, 2010.

12. National Treatment Agency. *Substance Misuse among Young People 2010–11*. London: NTA, 2011.

13. Home Office. *Blueprint Drugs Education: the response of pupils and parents to the programme*. London: Home Office, 2009.

CHAPTER 3

Prevalence and patterns of drug use in the UK and Europe

Malcolm Roxburgh and Clare Gerada

IN THIS CHAPTER

Introduction || *National Drug Treatment Monitoring System* ||
Estimating the number not in treatment || *Drug use in the UK* ||
Drug use in the UK compared with other European countries ||
Drug-related deaths || *Conclusion*

Introduction

How many people in Britain use illicit drugs? This question is deceptively easy to ask but difficult to answer. Reliable information on the extent and patterns of drug use and age of first use in the general population and specific populations is difficult to obtain from surveys. This is especially the case because people differ in their willingness to disclose personal use of illegal substances, even when anonymity is promised. So, to provide numbers, epidemiologists use a range of estimation techniques that combine information drawn from different sources. By doing this, researchers are able to provide estimates of the number of individuals who use drugs problematically, which are not reliant on the responses to survey questions. These techniques rely on there being reliable data about individuals who receive drug treatment, and individuals with problematic drug use who come into contact with the criminal justice system.

National Drug Treatment Monitoring System

In the UK, figures for drug users presenting for treatment are drawn directly from the National Drug Treatment Monitoring System (NDTMS), a development of the regional drug misuse databases, which have been in place since the late 1980s. In 2000/1, there were thought to be around 100,000 individuals treated for drug misuse in England.[1] By 2008/9, this peaked at 210,815, and has been declining since. The most recent published figure for 2011/12 is that 197,110 individuals were treated in the year.[2]

The increase in numbers treated from 2001–9 is consistent with the significant additional investment in the availability and accessibility of drug treatment in England over that period. However, the decrease seen since has taken place against a continuing background of low waiting times. This suggests that there is an underlying reduction in demand for treatment over this period. In particular, a significant reduction in the number of young, treatment-naïve individuals entering treatment is encouraging.

However, the monitoring system collects data on drug users presenting for treatment and those in treatment, though not on how many people are addicted to or having problems with drugs – the hidden population of users. To find this hidden population it is important to devise measures that find out, first, how many people are in treatment as a whole and, second, how many people have drug-related problems but are not seeking help.

Estimating the number not in treatment

There are statistical tools that can be used to make intelligent estimates of hidden populations of drug users.

Capture–recapture

A statistical technique known as the capture–recapture method can be used to estimate hidden populations. The method was originally used to estimate population sizes, such as the number of salmon in a pool.

The method involves 'tagging' a captured population and then in given settings calculating the overlap between tagged and untagged populations. Applied to drug users these settings would include various treatment areas, including non-statutory sectors. The size of the overlap between samples allows a statistical model to be created, which can then be used to estimate the size of the wider drug-using population.

To estimate the size of the total drug population, two other sources of data about drug users from criminal justice are matched against the NDTMS. These are the Drug Intervention Programme/prison system and the Police National Computer (PNC).

Multiple or Multivariate Indicator Method (MIM)

While the available data to support capture–recapture provides what are thought to be reliable estimates for a majority of the country, there are a number of areas where the technique does not fit the data so well, or provide estimates that do not seem feasible given the known population or estimates for use of other drugs. In these cases, a better estimate may be obtained by using the capture–recapture estimates from areas where these are available, and use these to anchor a stepwise regression to estimate prevalence in areas where there is no capture–recapture estimate.

Social survey data

Important data on the prevalence of drug use has been provided by a wide range of local and national surveys, which measure different aspects of a person's drug use, such as:

▸ any use during a person's lifetime (lifetime prevalence), often called 'lifetime use'

▸ any use during the previous year (past 12 months prevalence), often called 'recent use'

▸ any use during the previous month (past 30 days prevalence), often called 'current use'.

The figures for lifetime use are always higher than for the other two groups, as this group includes everyone who has ever tried drugs, no matter when. Recent-use figures are generally lower but reflect more accurately the current situation. A combination of lifetime experience and recent or current use can provide insight into drug use patterns.

National surveys used in the UK are the British Crime Survey (BCS, covering England and Wales), the Scottish Crime and Justice Survey, and the Northern Ireland Crime Survey. All of these are based on representative samples of the households in the countries they represent.

There are also a number of surveys that focus on vulnerable groups, for example substance use by young offenders[3] and school surveys.[4]

Drug use in the UK

General population

Capture–recapture and MIM have been used together to produce prevalence estimates for localities for 2004/5, 2005/6, 2006/7, 2008/9 and 2009/10 by Hay *et al.*[5] The latest version is expected in February 2013. Key findings are that:

▸ opiate and crack users have declined between 2005/6 and 2009/10 from about 330,000 to about 306,000

▸ the number of injecting drug users has declined from about 137,000 to about 103,000 over this period.

An annual estimate of the prevalence of drug use is undertaken through the BCS.[6] This drug use-declared component of the survey has been in place since 1996, and has tracked the prevalence of the use of different drugs over this time. Key findings include:

▸ last-year use of any illicit drug has fallen from 11.1% in the first 1996 BCS to 8.8% in the 2010/11 BCS. This is the lowest figure recorded. This represents about 2.9 million people who will admit to having taken drugs in the past year. They include one in five 16–24-year-olds, who mostly used cannabis

▸ most of this decline has been due to the significant fall in cannabis use

▸ Class A drug use among adults aged 16 to 59 in the 2010/11 BCS was 3.0%, a similar level as in the 1996 BCS (2.7%)

▸ although the long-term trend displays relatively constant levels of Class A drug use overall, within this category there are increases in powder cocaine use between the 1996 and 2010/11 BCS.

Young people

Information is also available relating to the prevalence of drug use among young people from *Smoking, Drinking and Drug Use among Young People in England in 2010*.[4] This is a survey carried out for the NHS Information Centre by the National Centre for Social Research and the National Foundation for Educational Research. The survey annually interviews school pupils aged between 11–15, and has been in place since 2001. Headlines for 2010 include:

▸ 18% of pupils said they had ever used drugs (29% in 2001)

▸ 12% responded they had taken drugs in the last year (20% in 2001)

▸ 7% had taken drugs in the last month (12% in 2001)

▸ 28% of pupils said they had been offered drugs (42% in 2001).

The NDTMS collects data on drug and alcohol treatment for young people (under 18), and produces official statistics bulletins.[1] However, it should be noted that young people's treatment figures are not comparable with statistics relating to adult drug treatment. This is because access to treatment for young people requires a 'lower severity of drug use and associated problems'.[7] Headlines for the number of under-18s include:

▸ accessing services in England during 2011–12 was 20,688

▸ treatment for problem drug use associated with primary use of heroin and crack has fallen each year for the past five years

▸ completing treatment successfully has more than doubled in five years.

Vulnerable groups

Drug use by care leavers is much higher than drug use by the general population. Ward *et al.*, in 2003,[8] surveyed care leavers aged between 14 and 24 years old and found that three-quarters of the sample responded positive to the question 'had ever used a drug' and over half 'had used a drug in the past month'. Not surprisingly, levels of drug use by the young homeless are much higher than by young people in general. Wincup *et al.*, in 2003,[9] sampled 160 homeless 16–25-year-olds and almost all (95%) had ever used drugs and equally almost all (89%) had used drugs in the past year and past month (76%), many of them using cocaine, heroin and/or amphetamine together with cannabis. This means that when a young homeless person presents to primary care, drug misuse should be considered even if the patient does not volunteer this information.

Drug use in the offending population

Drug use by the offending population is common. Information about drug use within this population is collected though the Drug Intervention Programme, which seeks to engage drug-using offenders with treatment services. It does this through a provision in the Drugs Act 2005, which introduced a mandatory drugs test for heroin, cocaine and crack cocaine from individuals arrested for specific 'trigger' offences (e.g. theft) known to be associated with high levels of drug misuse.

Initial findings published by the Home Office, relating to testing between July and October 2005, were that 7277 individuals tested positive from a cohort of 11,015 (73%).[10]

Prisons in England and Wales get 130,000 admissions every year, about 70% of whom have recently taken drugs. A busy remand prison treats over 3000 new drug-dependent prisoners a year. One study suggests a high rate of drug use among young offenders, where six out of ten had used some drug before entering prison. Among women, drug offences were more common, at one in five.[11]

Drug use in the UK compared with other European countries

Britain has often been portrayed in the media as the drug capital of Europe, with repeated claims from the media and others that it has higher cannabis use, higher cocaine use and higher alcohol use than its European neighbours. Indeed at first reading it does appear that Britain has among the highest levels of cannabis, ecstasy, cocaine and amphetamine use compared with most other members of the European Union (EU).

It is notoriously difficult, however, to make comparisons in use of illicit drugs across different nations. There are many factors that can interfere with establishing accurate comparisons. For example, sources of variation may reflect the differences in the urban and rural populations (where drug use is more prevalent in urban populations), age patterns/birth cohorts (these will affect measures of different drugs used as well as actual numbers using across the total population), the extent of the converging of lifestyles of young men and women (the more convergent, the higher the levels of use by women), and sociocultural factors, including income. As well as natural variation, the tools used to measure prevalence will vary across each country and hence comparative analysis across different countries using different survey tools needs to be made with caution, in particular where differences are small. Despite methodological limitations, however, some common patterns of drug use throughout the EU can be identified.

The European Monitoring Centre for Drugs and Drug Addiction (EMCDDA) produces an annual report on the state of drugs in Europe, attempting to bring coherence to the methods of collecting the data. Trends identified by the 2011 report [12] are described below.

Cannabis

In all countries in the EU, cannabis is the most commonly used drug, with many countries reporting lifetime prevalence rates in more than 25% of the general population. A conservative estimate would suggest that at least one in every five adults in the EU has tried the drug. Data suggest that the prevalence of cannabis use has stabilised and may now be decreasing in some European countries – including the UK.

Prevalence of cannabis use varies considerably across Europe, with Denmark, Spain, Italy, France and the UK all reporting over 30% for lifetime use. In all countries, estimates of the prevalence of recent use (within the past year) among the adult population are below 15%.

When young adults are considered, rates of use rise considerably. Recent use prevalence peaks in the 15–25-year-old age group, with Spain, France, the Czech Republic and Italy all above 10% for last-month use, and over 20% for last 12 months. Lifetime use estimates are higher, with most countries reporting lifetime prevalence estimates of between 20% and 50%. The UK lifetime-use prevalence rate is about one-third of the population.

The number of people using cannabis on a regular basis is small in overall population terms (generally less than 1%), although higher rates of regular use may be found in young people, and in particular in young men.

New or 'designer' drugs

A recent trend has been for an increasing number of new psychoactive substances being marketed through 'head-shops' and on-line vendors. The most common classes of drugs in this category are cathinones (e.g. mephedrone), synthetic cannabinoids and phenethylamines.

The harms caused by these new drugs are hard to assess, although in 2010 mephedrone was reported in the media to be a suspected cause in 65 UK drug-related death cases, of which toxicology confirmed the presence of mephedrone in 46 of these. However, the presence of a drug in a toxicology sample does not equate to the drug being responsible or contributing to the death, so these figures should be treated with some caution.

Between 1997 and 2010 there were 150 new substances notified through the EU early warning system, with 24 notified in 2009 and 41 in 2010. According to EMCDDA surveys of online availability of these drugs, in 2011 the UK had around 80 online vendors, up from about 20 in 2009. This is nearly double the reported number operating at that time in the Netherlands, which had the second highest number in Europe (41).

Amphetamines and ecstasy (MDMA)

Europe remains an important area for the production and use of amphetamines and ecstasy but less so for methamphetamine, the use of which is more significant to Australasia, Southeast Asia and the USA. Despite this, there have been significant increases in methamphetamine use in the Czech Republic and Slovakia where the drug is now a significant component of the countries' drug use. There is evidence from seizures that methamphetamine prevalence may be increasing in neighbouring countries and Scandinavia.

Rates of lifetime experience among the adult population for amphetamine use range between 0.1% (Greece) and 11.9% (UK). In the past, prevalence of amphetamine use was generally higher than prevalence of ecstasy use, but ecstasy has now become the more widely used. The 12-month prevalence for use of amphetamines varies from 0% (Greece) to 1.4% (UK). This compares with ecstasy, which ranges from 0.2% (Greece) to 1.9% (UK). As with cannabis, the highest rates of lifetime and recent use are found in young adults.

The proportion of clients entering treatment for an amphetamine problem in

Europe varies widely. In the Czech Republic (41%), Slovakia (32%), Poland (26%) and Sweden (22%), stimulants are a significant reason for seeking treatment. Rates in the rest of Europe are usually in the 3–10% range, with the UK rate being 4%.

A small number of deaths in Europe can be directly attributed to the use of ecstasy, but overall the numbers remain very low in comparison with deaths related to opioids. Although there have been some fluctuations in recent years, amphetamine powder seizures have increased in most European countries between 2004 and 2009. The quantities and number of methamphetamine seizures increased over this period, with a strong increase between 2008 and 2009, particularly in Sweden and Norway.

Cocaine and crack cocaine

Cocaine is now the second most tried drug in Europe, after cannabis, with prevalence rates for lifetime use highest in Spain (10%), the UK (9%) and Italy (7%). Across Europe, the rate is over 4%. Problematic crack cocaine use estimates are not available for most European countries, but are available for the UK, where this has been estimated at 184,000 in 2009/10, the majority of which are also heroin users.

The trend in the UK and Spain was that prevalence of cocaine use increased significantly in the 1990s, and has been relatively stable since then. In Denmark, Ireland, Italy and Cyprus the increase came later, but has now largely stabilised. In other European countries cocaine use is relatively low and generally stable.

Treatment data from the UK[2] indicates that the number of clients with a primary cocaine problem in treatment has fallen from 3684 in 2007–8 to 2279 in 2010–11, and from 1059 to 766 for crack cocaine over the same period. This suggests that there is a reducing prevalence of problematic cocaine use, which may be related to an increase in the availability of treatment, and also a reduction in the purity of street drugs, which has decreased from 62% measured in 1999 to 27% in 2008/09.[10]

The prevalence of use of crack cocaine in Europe appears to be relatively low, although sporadic local reports suggest a problem among marginal groups in some cities, for example within the sex industry. We know, however, that the health impact of crack cocaine use is disproportionately greater than that caused by cocaine powder use so the impact on health and social care services even with low prevalence use is significant.

Heroin and injecting drug use

Although few in terms of overall numbers, heroin users are responsible for a disproportionate share of the health and social problems resulting from drug consumption; regular injecting of heroin has a far greater health and social care

Figure 3.1   Trends in last-year prevalence of cocaine use among young adults in the six highest EU member states, Australia, Canada and the USA

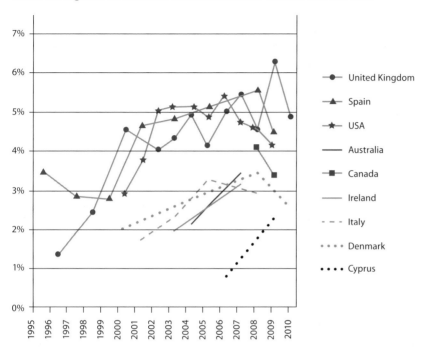

Source: European Monitoring Centre for Drugs and Drug Addiction. *Annual Report 2011: the state of the drugs problem in Europe.* Lisbon: EMCDDA, 2011. Used with permission.

cost than any other drug. In most countries in the EU, with the exception of Sweden and Finland where amphetamine use is more prevalent, problem drug use remains characterised by the use of heroin, often in combination with other drugs, so called 'polydrug use'.

Heroin use increased markedly in Europe after the 1970s, and its use became more prevalent until the late 1990s. Subsequently, the problem declined a little, although its use is thought to have been relatively stable since about 2003/4. This trend has been similar in the UK, although the prevalence of lifetime use is higher, at about 7.7 per 1000 population, against a European average of about 4. The estimated annual prevalence of problematic heroin use in the UK has decreased over from 273,000 to 264,000 between 2006/07 and 2009/10.[5]

Injecting drug users have a higher risk of experiencing ill health as a result of their drug use, particularly an increased risk of contracting blood-borne viruses and overdose fatalities. Injecting drug use is mainly associated with opiate use in Europe, although in some countries injecting is also associated with amphetamine use. The prevalence of injecting drug use in the UK has been estimated at

43

Figure 3.2   **Estimates of the annual prevalence of problem opioid use (among population aged 15–64)**

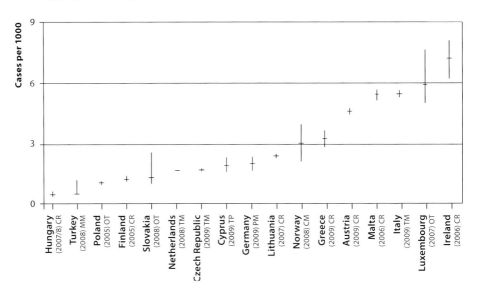

Source: European Monitoring Centre for Drugs and Drug Addiction. *Annual Report 2011: the state of the drugs problem in Europe*. Lisbon: EMCDDA, 2011. Used with permission.

about 4.0 per 1000 of the population, compared with a European average of about 3.6 per 1000.

Drug-related deaths

It is well documented that heroin users are at a substantially greater risk of pre-mature death than their non-heroin-using peers. However, about 12% of drug-related deaths are thought to be as a result of cocaine use.[13]

The number of drug-related deaths in the UK rose throughout the 1990s and early 2000s as it did in many other countries,[13] but has been fairly stable since then, at between about 1600 and 1900 deaths a year, with the trend falling over the past two years. This corresponds to a rate of about 59 deaths per million[14] (16–64 years) for the UK, compared with a rate of about 21 per million for Europe as a whole. However, it should be noted that data collection methods in some countries are not to the same standard as the UK's.

The Office for National Statistics reports that, between 2009 and 2010, the number of deaths from drug misuse fell by 6% in England to 1625, following on from the fall of 3% in the previous year.[15, 16] This reflects the NTA's official drug treatment statistics, which show that there are encouraging trends in drug treatment data, such as new presentations to treatment in the under-thirties falling.

While drug-related deaths have levelled off, they are still too high. This is thought to be related to the observed age profile of heroin injectors, who are growing older and are more likely to have a long history of drug dependency, engage in more dangerous injecting behaviour, and are consequently at greater risk of dying from an overdose.

It seems possible that the high water mark of the heroin epidemic that began in the 1980s has now passed, with relatively few presentations for opioid misuse among the under-25s, and a decline in presentations for heroin use generally – particularly in those parts of the country where the heroin epidemic took hold earlier.

Conclusion

Illicit drug use in the general population is at its lowest level since first being measured 16 years ago. This is a welcome reversal, following years of rising illicit drug use in society.

Very few use people use heroin, the most dangerous drug, with the potential for long-term addiction and overdose. Lifetime heroin use is in decline; having peaked at 1% in 2000, it is now 0.6%.

We have also recently seen reductions in the estimated size of the problem of heroin and crack users (from a peak of over 332,000 in 2005–7 to 306,000 in 2009–10). On top of this, declining overall use of illegal drugs in England seems to be feeding through into reduced treatment demand

The total number of adults in treatment peaked at 210,000 in 2008–9 and fell to 197,110 in 2011–12. The reduction is fastest in younger age groups with the number of heroin and crack users aged 1–24 coming into treatment more than halving since 2005–6.

For decades drug policy in the UK has concentrated on improving access to treatment and the prevention of drug-related harms. Over the last 15 years there has been a significant investment in drug treatment, both through open-access community services and through developing access routed into treatment through the Criminal Justice System.

Since the change of UK government in 2010, there has been a greater policy emphasis placed on 'recovery'-based treatment, which focuses on getting drug users free from drug use, and a reduced appetite to provide long-term methadone maintenance treatment.

The figures do suggest that the UK does have one of the higher rates of drug use within Europe, but that the trend is that this is now either stable or falling slightly. In particular, the use of opiates among young adults appears to have fallen significantly from the peaks recorded a decade or so ago.

45

Further reading

European Monitoring Centre for Drugs and Drug Addiction. *EMCDDA INSIGHTS Series, Number 3: reviewing current practice in drug-substitution treatment in the European Union.* Luxembourg: Office for Official Publications of the European Communities, 2000, www.emcdda.org.

Gabbay M (ed.). *The Evidence-Based Primary Care Handbook.* London: Royal Society of Medicine, 1999.

NHS Information Centre, Lifestyles Statistics. *Statistics on Drug Misuse: England, 2011.* Leeds: NHS Information Centre, 2011, www.ic.nhs.uk/webfiles/publications/003_Health_Lifestyles/Statistics%20on%20Drug%20Misuse%20England%202011/Statistics_on_Drug_Misuse_England_2011v3.pdf   [accessed October 2012].

References

1. National Treatment Agency for Substance Misuse. *Statistics from the National Drug Treatment Monitoring System (NDTMS) 1 April 2005–31 March 2006, Appendix 2.* London: NTA, 2006, www.nta.nhs.uk/uploads/ndtms_stat_report_05_06_11.06.08.pdf   [accessed November 2012].

2. National Treatment Agency. *Drug Treatment Activity in England 2011–12: statistical release.* London: NTA, 2012, www.nta.nhs.uk/statistics.aspx   [accessed October 2012].

3. Youth Justice Board. *Substance Misuse and the Juvenile Secure Estate.* London: YJB, 2004, http://yjbpublications.justice.gov.uk/en-gb/Resources/Downloads/SubstanceMisuseJSE summary.pdf   [accessed November 2012].

4. NHS Information Centre. *Smoking, Drinking and Drug Use among Young People in England in 2010.* Leeds: NHS Information Centre, 2011, www.ic.nhs.uk/statistics-and-data-collections/health-and-lifestyles-related-surveys/smoking-drinking-and-drug-use-among-young-people-in-england/smoking-drinking-and-drug-use-among-young-people-in-england-in-2010 [accessed November 2012].

5. Hay G, Gannon M, Casey J, *et al. Estimates of the Prevalence of Opiate Use and/or Crack Cocaine Use, 2009/10: sweep 6 report.* London: NTA, 2011, www.nta.nhs.uk/facts-prevalence.aspx [accessed November 2012].

6. Home Office. *British Crime Survey.* London: Home Office, www.homeoffice.gov.uk/science-research/research-statistics/crime/crime-statistics/british-crime-survey/ [accessed November 2012].

7. Department of Health (England) and the devolved administrations. *Drug Misuse and Dependence: UK guidelines on clinical management.* London: Department of Health (England), the Scottish Government, Welsh Assembly Government and Northern Ireland Executive, 2007, www.nta.nhs.uk/uploads/clinical_guidelines_2007.pdf   [accessed November 2012].

8. Ward J, Henderson Z, Pearson G. *One Problem among Many: drug use among care leavers in transition to independent living. Home Office Research Study 260.* London: Home Office, 2003.

9. Wincup E, Buckland G, Bayliss R. *Youth Homelessness and Substance Use: report to the drugs and alcohol research unit. Home Office Research Study 258.* London: Home Office, 2003.

10. Skodbo S, Brown G, Deacon S, *et al. The Drug Interventions Programme (DIP): addressing drug use and offending through 'Tough Choices'.* London: Home Office, 2007, www.ohrn.nhs.uk/resource/policy/HomeOfficeDrugs2.pdf   [accessed November 2012].

11. Lader D, Singleton N, Meltzer H. *Psychiatric Morbidity among Young Offenders in England and Wales*. London: ONS, 2000.

12. European Monitoring Centre for Drugs and Drug Addiction. *Annual Report 2011: the state of the drugs problem in Europe*. Lisbon: EMCDDA, 2011, www.emcdda.europa.eu/publications/annual-report/2011 [accessed November 2012].

13. Parliamentary Home Affairs Committee. *Trends in Cocaine Use*. London: PHAC, 2010, www.publications.parliament.uk/pa/cm200910/cmselect/cmhaff/74/7408.htm [accessed November 2012].

14. Griffiths C. Deaths related to drug poisoning: results for England and Wales, 1997 to 2001. *Health Statistics Quarterly* 2003: **17**; 65–71.

15. Advisory Council on the Misuse of Drugs. *Reducing Drug Related Deaths, 2000*. London: HMSO, 2000.

16. Office for National Statistics. *Deaths Related to Drug Poisoning in England and Wales, 2010*. Newport: ONS, 2011, www.ons.gov.uk/ons/rel/subnational-health3/deaths-related-to-drug-poisoning/2010/stb-deaths-related-to-drug-poisoning-2010.html [accessed November 2012].

CHAPTER 4

Prescribing of controlled drugs in primary care in England

Sue Faulding and David Lloyd

IN THIS CHAPTER

Introduction ‖ General trends in controlled drug prescribing during 2011 ‖ Analgesics ‖ Drugs used in the treatment of opioid dependence ‖ Stimulants ‖ Private prescribing ‖ Conclusion

Introduction

Controlled drugs are an important part of the prescribing armoury for GPs. They are used for analgesia, epilepsy and attention deficit hyperactivity disorder (ADHD) in children, and in the management of drug dependence. The actions of the convicted former GP, Harold Shipman, who used fraudulently obtained diamorphine to murder patients over a 23-year period exposed the apparent freedom that doctors in the UK had in relation to the prescribing of controlled drugs. Lady Justice Janet Smith, chairwoman of the Shipman Inquiry,[1] recommended practices and procedures to tighten the mechanisms for audit and monitoring, and the implementation of measures to identify potentially fraudulent or inappropriate prescribing. The Department of Health published guidance on the safer management of controlled drugs in June 2006.[2] This included:

▸ arrangements for private schedule 2 and 3 prescriptions to mirror those for NHS prescriptions. All private prescribers of controlled drugs are required to have a unique identifier code, and to use FP10PCD forms

▸ Primary Care Trusts became responsible for monitoring levels of prescribing of controlled drugs by both NHS and private prescribers

▸ all prescriptions for schedule 2 and 3 controlled drugs, whether NHS or private, are required to include the NHS number of the patient

▸ the validity period for all controlled drug prescriptions is 28 days

▸ all prescribers are strongly advised to restrict volumes to no more than 30 days' supply

▸ all details on prescriptions, except the signature of the prescriber, can be computer generated

▸ patients or other persons collecting medicines on their behalf are required to sign for them.

Additional changes to the legislation in April 2012 allow independent non-medical prescribers to prescribe controlled drugs.[3]

General trends in controlled drug prescribing in 2011

Using data from Prescription Services, a division of the NHS Business Services Authority (NHSBSA), it is possible to examine the prescribing patterns of controlled drugs. The data are for prescriptions dispensed in the community (by pharmacists, appliance contractors, dispensing doctors and items personally administered by practices) in England. While most of the data will relate to prescriptions issued in primary care by GPs and other primary care prescribers, hospital-generated items dispensed in the community and prescribing by dentists are also included.[4] Prescriptions issued in private practice are not included.

The prescription indicates nothing about the condition being treated. Therefore the classification of medicines that can be used for several purposes (e.g. methadone) is based on strength or formulation and not on any record of the indication. This means that drugs reported as being for one purpose (e.g. analgesia) may actually be used for another (e.g. substance dependence).

Figures 4.1 and 4.2 show the number of items and costs of controlled drugs over the period 2001 to 2011. Controlled drugs are divided into five schedules under the Misuse of Drugs regulations. Schedule 1 relates to such drugs as cannabis and lysergide, which are not normally used medicinally. However, in recent years medicines derived from cannabis have been introduced and these are now classified under schedule 1. Schedule 2 includes diamorphine, morphine and cocaine, and these are subject to the full controlled drug regulations. Schedule 3 includes barbiturates and buprenorphine and these drugs have less stringent regulations. Schedule 4 includes benzodiazepines (although some, such as temazepam, are in schedule 3) and zolpidem, and these are subject to minimal control. Schedule 5 includes those preparations that, because of their low strength, are exempt from virtually all requirements. Separate lines show the trend for each schedule. The drugs are classified here using the schedule to which they belonged in 2011, rather than the schedule to which they may have belonged at the time. The number of prescriptions for schedule 1 (medicines derived from cannabis) are very low and so cannot be seen at this scale.

Figure 4.1 shows that the use of schedule 2 medicines has increased while other schedules have been fairly stable or fallen. Schedule 5 drugs are the most commonly prescribed.

Figure 4.1 **Number of prescription items for controlled drugs dispensed in primary care in England 2001 to 2011, by schedule**

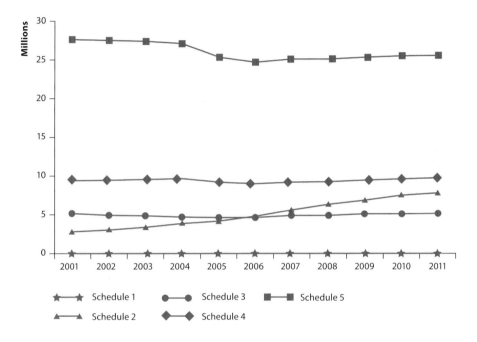

Source: adapted from Health and Social Care Information Centre.[4]

Figure 4.2 (overleaf) shows the dramatic increase in cost for schedule 2 drugs over the time period. The number of items increased by 178% over the period but cost increased by 285%, probably as a result of the availability of newer drugs and novel routes of administration such as patches.

Over 48.1 million prescriptions for controlled drugs were dispensed in 2011, representing 5.0% of all prescriptions of all categories of prescribed (controlled and non-controlled) medicines dispensed for that year. The increase in the number of prescription items for controlled drugs was 1.0% on the previous year. Note that these figures relate to all five schedules of controlled drugs as defined by the Misuse of Drugs Regulations 2011. Table 4.1 (overleaf) shows the number of items for each of the schedules.

Figure 4.2   **Net ingredient cost of controlled drug prescriptions dispensed in primary care in England 2001 to 2011, by schedule**

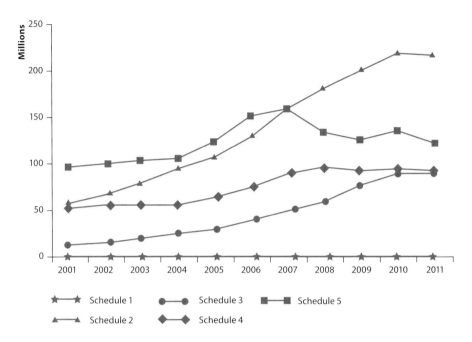

Source: adapted from Health and Social Care Information Centre.[4]

Table 4.1   **Number of items and percentage for each schedule for 2011, dispensed in primary care in England**

Schedule	Prescription items	Share of all controlled drugs (%)
1	2964	0.0%
2	7,810,448	16.2%
3	5,214,457	10.8%
4	9,649,083	20.1%
5	25,425,528	52.9%

Source: adapted from Health and Social Care Information Centre.[4]

Table 4.2 **Items and net ingredient cost (NIC) of medicines in schedules 1 and 2 in 2011**

	NIC	Items
Methadone hydrochloride	13.66%	37.04%
Morphine sulphate	9.27%	21.97%
Fentanyl	30.60%	13.60%
Oxycodone hydrochloride	23.34%	12.74%
Methylphenidate hydrochloride	13.04%	9.15%
Diamorphine hydrochloride (systemic)	3.38%	1.56%
Methadone hydrochloride	0.63%	1.03%
Oxycodone HCl/naloxone HCl	2.00%	1.00%
Pethidine hydrochloride	0.63%	0.63%
Dexamfetamine sulphate	1.46%	0.56%
Dipipanone hydrochloride	0.28%	0.29%
Hydromorphone hydrochloride	0.25%	0.14%
Morphine tartrate & cyclizine tartrate	0.03%	0.06%
Secobarbital sodium	0.16%	0.05%
Tapentadol hydrochloride	0.06%	0.05%
Cannabis	0.57%	0.04%

Source: adapted from Health and Social Care Information Centre.[4]

Only schedules 1 and 2 are subject to the full controlled drug requirements and subsequent analysis will focus only on medicines in schedules 1 and 2.

Items for schedule 1 (which consists solely of a treatment for multiple sclerosis based on cannabis) increased by 18.5% between 2010 and 2011. Items for schedule 2 increased by 4.5%.

Analgesics (*British National Formulary* [BNF] 4.7) accounted for 53.1% of schedule 1 and 2 controlled drug prescriptions. Over a third (37.0%) of all schedules 1 and 2 controlled drug items prescribed were for methadone solution for the treatment of substance dependence (BNF 4.10.3). See Table 4.2.

Methadone is the most frequently prescribed drug, followed by morphine. However, fentanyl and oxycodone account for the highest costs. Figure 4.3 (overleaf) shows the number of items for leading schedule 2 drugs from 2001 to 2011.

Figure 4.3   **Number of prescription items for the leading controlled drugs, by chemical substance, dispensed in primary care in England 2001 to 2011**

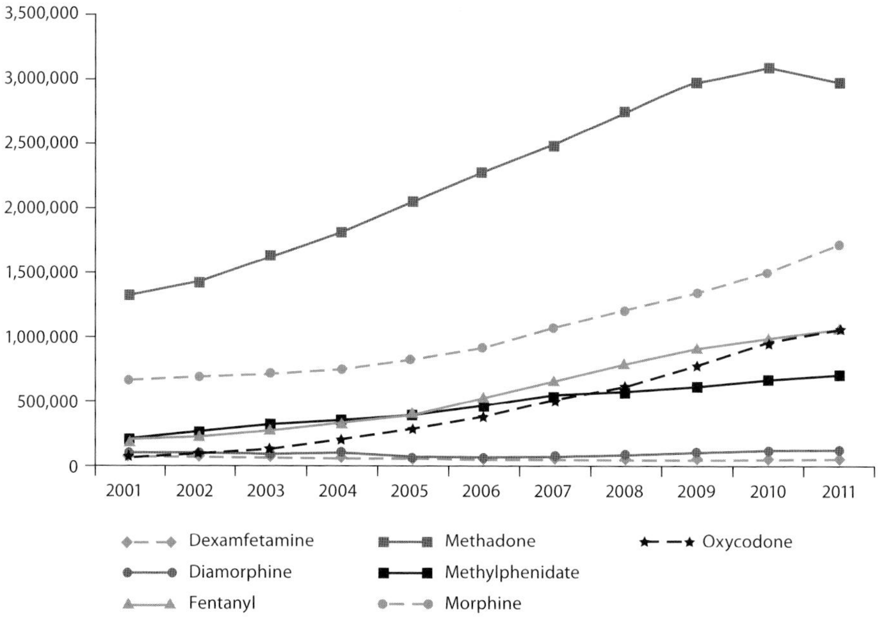

Source: adapted from Health and Social Care Information Centre.[4]

Over 4.1 million items were prescribed for 18 different analgesic drugs. Five drugs (methadone hydrochloride for substance dependence, morphine sulphate, fentanyl, oxycodone hydrochloride and methylphenidate hydrochloride) dominate controlled drug prescribing, and account for over 94% of total schedule 1 and 2 controlled items. Of these, three are analgesics (morphine, diamorphine and oxycodone).

Analgesics

Opioid analgesics are used to relieve moderate to severe pain, both acute and chronic, particularly of visceral origin.

Morphine sulphate

Morphine has been commercially available since 1827 and is the opioid of choice for oral treatment of severe pain in palliative care. It is available in a range of formulations, including: tablets, capsules, liquids, modified-release tablets, suppositories and injections. Morphine is available in several different salts and some low-strength preparations are classified as schedule 5. Use of schedule 2 morphine sulphate has grown by 156.5% in terms of the number of items and 45.8% in terms of cost over the period 2001 to 2011. The number of items grew by 14.7% between 2010 and 2011.

Fentanyl

Fentanyl was developed in the 1960s as an anaesthetic, and became widely used in palliative care following the development of patch formulations for transdermal administration in the 1990s.

Tablet and nasal spray formulations have more recently become available and are licensed for breakthrough pain in patients receiving opioid therapy for chronic cancer pain. Between 2001 and 2011, the number of items increased by 484.1% and the cost by 284.1%. In 2011 the number of items increased by 7.4% over use in 2010.

Diamorphine

The UK is one of the few countries in the world that recommends the use of diamorphine as a medicine. It has greater solubility than other opioids, which allows effective doses to be administered in smaller volumes, which is of value in palliative care. Between 2001 and 2011, the number of items increased by 27.3% and the cost by 115.5%. In 2011 the number of items increased by 7.3% over use in 2010. Figure 4.4 shows the annual figures for all forms of diamorphine classed as schedule 2.

The fall in use in 2005 is probably associated with the publicity around the use of diamorphine by Harold Shipman as the reports of the public inquiry were published between July 2002 and January 2005. The fifth report *Safeguarding Patients*, which covered regulation and care, and is the report most relevant to this chapter, was published in December 2004.[5]

Oxycodone

Oxycodone is also available in a range of oral and injectable formulations. It was initially introduced to the market as a better tolerated alternative to morphine, though this remains debatable. Prescribing of oxycodone in England increased by 11.7% from 2010 to 2011, but has increased by 1744.4% since 2001.

Figure 4.4   **Number of prescription items for diamorphine dispensed in primary care in England 2001 to 2011**

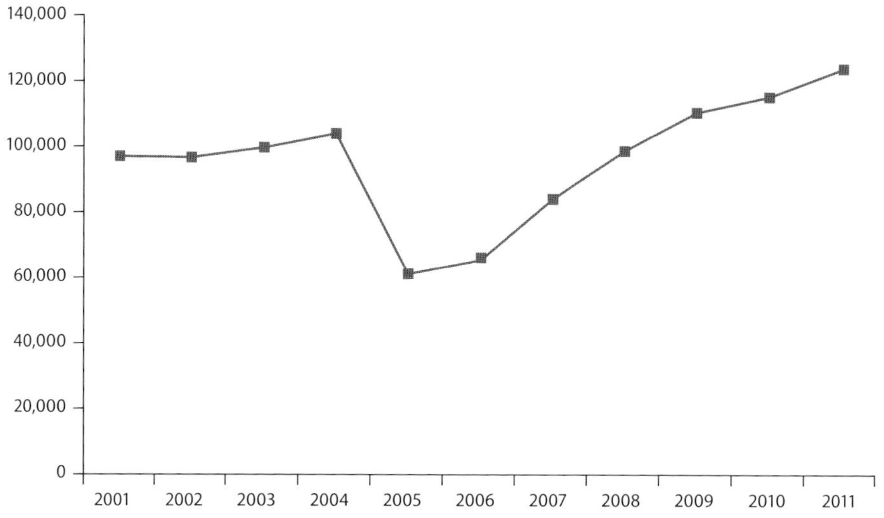

Source: adapted from Health and Social Care Information Centre.[4]

Drugs used in the treatment of opioid dependence

The National Institute for Health and Clinical Excellence (NICE) has published guidance on the management of opioid dependence. Both methadone and buprenorphine (controlled drugs schedule 3) are recommended for maintenance therapy alongside a supportive care programme.

Methadone

Overall methadone prescribing decreased by 4.0% between 2010 and 2011, and prescribing for methadone solution, classified by the *British National Formulary* as a drug for the treatment of substance dependence, also decreased by 3.9%, with over 3.8 million litres prescribed in 2011. However, this has increased by 125.7% since 2001.

Buprenorphine

Buprenorphine is a semi-synthetic opioid that is used to treat opioid addiction in higher dosages and to control pain in lower dosages. For treatment of opioid dependence there is a combination formulation with naloxone. As noted earlier, the classification of prescriptions is based on assumptions about strengths and not information on actual use. This means that some of the use classified by the BSA as for analgesia may actually be for dependence and vice versa. This is illustrated by the fact that 1% of the prescriptions issued in primary care in 2010 classified as buprenorphine for analgesia were on special Misuse of Drugs Act prescriptions intended for use in treating dependence.

Table 4.3   **Recent trends in buprenorphine prescribing**

Drug	Items in 2011	Change from 2010	Change from 2001
Buprenorphine for analgesia	1,371,694	14.9%	1083.7%
Buprenorphine for opioid dependence (including combination with naloxone)	791,281	7.2%	946.6%

Source: adapted from Health and Social Care Information Centre.[4]

Stimulants

Methylphenidate and dexamfetamine are licensed for use for ADHD and are also used for narcolepsy. In 2011 there was a growth of 8.1% in items for methylphenidate while items for dexamfetamine fell by 3.4%. Table 4.4 shows their relative use.

Table 4.4   **Recent trends in stimulant prescribing**

Drug	Items in 2011	Change from 2010	Change from 2001
Dexamfetamine sulphate	43,981	-3.4%	-39.1%
Methylphenidate hydrochloride	714,820	8.1%	242.9%

Source: adapted from Health and Social Care Information Centre.[4]

Other drugs for the treatment of ADHD are not controlled drugs. NICE recommends that treatment should be initiated only by child and adolescent psychiatrists or paediatricians with an expertise in ADHD, but responsibility for continued prescribing and monitoring may be passed to GPs under shared-care arrangements.

Private prescribing

Following the Shipman Inquiry, details of all private prescriptions for schedules 1, 2 and 3 controlled drugs dispensed in the community were required to be submitted to the Prescription Services division of the NHSBSA. This allows monitoring by the local Primary Care Trust and the Care Quality Commission.

In 2011 there were 43,731 private controlled drugs prescriptions recorded in the system, 83.5% of which were schedule 2. Half of all items were prescribed in Westminster PCT, and London SHA comprised 84.4% of total items. Private prescribing of controlled drugs is much lower than prescribing rates in the NHS. Note that these data exclude controlled drugs prescribed within private hospitals.

Methadone was the most frequently prescribed chemical, comprising 42.7% of all items (27.6% classified as for analgesia and 15.1% for substance opioid dependence). Table 4.5 shows the top 10 drugs by number of items and the figure for all other drugs.

Table 4.5   **Private prescribing of controlled drugs for 2011 in England**

BNF name	Items	Percentage of total
Methadone hydrochloride for analgesia	12,055	27.6%
Dexamfetamine sulphate	6932	15.9%
Methadone hydrochloride for substance dependence	6596	15.1%
Morphine sulphate	3964	9.1%
Methylphenidate hydrochloride	3899	8.9%
Temazepam	3644	8.3%
Buprenorphine hydrochloride	2030	4.6%
Oxycodone hydrochloride	1315	3.0%
Buprenorphine	627	1.4%
Fentanyl	601	1.4%
Others	2068	4.7%

Source: adapted from Health and Social Care Information Centre.[4]

Conclusion

Medicines classified as controlled drugs have a range of therapeutic uses. Schedule 5 controlled drugs, which have the lowest level of control, are the most frequently prescribed. Schedule 2 medicines, which are subject to the greatest control, account for the highest costs in primary care in England. Methadone, used for the management of opioid dependence, is the most frequently prescribed controlled drug. However, use of methadone has declined slightly in the last year, while the use of buprenorphine for opioid dependence has increased.

Over the last five years, following the Shipman Inquiry, there have been significant changes to the legislation relating to controlled drugs. There are now tighter processes in place for monitoring the prescribing of controlled drugs, including closer scrutiny of private prescriptions. Additional changes enacted in 2012 mean that independent non-medical prescribers are permitted to prescribe controlled drugs.

Further reading

The BNF is a useful resource. Under the 'Guidance on prescribing' at the start of the book are sections on: 'Controlled drugs and dependence' and 'Prescribing in palliative care'. The BNF also contains information on individual drugs and preparations.

References

1. Department of Health. *The Regulation of Controlled Drugs in the Community* (Shipman Inquiry, Fourth Report). London: HMSO, 2004.

2. Department of Health. *Safer Management of Controlled Drugs: guidance for implementation.* London: HMSO, 2006.

3. Home Office. Nurse and pharmacist independent prescribing, 'mixing of medicines', possession authorities under patient group directions and personal exemption provisions for schedule 4 part II drugs. Home Office Circular 009/2012. April 2012.

4. Health and Social Care Information Centre. Prescription cost analysis, England – 2011, April 2012.

5. Department of Health. *Safeguarding Patients: lessons from the past – proposals for the future.* London: HMSO, 2004.

CHAPTER 5

General practitioners and the care of drug users: past, present and future

Linda Harris

Introduction: the current role of GPs in providing care to those who misuse drugs

Across the country GPs are playing a central role in dealing with the impact of drug misuse. A survey of English GPs conducted by the National Addiction Centre showed that about half of GPs had seen a drug user in the preceding month, with half of these GPs prescribing substitute medication.[1]

The latest figures from the National Treatment Agency for Substance Misuse (NTA) show that, across the country, 32% of GPs are involved in the care of drug users and it can be said that the majority of substitute medication now takes place within a primary care context, albeit mostly supported by specialist services through shared care. In fact, in some areas of the country, the involvement of GPs in the shared care of drug users has reached 80%.[2]

Many of these GPs provide only core services, in partnership with local specialist services. Some are GPs with a special clinical interest, who are able to provide an intermediate level of support to their colleagues, and the General Medical Services contract for GPs has opened up further opportunities for practices to be engaged with drug users.

GPs are well placed to continue to play an important role in both preventing and dealing with substance misuse. A key strength of general practice is the ability of GPs to form strong interpersonal bonds within professionally appropriate limits. Medical generalists are able to deal with health issues that require delicate discussions about emotional vulnerability, lifestyle and behavioural choice, such as substance misuse. Systems for tackling drug misuse must look to build on, and maximise the potential of, these strengths to achieve the best outcomes for patients. There is a need for continuing investment in primary care to enhance the contribution that GPs can make in this area.[3]

Primary care: rising to the healthcare challenges of the future and the changing landscape of care

Major progress has been made in improving the performance of the NHS and in so doing the care and experience of patients. General practice and the specialist realms within it, including substance misuse treatment and care, have been major contributors to this success. Primary care has been a passionate advocate for those from vulnerable groups who face the burden of inequity of care.[4]

Notwithstanding this progress, there is robust evidence that the current health and social care delivery system is failing to keep pace with the needs of an ageing population, the changing burden of disease, and rising patient and public expectations.[5] This is no different for primary care substance misuse treatment and care, which is now competing with other priorities in public health and wellbeing, and adapting to the changing presentation and impact of substance misuse amongst an ageing population and new drugs.[6]

The GP now and even more so in the future will need to be an active contributor to some of the most fundamental changes to the ways in which care is organised and delivered. It must be ensured that there is a greater emphasis on:

▸ preventing illness and tackling risk factors, such as obesity, smoking and substance misuse, to help people remain in good health

▸ supporting people to live in their own homes and offering a wider range of housing options in the community

▸ providing high standards of primary care across all practices to enable more services to be delivered in primary care, where appropriate

▸ making more effective use of community health services and related social care, and ensuring these services are available 24/7 when needed

▶ using acute hospitals and care homes only for those people who cannot be treated or cared for more appropriately in other settings

▶ integrating care around the needs of people and populations.[7]

The provider landscape is changing rapidly and commissioning structures are being radically reformed, including the establishment of Clinical Commissioning Groups and Public Health England (PHE). PHE is the new central body with responsibilities to drive the national public health agenda forward.[8] It is the authoritative national voice for public health, providing specialist skills, expert services and expertise, information and advice, based on the best available evidence of what works.

PHE will be providing oversight to local authorities who have subsumed the local public health workforce. They in turn will be supported by the organisational memory and expertise of professionals formerly part of the NTA and the Health Protection Agency who are now integrated within the new PHE structure.[9]

While health professionals may have become used to and in some ways taken comfort from the raft of top-down performance targets (e.g. numbers of users retained in treatment, numbers of GPs engaged in shared care), the most recent national strategies for health, social care and criminal justice rarely advocate centrally driven performance targets. These have been replaced by a series of locally focused health and social care priorities and outcomes based on the findings of the local joint strategic needs assessment. The public health white paper *Healthy Lives, Healthy People* sets out the government's long-term vision for the future of public health in England.[10]

Following the launch of this paper in 2010 and the subsequent pause and published findings of the NHS Future Forum [11] primary care is now firmly signed up to the ideologies of integrated care, marketisation, patients empowered by more choice and control, services commissioned as whole systems and performance managed on outcomes.

The continuing need for the GP champion

In spite of the huge upheaval and uncertainty created by a reform agenda that is affecting almost every part of every public service, the role and responsibility of the clinical leader or champion remains critical to the successful implementation of effective, evidence-based care.

Effective clinical leaders understand the importance of relationships across primary and secondary care, and the need to be able both to understand and effectively articulate the evidence that underpins clinically effective treatment.[12]

Effective clinical leaders understand too the importance of keeping abreast of the evidence, to challenge where resources are at risk or inequitable and to adopt innovation early where relevant and safe to do so. They serve as 'beacons of good practice' in a local area always on the lookout for ways to effect the best results for their patients.

The effective clinical leader is committed to education and training, and makes time to develop the skills of others, such as fellow professionals or peers. Education and training needs to be flexible, accessible and offered through a variety of different means, be that through clinical attachments, the facilitation of action learning, tutoring and mentoring or didactic presentations.

The effective clinical leader is known within the locality as an enthusiastic advocate whose leadership is visible through his or her representation at the meetings that matter. Particularly important are strategic commissioning and service development meetings, where clinical leaders can be found making a contribution and owning actions to ensure that managed change takes place.

Complex patients whose lives are blighted by stigma and discrimination require care that is 'better than the best' in view of the legacy that health inequality leaves in terms of quality of life and morbidity and mortality. Cuts in services often lead to the most vulnerable being hit the hardest due to the deterioration of partnership working and the fragmentation of care.

A cohort of effective clinical leaders will be needed to maintain and improve the outcomes of patients with substance misuse. These leaders must be equipped with skill, enthusiasm and resilience to work to raise standards, challenge inequitable care and promote the holistic needs of those with hepatitis, bearing in mind the competing priorities within the public health pool of resources.

RCGP Substance Misuse and Associated Health: developing and supporting clinical champions in primary care substance misuse

The RCGP Substance Misuse and Associated Health's (SMAH) suite of training [13] is designed to increase confidence through skills acquisition and enthuse participants to become the effective clinical champions of the future. The training offered by SMAH supports leadership development and encourages participants to maintain a strong clinical network as a means of sharing good practice and garnering support for the prioritisation of hepatitis treatment and care as an area for targeted investment.

In addition primary care practitioners can gain specialist advice and signposting to the latest workforce development programmes by joining and engaging with Substance Misuse Management in General Practice (SMMGP) [14] and the industry-wide body, the Substance Misuse Skills Consortium. [15] The latter works collaboratively with the NHS and voluntary-sector providers to promote specialist skills in substance misuse.

The Consortium takes account of all the current drivers and the recovery agenda. It has produced a strategic statement on the drug and alcohol workforce. In conjunction with Skills for Justice it has produced a blueprint for roles and responsibilities from various levels of accountability within the drug and alcohol workforce, including commissioners, managers, individuals, learning and development providers, members of the non-traditional workforce, i.e. mutual aid, and service users, families and carers.

The future, while challenging, provides opportunities for the well-organised and systematic clinical leader. Leaders must be capable of rising to the challenge posed by unprecedented funding pressures that will not only affect health and social care but also the body of primary care professionals. Clinical leaders should welcome the opportunities provided by this major shift in the location of care delivery and the ways in which patients and service users relate to health and social care professionals.

Drug policy, primary care and public health

Investment in drug treatment services has been a significant element in successive drug strategies since the first needle and syringe exchanges were piloted in 1986 by Margaret Thatcher's administration. Drug treatment in Britain is by and large a success story. Primary care and the growth and spread of shared-care schemes means that treatment is now available to anyone who needs it in England. Ninety-six per cent of clients start treatment within three weeks and the average wait for treatment fell from nine weeks in 2002 to five days.[16]

Since then treatment services have expanded to include protecting the public and drug users from blood-borne viruses and injecting risks, preventing overdose death by promoting safer practices among users, and stabilising troubled families to protect children and vulnerable adults.

The University of Glasgow prevalence research showed that the number of injecting drug users in England fell by a quarter from a peak of 137,141 in 2004–5 to 103,185 in 2009–10.

Data from the National Drug Treatment Monitoring System show a 10% fall in the proportion of new treatment entrants currently injecting over the last six years. The UK now has one of the lowest rates of HIV among injecting drug users in the Western world. The overall incidence of hepatitis C among current injectors in England (around 45%) is also one of the lowest in Europe.[17]

Drug-related deaths increased steadily in England during the 1990s to 1697 in 2001, then fell as treatment expanded. Despite a small rise in the late 2000s the 2010 figure was 1625. The flat trend is reassuring because the injecting population is ageing and becoming more vulnerable.[18]

The evidence base for drug treatment was evaluated by the National Institute for Health and Clinical Excellence (NICE) and its recommendations enshrined in NICE guidance and UK clinical guidelines (2007).[19–23] These promote a range of therapeutic interventions – involving psychosocial, pharmacological and social approaches – to help people overcome addiction and reduce the physical and psychological harms it causes. Since then the Strang Report *Reorienting Drug Treatment* has been published, which argues that recovery status is best defined by factors other than medication status.[24] Neither medication-assisted treatment of opioid addiction nor the cessation of treatment by itself constitutes recovery. Recovery status instead hinges on broader achievements in health and social functioning – with or without medication support.

Rather than seeing addiction treatments with and without medication as philosophically incompatible, the Expert Group that contributed to the report suggested it is more useful to consider medications and all other therapeutic components of contemporary care as a menu of medical and non-medical recovery support options. These can be combined, separated and sequenced to meet individual or family needs over the course of the recovery process.

The 2010 drug strategy set two aims: to reduce illicit and harmful drug use, and to increase the numbers recovering from dependence.[25] Treatment and recovery services contribute indirectly to the former and directly to the latter.

The previous strategy (2008) measured activity, with a Public Service Agreement target (which was achieved) to increase by 3% the numbers in effective treatment for 12 weeks or more, in order to reflect increased investment. In line with the recovery ambition of the 2010 strategy, the focus of measurement is now on outcomes (through individuals completing treatment free of dependence).

The numbers successfully completing treatment free of dependence doubled from 11,208 in 2005–6 to 23,680 in 2009–10. There was a further 18% increase in 2010–11 to 27,969, and NTA figures for the first six months of 2011–12 suggest this improvement is being sustained.[17]

A retrospective analysis in the most recent national statistics found that, of the 255,556 unique individuals who started treatment for the first time since 2005, 71,887 (28%) left free of their dependence and did not subsequently present again to treatment services. Further analysis by the NTA showed that the proportion of unique individuals starting treatment for the first time in the past three years who left free of dependence and did not return to services was 33%. This rate of successful completion and non-return is accepted across government as a key benchmark for measuring recovery. It will be one of the national outcome indicators by which local authorities will be held to account by PHE from 2013.[16]

Shift in commissioning of substance misuse treatment

From April 2013, full responsibility for commissioning drug and alcohol treatment and recovery services will move from existing partnerships to local authorities, as part of a new duty on councils to promote the health of their local populations. This role will be supported by PHE.

As set out in the 2010 white paper *Healthy Lives, Healthy People*,[10] the NTA's critical functions will transfer to PHE in April 2013, contributing to its overall mission to protect and improve the health and wellbeing of the population, and to reduce inequalities in health and wellbeing outcomes. Part of PHE's role is to help authorities discharge their responsibilities in a way that reflects both local priorities and the interest of the Secretary of State for Health and other government ministers. How this balance is struck will become apparent as PHE takes shape during 2012.

Bringing together responsibility for tackling drug addiction and severe alcohol dependence, at both national and local level, is supported by primary care. It has been welcomed by the field, since many drug users have serious alcohol problems and GPs already treat both sets of clients.

Locating responsibility for commissioning drug and alcohol treatment with local authorities, under the leadership of local Directors of Public Health, also offers the exciting prospect of integrating treatment with the local factors that sustain recovery – access to jobs, stable homes, education opportunities and children's services.

The local public health system will be coordinated with NHS and social care services through new Health and Wellbeing Boards and the current central funding for drugs (the Pooled Treatment Budget) will be subsumed into a wider ring-fenced public health budget.

Over the past year, the commissioning of integrated treatment in prisons and the community has been aligned to improve the continuity of care and reduce the risk of overdose, relapse and reoffending among ex-prisoners. From 2013 responsibility for prison treatment will move to the NHS Commissioning Board.

Payment by results

The rate of completion and non-return is also one of the agreed outcomes for the eight local areas that are piloting methods of payment by results for drugs recovery. The other measureable outcomes are reduced drug use and reduced offending. At the time of writing a significant proportion (20%) of the central pooled budget for drug treatment (approximately £400m) will be allocated to local partnerships on the basis of their rate of completion and non-return, in order to incentivise them to further improve recovery outcomes

Payment for primary care drug and alcohol treatment has typically been based upon numbers in treatment and not results. Outcome-focused payments, not a new concept for primary care,[26] may allow the opportunity for primary care to evidence and promote a range of activities that it is perfectly placed to offer. These activities may have gone unnoticed in the past, for example improved health outcomes, signposting, multiagency collaboration and work with families, all from a community base that provides a non-stigmatising environment from which to receive treatment.[27, 28]

Delivering recovery-oriented treatment in primary care

The 2010 drug strategy introduced a new emphasis on building recovery in communities – not just tackling the symptoms and causes of dependence, but enabling former addicts to get off drugs for good and successfully reintegrate into society. One vital aspect of this agenda is the recognition that, to sustain recovery and form positive relationships, people need something to do and somewhere to live. The other aspect of the recovery agenda was a drive to transform the treatment system into a recovery system, so individuals became free of dependence, no longer needed to offend, stopped harming themselves and their communities, and contributed to society.

Local systems are already reconfiguring to deliver recovery-oriented treatment, with greater emphasis put on enabling individuals to overcome dependence and on working with the support services needed to achieve full recovery. Providers who deliver recovery outcomes are gaining market share and primary care services need to be a part of this transformation. This will only be achieved by forging new relationships with mutual-aid networks like Narcotics Anonymous and establishing new pathways between treatment and recovery support. New models of intervention should be used such as SMART recovery, which delivers peer-led support in partnership with conventional treatment providers.

Key themes of recovery-oriented treatment applicable to primary care

Below is a series of key themes followed by a checklist of how a practice or GP-led community service can provide evidence that services are working towards these themes. In doing so they can provide evidence to commissioners that they are working in a recovery-focused way.

Good-quality opioid substitute treatment: a positive role in recovery

Entering and staying in treatment, coming off opioid substitution treatment (OST) and exiting structured treatment are all important indicators of an individual's recovery progress, but they do not in themselves constitute recovery. Coming off OST or exiting treatment prematurely can harm individuals, especially if it leads to relapse, which is also harmful to society. Recovery is a broader and more complex journey that incorporates overcoming dependence, reducing risk-taking behaviour and offending, improving health, functioning as a productive member of society and becoming personally fulfilled. These recovery outcomes are often mutually reinforcing.[24]

The 2010 drug strategy and the 2012 Strang Report make clear that recovery is not an end state (e.g. abstinence) but rather a journey of improvements and that there remains an important role for OST within this. However, the report also highlights the importance of having a balanced and ambitious system that encourages patients to consider a full range of options, including detoxification. Primary care is able to deliver a full range of effective OST interventions, including detoxification.

Practice/service checklist

▶ Have the clinicians completed appropriate training to provide treatment in a primary care setting (RCGP Certificate in the Management of Drugs/Alcohol Part 1)?

▶ Do clinicians access regular opportunities for continuing professional development (e.g. local training, meetings of the multidisciplinary team?)

▶ Are patients able to receive a full range of clinical services from primary care (titration, detoxification, blood-borne virus services, long-term conditions management)? If not, are there accessible care pathways to these parts of the system?

▶ Do regular audits of clinical practice take place and are results fed back to clinicians, with action plans for improvements where appropriate?

▶ Is mentoring/clinical support for clinicians available?

▶ Are there mechanisms for dealing with poor performance?

▶ Are caseloads audited to ensure that there is a balance of harm reduction and overcoming dependence?

▸ Do individual clinicians apply a personalised assessment for each patient, repeat it regularly and based upon its findings readjust the treatment plan with the patient?

▸ Is data accurately recorded for all patients in primary care on the National Drug Treatment Monitoring System?

Drug treatment should integrate with and benefit from other support

An integrated recovery-oriented system of care should be commissioned in each locality that includes other health and social care services with drug treatment to provide recovery support, including mental health, employment, housing, mutual aid and recovery communities.

Primary care is able to deliver a range of services from a community base, from clinical services for substance use, to General Medical Services and also a range of psychosocial services. An enormous range of diverse services is available from primary care including interpreter services, Citizens Advice clinics, the Improving Access to Psychological Therapies programme, help to quit, quick access to dental services, midwifery services, counselling … the list is endless. Primary care is also expert at signposting individuals to services when they are not available 'on site' and working with care pathways between agencies. Primary care includes community pharmacy and dentistry, and GP surgeries often have strong links with their colleagues.

Practice / service checklist

▸ Are clinicians/keyworkers aware of the range of services available, such as housing or employment support, to families and carers?

▸ Are GPs/clinicians involved in care planning with the keyworker and patient? Is the regular communication between the keyworker and GP about patient care? Does the GP see patients regularly (at least every three months)? Are patients offered a full range of recovery-oriented services?

▸ Do effective care pathways exist between all parts of the treatment system? Are they monitored and is there a forum to troubleshoot problems?

▸ Are clinicians/keyworkers trained to deliver recovery-focused care planning?

▸ Are commissioners aware of the full range of services available from primary care?

Improvement in health is an essential element of recovery

For some people – and especially as the treatment population ages – physical health problems may be a persistent barrier to recovery. … The provision and organisation of physical (as well as mental) healthcare for those in drug treatment needs to reflect the problems of access and stigmatisation commonly faced by drug users. Support may be needed for them to effectively use health and care services. … Primary health care services can play a pivotal role in providing for the physical health needs of drug users but may need support from drug services.[24]

Drug treatment from primary care allows people's general health needs to be addressed as well as their substance use issues from a non-stigmatising community base. This is a unique and important characteristic of primary care treatment in light of the general poor health of this group, together with the co-morbidity issues of an ageing population of opioid users.

Practice / service checklist

▸ Are patients' general health needs reviewed on a regular basis?

▸ Is primary care evidencing the general health services and outcomes people are achieving (e.g. contraception, blood-borne virus immunisation and testing, help to quit, mental health interventions), and is this audited on a regular basis? Can Read codes / templates be used to evidence the interventions that are being carried out with this group?

Active promotion of mutual aid networks will be essential

There is a growing evidence base for mutual aid. Evidence also suggests that people do better when they access mutual aid while in treatment. Primary care is used to signposting and can develop links with local community groups. The 2012 Strang Report suggests that recovery is made visible to people at all stages of their treatment journey.

Practice / service checklist

▸ Are keyworkers/clinicians aware of the full range of mutual aid meetings in their area? Are they aware of the benefits of patients' attendance at these groups? Are they assertively encouraging people to attend?

▸ Do patients have access to recovery champions throughout their treatment journey?

▶ Do they have access to people who will take service users to meetings? Have clinicians been to a mutual aid meeting themselves?

▶ Could mutual aid meetings be held at the surgery?

Evidence shows that treatment is more likely to be effective, and recovery to be sustained, where families, partners and carers are closely involved

Patients' families or partners tend to be known in primary care, and it is more likely that they will be seen and involved in recovery planning with the patients (when appropriate). There is evidence that primary care can also provide effective support to families and carers of people who use drugs and alcohol in their own right.[29] As the age of people on OST rises, a number of service users are becoming carers of their parents and primary care can also support this.

Primary care tends to build up relationships with local schools/children's services and provides invaluable support from health visitors. It is well placed to provide support for parenting and safeguarding of children.

Practice / service checklist

▶ Do clinicians/keyworkers involve and record the involvement of other family members in the care of patients?

▶ Do clinicians/keyworkers record independent interventions with families and carers of drug users?

▶ Do clinicians/keyworkers record the multiagency work that takes place with children's services / health visitor interventions?

Substance misuse treatment should be widening the focus to consider dependence on all drugs and alcohol (2010 drug strategy)

Primary care is perfectly positioned to provide recovery-oriented treatment for people who use drugs *and* alcohol. The reasons for this include, first, that primary care can act as a discrete beginning-to-end service in a patient's community. It can deal with a range of drug and alcohol problems, including new trends such as over-the-counter medication misuse, misuse of prescribed medications and legal highs.

Second, primary care is accessible because it exists in the patient's community. Appointments can usually be made on the day and primary care understands and is able to deal with the full range of diversity of its community. Primary care is designed to work with people with disabilities and people from a range of ethnic backgrounds, sensitive to the specific needs of its community. It is a non-stigmatising community service.

Practice/service checklist

▸ Are your clinicians/keyworkers trained to deal with a range of drug and alcohol problems?

▸ Are your care pathways fit for purpose to deal with 'non-opioid' substance use from a primary care base?

Delivering Quality Care for Drug and Alcohol Users: the roles and competencies of doctors

In 2012 the RCGP and the Royal College of Psychiatrists published *Delivering Quality Care for Drug and Alcohol Users*, their revised competency framework for all doctors involved in caring for those recovering from drugs and alcohol.[30]

The guidance document acknowledges that doctors working to support recovery come from a variety of backgrounds (usually psychiatry and general practice), and have a range of different qualifications and specialist competencies. In order to satisfy regulatory requirements from the Care Quality Commission (CQC)[31] and the General Medical Council (GMC), and achieve the best outcomes for patients, doctors' competencies need to match their roles.

The Working Group that produced the guidance identified three levels of competency: generalist, e.g. doctors in emergency departments, GPs working in general practice; intermediate, e.g. GPs with a special clinical interest (GPwSIs); and specialist, e.g. addiction psychiatrists. The competencies at each level are described in detail and there is support in the document for a proposal by the RCGP whereby doctors following an agreed programme of qualifications and experience, and who reach the competencies associated with addiction specialists, can be approved by the RCGP as 'Primary Care Specialists in Substance Misuse'. The document has been well received by the field and highlights the extensive range of certificated, quality-assured training provided by the RCGP, leading to competencies in a range of areas up to and including the intermediate practitioner.

Investing in general practice to achieve improved outcomes in relation to drug misuse

Strategies to tackle substance misuse should look to build on the strengths of general practice. The role of the GP is becoming more complex and demanding, linked to demographic change and the movement of more care into primary care settings. GPs also have an important role in reducing health inequalities as they have unrivalled access to the heart of communities and can influence the health inequalities agenda as practitioners, commissioners and community leaders.

The RCGP believes we need more GPs, spending more time with patients and with access to a longer postgraduate education, because there is evidence that this leads to safer, more effective care.

The College is calling for longer consultation times in order to help GPs uncover hidden health problems, including time to identify underlying issues that may not be the first and most obvious reason for a patient presenting to the GP. It must be looked into how to recruit more doctors into general practice in order to achieve this and to encourage more to consider working with vulnerable patients, such as those with substance misuse problems, or delivering care in secure and forensic environments. Recent reports published by the Centre for Workforce Intelligence have recommended an increase in the GP workforce to reflect the growing demands on primary care and the increasingly complex GP role.[32,33]

There is a particular need to increase the number of GPs in deprived areas as the relationships between deprivation and illegal drug use have been highlighted in a number of research studies including the Advisory Council for the Misuse of Drugs report *Drug Misuse and the Environment* (1998). The report stressed that deprivation is associated with the problematic use of particular drugs such as heroin and crack cocaine.

The approval of extended training for general practice from three years to four will equip the GPs of the future with increased skills to identify substance misuse early and provide effective interventions in primary care to tackle harmful drinking. All GP trainees will receive training to enable them to deliver targeted alcohol screening and harm reduction strategies, and there will be greater opportunity for trainees to gain direct experience of working with specialist services providing treatment for substance misuse.

RCGP 2022 Vision

The RCGP's General Practice 2022 is an eight-year strategic initiative that, subject to Council approval, will protect and develop primary care so that GPs can continue to develop and deliver excellent care for our patients and our communities.[34] Primary care is 'mission critical' to the NHS but rising patient needs and consequent costs need to be addressed within a restricted cash envelope. Investing in more GPs, spending longer with their patients and communities, and with longer training will provide an excellent solution to meeting this challenge. Extended training will offer opportunities for more GP trainees to be able to access training in less traditional settings where there is a higher exposure to patients with multiple and complex needs including substance misusers and individuals with coexistent substance use, mental health and offending.

There is strong international evidence that effective primary care improves the quality of patient care, contains costs and is associated with reduced health inequalities and better disease prevention.[35] The role of general practice in contributing to these outcomes is crucial.

The RCGP's recent report *Medical Generalism: why expertise in whole person medicine matters* examines in detail the role of GPs' generalist skills in delivering these benefits. It explores how generalist models of care can be developed to enable general practice to deliver the best possible care to patients in future.[36]

Changes in the nature and delivery of health care means that the NHS faces a number of major challenges over the coming years. Key factors include:

▶ an increase in the volume and complexity of health and social care needs, as more people live for longer with *long-term and often multiple conditions*

▶ *financial constraints* as a result of the economic situation and the resultant need to find ways of transforming services to reduce costs while maintaining and increasing quality

▶ the shift of care out of the hospital and into the community, both as a means of bringing it closer to patients and their families, and of reducing costs, as well as barriers to better integration with community and social care

▶ major structural changes, particularly in England

▶ the potential for *service fragmentation* as a result of competition and the use of multiple providers

▶ growing *health inequalities*

▶ the challenge of *engaging patients more in their own care* and of promoting healthy lifestyles and behaviours.

Conclusion

So what does the future hold for primary care drug misuse treatment? In the view of the author it is most definitely positive and exciting. Many GPs remain willing to be involved in providing general medical care to drug misusers and are seen as an experienced and trusted resource.

With appropriate support and funding, many of the remaining 'dormant' GPs might be stimulated into action. Also, through the development of federated models of care, GPs can become affiliated to an associated practice where they can refer their own registered patients with problems to get treatment in a primary care setting.

Unfortunately there is now real evidence of service users suffering the impact of years of health neglect coupled with the inevitable increased risk of long-term conditions. In this context the general practice setting becomes a compelling and cost-efficient area where these issues of health and social care can be targeted and managed.

In addition iatrogenic problems associated with addiction to medications and over-the-counter medicine abuse have grown. There is a need for ongoing vigilance against the tide of 'new drugs' coming in via new sources and spreading through the new social media spawned by the World Wide Web.

Tomorrow's Doctors[37] along with the RCGP's 2022 vision[34] now give GPs in training many opportunities to extend their training into the substance misuse field. Today's GP champions and clinical leaders need to support and coach the leaders of tomorrow to ensure as many of tomorrow's doctors will take up the challenge. This can be done by providing shadowing opportunities, observerships, contributing on a regular basis to VTS training sessions and proactively seeking funding for innovative modular attachments.

As with all patient groups the substance misuse population will be better served and make progress towards their recovery goals if the GPs caring for them are well trained, alert to new initiatives and grounded in the delivery of evidence-based, personalised care.

Care should be delivered in treatment systems where:

▸ service users are co-productive partners in their care

▸ service users are cared for by staff teams working flexibly where full use is made of the range of skills available

▸ service users are cared for in the right place at the right time and where every effort is made to reduce the over-reliance of the care of the most complex and challenging on hospitals and institutions

▸ information and communication technologies are being used to revolutionise service users' experiences

▸ there is the potential for new medical technologies being used more effectively

▸ there is intelligent use of data and information to empower the service users and to supporting professionals in delivering high-quality care.

Finally, with the recovery agenda comes a reversal in years of trying to increase numbers in treatment. There is now a move to concentrate on consolidating quality and providing better-coordinated services for drug users, which match their needs and promote their assets. To a large degree GPs are already embedded in the response to the challenge of the management of drug users. Collectively they are undoubtedly the backbone of drug misuse treatment services, including the provision of substitute medication. However, this is not the time to sit back and wait on the changes and meet them half way. Rather, GPs should build on their well-earned and trusted platform of expertise and talk up the compelling case for the paradigm shift in drug treatment to be led from primary care.

References

1. Strang J, Sheridan J, Hunt C, *et al*. The prescribing of methadone and other opioids to addicts: national survey of GPs in England and Wales. *British Journal of General Practice* 2005; **55(515)**: 444–51.

2. Royal College of Psychiatrists and Royal College of General Practitioners. *Roles and Responsibilities of Doctors in the Provision of Treatment for Drug and Alcohol Misusers*. London: RCPsych, 2005.

3. National Treatment Agency for Substance Misuse. *NTA Business Plan 2010–11*. London: NTA, 2010.

4. Ryrie I, Ford C. The primary care treatment of drug users: is shared care really the best approach? *Journal of Substance Use* 2001; **6(1)**; 3–6.

5. European Monitoring Centre for Drugs and Drug Addiction. *Treatment and Care for Older Drug Users*. Luxembourg: Publications Office of the European Union, 2010.

6. McGrath A, Crome P, Crome I B. Substance misuse in the older population. *Postgraduate Medical Journal* 2005; **81(954)**; 228–31.

7. Goodwin N, Smith J, Davies A, *et al*. *A Report to the Department of Health and the NHS Future Forum: integrated care for patients and populations*. London: King's Fund, 2012.

8. Department of Health. *Equity and Excellence: liberating the NHS*. Norwich: TSO, 2010.

9. Health and Social Care Bill 2010–12, www.dh.gov.uk/healthandsocialcarebill [accessed January 2013].

10. Department of Health. *Healthy Lives, Healthy People: our strategy for public health in England*. Norwich: TSO, 2010.

11. NHS Future Forum. *Summary Report on Proposed Changes to the NHS*. London: DH, 2011.

12. NHS Leadership Academy, www.leadershipacademy.nhs.uk.

13. RCGP Substance Misuse and Associated Health (SMAH), www.rcgp.org.uk/revalidation-and-cpd/substance-misuse-and-associated-health.aspx [accessed January 2013].

14. Substance Misuse Management in General Practice (SMMGP), www.smmgp.org.uk.

15. National Treatment Agency Substance Misuse Skills Consortium, www.nta.nhs.uk/healthcare-skills-consortium.aspx   [accessed January 2013].

16. National Treatment Agency Facts & Figures, www.nta.nhs.uk/statistics.aspx [accessed January 2013].

17. National Drug Treatment Monitoring System, www.ndtms.net.

18. Ghodse H, Corkery J, Oyefeso A, *et al. Drug-Related Deaths in the UK: annual report.* London: International Centre for Drug Policy, St George's University of London, 2009.

19. National Institute for Health and Clinical Excellence. *Technology Appraisal Guidance 114, Methadone and Buprenorphine for the Management of Opioid Dependence.* London: NICE, 2007.

20. National Institute for Health and Clinical Excellence. *Clinical Guideline 51, Drug Misuse: psychosocial interventions.* London: NICE, 2007.

21. National Institute for Health and Clinical Excellence. *Technology Appraisal Guidance 115, Naltrexone for the Management of Opioid Dependence.* London: NICE, 2007.

22. National Institute for Health and Clinical Excellence. *Clinical Guideline 52, Drug Misuse: opioid detoxification.* London: NICE, 2007.

23. Department of Health (England) and the devolved administrations. *Drug Misuse and Dependence: UK guidelines on clinical management.* London: DH (England), Scottish Government, Welsh Assembly Government and Northern Ireland Executive, 2007.

24. National Treatment Agency for Substance Misuse. *Medications in Recovery: re-orientating drug dependence treatment.* London: NTA, 2012.

25. HM Government. *Drug Strategy 2010. Reducing demand, restricting supply, building recovery: supporting people to live a drug free life.* London: Home Office, 2010.

26. Sturgess G L, Cumming L. *Payment by Outcome: a commissioner's toolkit.* London: 2020 Public Services Trust, 2010.

27. Culley D, Disley E, Donmall M, *et al. Scoping & Feasibility Report.* Manchester: University of Manchester, 2012.

28. Department of Health. *Report from the Gaming Commission on Drug and Alcohol Recovery PbR Pilots.* London: DH, 2012.

29. Copello A, Templeton L, Orford J, *et al.* The relative efficacy of two levels of a primary care intervention for family members affected by the addiction problem of a close relative: a randomized trial. *Addiction* 2009; **104(1)**: 49–58.

30. Royal College of Psychiatrists and Royal College of General Practitioners. *Delivering Quality Care for Drug and Alcohol Users: the roles and competencies of doctors.* London: RCPsych, 2012.

31. Care Quality Commission, www.cqc.org.uk.

32. Centre for Workforce Intelligence. *Shape of the Medical Workforce: informing medical training numbers.* London: CfWI, 2011.

33. Centre for Workforce Intelligence. *Shape of the Medical Workforce: starting the debate on the future consultant workforce.* London: CfWI, 2012.

34. Royal College of General Practitioners. General Practice 2022, www.rcgp.org.uk/policy/rcgp-policy-areas/general-practice-2022.aspx   [accessed January 2013].

35. Gerada C, Mathers N, Thomas M. *Patients, Doctors and the NHS in 2022.* London: RCGP, n.d.

36. Royal College of General Practitioners. *Medical Generalism: why expertise in whole person medicine matters.* London: RCGP, 2012.

37. General Medical Council. *Tomorrow's Doctors.* London: GMC, 2009.

CHAPTER 6

The role of the nurse

Jane Haywood and David Harding-Price

Introduction

Nursing has changed over the past three decades and the modern nurse now is often a practitioner in his or her own right, developing treatment plans based on a medical diagnosis and seeing treatment packages through to completion. The aim of this chapter is to offer the reader an overview of the role of the modern nurse in the clinical setting, an update on the National Treatment Agency's 'models of care', and a summary of the role of the nurse in prescribing for patients who are coping with an addiction.

In modern health care there is a wide range of nurses working in primary care, ranging from the practice nurse based in the surgery, to the district nurse, health visitor, and community psychiatric nurse working in patients' homes, to the school nurse and the occupational health nurse based in places of work. All of these nurses often have an input into the life of a substance user and increasingly their family and friends.

Twenty-first-century health care is evolving and the new Health and Social Care Bill is going to change radically in the coming years the way people access health care. Nurses need to be at the forefront of the process and be able to provide a myriad of roles for their patients. The skills they develop – be they in substance misuse, mental health, care of the elderly, physical health care or any of the aspects of modern health care – will be of paramount importance not only to the patient but also to their colleagues in the wider primary care team. Nurses will play a pivotal role in the care and management of people addressing their addictive behaviour, whether drugs, alcohol, gambling or any of the more modern addictions, for example computer gaming.

As a result of the planned changes it is not only an exciting time but also provides a window of opportunity for nurses. Nursing roles have expanded and changed over the past decade and now there is a prospect that, in many areas of health care, nurses can take the lead. To assist nurses in this there are accredited training programmes and modular packages in a range of fields, wherever the nurse may be working.

Affara and Styles defined the nurse specialist as 'a nurse prepared beyond the level of a generalist nurse and authorised to practice as a specialist with advanced expertise in a branch of the nursing field. Specialist practice includes clinical, teaching, administration, research and consultant roles'.[1] However, in modern nursing many of the elements of specialist nursing present themselves to the nurse on a regular if not daily basis, substance misuse being one of them. As a result, managing people with addictive illnesses brings into play many of the core components of nursing and these will be addressed in this chapter.

As Parrott *et al.* note, drug dependence is not a twentieth-century disease but can be traced back thousands of years. Circe (in Homer's *Odysseus*) was a practised chemist able to drug Odysseus's crew, while the Mesopotamians had laws to control alcohol use. Today, with the relaxation of gambling laws and the development of interactive computer games, new forms of addiction are developing. Consequently, within this chapter the reader should read for 'substance' a wider gamut of addictive behaviours including drugs (both licit and illicit), alcohol, solvents, gambling, pornography, computer games and arguably any other behaviour that can control part of the person's life. The authors will use the word 'substance' to denote this wide panoply of products.

Role of the nurse

Modern nurses working in primary care have a variety of roles that they have to address in their daily practice. Depending on their main clinical area these will vary, but for all nurses the basic tenet of nursing remains the same, whichever model of nursing they follow, from Henderson to Tidal. Ultimately, the role of the nurse is 'to assist the individual, sick or well, in the performance of those activities contributing to health or its recovery … that he would perform unaided if he had the necessary strength, will or knowledge'.[3] Nurses working in primary care have to address the issues raised by addictive behaviour and to achieve this will need to understand their patient and their attitude towards the 'substance' that is causing the variant behaviour. It is important to understand that some 'substances' are described as habituating and others as addictive. Also, one individual might be considered addicted to a 'substance' whereas another merely habituated to the same 'substance'.[4] A nurse will need to understand the patient's view on his or her 'substance' to enable the nurse to plan the appropriate treatment package and in some cases even address the issue.

Nurses perform a number of roles within their field of care, including:

▶ treatment planner – provider of care

▶ advocate

▶ counsellor/therapist

▶ educator

▶ resource director

▶ consultant

▶ promoter of health

▶ supervisor/leader

▶ researcher

▶ monitor.

Rassool defined addiction nursing as 'a clinical specialty concerned with the care and treatment interventions aimed at those individuals whose health problems are directly related to the use and misuse of psychoactive substances and to other addictive behaviour such as eating disorders and gambling'.[5] It is clear that in modern society nurses and nursing have moved on from this basic position to include the provision of treatment for any element that can lead to a disablement of a person's life or family. It is now recognised that 'substance' misuse does not just affect the patient but also has a wider effect on his or her family, carers and friends. The problems of, for example, binge drinking now spill out onto the streets many nights a week and the end results come into contact with nurses in a wide range of settings.

The practice nurse

The 1999 Clinical Guidelines (often referred to as the Orange Book) present the treatment of people with drug use problems as being the role of the GP. Since it being written over two decades ago nursing has advanced to the point where now practice nurses are using their skills and knowledge to develop and then provide treatment packages for patients. Increasingly GPs are struggling to meet the demands on them and a skilled practice nurse is an invaluable asset to a health centre, with nurses now providing many of the roles and resources that once were the sole domain of the GP.

The practice nurse is the first point of clinical contact users have when they register with the surgery. The new patient screening session is a good place to ask about drug and alcohol use once a rapport has been established. Nurses use screening tools to determine 'substance' use, notably smoking and drinking. Nurses may need to consider also looking at drug use and associated risk behaviours. History taking needs to extend beyond the fundamentals of blood pressure, urinalysis and blood sugar level, with the nurse considering what effect the patient's actions/health are having on themselves and their wider social network. In the modern NHS social care is as much a part of the integrated care delivery as is health care. The Treatment Outcomes Profile (TOP) was first developed by the National Treatment Agency. This questionnaire covers substance use, injecting, crime and health, and social functioning, as well as giving an indication of potential problems. TOP should be used at first contact, review and discharge. If possible, it should also be used post-discharge for lifestyle monitoring and health improvement. Nurses have an important role in health promotion and should bear this in mind when completing a new patient screening session. It has been shown that simple advice from nurses during routine care is effective in smoking cessation. Often this can be extended to computer gaming, gambling and other non-chemical addictive behaviours.

All nurses working in primary care should have a foundation level of knowledge regarding 'substance' misuse. The RCGP's National Drug Misuse Training Programme Certificate Part 1 can provide any nurse working in primary care with the necessary general knowledge and skills to work with this patient population. Practice nurses will increasingly find themselves having to address the issues around 'substance' use and misuse not only with their patients directly but also in supporting patients who are affected by a family member's usage. This latter effect is more than likely to draw the practice nurse into the realms of social care and away from his or her comfort zone of health care. There is one group of nurses who can support the practice nurse in this area – the community psychiatric nurse (CPN).

The community psychiatric nurse

Many CPNs will have the theoretical knowledge on how to work with the person who is facing an addictive behaviour. For many, though, their contact with such patients has been limited to people drinking hazardously or where drugs are secondary to the presenting mental health condition. The CPN should consider how he or she can support patients as they move their life through the stages of being unaware of or unable to address their 'substance' use to a point where they can either maintain a socially acceptable level of usage or be abstinent. Prof. Strang, speaking at the RCGP conference on 11 May 2012, noted that, 'the relationship between recovery and abstinence is an area that needs careful attention'. This highlights the need for nurses to become active within the recovery process, which means different things to different people.

For many CPNs this will require them to start working with practice nurses directly in health centres or GPs' surgeries: working with patients to empower them to come to terms with why they are using the 'substance' and how it is affecting their lives and the lives of their families. Many CPNs will recognise this as the Recovery Model. For some CPNs their contact will be in non-health-based centres, for example Salvation Army or YMCA hostels, in local cafés or on the streets.

The stigma of mental health and the association of 'substance' use to psychiatry will present a barrier that the CPN is skilled in knowing how to overcome. In working with patients to address the issues behind their 'substance' use the CPN can start the lengthy process of life change that is necessary to enable service users to make the changes to their life and so be able to function with abusing their 'substance' of choice.

The use of personal budgets to provide patients with the tools they require to reduce or stop their 'substance' use is essential. Increasingly, personal budgets for social care are becoming the norm and may well become the norm for some elements of health care. CPNs should become skilled in lateral thinking to develop care plans that a service user can live with and that can be funded from a range of sources.

The Nurse with a Special Interest

Nurses who develop enhanced skills, having a special interest in 'substance' misuse, are increasingly becoming the lead within a healthcare team or GP surgery. They often start the process of developing a local service within a surgery. Nurses who decide to take on this role should in the first instance ensure that they have gained more than basic knowledge about 'substance' misuse. With the developments within society many more activities and chemicals are falling into the remit of the nurse working with 'substance' misuse.

Nurses with a Special Interest can develop early practice interventions, for example health promotion for safer injecting, brief interventions for alcohol overuse, groups for people addicted to gambling, or completing more complex assessments using recognised assessment tools.[6,7] Nurses working at this level can also be instrumental in developing in-house support for users, for example immunisation of users' children or production of a leaflet providing information about local services. The nurse will also probably have a working relationship with the local secondary drugs/alcohol teams. They are in the best position to refer patients to the most appropriate local service.

Nurses with a Special Interest can also provide other functions, including:

▸ improving the skills of GPs and primary care nurses in identifying and managing patients with 'substance'-related problems, by training and the development of written material that can be made locally available

▸ enabling 'substance' misusers to access the full range of primary healthcare services

▸ improving the quality of care these patients receive by supporting the implementation of the clinical guidelines

▸ redistributing the care of specific 'substance' users – for example drug users – more equitably across primary care group teams.

The specialist nurse

There are a number of nurses who have extended their knowledge beyond the basic level to become specialists in their chosen field. These nurses have developed their interest in 'substance' misuse beyond the provision of localised care in their surgery or clinical team and most are now developing their service to a whole locality. These nurses, often consultant nurses or clinical nurse specialists, can be found in the 'substance' misuse fields, notably drugs, alcohol and smoking. Increasingly they are also developing these skills within hospital settings, for example A&E and liver specialists.

While nurses working in primary care are ideally placed to respond quickly and meet the needs of GPs and primary care staff, the consultant nurse is drawing on previous experience from specialist services, relevant post-registration training and continuous clinical supervision to provide a service to the wider health community. Such nurses are essential independent practitioners supporting and developing shared care, often across wide geographical and clinical areas.

There are a number of models where specialist nurses can support the integrated care of 'substance' misusers in the primary care setting. Many addiction nurses work within a liaison and consultancy model where the nurse meets the primary care team to discuss and agree the management plan of their patients. This aims to support the GPs in the management of their patients rather than the nurses taking over the care themselves. The nurse here is the person with specialist clinical knowledge. The nurse can also facilitate linking the patient and GP with an appropriate agency for continuing psychosocial interventions. Specialist nurses with advanced training can take over the clinical care of the patient, with the surgery providing facilities and the nurse addressing the treatment plan and following the package through support by a community support worker (CSW).

Table 6.1 **Responsibilities of different nursing roles**

Nursing process	Assessing	Planning	Implementing	Evaluation
Practice nurse (primary tier)	New patient screening, identification of problems, brief interventions, family liaison	Health screening and referral for detoxification services	Viral screening, vaccination, wound care management, family planning. Referring to secondary services. Relapse prevention	Monitoring audit trails, feedback on outcomes
Community psychiatric nurse (secondary tier)	Assessments of mental health, capacity and Wellness Recovery Action Plan (WRAP) or similar, family liaison	Develop individual care plan taking into account biopsychosocial needs	Personal budgets, social care, mental health care pathways, referral to tertiary services. Relapse prevention	Monitoring care pathways and personal budgets, feedback on outcomes
Nurse with Special Interest (secondary tier)	Harm reduction assessment, assess suitability for primary care treatment	Liaison with specialist agencies, community pharmacists and other members of primary care team	Goal setting, support, stabilisation, referral to tertiary services, working with prescribers. Relapse prevention	Regular monitoring of treatment and achievement goals with patient and GP team, feedback on outcomes
Consultant nurse, clinical nurse specialist (tertiary tier)	In-depth assessment, formulation of complex treatment plans, working with complex cases	Patient contracts, medication concordance, develop clinical management plans, independent prescriber	Regular patient contact, re-assessing and changing treatment packages where necessary, liaison with professionals. Relapse prevention	Audit treatment packages, satisfaction surveys – patient and other staff, implementing changes to protocols, attending monitoring meetings, publishing outcomes

Jacksley *et al.* described a clinical nurse specialist service in one London borough, which consisted of a five-point model for the role of the specialist nurse in primary care.[8] While it remains a good standard, it is no longer the sole preserve of the specialist nurse. A Nurse with a Special Interest in the health centre or GP practice should be able to meet the five points. These are:

▸ one-off expert substance misuse/health assessment with recommendations for treatment

▸ shared care – formal therapeutic package, leading to stabilisation or abstinence, with referral to specialist services (detoxification or rehabilitation if necessary)

▸ continuous support – reviews monthly, two-monthly and stabilised at three-monthly intervals; rapid response if the GP feels the client needs to be seen in the interval between review meetings

▸ on-site and immediate information exchange and advice while in treatment at the practice

▸ fast tracking into specialist treatment services for clients who have encountered a crisis.

In addition to the nursing roles set out above, for those practices that are providing either a local or a nationally enhanced service for 'substance' misusers this provides the opportunity for primary care practitioners, including nurses, to develop a variety of models to provide seamless care to patients within their surgeries.

All nurses, at whatever levels they are practising at, have a duty of care and this includes addressing harm minimisation issues. In 'substance' misuse these present in a wide variety of ways and the nurse has to be mindful of them, from both a health and social care aspect.

Social care

The advent of personal budgets and the drive by the government for people to take more responsibility for their care has resulted in an increasing number of nurses becoming involved with social care. Many may argue that this is the role of the social worker but increasingly the nurse addressing a patient's 'substance' misuse problems will also have to address the social elements of his or her health care. It is well known that drug and alcohol misuse leads to family problems, whether that be lack of money, criminal activity or child protection issues. There is evidence that gambling is also becoming problematic from the social care viewpoint and this has the knock-on effect on people's health for the same reasons as with drugs and alcohol. The gaming industry currently funds a charity that provides services to people with a gambling addiction, which is recognition that there is a problem.

With rising unemployment, the 'substance' user is at greater risk of finding him or herself out of work. There is a definite role for nurses working in mental health and Nurses with a Special Interest in a health centre to become involved in the social care of patients. The creative use of personal budgets will enable service users to develop the skills they require to keep or gain employment. Nurses need to develop links with their local Jobcentre Plus,[i] where financial support to assist patients in keeping or gaining a job is available under the Welfare to Work programme (www.dwp.gov.uk/healthcare-professional).

All nurses working in primary care need to take a holistic approach to patient care and in the case of people presenting with 'substance' problems this includes the family of the user. Nurses are often the first point of contact a user has with the system and if the family is suffering because of the user's use the nurse needs to consider how the family can be supported. This can range from signposting the family to food banks, for example the Trussell Trust (www.trusselltrust.org), to making contact with local social services to enable psychosocial interventions to be developed. The provision of a holistic package for a patient will in the long term provide wider benefits.

Young people

Young people are increasingly looking to be independent for as much of their life as they can. This often leads them into difficult situations, which they are unable to escape from without support from a professional. Drug and alcohol use in the young homeless is so prevalent that it should be considered to be present until proven otherwise. The practice nurse plays a vital role in encouraging the young person to seek specialist help, while providing some elements of care that can assist the young person in making any needed or wanted adjustments to be able to move forward. Additionally, with young people the risks from excessive computer gaming should not be overlooked. Health visitors, school nurses, midwives and other nursing colleagues will come into contact with young teenagers in a wide range of settings.

Health practitioners working with children between the ages of 10 and 16 need to be mindful that they have to be able to answer yes to all the questions below.

1. The child will understand the advice being offered

2. The nurse cannot persuade the child to inform its parents or allow the nurse to inform the parents about the issue

---

i Jobcentre Plus ceased on 4 October 2011 as an executive agency and is now a brand name within the Department of Work and Pensions.

Figure 6.1   **Social contract version of Prochaska and DiClemente's model of change**

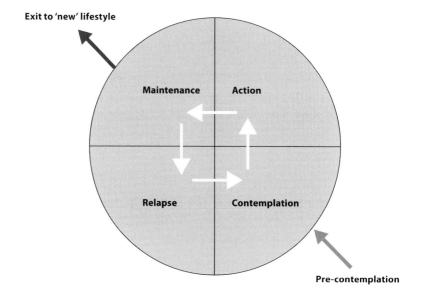

Source: adapted by David Harding-Price for Skegness Recovery Team (2007).

3. That the child is likely to begin or continue the activity with or without protection

4. That without protection the child's physical or mental health or both are likely to suffer

5. That it is in the child's best interest to provide advice, treatment or both without the parental consent.[9]

Relapse prevention

The art of relapse prevention has been taken up by nurses, in particular mental health nurses, and now has to be part of the treatment package offered to all patients using a 'substance'. Adapting Prochaska and DiClemente's cycle of change [10] shows that relapse prevention takes place in the maintenance phase. Successful relapse prevention requires a care package to be developed that enables the user to maintain his or her abstinence or reduced use, and address the issues that lead to the 'substance' misuse. Relapse occurs when the person moves from

Figure 6.2   **Timeline using Prochaska and DiClemente's model of change**

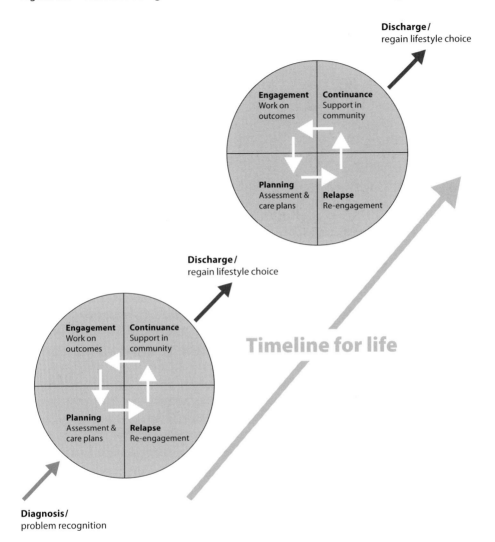

Source: adapted by David Harding-Price for Skegness Recovery Team (2007).

the maintenance or action phase back to the contemplation phase. A person may be in the relapse phase for a few minutes or many days. The role of any nurse at this point is to support the person back into the contemplation phase and assist him or her to move into the action phase.

For a relapse prevention package to be effective the nurse needs to address all elements of the biopsychosocial-physical needs of the patient. It is here that lateral thinking with the patient's personal budget can be most effective. There is an argument that, for a patient to maintain 'abstinence', a new 'addiction' or life issue needs to be addressed or introduced. The use of a personal budget can enable this to take place. The nurse needs to have a holistic approach to the provision of care and follow the patient through the process. However, as can be seen in Figure 6.2, if the 'cycle of change' is one of continuance through life the nurse is able to step in at the time when a 'diagnosis' is on the horizon. If 'diagnosis' is substituted for 'recognition of a problematic behaviour' then nursing is well placed to provide the clinical and social support people need in modern society to maintain a positive lifestyle. Alternatively, nurses working directly in the GP practice or health centre can maintain working contact with the service user, and support him or her and the rest of the primary care team in maintaining the patient's wellbeing.

An overview of the development of nurse prescribing and wider non-medical prescribing

History and background

This has been a fascinating and complex area of continual change over the past 20 years, resulting in opportunities and challenges for nurses to extend their role. It is recommended that any nurse interested in becoming a nurse prescriber or who is already prescribing should seek additional information.

In 1992 legislation changes enabled nurses to prescribe but were not implemented until 1998, and then restrictions were such that, after completing appropriate accredited training, nurses could only prescribe from a very basic, limited formulary.

The Crown Report of 1999 reviewed 'prescribing, supply and administration of medicines' and since then there have been regular legal and policy changes. These have extended prescribing responsibilities to professionals allied to medicine who have received additional specialist training.

The founding principles of non-medical prescribing are to:

▸ make more effective use of the skills and expertise of groups of professionals

▸ improve patients' access to treatment and advice

▸ improve patient choice and convenience

▸ contribute to more flexible team working across the NHS.[11]

Since 1999, training specifically related to prescribing of medicines has been included in all training for district nurses and health visitors. This is now integral to all district nurse and health visitor training, and for some practice nurses. Their prescribing status is noted on the professional register. Legislation changed on

4 April 2003 to enable nurses and pharmacists who had completed an approved programme of training and preparation to prescribe prescription-only medicines, pharmacy medicines and general sale list medicines. In 2004 the formulary was revised to include certain controlled drugs for which additional training was required. Now this has extended to include optometrists, physiotherapists, podiatrists and radiographers.

There are various terms and sets of competencies attached to types of prescribing by nurses, including 1) the Extended Nurse Formulary, 2) Patient Group Directions, 3) Supplementary and 4) Independent Nurse Prescribing. Nurses working in the field of substance misuse need to be familiar with these.

In 2010 the Nursing and Midwifery Council (NMC) produced and updated the 2004 *Standards for Medicines Management*,[12] which states:

> *The administration of medicines is an important aspect of the professional practice of persons whose names are on the Council's register. It is not solely a mechanistic task to be performed in strict compliance with the written prescription of a medical practitioner (can now also be an independent and supplementary prescriber). It requires thought and the exercise of professional judgement.*

The *Standards for Medicines Management* provides a glossary that gives definitions relating to nurse prescribing.

Scope of practice

The UK Central Council for Nursing Midwifery and Health Visiting (now the NMC) defined the scope of nursing practice as:[13]

> *The range of responsibilities which fall to individual nurses, midwives and health visitors ... related to their personal experience and skill.*

Individual organisations or employers may require nurses to complete an 'Intention to Prescribe' document. Typically, this will detail the following clinical domains:

- ▶ medicine types including the relevant sections of the BNF, set out in a locally agreed competency framework document
- ▶ evidence of competency such as training and work experience
- ▶ evidence of recent continuing professional development
- ▶ any local or nationally recognised protocols and/or procedures utilised by the employer.

This document may then be presented to the local Medicines Management Committee or equivalent for sign-off and then reviewed at least annually.

Guidance for drafting such documents should be sought from organisations such as the Royal College of Nursing and medical royal colleges.

Supplementary prescribing

The Department of Health described supplementary prescribing as:[14]

> *A voluntary partnership between an independent prescriber (a doctor or a dentist) and a supplementary prescriber, to implement an agreed patient-specific clinical management plan, with the patient's agreement.*

Supplementary prescribing is not restricted to specific medical conditions but to an agreed treatment plan for an individual patient. Legislation details the particulars to be contained in the clinical management plan and requires supplementary prescribers to have access to the patient's medical records. The clinical management plan must be devised in agreement with the patient.[ii]

Independent prescribing

The former Nurse Prescribers' Extended Formulary was discontinued in May 2006. The National Prescribing Centre (NPC) stated that: 'qualified Nurse Independent Prescribers, formerly known as Extended Formulary Nurse Prescribers, can prescribe any medicine for any medical condition within their competence, including some controlled drugs for specified medical conditions.'[15]

Expanding prescribing rights to nurses seems to be a move in a sensible direction and changes to controlled drug legislation came into force on 23 April 2012. These changes affect nurse and pharmacist independent prescribers.

Amendments to the Misuse of Drugs Regulations were put before parliament on 30 March 2012 and came into effect on 23 April 2012. They concern nurse and pharmacist independent prescribing, and the mixing of controlled drugs.

The changes allow:

▶ nurse independent prescribers to prescribe any schedule 2–5 controlled drug within their clinical competency, removing the previous limitations

▶ pharmacist independent prescribers to prescribe any schedule 2–5 controlled drug within their clinical competency

▶ nurse and pharmacist independent prescribers, and supplementary prescribers when within the terms of a clinical management plan, to mix schedule 2–5

---

ii At the time of writing, this element was under review by the government.

controlled drugs for administration to a patient and provide written directions for others to do so

▶ nurse and pharmacist independent prescribers to possess, supply, offer to supply, administer and give directions for the administration of any controlled drug specified in schedule 2–5.

▶ registered nurses and pharmacists to supply or offer to supply morphine or diamorphine under a PGD for the immediate and necessary treatment of a sick and injured person in any setting.

These changes *do not* apply to the prescribing of cocaine, diamorphine or dipipanone for the treatment of addiction (which is restricted to Home Office-licensed doctors).

Single competency framework

This was published by the NPC (provided by the National Institute for Health and Clinical Excellence) in May 2012.[16] It is 'an outline framework of prescribing competencies relevant to all prescribers. The statements in this framework should be interpreted in the context in which individuals are prescribing, taking into account their scope of practice.'

The framework outlines the domains in which a nurse (any prescribing practitioner) has to be competent. They are:

▶ the consultation

▶ prescribing effectively

▶ prescribing in context.

The NPC acknowledges that 'a common set of competencies underpin prescribing regardless of professional background'. From a patient persepective, timely access to a competent practitioner is probably the most important priority. In diagrammatic form the NPC sets out the cycle as a circle (see Figure 6.3, overleaf).

To assist the prescriber there are a number of websites providing information, including updates and support for nurses:

▶ **www.npc.co.uk/** – from 2012 future medicines and prescribing outputs will be published on the NICE website and signposted from the Medicines and Prescribing homepage (www.nice.org.uk/mpc/)

▶ **www.smmgp.org.uk/** – has a supplementary prescribing forum

▶ **www.nurseprescribing.com/** – is dedicated to nurse prescribing

▶ **http://anp.org.uk/** – is dedicated to nurse prescribing.

Figure 6.3   **Competency framework domains**

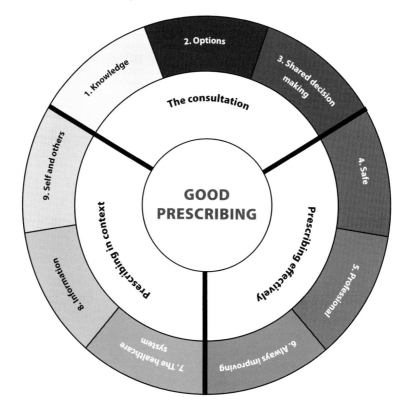

Accountability and professional responsibility

All nurses are accountable for their actions and must be able to provide clinical evidence for their actions. The NMC (2008) Code of Conduct [17] states that nurses 'must deliver care based on the best available evidence or best practice'. In the modern age, with technology and practice evolving rapidly, it can be difficult for nurses to keep abreast of the current practice. Any nurse working in the field of 'substance' misuse needs to be sure that his or her practice is based on the 'best available evidence'. This may not of necessity be the latest.

Independent nurse prescribers, whether operating within or outside the NHS, are clinically responsible and professionally accountable for the care of their patients and their own actions. Where a nurse is appropriately trained and qualified as an independent prescriber, and prescribes as part of his or her nursing duties with the consent of the employer, the employer may also be held vicariously responsible for the nurse's actions. The Department of Health's 2004 guide to implementation of independent nurse prescribing advised all nurse prescribers to ensure that they have professional indemnity insurance for their prescribing activities,[18] for example through membership of a professional organisation or trade union.

Support for nurses

How can nurses protect themselves as nursing moves into the twenty-first century? Many nurses shy away from clinical supervision, fearful that it will lead them into conflict with management. The contrary is the case. Nurses who undertake regular review of their own practice by engaging in reflection, critical examination and evaluation, as well as seeking peer review, will find that their practice improves and management will be less likely to 'be on their back'.

It is a sad fact that, as a Royal College of Nursing steward, one of the authors has seen first hand the problems that nurses bring upon themselves by failing to maintain their clinical knowledge. Equally nurses need to be mindful of modern technology. The social network sites like Facebook, Twitter or Bebo can easily lead nurses into trouble. Nurses should remember that while they may be putting something on Facebook for a friend it can almost instantly be bouncing around the globe and, somewhere along the line, a friend of a friend may be the friend of their manager. Using modern technology to access information is an excellent way of getting up-to-date information. However, nurses or indeed any clinician should never put patient information or even how their day at work was on social network sites.

The Royal College of Nursing's Mental Health Forum provides all forum members with access to an online learning zone [iii] and has developed a section about substance misuse for non-experts in the field. Members of the Royal College of Nursing can also gain access to wider professional knowledge through the Forum,[iv] allowing them to develop their own personal practice.

As practitioner, nurses are in an exceptional position of being able to identify and support colleagues who find themselves facing difficulties with 'substance' misuse and/or mental health. Being able to provide a basic service to a colleague will assist him or her in their recovery pathway.

The RCGP provides nurses with a range of 'substance' misuse-specific courses that address the risk issues nurses face within their clinical practice.

---

iii www.rcn.org.uk.
iv www.rcn.org.uk/development/communities/rcn_forum_communities/mental_health.

Models of care

The National Treatment Agency for Substance Misuse (NTA) is a special health authority within the NHS, established by government in 2001, to improve the availability, capacity and effectiveness of treatment for drug misuse in England. In 2006 the NTA reviewed its 'Models of Care' document. The overall aim remained unchanged, as did the basics of the four tiers. They are set out on Table 6.2.

Table 6.2   **A tiered model of care for the treatment of drug users**

Tier 1	Provision of drug-related information and advice, screening and referral to specialised drug treatment
Tier 2	Provision of drug-related information and advice, triage assessment, referral to structured drug treatment, brief psychosocial interventions, harm reduction interventions (including needle exchange) and aftercare
Tier 3	Provision of community-based specialised drug assessment and coordinated care, planned treatment and drug specialist liaison
Tier 4	Provision of residential specialised drug treatment, which is care planned and coordinated to ensure continuity of care and aftercare

Following feedback from people in the drugs field the 2006 version of 'Models of Care' did review care planning, looking to put more emphasis on clients achieving treatment goals through the delivery of a care plan and the client treatment journey. As a result, while the key principles of care planning and the coordination of care set out in Models of Care 2002 remained the same, there were some differences, which are consistent with a greater focus on the patient's treatment journey. These are:

▸ the care planning process as the essential component of the client treatment journey

▸ the importance of all clients receiving keyworking as a crucial element of care-planned treatment

▸ a greater focus on clients' participation in the care planning process, where they are involved in producing and agreeing their care plans. This is consistent with the consultation response where an overwhelming majority of respondents wanted to see more service user involvement in care planning and review

▸ ensuring the care plan actively covers meeting client needs in the four key domains of substance misuse, health (physical and psychological), social functioning (including employment and education) and offending behaviour. This will require providers to work together to meet these multiple needs and greater coordination of elements of the care plan

▸ the focus in care plans and keyworking on the main elements in the treatment journey: engagement, delivery and completion or maintenance.[19]

Conclusion

Nurses have been a major component of the alcohol and drug addiction workforce for at least three decades. Now nurses need to be able to address the wider problems of 'substance' misuse. With the changes in the way health care is to be provided with the new Health and Social Care Bill, nurses are well placed to take the lead in the care of the patient with a 'substance' misuse problem.

The basic qualities of any nurse, that of empathy and kindness, form the foundation of any care plan being set out for a patient. Nurses should ensure that they maintain their professionalism in whatever situation they find themselves, whether at work or off duty. The NMC Code of Conduct requires all nurses to be mindful of their peers and to work as a member of the team, supporting colleagues and sharing their expertise.

Modern nursing covers a multitude of facets and 'substance' misuse is just one of them. No nurse is expected to be able to provide 100% of the care for a patient. However, nurses should be mindful of their requirement to be able to signpost patients to appropriate professionals, who can address the element of that patient's care when the nurse recognises require healthcare input.

Nurses are members of a multidisciplinary team that provides integrated care packages to the people of their community.

Further reading

Peterson T, McBride A. *Working with Substance Misusers*. London: Routledge, 2002.

Rassool G H (ed.). *Substance Use and Misuse: nature, context and clinical interventions*. Oxford: Blackwell Science, 1998.

References

1. Affara F A, Styles M M. *Nursing Regulation Guidebook, from Principle to Power*. Geneva: International Council of Nurses, 1992.

2. Parrott A, Morinan A, Moss M, *et al. Understanding Drugs and Behaviour*. Chichester: Wiley, 2004.

3. Henderson V. *The Nature of Nursing*. New York: Macmillan Publishing, 1966.

4. Ghodse H. *Drugs and Addictive Behaviour, a Guide to Treatment*. Cambridge: Cambridge University Press, 2002.

5. Rassool G H. Addiction nursing: towards a new paradigm: the United Kingdom experience. In: G H Rassool, M Gafoor (eds). *Addiction Nursing: perspectives on professional and clinical practices*. Cheltenham: Stanley Thornes, 1997.

6. Peterson T, McBride A. *Working with Substance Misusers*. London: Routledge, 2002.

7. Rassool G H. *Substance Use and Misuse: nature, context and clinical interventions*. Oxford: Blackwell Science, 1998.

8. Jacksley H, Dicker A, Coyne P. G P contract killing you? Time to call a nurse. *Drugs and Alcohol Today* 2004; **4(2)**: 15–18.

9. Harding-Price D, *et al. Drug Misuse and Caring for Children*. Grimsby: Grimsby Health Authority, 1991.

10. Prochaska J O, DiClemente C C. Stages and processes of self-change of smoking: toward an integrative model of change. *Journal of Consulting and Clinical Psychology* 1983; **51(3)**: 390–5.

11. National Prescribing Centre. Non-medical prescribing, www.npc.nhs.uk/non_medical/ [accessed October 2012].

12. Nursing and Midwifery Council. *Standards for Medicines Management*. London: NMC, 2010, www.nmc-uk.org/Publications/Standards/ [accessed October 2012].

13. UK Central Council for Nursing, Midwifery and Health Visiting. *Scope of Professional Practice*. London: UKCC, 1992.

14. Department of Health. *Supplementary Prescribing by Nurses and Pharmacists within the NHS in England. A guide for implementation*. London: DH, 2003.

15. National Prescribing Centre. Changes to controlled drugs legislation for nurse and pharmacist independent prescribers: coming into force on 23rd April 2012, *Controlled Drugs Alert* 2012 (April), http://lists.npc.nhs.uk/list/fe03n4zc/120417B/kgfp2q.vib [accessed October 2012].

16. National Prescribing Centre. *A Single Competency Framework for All Prescribers*. London: NICE, 2012, www.npc.co.uk/improving_safety/improving_quality/resources/single_comp_framework.pdf [accessed October 2012].

17. Nursing and Midwifery Council. *The Code: standards of conduct, performance and ethics for nurses and midwives*. London: NMC, 2008.

18. Department of Health. *Extending Independent Nurse Prescribing within the NHS in England: a guide for implementation* (2nd edn). London: DH, 2004.

19. National Treatment Agency. *Models of Care for Treatment of Adult Drug Misusers. Update 2006*. London: NTA, 2006.

CHAPTER 7

The management of drug misuse in primary care: exploring wider opportunities in community pharmacy

Janie Sheridan and Jenny Scott

IN THIS CHAPTER

Introduction || *Pharmacists and the management of drug users* ||
Areas of health care where pharmacists can have an impact || *Delivering
services to drug users* || *How can pharmacists take on additional roles?*

Introduction

This chapter aims to explore roles for community pharmacists providing services
for drug misusers. These roles go beyond those such as dispensing opioid substitution therapies and the provision of needle exchange. Community pharmacists,
like GPs, are able to provide brief interventions, and their more frequent contact
with patients lends itself to multiple staged interventions. Pharmacists are often
a first point of healthcare contact and are, therefore, also a signposter to the rest
of the health services. The introduction of new pharmacy contracts in England,
Wales and Scotland in the mid-2000s consolidated opportunities for pharmacists as a diagnostician, prescriber and manager of long-term chronic conditions.
Under these arrangements, pharmacists, like GPs, can be paid according to the
type and quality of care they provide and they are able to develop special interest
areas in order to provide local pharmaceutical services to specific populations
of patients. The challenge for community pharmacists is the re-engineering of
everyday practice to incorporate the many elements of the extended role against a
background of increasing prescription volumes and patient expectation.[1]

The chapter has a mainly UK focus in terms of the law, regulations and examples.

Pharmacists and the management of drug users

Traditionally the dispensing of medicines has dominated the role of community pharmacists. With regard to the management of drug misuse this role has included dispensing prescriptions for opiate substitution therapy (OST) to drug users and supplying clean injecting equipment and health promotion literature by means of pharmacy-based needle exchange schemes.

Since the publication in 1999 and 2007 of UK clinical guidelines,[2,3] increasing importance has been placed on the roles that both community and hospital pharmacists can play in the care and treatment of people who have problems with their drug use. Community pharmacists provide a significant point of contact with drug misusers and have regular (often daily) contact with the patient through OST dispensing. Research confirms that up to 79% of community pharmacists are involved in the provision of pharmacotherapies such as methadone and buprenorphine for opiate-dependent patients.[4,5]

While pharmacists have embraced these roles, many have expanded on them to include the management of a wider range of health issues relating to problem drug use. However, one of the challenges pharmacists face is that contact with drug misusers, although frequent, is not always very long. Similarly, pharmacists who delegate drug users to medicines counter assistants or technicians may miss opportunities to maximise their role.

Community pharmacists are trained to take a holistic approach when working with patients. They are in a position to respond to requests from patients for medications to relieve symptoms of self-limiting conditions that are presented to them in the pharmacy, and are able to prescribe both general sales list and pharmacy medicines, where appropriate, as well as providing any necessary advice. They are in a prime position to signpost patients, as necessary, to a GP, dentist, accident and emergency department or drug service. Finally, because they are situated in the community and have contact with their patients/customers when they are well, as well as when they are ill, they have the opportunity to follow up patients and may therefore be a valuable initial contact point when a relapse occurs.

In practice, patients with chronic long-term disorders probably have as good a relationship with their local pharmacist as they do with their GP. The extent to which pharmacists can effectively intervene in patient care, however, even to suggest alterations to treatment regimens, is limited by lack of access to patients' medical records and access to the details of patients' involvement with other relevant agencies. Pharmacists may, therefore, be limited in their ability to recognise events and conditions that require referral to or from other agencies or treatment providers. However, even considering these potential barriers, there is current evidence of innovative and relevant practice. The success of extending the role of pharmacists depends upon a proactive approach, good communication and appropriate training.

The rest of this chapter will consider a number of innovative ways in which pharmacists' input into the management of drug misuse in the community can be expanded to benefit patients and to optimise their care. Two approaches will be taken: the first will explore areas of health care where pharmacists can have an impact on problem drug use, and the second will look at other services delivered to drug users by exploring processes and activities that may facilitate the provision of a more comprehensive system of care for patients.

Areas of health care where pharmacists can have an impact

Management of minor ailments schemes

It is important for the pharmacist to recognise that patients on a substitute medication programme for the treatment of substance misuse, and those utilising needle exchange services, may also experience concurrent self-limiting diseases or minor ailments. Research indicates that OST clients want help for primary healthcare problems such as headache (18%) and constipation (22%),[6] and that 24% have suffered from a cold, 56% from headache and 23% from indigestion in the previous three months.[7] Thus it is important to remember that requests for the supply of over-the-counter products to treat such conditions may be genuine rather than a ploy to obtain medicines that can enhance the effects of illicitly obtained psychoactive substances or themselves be misused. See below for more information on specific issues.

Community pharmacists are ideally placed to develop guidelines and protocols for the supply and/or sale of any necessary treatments and to ensure that the medications proposed do not interact with prescribed methadone, buprenorphine or other treatment medicines, or interfere with drug screens. With the development of minor ailment schemes, which allow pharmacists to supply such remedies as part of the NHS in specified circumstances, it is essential that patients on drug treatment programmes are not inappropriately excluded from such schemes.

The treatment of minor ailments by pharmacists has been a feature of the daily routine of community pharmacy for many generations. Clinical governance issues and the need for pharmacists to use evidence-based practice when responding to requests from the public mean that such requests are handled in a professional and considered manner. Medicines counter staff in the UK are required to undertake specific training and to refer requests to the pharmacists as appropriate.

Pilot schemes undertaken in several Primary Care Trust areas have demonstrated that community pharmacists can help to shift the management of minor ailments from the care of the GP to the community pharmacy and hence reduce the GP's workload.[8] Research indicates, however, that patients on an OST programme may be refused access to self-medication and treatment for self-limiting conditions such as coughs, colds, headaches or sleep disturbances because it is assumed that their requests for antihistamines, decongestants or analgesics are not genuine.[8,9] It is important to recognise that methadone and buprenorphine patients are not immune to coughs, colds and headaches. It would be beneficial for such conditions to be treated appropriately by the pharmacist supplying OST rather than that the patient seeks such medication elsewhere, where the counter staff and/or pharmacists are not aware of the patient's medication history. Minor ailment schemes that cover OST clients should be set up in collaboration with local drug services.

Prevention of overdose

Accidental overdose is a risk for drug users and a common occurrence. Most drug users have witnessed overdose in a friend or drug-using peer. The National Treatment Agency and the Department of Health have responded to the Advisory Council on the Misuse of Drugs (ACMD) report on drug-related deaths [10] in many ways. This includes the publication of several guidance documents by the National Treatment Agency and guidance notes on harm reduction services. Pharmacists can reinforce these endeavours by the provision of advice to those receiving medication and to needle exchange clients on how to avoid overdose and what to do if they are present when someone else experiences one. Materials that are suitable for use include those published by:

▸ Exchange Supplies (www.exchangesupplies.org)

▸ Department of Health-funded 'Talk to FRANK', a 24-hour drugs information and telephone helpline and website (www.talktofrank.com/search/node/overdose)

▸ Scottish government (http://knowthescore.info/).

Pharmacists should ensure that all medicines are stored safely so that accidental poisoning of children is prevented. Again, the provision of both verbal and written advice/information can be helpful in reinforcing safety messages, as can the addition of special warning labels on dispensed methadone or buprenorphine containers. Pharmacists should liaise with local drug services to find out whether lockable storage boxes are supplied to drug users locally for the safekeeping of take-home doses of OST.

It has been argued that naloxone should be made more generally available, for example to those who are likely to witness opioid overdoses.[11,12] The ACMD drug-related deaths report was of the view that, as a matter of principle, naloxone should be made more widely available, but that careful consideration should be given to prevention, first aid and resuscitation (placing person in recovery position, keeping airways open, etc.).[10] Some community pharmacists supply naloxone under patient group direction, for example in Grampian.[13] Whether or not all pharmacists are willing to be trained to supply and administer naloxone under a patient group direction is open to debate.[5] Pharmacists can be involved in drawing up patient group directions for the supply and administration of naloxone by nurses in the NHS, prisons or some other settings where overdoses may occur.

Nutrition

Drug users may not eat a balanced diet, and may often miss out on meals and consume high levels of sugary foods.[14,15] Concurrent alcohol dependency can increase their risks of developing nutritional deficiencies including thiamine deficiency, which can lead to Wernicke's encephalopathy. Pharmacists can provide advice on healthy eating, and may refer patients to a doctor or a dietician for the provision of prescribed vitamin supplementation or advice on nutrition.

Drug users may ask for dietary supplements, such as high-calorie drinks. There is no empirical evidence to guide the clinician in either prescribing or selling these products, and they are probably best avoided except in the most nutritionally deprived individuals. They are not advocated in the UK clinical guidelines unless there is a specific clinical indication. In otherwise healthy, non-debilitated individuals, dietary supplements are no substitute for a balanced diet. When discussing the use of supplements in the homeless population, Wright suggests that they should be considered only when the body mass index falls below 19.[16] Community pharmacists should consider contacting their local dietician for specific information to supply to drug users. It may even be possible to develop such information as a joint project between the local pharmacy, drug and dietetic services.

Constipation

One of the most common and uncomfortable adverse effects of opioids (prescribed or otherwise) is constipation. Research indicates that 46% of OST patients report this problem and 22% would like help for it.[6,7] Unlike some of the opioid effects, tolerance to this does not always occur. Asking patients who are on an OST prescription about their bowel habits could be something routinely undertaken by the pharmacist. Patients should be told early on in treatment that constipation is likely to be a problem. Dietary advice and laxative treatment where appropriate can be provided by their pharmacist. Advice to patients can include increasing the amount of fruit and vegetables that they eat and reducing their alcohol consumption. Laxatives that work by softening stools will be more helpful than those that act on muscle tone. Bulking laxatives are not recommended as they can lead to bowel impaction in combination with reduced bowel tone caused by opioids.

Sleep problems

Psychoactive drugs often interfere with sleep patterns. The most obvious culprits are caffeine, cocaine/crack, cannabis and amphetamines, though many other drugs can cause this problem. Many drugs interfere with normal sleep, especially following a reduction of dose, such as during detoxification. Sleep disturbance after an opioid detoxification can be a major contributor to relapse, and is a major feature of benzodiazepine withdrawal.

Although the prescribing of drugs to aid sleep may be inappropriate for some drug users, especially long term, advice on sleep hygiene, the use of sleep diaries and herbal remedies, plus a listening ear are all useful interventions that can be provided by pharmacists. An informative leaflet on sleep is available from www.exchangesupplies.org/shopdisp_P105.php.

Sweating

Spontaneous sweating is a common long-term problem in methadone patients with 70% reporting suffering it in the last three months;[7] histamine release may be a partial cause of this phenomenon.[17] The sweating can be severe and is often present in the absence of other histamine-related effects, which suggests that other mechanisms may be involved. Whereas sedating antihistamines may be helpful in both inducing sleep and in countering the sweating caused by histamine release, they are also known to potentiate the effects of methadone and have been specifically sought by drug users for this purpose and therefore should be avoided.[18] In addition antihistamines associated with QTc prolongation should be avoided. There are two case reports suggesting that the non-sedating antihistamine desloratadine is beneficial although there is a need for a trial to confirm whether this can indeed relieve symptoms.[17]

Excessive sweating can be a cause of severe distress to patients on high doses of methadone. Wearing loose cotton clothing, avoiding coffee and strong tea or soft drinks that contain high amounts of caffeine, and cold baths can sometimes be helpful. Taking methadone early in the day rather than later may also be helpful in reducing night sweats, although there is no evidence to support this.

Smoking cessation

A high proportion of drug users smoke. Studies of methadone maintenance patients indicate that more than 90% of the patients smoked cigarettes and many others also smoked cannabis.[19, 20] Research has indicated that many patients in methadone treatment are interested in quitting smoking[21] and are interested in smoking cessation services being offered in treatment programmes.

Community pharmacists have been shown to be effective in enhancing smoking cessation[22] and are knowledgeable about smoking cessation products. There may be a useful role for pharmacists working in collaboration with drug treatment services that wish to instigate smoking cessation services for their patients to develop enhanced services that involve smoking cessation.

The pharmacist should bear in mind that it may be inappropriate to promote smoking cessation as a high-priority goal at a time when the patient has many other more immediate problems to deal with. It may be more appropriate to discuss smoking cessation options once a successful drug detoxification has been completed rather than before or once the client is stable on OST maintenance. However, there is some evidence that suggests addressing smoking does not have an adverse effect on recovery from alcohol or other drug dependence.[23,24] It is important not to minimise significant health gains from cessation of smoking and there is a tendency for alcohol and drug workers to not address smoking. So there is an opportunity for pharmacist intervention. Additional advice on how and when to offer information about the various treatments that are available to assist smoking cessation should be explored.

Hepatitis

The incidence of hepatitis B and C among injecting drug users is of concern, as the viruses can be transmitted through the sharing of contaminated injecting equipment. Co-infection with hepatitis A may lead to serious consequences for those who already have liver damage. Whereas no vaccination is available against hepatitis C, both hepatitis A and B are preventable conditions.

Giving advice on hygiene to needle exchange clients can help to reduce infection. Vaccination against hepatitis A and B is possible for those not already infected. Many injecting drug users have not been vaccinated and many are not aware of their hepatitis B status. Pharmacists should be encouraged to ask whether the user has ever been tested and/or vaccinated, and make the appropriate referral for testing and immunisation. Where a pharmacy needle exchange has a private consulting room on site it may be possible to allow the room to be used for a nurse- or pharmacist-based vaccination facility using patient group directions[25,26] to administer hepatitis B or the combined A and B vaccine using accelerated regimens. Furthermore, research indicates a role for hepatitis B and C testing in the community. A pilot study that explored hepatitis B and C testing in community pharmacies found that this could be feasible and acceptable. The same research also found that rates of hepatitis C identified in community pharmacies are higher than those identified in general practice, making pharmacies a good potential site for testing.[27] Pharmacists can also play an important role in encouraging or supporting clients to seek treatment for hepatitis C (interferon). Those undergoing interferon treatment can benefit from support and monitoring of mood in particular.

Dental health

Community pharmacists are in a position to identify dental problems when the user enquires about over-the-counter remedies, and can encourage the person to seek dental treatment. In a study in London, pharmacists were able to link with local dentists and make direct referrals for drug users to NHS dental care.[28, 29]

Research has shown that drug users suffer numerous problems with their teeth yet they often have trouble accessing dental care owing to fear of pain, fear of stigmatisation, previous bad experiences and cost of treatment.[28, 30] Dental problems may result as a consequence of drug use, for example bruxism associated with stimulant use, or as a result of a lifestyle that is often associated with problematic drug use, or from eating high-calorific sugary foods, or having poor general diet, bad dental hygiene and poor access to health care when problems arise, such as dental abscesses or cavities. Brondani provides an excellent review article.[31] Furthermore, opioids may mask dental pain, something that becomes apparent only when the patient stops using opioids for whatever reason. Methadone is often cited as a 'cause' of dental problems and many patients will request sugar-free methadone solution. It is true that methadone solution has the potential to provide an environment in which tooth decay occurs, as the solution is acidic and has high sugar content. Because opiates reduce saliva flow, they are a risk factor for dental decay. Both sugar-free and sugar-based solutions of methadone are acidic, and can cause erosion of dentine and reduce saliva.

It is important that patients are aware that they need to practise good dental hygiene whichever formulation they are taking. Giving the advice to suck the methadone solution through a straw and to rinse the mouth with plenty of water after the dose is swallowed, or to chew sugar-free gum, can all minimise the risks of tooth decay. Other problems may be associated with the use of sugar-free formulations, not the least being the ease with which it can be injected, and that some of the sweetening agents used in sugar-free preparations have laxative effects. The latter can be severe where large doses result in a considerable volume of mixture being consumed on a daily basis.

Children of problem drug users

It is important that pharmacists, like all professionals who work with the drug-using population, recognise that the wellbeing of children is of paramount importance and overrides the duty of confidentiality to their parents or other patients. Although being a drug user does not automatically make an individual a bad parent, the nature of addiction may result in inappropriate parenting. Children of some drug users may experience significant harm and neglect. Therefore, all health professionals have to be alert to the possibility of risk to children. The Advisory Council on the Misuse of Drugs in their report, *Hidden Harm*,[32] considered the particular problems faced by the children of drug users. Although the role of pharmacists was not specifically mentioned in the report, there are nevertheless a number of ways in which pharmacists could assist both the parents and their children. These include:

▸ contributing positively to the stabilisation of the parent's drug use through the provision of methadone and/or needle exchange services

▸ alerting the GP when the patient is not well or is behaving out of character

▸ asking about the home situation

▸ observing the condition of any children brought into the pharmacy

▸ advising that children are registered with a GP

▸ advising on safe storage of medicines and injecting equipment in the home

▸ providing contraception advice

▸ providing advice on immunisation for both parent and children

▸ referring pregnant drug users to antenatal services if necessary.

Pharmacists should report childcare concerns to GPs, social workers or key drug workers, or in exceptional cases directly to the police. A useful first point of contact is the Primary Care Trust child protection lead who can discuss and give advice on initial concerns.

Delivering services to drug users

There are many ways for pharmacists to become involved in delivering services to OST patients. One long-established example is the Four Way Berkshire Agreement service.[33] This scheme, developed by a pharmacist, provides a mechanism for helping professionals comply with good prescribing practice and improve multiprofessional collaboration. The scheme provides remuneration for GPs and pharmacists, and also established well-defined channels of communication, also including key workers and the patient. In addition, the community pharmacist has a prime role in providing supervised consumption of OST and shared care, and also in helping monitor outcomes. This scheme has informed the development of many other localised models for drug treatment provision where community pharmacy involvement is formalised.

Other services and interventions, such as needle exchange, offering advice on dental care, hepatitis screening and any other areas mentioned above, should be set up in conjunction with local Primary Care Trusts or drug and alcohol services, where required. It is essential that such services and interventions are developed in collaboration with key stakeholders.

Prescribing services

Patient group directions

A patient group direction (PGD) is a written direction relating to the supply and administration, or administration only, of a prescription-only medicine to persons generally (subject to specified exclusions) and is signed by a doctor or a dentist and a pharmacist (see: www.nelm.nhs.uk/en/Communities/NeLM/PGDs). Over recent years pharmacists have demonstrated their ability to supply prescription-only medicines under such directions, for example for the supply of emergency hormonal contraception.[34] Consideration could be given to developing PGDs for the following situations:

▸ supply and administration of naloxone for opioid-induced overdose

▸ administration of hepatitis B or the combined hepatitis A and B vaccination to pharmacy needle exchange clients/patients

▸ provision of antibiotics to treat injection-related injuries.

Although it is recognised that not all pharmacies have an appropriate private area to undertake all three of the above activities, the majority of pharmacies in the UK do.

Medication reviews

Medication Use Review (MUR) is an enhanced-level service within the current community pharmacy contract. Although most reviews have targeted the elderly or patients on long-term medication for cardiovascular or respiratory conditions, there is no reason why consideration should not be given to pharmacists undertaking medication reviews for patients on methadone or buprenorphine programmes. Some of these patients may be receiving concurrent medications that interact with methadone or buprenorphine or they may develop problems that necessitate the administration of additional medications. In such cases, for instance patients receiving medication to treat HIV/AIDS, tuberculosis, epilepsy, hepatitis C or alcoholic liver disease, it is important to monitor the patient to reduce the possibility of adverse drug reactions. Furthermore, there is evidence of an ageing OST treatment population, who are likely being prescribed medications for cardiovascular and other age-related conditions.[35, 36]

Pharmacist prescribing

In 2006 legislation was introduced in the UK to allow appropriately qualified pharmacists to act as independent prescribers. One of the areas where pharmacists have made a significant contribution as prescribers is in the management of drug misuse. There are many examples from around the UK of pharmacists contributing to the work of specialist addiction services and drug treatment within primary care. Until April 2012, pharmacists had to act as supplementary prescribers when prescribing controlled drugs under a clinical management plan agreed with a doctor and the patient. However, legislation that came into force on 23 April 2012 now permits pharmacists independent prescribing of controlled drugs. In practice, the importance of pharmacists working in teams with other professionals including doctors and drugs workers remains. Many drugs services now use non-medical prescribers (NMPs) to provide some of the prescribing for clients, especially what may be seen as more routine prescribing, allowing best use of the doctor's time to be made. The unique contribution that pharmacists can make, compared with other NMPs, is around the management of cases where pharmacotherapy presents a particular challenge. Examples include managing drug interactions, controlling side effects and liaising with other healthcare teams that may prescribe for the patient, e.g. HIV clinicians, neurologists or psychiatrists.

Computer-generated prescriptions and electronic record keeping

The introduction of computer-generated prescriptions and record keeping for controlled drugs and the electronic transfer of prescriptions should release time to allow pharmacists to take an even more proactive clinical role in the care of all patients, including those with drug or alcohol use problems. One welcome recommendation from the Fourth Shipman Report[37] that is benefiting practice is that pharmacists in the UK can now correct technical errors on prescriptions for controlled drugs without the prescription having to be returned to the prescriber. There is a limit to what these technical errors are classed as. For example, the pharmacist can add the quantity in words or figures when one or other is missing but cannot add the quantity when it is not stated in any format.

Information and advice to drugs services

Although pharmacist-led medicines information centres are well established in hospitals throughout the UK and elsewhere, the expertise of such centres is, with some notable exceptions, in the field of medicines rather than substances liable to misuse. Those pharmacists who have acquired relevant knowledge and expertise in the field of substance misuse have already demonstrated their potential to provide valuable support and information to local drugs agencies and their clients.

How can pharmacists take on additional roles?

What is needed to facilitate these developments? In the first place, a willingness and acceptance of these roles among pharmacists is essential. Descriptions of appropriate levels of competency are currently being developed, and training put in place to enable pharmacists to achieve and maintain them. Furthermore, a whole of pharmacy approach is required, where all pharmacists and support staff are aware of, and support, these initiatives. Evidence exists that some staff are keen to be involved in these services, although many have negative attitudes,[38] and such attitudes can jeopardise new services. Support staff training must not be forgotten – at the very least training in understanding drug misuse and concepts of harm reduction should be provided.

Pharmacists should be proactive in forming partnerships with local drugs service providers, including GPs, specialist drugs services and non-pharmacy needle exchanges. The expansion of shared-care arrangements to encompass these additional interventions could ensure that all partners in the care of a client are aware of what has taken place.

In its report on the commissioning and management of community drug treatment services for adults, the Audit Commission (UK) reported that pharmacists can play an important role in the management of drug misusers, but noted that research has shown that many pharmacists are an underused point of contact to the drug-misusing population and would benefit from a closer working relationship with prescribing services.[39] The only way those services can become more aware of the important role that pharmacists have in the treatment and care of drug misusers is if the pharmacists themselves take the initiative and contact services with a description of what they can offer.

The provision of acceptable levels of privacy to encourage and enable appropriate discussion to take place is essential. Most pharmacies now have a private room to enable consultations to take place in confidence. Such facilities enhance the level of services that can be offered to all pharmacy clientele and not just drug users.

When taking on additional roles in the field of substance misuse it is essential that pharmacists ensure that they have optimum levels of security to protect themselves, their staff and the premises. Useful advice on how to optimise security and deal with difficult situations can be obtained from local police community safety officers. Pharmacists should also check whether their personal and liability insurance covers these services.

Acknowledgements

We would like to acknowledge the input of Kay Roberts who was a co-author of this chapter in the first edition and for Carina Walters, Auckland Community Alcohol and Drug Services, Waitemata District Health Board, Auckland, for feedback on the manuscript.

References

1. Ghalamkari H. Pharmacists are willing to extend their roles and change their practice. *Pharmaceutical Journal* 2004; **273**: 82.

2. Department of Health. *Drug Misuse and Dependence: guidelines on clinical management.* London: HMSO, 1999.

3. Department of Health (England) and the devolved administrations. *Drug Misuse and Dependence: UK guidelines on clinical management.* London: DH (England), the Scottish Government, Welsh Assembly Government and Northern Ireland Executive, 2007.

4. Matheson C, Bond CM, Tinelli M. Community pharmacy harm reduction services for drug misusers: national service delivery and professional attitude development over a decade in Scotland. *Journal of Public Health* (Oxford) 2007; **29(4)**: 350–7.

5. Sheridan J, Manning V, Ridge G, *et al.* Community pharmacies and the provision of opioid substitution services for drug misusers: changes in activity and attitudes of community pharmacists across England 1995–2005. *Addiction* 2007; **102(11)**: 1824–30.

6. Winstock A R, Lea T, Sheridan J. Patients' help-seeking behaviours for health problems associated with methadone and buprenorphine treatment. *Drug and Alcohol Review* 2008; **27(4)**: 393–7.

7. Sheridan J, Wheeler A, Walters C. Health problems and help-seeking activities of methadone maintenance clients at Auckland Methadone Service (AMS): potential for community pharmacy service expansion? *Harm Reduction Journal* 2005; **2**: 25 (doi:10.1186/1477-7517-2-25).

8. Akram G, Roberts K. Pharmacists' management of over-the-counter medication requests from methadone patients. *Journal of Substance Use* 2003; **8(4)**: 215–22.

9. Roberts K, Coggans N, King J. Do problem drug users only purchase 'over-the-counter' (OTC) medications for the purpose of misuse? *Proceedings of 11th International Conference on the Reduction of Drug Related Harm.* Jersey: IHRA, 2000.

10. Advisory Council on the Misuse of Drugs. *Reducing Drug Related Deaths.* London: HMSO, 2000.

11. Strang J, Hall W, Farrell M, *et al.* Heroin overdose: the case for take-home naloxone. *British Medical Journal* 1996; **312(7044)**: 1435–6.

12. Strang J, Manning V, Mayet S, *et al.* Overdose training and take-home naloxone for opiate users: prospective cohort study of impact on knowledge and attitudes and subsequent management of overdoses. *Addiction* 2008; **103(10)**: 1648–57.

13. NHS Grampian. Launch of life-saving training programme on International Overdose Awareness Day. 2011, www.nhsgrampian.org/nhsgrampian/gra_display_simple_index. jsp?pContentID=7843&p_applic=CCC&p_service=Content.show& [accessed April 2013].

14. Best D, Lehmann P, Gossop M, *et al.* Eating too little, smoking and drinking too much: wider lifestyle problems among methadone maintenance patients. *Addiction Research and Theory* 1998; **6(6)**: 489–98.

15. Zador D, Wall P M L, Webster I. High sugar intake in a group of women on methadone maintenance in South Western Sydney, Australia. *Addiction* 1996; **91(7)**: 1053–61.

16. Wright N. *Homelessness: a primary care response*. London: RCGP, 2002.

17. Al-Adwani A, Basu N. Methadone and excessive sweating [letter]. *Addiction* 2004; **99(2)**: 259.

18. Roberts K, Gruer L, Gilhooly T. Misuse of diphenhydramine soft gel capsules (Sleepia): a cautionary tale from Glasgow. *Addiction* 1999; **94(10)**: 1575–7.

19. Calsyn D A, Saxon A J. An innovative approach to reducing cannabis use in a subset of methadone maintenance clients. *Drug and Alcohol Dependence* 1999; **53(2)**: 167–9.

20. Clemmey P, Brooner R, Chutuape M A, *et al*. Smoking habits and attitudes in a methadone maintenance treatment population. *Drug and Alcohol Dependence* 1997; **44(2–3)**: 123–32.

21. Nahvi S, Richter K, Li X, *et al*. Cigarette smoking and interest in quitting in methadone maintenance patients. *Addictive Behaviors* 2006; **31(11)**: 2127–34.

22. Maguire T A, McElnay J C, Drummond A. A randomized controlled trial of a smoking cessation intervention based in community pharmacies. *Addiction* 2001; **96(2)**: 325–31.

23. Bird Gulliver S, Kamholz B, Helstrom A. Smoking cessation and alcohol abstinence: what do the data tell us? Bethesda: National Institute on Alcohol Abuse and Alcoholism (NIAAA), http://pubs. niaaa.nih.gov/publications/arh293/208-212.htm [accessed April 2013].

24. Lemon S C, Friedmann P D, Stein M D. The impact of smoking cessation on drug abuse treatment outcome. *Addictive Behaviors* 2003; **28(7)**: 1323–31.

25. Lanarkshire Health. *Annual Report of the Hepatitis B Vaccination Programme 2003–2004*. Lanarkshire Health, 2004.

26. Isle of Wight Primary Care Trust. Patient Group Direction for the supply/administration of Hepatitis B vaccination in those adults considered to be at high risk (excluding those presenting with a needlestick injury) by qualified and suitably trained community pharmacists. www. hampshirelpc.org.uk/webfm_send/3134 [accessed January 2013].

27. Hepatitis C Trust. *Diagnosing Viral Hepatitis in the Community: a 3-month pharmacy testing pilot*. London: Hepatitis C Trust, 2010, www.hepctrust.org.uk/Resources/HepC/HCV%20Reports/ Trust/Diagnosing%20viral%20hepatitis%20in%20the%20community%20A%203%20month%20 pharmacy%20testing%20pilot.pdf [accessed April 2013].

28. Sheridan J, Aggleton M, Carson T. Dental health and access to dental treatment: a comparison of drug users and non-drug users attending community pharmacies. *British Dental Journal* 2001; **191(8)**: 453–7.

29. Sheridan J, Carson T, Aggleton M. Providing dental health services to drug users: testing a model for a community pharmacy advice and referral scheme. *Pharmaceutical Journal* 2003; **271**: 180–2.

30. Metsch L, Crandall L, Wohler-Torres B, *et al*. Met and unmet need for dental services among active drug users in Miami, Florida. *Journal of Behavioral Health Services and Research* 2002; **29(2)**: 176–88.

31. Brondani M, Park P E. Methadone and oral health: a brief review. *Journal of Dental Hygiene* 2011; **85(2)**: 92–8.

32. Advisory Council on the Misuse of Drugs. *Hidden Harm. Responding to the needs of children of problem drug users. The report of an inquiry by the Home Office*. London: Advisory Council on the Misuse of Drugs, 2003.

33. Walker M. Shared care of opiate substance misusers in Berkshire. *Pharmaceutical Journal* 2001; **266**: 545–52.

34. Bissell P, Anderson C, Savage I, *et al*. Supplying emergency hormonal contraception through patient group direction: a qualitative study of the views of pharmacists. *International Journal of Pharmacy Practice* 2001; **9(S1)**: 57.

35. Lofwall M R, Brooner R K, Bigelow G E, *et al.* Characteristics of older opioid maintenance patients. *Journal of Substance Abuse Treatment* 2005; **28(3)**: 265–72.

36. Rosen D, Smith M L, Reynolds C F, III. The prevalence of mental and physical health disorders among older methadone patients. *American Journal of Geriatric Psychiatry* 2008; **16(6)**: 488–97 (10.1097/JGP.0b013e31816ff35a).

37. Smith J. *The Shipman Inquiry. Fourth report: the regulation of controlled drugs in the community.* Command Paper Cm 6249. London: Stationery Office, 2004.

38. Mackridge A J, Scott J. Experiences, attitudes and training needs of pharmacy support staff providing services to drug users in Great Britain: a qualitative study. *Journal of Substance Use* 2009; **14(6)**: 375–84.

39. Audit Commission. *Changing Habits: the commissioning and management of community drug treatment services for adults.* London: Audit Commission 2002.

CHAPTER 8

The management of opioid addiction: evidence-based treatment

Clare Gerada, Jenny Keen and Steve Brinksman

IN THIS CHAPTER

Introduction ‖ *Prevalence of opioid users in general practice* ‖ *Opioid treatment options* ‖ *Opioid withdrawal/detoxification* ‖ *What to choose for detoxification* ‖ *Maintenance treatment for opioid dependence* ‖ *Relapse prevention* ‖ *Conclusion*

Introduction

Chapter 9 describes the practical treatment in the management of opioid addiction. This chapter deals with more general issues around opioid treatment, including the evidence base for the various options. An awareness of the reasoning behind each treatment promotes effective practice. There is, however, a lack of sound evidence on which to base some of our prescribing decisions. Even where a body of evidence exists it seldom includes primary care patients or practitioners as part of the research methodology.

Prevalence of opioid users in general practice

The number of illicit opioid users in the UK is generally estimated at just over 300,000 and over 50% of GPs will have seen a known heroin user in the past month. The number of patients using illicit drugs registered with a practice varies with location and with the interest that practice has in working with this population. It would be unusual for a practice to have heroin users comprise more than 1–2% of its registered list. Equally it would be unusual for a practice to have none, such is the ubiquitous nature of this problem.

Opioid treatment options

There is a variety of treatment options available for treating opioid dependence, both in the pharmaceutical agents available and the regimes used (see Table 8.1).

Table 8.1   **Summary of treatment options for opioid dependence**

Stage of treatment	Options
Withdrawal/detoxification	The opioid-dependent individual is taken off the drug, either abruptly, or gradually so as to eliminate physical dependence with the minimum of discomfort from withdrawal. Detoxification alone cannot be expected to achieve long-term abstinence and is best considered as a precursor to, or first stage of, treatment.
	Options available include tapered doses of methadone or buprenorphine or an alpha-2 adrenergic agonist, such as lofexidine. Other medications are antiemetics for nausea and vomiting, antidiarrhoeals, and analgesics for muscle cramps. Some clinicians use dihydrocodeine for short-term detoxification, though evidence for effectiveness of this is limited
Maintenance	There is a wealth of evidence for the effectiveness of high-dose methadone in combination with psychosocial support in a number of outcomes. Also evidence is growing for effectiveness of maintenance on buprenorphine for opioid substitution therapy
Relapse prevention	Naltrexone treatment is a useful adjunct to other psychosocial interventions to prevent relapse

The treatment of opioid dependence has often been subjected to political imperative and the drug strategies in many countries are rarely devised purely on the evidence base. It is only by having an understanding of all the treatment options and the evidence that underpins these that a clinician can work with the individual patient to decide on an appropriate management for him or her.

Methadone is the best-known treatment used as opioid substitution therapy. It is a synthetic opioid and was originally synthesised in Germany as a substitute for morphine when supplies of this became unobtainable during the Second World War. It is a full agonist in terms of its activity on the opioid receptors in the brain. There are many decades of research and evaluation of methadone and its use in treating opioid dependence and it has been described as the most researched medication in the world. Where correctly implemented it is a treatment that has been shown to produce remarkable improvements in patients who have been highly dysfunctional as a consequence of their heroin use. Where treatment is provided for a long period there are improvements in not just physical and mental health but also social functioning, allowing patients to resume what would be recognised as a normal life by non-opioid users.

Before the work of Dole and Nyswander in 1965 looking at methadone as a long-term maintenance therapy [1] it was previously used as a detoxification agent to facilitate withdrawal from heroin. The evidence base garnered since the 1960s informed previous drug strategies to promote long-term maintenance. However, the 2010 drug strategy shifted the emphasis to 'recovery' and, despite the fact that this makes it clear that this is an individually defined concept, there is some ideological pressure that this should be categorised as abstinence from both illicit and prescribed medication. This may be achievable for some but the evidence base still provides ample justification for the use of long-term opioid substitution therapy for those who are not yet ready or able to become abstinent.

Buprenorphine is another man-made opioid first synthesised in the 1960s. It differs from methadone in its effects, as it is only a partial agonist of the opioid receptors. It is highly soluble and is used as a sublingual preparation. There is a growing body of evidence for its use both in long-term substitution therapy and detoxification. Both it and methadone have been the subject of National Institute for Health and Clinical Excellence (NICE) technical appraisals.[2]

Buprenorphine is also available in a combined preparation with naloxone. Naloxone is a short-acting opiate antagonist that is inactive if taken sublingually. However, if injected or snorted it has the effect of blocking the effect of the buprenorphine. This has led to its use where diversion and illicit use of buprenorphine can be a problem such as in prison settings.

Lofexidine is an alpha-2-adrenergic agent licensed for use in opioid detoxification. It is a non-opiate and used to reduce the severity of withdrawal symptoms. It may also be used in combination with other common medications for symptomatic relief such as antidiarrhoeals, antiemetics and non-opioid analgesics.

Naltrexone is a long-acting opiate antagonist that, taken orally once a day, produces opioid receptor blockade, thus preventing any effects of opioid use. It can therefore be of use in well-motivated patients after detoxification as an aid to relapse prevention.

Opioid withdrawal / detoxification

Methadone at gradually tapering doses

We have already discussed the use of methadone in long-term opiate substitute treatment and also as an agent to use in a detoxification process. It can however be used as part of a gradually tapering reduction.[3] It is often used this way in primary care where, after a period of stability, a patient may wish as part of his or her recovery journey to slowly reduce the dose rather than have a formal detoxifica-tion. These patient-led reductions can be very effective, especially if there is con-current psychosocial support, whereas enforced reductions are associated with poor outcomes.[4]

There has also been a significant change in the way opioid-dependent people are dealt with in the prison system. Many of those in receipt of a methadone or buprenorphine prescription who are on remand or receive short custodial sen-tences are now maintained on medication, albeit many prisons will have an arbi-trary dose ceiling which is often lower than that supported by clinical evidence and used in a community setting. Those serving longer settings will usually now have the option of a formal detoxification, often with buprenorphine.

When to use methadone detoxification

Detoxification should be seen as a brief (although an important) technical step between maintenance and relapse prevention in the treatment of opiate addiction and not as a treatment for dependence by itself. Mattick and Hall suggest that the criteria for assessing effectiveness should be: [5]

1. Rates of completion of the process

2. Severity of withdrawal symptoms (both psychological and physical distress)

3. Medical complications, rather than, for example, relapse rates.

This means that outcome is not based on long-term abstinence, implying that detoxification alone is not an effective treatment if abstinence is the final outcome measure.

Buprenorphine for treatment of withdrawal

A systematic review of studies comparing buprenorphine with other withdrawal regimens was carried out in 2004 by Gowing *et al.*[6] The overall conclusion was that buprenorphine regimens resulted in lower withdrawal severity than ben-zodiazepines or alpha-2-adrenergic agonists, and with fewer adverse side effects.

Alpha-2-adrenergic agonists

A systematic review of the use of alpha-2-adrenergic agonists in patients with opioid dependence found that methadone dose reduction was more effective than alpha-2-adrenergic agonists in improving treatment retention and ameliora-tion of withdrawal symptoms. Methadone detoxification took longer than with alpha-2-adrenergic agonists. Clonidine and lofexidine were equally effective but hypotension was less likely to occur with lofexidine. There were more adverse effects for clonidine than for methadone and clonidine does not currently have a licence for use in opioid detoxification.[7] It is therefore suggested that clonidine is not used for opioid detoxification.

What to choose for detoxification

Given the evidence of effectiveness for different treatments used in detoxification the following criteria can be used by the clinician when choosing the drug for detoxification treatment.

Desired duration of treatment

▸ If a very short duration of treatment is the aim, alpha-2-adrenergic agonists are preferable to methadone.

▸ Methadone treatment is more successful if carried out slowly with gradual stepwise reduction rather than rapid reductions in dose.

Adverse effects

▸ Buprenorphine is preferable to alpha-2-adrenergic agonists if there are concerns about bradycardia or hypotension.

Withdrawal severity

▸ Buprenorphine results in lower severity of withdrawal symptoms than alpha-2-adrenergic agonists.

Specific patient groups

▸ Methadone can be used during pregnancy and there is emerging evidence that buprenorphine is safe and effective though it does not have a Medicines and Healthcare products Regulatory Agency (MHRA) licence for use during pregnancy. Alpha-2-adrenergic agonists should not be prescribed during pregnancy.

▸ In situations where a quick detoxification is planned, and methadone contraindicated, experienced practitioners would suggest buprenorphine as the first-line treatment.

Maintenance treatment for opioid dependence

The objectives of maintenance treatment are to:

▶ suppress signs and symptoms of opioid withdrawal

▶ extinguish opioid drug craving

▶ block the reinforcing effects of illicit opioid 'blockade'.

Methadone maintenance

There are a number of treatment options available for maintenance treatment. The use of methadone is the most researched treatment for heroin dependence, was the first widely used opioid replacement therapy designed to treat heroin dependence, and is used in many countries. There are Cochrane reviews comparing the effectiveness of methadone maintenance therapy with no opioid replacement therapy, the most recent published in 2003.[8] Other reviews include those by Keen *et al.*[9]

Numerous studies (summarised in both Cochrane and NICE reviews), several with double-blind placebo controlled design, clearly demonstrate that long-term treatment with methadone and buprenorphine are effective treatments for opioid dependence, reducing illicit drug use, risk of HIV, death, crime and unemployment. It also improves social stabilisation, retention rate in treatment and patients' contribution to society.[2,8]

Studies of the effectiveness of methadone maintenance programmes, however, vary widely in terms of the nature and quantity of psychosocial support delivered in addition to the medication. Nevertheless, in broad terms the prescribing of opioid substitution therapy (OST) with good-quality psychosocial interventions is superior to just a prescription, although this on its own is of some benefit. Studies also vary in terms of the degree of supervision of methadone consumption. It is also important to note that the research evidence has generally been based on programmes with supervised consumption of methadone, while in practice many treatment programmes, especially those in primary care and private practice settings, have no supervised consumption or indeed additional psychosocial support systems. Reassuringly, studies such as those by Keen *et al.* suggest that primary care provision of methadone prescribing can be done without an increase in methadone-related mortality (see Box 8.1).[10]

Box 8.1 **Benefits of methadone maintenance treatment for the management of opioid dependence**[8]

✓ Reduced levels of opioid use.

✓ Reduced levels of crime.

✓ Reduced levels of injecting and other risk behaviour.

✓ Improved quality of life.

✓ Increased sense of wellbeing.

✓ Better physical health.

✓ Reduced drug-related death rate.

✓ Reduced non-opioid misuse.

Adequate dose methadone

Although the original work by Dole and Nyswander recognised the need for adequate dosing in opiate substitution therapy it is only over the past decade that this has been a key component of UK treatment regimes. Flexible dosing determined by the individual patient not only reduces the increased mortality and morbidity in this group but also reduces the amount of illicit opioids used.

Over the years there have been many clinical trials comparing various doses of methadone for maintenance treatment and it is consistently reported that patients receiving a higher methadone dose compared with those at lower doses exhibit better outcomes. Studies have shown that an adequate dose of methadone is typically 80–100 mg/ml. Many methadone maintenance treatment programmes, however, prescribe low dosages of methadone for political, psychological, philosophical or moral reasons. There are also an increasing number of studies that suggest when using buprenorphine again there is an association between higher doses and more positive outcomes.[8]

Another point of disagreement amongst prescribers is the use of dosages of over 100 mg/day. A review of methadone dosages strongly suggests that methadone dosages higher than, and sometimes greatly higher than, 100 mg/day may be beneficial in some patients. Current guidance to treatment providers such as the Department of Health 2007 clinical guidelines, models of care and the recent National Treatment Agency Research into Practice briefings on methadone maintenance treatment all emphasise the greater benefits associated with daily methadone doses of 60–120 mg (and higher doses in exceptional cases).[11]

For GPs there has always been an anxiety about increasing doses of methadone and many GPs have placed an arbitrary ceiling of 40–60 mg/day. Methadone maintenance treatment is a worthless exercise if individuals who need high doses of methadone to keep away from crime and illicit drugs are denied this because of a general unwillingness to prescribe over a certain amount. This does not mean indiscriminately placing a patient on high starting doses of methadone. The dose increase should be incremental and safeguards such as supervised ingestion and daily dispensing should reduce the fear of diversion.

In a primary care setting there may be anxiety about higher doses of methadone relating to worries about diversion and also the recent evidence regarding prolongation of the QT interval in patients on high-dose methadone.[12] However, there is a positive correlation between a higher prescribed dose and a reduction in the use of 'on top heroin' (see Figure 8.1). While higher doses should be provided for those who need them to stabilise in terms of on-top heroin use and/or stopping criminal behaviour, it is still important that doses are increased incrementally and that the use of supervised consumption and daily dispensing are employed to reduce the risk of diversion.

Figure 8.1   **Illicit heroin use and methadone dose**

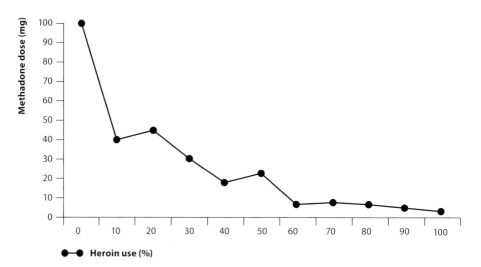

While it has been shown that methadone does prolong the QT interval, especially at higher doses, there have been no recorded fatalities from Torsades de Pointes in the UK in this treatment population. It has however been suggested that good practice would be to measure the QTc (see www.mdcalc.com/

corrected-qt-interval-qtc/) in all those patients receiving a daily dose of 100 mg or more of methadone.

Although the evidence supports higher doses, there is no consensus on ceiling dose. Individuals vary in their metabolism and so-called 'fast metabolisers' may require higher doses. Some commonly prescribed medications enhance methadone metabolism.

At very high doses it is advisable that the primary care practitioner works closely with the specialist service that may have the facilities to admit patients for dose titration. Therapeutic plasma level monitoring may provide additional guidance, though this form of monitoring is rarely used and impractical in those patients with poor venous access.

Methadone tablets

The 1999 and 2007 clinical guidelines, the Department of Health Task Force and the Advisory Council on the Misuse of Drugs (2000) have all advised that tablets should not be prescribed, as they are liable to be abused by being crushed and injected. They are also only licensed for use as an analgesic and not for the treatment of opioid dependence. Despite these recommendations significant amounts are being prescribed in a primary care setting.

In practice, GPs find that patients request tablets for many reasons – either patients claim that they cannot tolerate the solution or that they find tablets easier to take – especially when large volumes of methadone have to be ingested. Patients also find tablets easier to transport, especially when travelling, and do not have to deal with dropped bottles or leaking bottle tops. More research is needed as to who would benefit from tablet formulations; in the mean time clinicians ought to be cautious when prescribing them to patients.

Buprenorphine for opioid maintenance

There is a growing body of evidence for buprenorphine for maintenance treatment of opioid dependence and that buprenorphine should now be considered a well-researched, evidence-based addition to the range of pharmacological maintenance treatments. The goals of treatment are the same as those of methadone maintenance treatment: the reduction of illicit drug use and the associated risks and harms.

The effectiveness of buprenorphine maintenance treatment has been examined in a Cochrane review.[6] In comparison with placebo, there is evidence that buprenorphine is superior in terms of retention in treatment at low or moderate doses and at high doses. It is superior to placebo in terms of reduction in opioid positive urine tests at moderate doses and high doses, but not at low doses.

It is advisable to delay the first dose of buprenorphine until the patient is experiencing features of opioid withdrawal (this typically means at least eight hours after last heroin use, or 24–48 hours after last methadone use). Commence with an initial dose of 4–8 mg and increase the dose on each day for the next three to four days thereafter according to clinical response. Daily increases of up to 4–8 mg/day are possible up to a maximum dose of 32 mg/day.

Transition to buprenorphine from heroin or low-dose methadone (30 mg or below) can usually be accomplished with minimum complications, although restlessness, insomnia and diarrhoea are commonly reported in the first one to three days. Some patients experience problems for up to two weeks.

Patients wishing to transfer from higher-dose methadone (over 30 mg) straight onto buprenorphine risk precipitated withdrawal. This can occur one to three hours after the first buprenorphine dose, peaking in severity over three to six hours and then gradually subsiding. Lofexidine can be used to alleviate symptoms. Induction from methadone doses over 30 mg should, ideally, be undertaken only in specialist settings by a clinician with the relevant experience. The dose of buprenorphine for maintenance prescribing is typically 8–32 mg/day.

Buprenorphine produces comparable outcomes to lower-dose (e.g. 30–60 mg) methadone. Higher-dose methadone maintenance treatment (> 60 mg) appears more effective than buprenorphine, especially in terms of treatment retention, but adequate comparisons of higher-dose (16–32 mg) buprenorphine with high-dose methadone maintenance treatment (60–120 mg) are lacking.

Choosing between buprenorphine and methadone

Current evidence suggests that buprenorphine and methadone are of similar efficacy in retaining patients in treatment and reducing heroin use.[8] The decision as to which medication to use should be made in consultation with the patient. As with methadone, higher daily doses of buprenorphine (8–16 mg) are superior to lower doses, while doses in the region of 12–24 mg/day are preferable for maintenance treatment.[13]

Duration of maintenance treatment

A common question posed by clinicians treating drug users with methadone or buprenorphine maintenance is how long treatment should continue. Rigorous research is generally lacking and many longitudinal studies suffer from selection bias. Here, the more problematic patients tend to leave early, meaning that the performance of the remaining patients appears to improve when in fact the reported outcome measures, such as continued heroin use, are diminishing owing to changes in the composition of the group rather than the accumulated impact of the treatment provided.

Some studies attempt to control for this and overall the finding is that the longer patients spend in maintenance treatment the more likely they are to benefit. The conclusion reached by Ward et al.[14] is that only a small number of patients will benefit from relatively short periods of methadone maintenance; these patients tend to have a short history of heroin use and significant social and psychological resources at their disposal, which can be deployed in the recovery process. For the majority of entrants into treatment, it is more appropriate to have maintenance as a goal and to maximise retention rates so that the benefits of treatment are realised for both the individual and the community. There is no specifiable, optimal duration for methadone maintenance treatment. It is likely that this will be equally true for buprenorphine. The duration of maintenance should therefore be dictated by the needs of the patient rather than an artificially created end date.

Maintenance treatment involving injectable preparations

Two injectable preparations have been investigated, diamorphine, which is pharmaceutically produced heroin, and methadone. The very first drug dependence clinics prescribed injectable heroin but over time methadone and subsequently buprenorphine became the treatments of choice based on their easier administration, once-daily dosing and minimal if any euphoriant effect. Studies however have shown that up to 10–15% of injecting opioid users continue to inject regular illicit heroin despite substitution therapy. This hard-to-treat group has been suggested as being suitable for injectable treatments. Previous drug strategies recommended pilot studies be carried out in the UK to complement those that had already been carried out elsewhere and shown positive benefits.[15, 16]

From 2006, the Randomised Injectable Opiate Therapy Trial (RIOTT) study was undertaken in the UK.[17] This was a multicentre randomised controlled trial comparing injectable heroin with injectable methadone and optimised oral methadone in heroin users unresponsive to standard treatment. It reported a significant reduction in illicit heroin and other drug use (confirmed by drug testing, not just self-reports), and a reduction in risky injecting practice. This study is important as it compared injectable heroin and methadone with oral methadone at adequate dose levels, with additional psychosocial support and sufficient duration, thus addressing the prior criticism that previous studies had only compared injectable treatments with inadequate alternative treatment options.

While any doctor can prescribe injectable methadone, to use diamorphine as a treatment for opioid addiction requires a special licence from the Home Office. However, it can be prescribed by any medical practitioner as an analgesic for acute pain.

Arguments for and against injectable preparations

Arguments for injectable prescribing are mainly centred on harm reduction: it decreases crime and provides a drug that is free from contaminants. Those opposed to this treatment point out that it perpetuates injecting behaviour and may postpone by years eventual abstinence from heroin use, and that it runs contrary to the duty of doctors to improve or maintain the physical health of their patients.[18]

Injectable methadone treatment is very different from oral methadone treatment. Whereas the drug itself is the same, the differences far exceed the similarities. These differences include the euphoric effect that results from intravenous methadone (in contrast to oral methadone). When prescribing injectable opioids in clinical practice in the UK, a typical experience was described by Strang and colleagues:[19]

> The committed injector seeking a prescribed supply of injectable drugs would usually be quite amenable to moves between heroin and methadone in injectable form – in sharp contrast to the determined opposition which may be encountered to suggestions of moving from injectable methadone to its oral form.

Methadone ampoules have a black market value – especially the higher-dose 30 mg and 50 mg preparations, which is similar to heroin when both drugs are compared in their injectable forms. A small number of patients might require prescriptions of injectable medications to keep them in treatment and/or ease the change from injecting the drug of dependence to taking a substitute orally. However, this decision should only be taken after obtaining specialist advice.

Other pharmacotherapies

There are a number of other pharmacotherapies that have been used for opioid treatment, though none of them has been as well researched as those described above.

Dihydrocodeine

Dihydrocodeine (DHC) is a minor opioid that seems to produces less dependence than methadone. It may be useful at the tail end of methadone detoxification or for short-term (7–10 days) detoxification in well-motivated patients. It has little use for the long-term management of dependence and as yet there are only a few studies comparing DHC with other substitute medication. One such study carried out in Edinburgh audited the progress of 200 patients in substitution treatment in a primary care setting. There were no significant differences in patients prescribed methadone and those prescribed DHC in terms of retention in treatment, death rate and behaviour change.[20, 21]

These findings were reported when DHC was compared with oral methadone in a randomised controlled trial in Scotland. There were no differences at six and 18 months in the two groups in terms of retention in treatment, criminal behaviour and injecting drug use.

Many clinicians and the national clinical guidelines, however, continue to discourage the use of DHC. Large numbers of tablets are required (approximate milliequivalents 3 mg methadone = 30 mg DHC), it has a short half-life, and its administration in tablet form makes it an impractical opioid substitute.

DHC is not licensed for the treatment of drug users and the fact that it is in short-acting tablet form excludes supervised consumption and facilitates injection. Furthermore it cannot be dispensed on an FP10 (MDA) in England.

Morphine

Morphine in slow-release oral formulations suitable for once-daily dosing is now available for the management of pain and may also possess clinical utility for maintenance treatment for opioid dependence.[22–24]

Although morphine is likely to be beneficial as an alternative for patients who respond poorly to methadone, and has been tried for this purpose in several countries (Austria, Australia, the UK),[25,26] quantitative assessments of patient outcomes and acceptability of morphine are impeded by the paucity of information regarding oral dose equivalence of methadone and morphine, and the means by which patients should be transferred between these medications.

Mitchell et al. have recently conducted a study that evaluated morphine as an alternative to methadone in patients who were finding that they experienced breakthrough craving on methadone maintenance.[27] The study found that transfer to and from methadone was associated with few ill effects, in particular without any significant withdrawal symptoms. The final mean morphine: methadone ratio was found to be 4.6:1, though the range varied from 3.5:1 to 8:1 in the patients being studied. This study found that, compared with methadone, morphine was associated with improved social functioning, weight loss, fewer and less troublesome adverse effects, greater acceptability of the prescribed drug, reduced heroin craving, an enhanced sense of feeling 'normal', and similar outcomes for unsanctioned drug use. Slow-release morphine preparations could be considered as an alternative to methadone. However, much more research is required in establishing which patients are best suited to this treatment, and which has greater intrinsic risks of overdose and diversion than methadone.

Dextromoramide

Dextromoramide (trade name Palfium) has been suggested as having a role in the treatment of opioid addiction. Some studies from the Netherlands have looked at it as an adjunct to methadone maintenance in a group of patients who continued to use heroin despite receiving prescribed methadone. While there were some benefits, they were not sufficient to outweigh the concerns over diversion of medication and the need for a very structured treatment programme. The evidence has not altered current UK practice and it would be preferable for a primary care practitioner to consider referral for consideration of injectable methadone or diamorphine rather than to add in dextromoramide as an adjunct.[28]

Relapse prevention

Naltrexone is a long-acting competitive opioid antagonist, which is effective when taken orally. It can be used to precipitate withdrawal in accelerated detoxification from opiates but its main use is for relapse prevention. The goal of naltrexone treatment is maintenance of abstinence from opioid drugs in previously dependent patients following detoxification. It is prescribed for oral use as a 50 mg tablet. The principle of treatment is that, on establishing a dose of 50 mg per day, any ordinary amounts of opiates that are then taken are completely ineffective, the medication therefore acting as a strong deterrent to further use. This resembles disulfiram in alcohol abuse. However, it doesn't produce any adverse physical effects if opiates are taken. Interestingly there is now some crossover with naltrexone being used post-detoxification in alcohol-dependent patients.

Since the mid-1990s some practitioners have used naltrexone implants though these products do not have a licence in the UK. A Cochrane review concluded that the evidence available did not allow an objective evaluation of naltrexone, but that it may be efficacious in highly motivated patients.[29] Probation-linked supervised naltrexone has been used as an alternative to custody in opiate-misusing offenders;[30] providing there is an average 50 mg dose each day, treatment can be given two or three times a week.

GPs can prescribe naltrexone, although it is wise first to ensure that there are no opioids in the patient's system (which usually means commencing treatment 7–10 days after last opiate use) and that there is normal liver function before commencement. There is little to guide the clinician as to the length of treatment on naltrexone and, therefore, until the evidence is clear it is probably wise to tailor the length of treatment on the outcome in individual patients.

There are no controlled studies of naltrexone implants or the newer preparation, naltrexone depot.

Conclusion

There are several options available to the practitioner when prescribing treatment for opioid dependence. Practitioners would be well advised to start with treatments that are well used and well researched. Detoxification and long-term abstinence should be a primary goal for all opioid addicts, but practitioners should be aware that longer-term treatment stands the best chance of keeping many individuals away from crime and illicit drugs. All patients on opioid substitution therapy should be regularly assessed to determine with them whether a move towards detoxification is appropriate. More controversial and less common treatments such as injectable methadone or dihydrocodeine should not be prescribed in primary care without serious consideration of their suitability.

It is essential that practitioners read Chapter 9 on the practicalities of opioid treatment prescribing. Even when a method of treatment is decided upon, there are many issues that need to be addressed in order to tailor the treatment to an individual patient. Whatever the treatment chosen, prescribing should be tailored to the needs of the individual, and prescribing practices should reflect the evidence base that currently exists; this evidence base should also be expanded through the evaluation and research of other interventions.

Further reading

Carnwath T, Smith I. *Heroin Century.* London: Routledge, 2002.

Ford C, Halliday K, Lawson E, *et al. Guidance for the Use of Substitute Prescribing in the Treatment of Opioid Dependence in Primary Care.* London: RCGP, 2011.

National Institute for Health and Clinical Excellence. *Technology Appraisal Guidance 114, Methadone and Buprenorphine for the Management of Opioid Dependence.* London: NICE, 2007.

References

1. Dole V, Nyswander M. A medical treatment for diacetylmorphine (heroin) addiction: a clinical trial with methadone hydrochloride. *Journal of the American Medical Association* 1965; **193**: 80–4.

2. National Institute for Health and Clinical Excellence. *Technology Appraisal Guidance 114, Methadone and Buprenorphine for the Management of Opioid Dependence.* London: NICE, 2007.

3. Amato L, Davoli M, Ferri M, *et al.* Methadone at tapered doses for the management of opioid withdrawal. In: *The Cochrane Database of Systematic Reviews.* Issue 3, Chichester: John Wiley, 2004.

4. Gossop M, Marsden J, Stewart D, *et al.* Outcomes after methadone maintenance and methadone reduction treatments: two-year follow up results from the National Treatment Outcomes Research Study. *Drug and Alcohol Dependence* 2001; **62(3)**: 255–64.

5. Mattick R P, Hall W. Are detoxification programmes effective? *Lancet* 1996; **347(8994)**: 97–100.

6. Gowing L, Ali R, White J. Buprenorphine for the management of opioid withdrawal. In: *The Cochrane Database of Systematic Reviews*. Issue 3, Chichester: John Wiley, 2004.

7. Gowing L R, Farrell M, Ali R L, *et al.* Alpha2-adrenergic agonists in opioid withdrawal. *Addiction* 2002; **97(1)**: 49–58.

8. Mattick R P, Breen C, Kimber J, *et al.* Methadone maintenance therapy versus no opioid replacement therapy for opioid dependence. In: *The Cochrane Database of Systematic Reviews*. Issue 4, Chichester: John Wiley, 2003.

9. Keen J, Oliver P, Rowse G, *et al.* Does methadone maintenance treatment based on the new national guidelines work in a primary care setting? *British Journal of General Practice* 2003; **53(491)**: 9461–7.

10. Keen J, Oliver P, Mathers N. Methadone maintenance treatment can be provided in a primary care setting without increasing methadone related mortality: the Sheffield experience 1997–2000. *British Journal of General Practice* 2002; **52(478)**: 387–9.

11. National Treatment Agency for Substance Misuse. *Methadone Dose and Methadone Maintenance Treatment. Briefings for drug treatment providers and commissioners. Research into practice briefing.* London: NTA, 2004.

12. Medicines and Healthcare products Regulatory Agency. Risk of QT interval prolongation with methadone. *Current Problems in Pharmacovigilance* 2006; **31**: 6.

13. Ling W, Charuvastra C, Collins JF, *et al.* Buprenorphine maintenance treatment of opiate dependence: a multicenter, randomized clinical trial. *Addiction* 1998; **93(4)**: 475–86.

14. Ward J, Mattick R, Hall W. How long is long enough? Answers to questions about the duration of methadone maintenance treatment. In: *Methadone Maintenance Treatment and Other Opioid Replacement Therapies*. The Netherlands: Harwood Academic Publications, 1998, pp. 265–305.

15. Cummins M. The supervised injecting clinic: a drug clinic's experience of supervising the intravenous self-administration to prescribed injectable methadone. In: G Tober, J Strang (eds). *Methadone Matters. Evolving community methadone treatment of opiate addiction*. London: Martin Dunitz, 2003, pp. 119–28.

16. van den Brink W, Hendriks VM, Blanken P, *et al.* Medical prescription of heroin to treatment resistant heroin addicts: two randomised controlled trials. *British Medical Journal* 2003; **327(7410)**: 310–12.

17. Strang J, Metrebian N, Lintzeris N, *et al.* Supervised injectable heroin or injectable methadone versus optimised oral methadone as treatment for chronic heroin addicts in England after persistent failure in orthodox treatment (RIOTT): a randomised trial. *Lancet* 2010; **375(9729)**: 1885–95.

18. Zador D. Injectable opiate maintenance in the UK: is it good clinical practice? *Addiction* 2001; **96(4)**: 547–53.

19. Strang J, Gossop M. The 'British System': visionary anticipation or masterly inactivity? In: *Heroin Addiction and Drug Policy: the British System*. Oxford: Oxford University Press, 1994, pp. 342–51.

20. MacLeod J, Whittaker A, Robertson JR. Changes in opiate treatment during attendance at a community drug service: findings from a clinical audit. *Drug and Alcohol Review* 1998; **17(1)**: 19–25.

21. Banbery J, Wolff K, Raistrick D. Dihydrocodeine: a useful tool in the detoxification of methadone maintained patients. *Journal of Substance Abuse Treatment* 2000; **19(3)**: 301–5.

22. Fischer G, Presslich O, Diamant K, *et al*. Oral morphine sulfate in the treatment of opiate dependent patients. *Alcoholism* 1996; **32**: 35–43.

23. Mitchell T B, White J M, Somogyi A A, *et al*. Comparative pharmacodynamics and pharmacokinetics of methadone and slow-release oral morphine for maintenance treatment of opioid dependence. *Drug and Alcohol Dependence* 2003; **72(1)**: 85–94.

24. Kraigher D, Ortner, R, Eder H, *et al*. Slow release of morphine hydrochloride for maintenance therapy of opioid dependence. *Wiener klinische Wochenschrift* 2002; **114(21–2)**: 904–10.

25. Brewer C. Recent developments in maintenance prescribing and monitoring in the United Kingdom. *Bulletin of the New York Academy of Medicine* 1995; **72(2)**: 359–70.

26. Sherman J P. Managing heroin addiction with a long-acting morphine product (Kapanol). *Medical Journal of Australia* 1996; **165(4)**: 239.

27. Mitchell T, White J, Somogyi A, *et al*. Slow release oral morphine versus methadone: a crossover comparison of patient outcomes and acceptability as maintenance pharmacotherapies for opioid dependence. *Addiction* 2004; **99(8)**: 940–5.

28. de Vos J W. Ufkes J G, van den Brink W, *et al*. Craving patterns in methadone maintained treatment with dextromoramide as adjuvant. *Addictive Behaviors* 1999; **24(5)**: 707–13.

29. Kirchmayer U, Davoli M, Verster A. Naltrexone maintenance treatment for opioid dependence. In: *The Cochrane Database of Systematic Reviews*. Issue 4, Chichester: John Wiley, 2001.

30. Brahen L S, Brewer C. Naltrexone in the criminal justice system. In: *Treatment Options in Addiction, Medical Management of Alcohol and Opiate Abuse*. London: Gaskell, 1993, pp. 46–53.

CHAPTER 9

Practical aspects of methadone treatment

Martyn Hull and Clare Gerada

IN THIS CHAPTER

Introduction || *How does methadone work?* || *The importance of tolerance* || *Tolerance testing in primary care* || *Methadone deaths* || *Methadone induction and effective doses* || *Factors affecting response to methadone* || *Therapeutic drug monitoring* || *Injectable preparations* || *Prescribing issues* || *Tests of compliance/screening* || *Using on top* || *Drug interactions* || *Conclusion*

Introduction

This chapter will explore the practical issues in administering methadone in order to avoid potentially dangerous consequences, while ensuring that individual patients are prescribed the dose that suits their situation.

How does methadone work?

Methadone mixture is seen as the gold standard for treatment of opioid dependence as it has low addictive potential, low potential for injection when prescribed as 1 mg/ml solution and relatively low 'street' value if diverted onto the illicit market.[1] Methadone is a long-acting synthetic opioid originally synthesised in 1939 and has been the mainstay of substitute treatment for over 40 years.

Pharmacology

It reaches peak plasma concentration at four hours (range 2–6) after oral administration, but takes 4–5 days for levels to stabilise in tissue and plasma when initiated, finally reaching a steady state ten days after induction. The plasma half-life varies, with a single-dose half-life lasting 12–18 hours, and a mean half-life of 37 hours in the first few days of daily dosing.[2]

Methadone works predominantly by binding itself to opioid receptors in the brain, where, if given in sufficient quantities, it blocks the effects of other opioid drugs such as heroin. It thereby prevents the unpleasant side effects of withdrawal and avoids the same euphorigenic effects. It is nearly completely absorbed across the gastrointestinal tract with a bioavailability of more than 80%. Methadone is stored extensively in the liver and secondarily in other body tissues, but not 'in the bones' – a common urban myth among drug users and doctors.[3] The amount in the bloodstream is kept relatively constant by the slow release of methadone from tissues, which helps account for its long half-life.[4] It is metabolised through the liver via cytochrome P450 enzymes, so is susceptible to interactions with drugs that inhibit the P450 system. It is also worth noting that its metabolism varies significantly between people, contributing to the fact that patients require widely different doses to achieve satisfactory clinical responses.

Steady state occurs after an interval of five times the elimination half-life, which is approximately five to ten days, although in some patients it can take longer.[5] The extent of plasma binding is high – approximately 90%.

The advantages of methadone include:[1]

▶ its clinical effectiveness is supported by extensive research

▶ it alleviates opioid withdrawal symptoms

▶ it is taken orally, thus reducing the risk of injection

▶ it has a long half-life, which means only a single daily dose is required for most patients

▶ the dose can be carefully titrated to the optimal level

▶ blood levels can be kept stable, thus eliminating post-dose euphoria and pre-dose withdrawal

▶ it has no serious long-term side effects when used on a long-term basis.

Methadone itself is addictive in that it produces dependence and a recognised withdrawal syndrome, but less so than heroin. Nevertheless, many users complain bitterly about symptoms that can go on for weeks, in some cases even for months, after stopping methadone. Methadone is less potent and it has a long duration of actions, which avoids the need for regular 'topping up' that is characteristic of shorter-acting opioids.

Main problems with methadone

The main problems are predominantly ones that are shared with all opioids. These problems are:

▶ constipation

▶ lethargy and depression

▶ loss of libido

▶ weight gain, more likely to be related to increased wellbeing rather than the calories in methadone itself

▶ dental problems, even with sugar-free preparations – thought to be related to reduction in salivary flow and a high-sugar diet, rather than to the methadone itself

▶ nausea

▶ sweating, due to histamine release

▶ menstrual disturbances.

The importance of tolerance

Despite its advantages, like all opioids methadone is dangerous to anyone who is not tolerant to opioids and a single dose of around 30–40 mg can cause life-threatening respiratory depression.[6] An opioid-tolerant person, however, can function normally at doses that can be fatal to a non-tolerant person. Opioid tolerance is a complex process of neuroadaptation and even experienced opioid users can be at risk of toxic methadone effects.[7] It is essential, therefore, to estimate an individual's opioid dependence and level of tolerance before starting methadone treatment, and again after a period of abstinence lasting more than a few days.

Tolerance develops more quickly to some effects of opioids than others. For example, tolerance develops quickly to the euphoric effects, whereas tolerance to gastrointestinal effects (e.g. constipation), sedation or respiratory depression is slower to develop. This can be potentially fatal if users start to ingest increasingly greater amounts of opioids for its euphoric effect. In the case of methadone, tolerance development is incomplete, so the respiratory depressant effects of other agents such as alcohol, sedatives and other opiates, or acutely excessive methadone, may not be completely blocked even in a person stabilised on methadone maintenance doses.

Tolerance testing in primary care

Observing a patient after a first dose of methadone may not be sufficient to establish a level of tolerance. Often it can be inferred only that the dose given is not a significant overdose. Careful dose induction, starting with a low dose and increasing gradually over the course of several days, is preferable and should provide reasonably confident grounds for identifying non-tolerant patients and adjusting their dose (or even reviewing the appropriateness of methadone treatment) accordingly (see Box 9.1 and Table 9.1).[1,8]

Box 9.1   **Risk factors in starting methadone**

✓ First presentation or where drug and alcohol history is unclear.

✓ Initial dose over 30 mg.

✓ Concomitant use of other drugs, especially benzodiazepines and alcohol.

✓ General health of the patient, especially impaired liver function (and also respiratory disease and HIV).

✓ Intolerance to opioids.

✓ Failure to inform patients of the danger of overdose if they use other drugs at the same time.

Table 9.1   **Subjective and objective characteristics at various doses of methadone**

Overdoses	Respiratory depression, pinpoint pupils unreactive to light, snoring giving way to shallow respirations, bradycardia and hypotension, varying degrees of reduced consciousness and coma
Overmedication	Sedation, small pupils, itching, low blood pressure, flushing, depressed respiration, cognitive decline, spasticity
Comfort range	Comfortable, neither withdrawing nor intoxicated
Subjective withdrawal	Craving, anxiety, dysphoria, irritability, fatigue, insomnia, myalgia, anorexia, nausea, stomach cramps, restlessness, hot and cold feelings
Objective withdrawal	Dilated pupils, sweating, gooseflesh, muscle twitching, diarrhoea and vomiting, running nose and eyes, sneezing, yawning, fever, tachycardia, high blood pressure

Clinical assessment using history taking and examination

Robust clinical assessment of tolerance involves observing the effects of methadone administered, and is the most direct and least ambiguous way of assessing methadone tolerance. Such observation can be supplemented by questionnaires and obtaining corroborative evidence from previous doctors or dispensing pharmacists.

Methadone deaths

Increases in methadone-related deaths over recent years have led to evaluation of the safety of the drug and guidance on its use.[9,10] Early research with methadone-maintained patients revealed that methadone-related deaths were predominantly due to respiratory depression, occurred predominantly in the induction phase, and often against a background of polysubstance use.[11,12] Recent reports emphasise chronic pain patients (predominantly in the USA where methadone is more widely used as an analgesic), but also flag up the role of methadone in causing QTc prolongation and the possibility of inducing Torsades de Pointes, a potentially fatal ventricular arrhythmia.

Respiratory depression

Methadone accumulation can lead to fatal respiratory depression in doses as low as 30 mg in non-tolerant patients,[13] and these effects can also occur in those tolerant to opioids, albeit at higher doses. The risk of death during methadone induction has been calculated as nearly seven-fold greater than the patient's risk of death prior to entering methadone treatment,[12] and nearly 98 times higher than those who have been safely receiving methadone for more than two weeks.[14] Prescribing too high a dose too soon seems to be implicated in this, and this risk – while statistically low – reiterates the need for caution in induction.

A significant proportion of methadone-related deaths involve individuals who are in poor health and have other diseases, particularly HIV, hepatitis and other infections, which may have also contributed to their deaths. The risk of death from overdose is greatest in the first two weeks of methadone maintenance treatment.

Prolonged QTc interval and Torsades de Pointes

In addition to its respiratory depressive effect, methadone is associated with QTc prolongation. The QTc interval is an ECG measure of the electrical depolarisation (Q wave) and repolarisation (T wave) of the myocardium. Prolongation of the QT interval is associated with Torsades de Pointes, a distinct pattern of ventricular tachycardia manifested by syncope or sudden death. The association of Torsades de Pointes with high-dose methadone was first noted in 2002 and a review of the literature in 2006[15] found 40 cases of Torsades de Pointes associated with methadone, though none was fatal and 85% had an additional factor predisposing to the arrhythmia.

A Norwegian study[16] estimated that the maximum attributable mortality risk was in the region of 0.06 deaths caused by methadone-induced QTc prolongation for every 100 patients on methadone per year. The Medicines and Healthcare products Regulatory Agency has stated that patients with risk factors for QTc prolongation should be carefully monitored while taking methadone[17] and the 2007 Department of Health guidelines reiterated this.[7]

There seems likely to be a dose-dependent response between methadone and QTc prolongation. Additionally, there are a number of other drugs that are known to cause QTc prolongation, including lithium, TCAs, SSRIs (notably citalopram and escitalopram), macrolides, sotalol and venlafaxine. Cocaine has been shown to increase QT intervals acutely[18] and confounding factors may be the use of antipsychotics and tricyclic antidepressants.[19]

If a patient is felt to be at risk, ECG should be undertaken and the risks discussed. If ECG is normal, then consideration of repeat ECG at 6–12 month intervals should be undertaken if risks of QT prolongation remain high. If QTc is prolonged (more than 500 ms), alternative medications should be considered, and advice given on use of stimulants and alcohol. Further investigations and/or referral to cardiology should be considered. Consideration should also be made regarding possible detoxification, reduction in the dose of methadone or switch to buprenorphine. This should however be undertaken with consideration of the risks of relapse or increased illicit drug use.

Methadone induction and effective doses

Testing for tolerance is the first stage of initiating a patient safely onto methadone. Dose induction involves reaching steady-state plasma methadone levels. Prior to steady state, it is important clinicians understand that half of each day's dose remains in the body and is added to the next day's, producing rising serum methadone levels even without any increase in dose.[20] Until steady state is reached, any dose increase should be made with caution. With methadone treatment, it may take up to 12 half-lives before steady state is reached (see Figure 9.1 and Box 9.2).

Box 9.2 **Summary of methadone induction**

✓ Death can occur owing to lack of tolerance.

✓ Methadone blood concentration can take a week to reach a steady state.

✓ The use of other central nervous system (CNS) depressant drugs, for example heroin, benzodiazepines, alcohol, etc., in significant concentrations can reduce the quantity of methadone needed for a fatal dose.

✓ The presence of significant natural disease can increase the toxic potential of methadone.

Figure 9.1   **Serum methadone levels take on average 4–5 days to reach steady state half-lives**

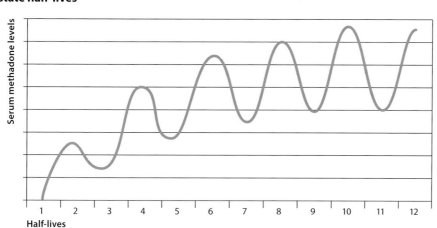

Source: reproduced with permission of J. Thomas Payte.

During methadone induction, patients may be in mild withdrawal towards the end of the dosing interval, so doses should not automatically be increased based on how the patient feels at 12 hours or more after dosing. Instead, a patient should be asked how he or she feels at three to eight hours after the last dose. If the patient is relatively comfortable no increase is needed (see Table 9.2).

Table 9.2   **Improving safety during induction**

Good clinical assessment	Use of corroborative evidence such as urine tests and examination of veins for evidence of injecting drug use
	Contact previous prescribers
	Contact previous dispensing pharmacist
	Contact previous prison doctor
Dose with caution: 'start low, go slow'	Review regularly in the early stages of dose induction

Induction dose recommendations

Given that it can take four to five days until steady state is reached, and that it has been shown that methadone's half-life can result in an accumulation of methadone and a resulting overdose one or two weeks after treatment begins, it is important that the clinician proceeds with care during the induction stage. Since there is no exact formula to guide the clinician in calculating opioid tolerance the recommendation for methadone induction is to 'start low, go slow'. Table 9.3 gives different examples of international induction regimes.

Table 9.3   **Induction dosing guidelines**

Methadone dose range	Country
Initial dose not to exceed 30 mg or 40 mg total in the first day	USA [15]
Initial dose 10–20 mg if tolerance low or uncertain; 25–40 mg if opioid tolerance established	UK [clinical guidelines]
Initial dose 10–20 mg if tolerance low or uncertain; 25–40 mg if tolerance high	Europe [16]
15–30 mg/day during the first three days (which represents time to 87.5% of steady state)	Canada [17]

Authorities in various countries have produced guidelines to cover the induction stage. Most give starting doses of methadone of 20–30 mg. The purpose of titration to methadone is to establish the patient, in a safe manner and as quickly as possible, on a dose of methadone that prevents opioid withdrawal, reduces the need to take additional illicit opioids and keeps side effects to a minimum.[7] If not done expediently enough, on-top illicit opioid use is likely to continue and the cumulative effect of methadone can then lead to overdose.

The starting dose should be between 10 mg and 30 mg (though starting as low as 10 mg is very rare in clinical practice), based on assessment of the person's opioid tolerance, route of administration (e.g. injecting) and the use of other drugs such as benzodiazepines or alcohol. Methadone should be increased no quicker than 30 mg per week for the first two weeks, and each dose increase should be undertaken after careful clinical review.

It normally takes 4–5 days for plasma levels of methadone to stabilise after dose commencement or titration, but may take up to ten days to reach a steady state. The patient should be warned of this 'increasing effect' and – if using illicit opioids on top of the prescribed methadone – needs to be aware of the increasing risk of this as the methadone effect accumulates.

The optimal dose of methadone for most people is 60–120 mg, though some will need more or less to provide an adequate clinical response.[1] Doses of between 60–120 mg will normally exert a clinical effect for 24–36 hours. Methadone can be successfully used for maintenance prescribing and for detoxification from opioids.

Factors affecting response to methadone

Body weight, age, sex, individual differences in metabolism and excretion rate, certain physiological or pathological states, and other drugs, in particular enzyme inducers, can all influence the rate of methadone metabolism. Flexibility in dosing is required to stabilise patients in whom methadone's effects can be so variably altered.

The most notable physiological state associated with changes in methadone metabolism is pregnancy. Pregnancy is associated with lower than expected methadone plasma levels in the third trimester. Liver disease is common in methadone maintenance patients owing to hepatitis infection or in some cases alcohol dependence. Liver disease may result in a slowing of the rate of elimination of methadone and such individuals should be dosed with care to avoid toxicity.[21,22]

Some drugs have been shown to influence the amount of methadone present in blood plasma by speeding up the elimination of methadone from the body. Rifampicin, phenytoin, barbiturates, benzodiazepines, carbamazepine and disulfiram have all been associated with lowering of plasma methadone levels and onset of withdrawal symptoms in methadone-maintained patients. Concurrent use of fluvoxamine and desipramine have been associated with higher plasma levels and increased risk of toxicity.[23] Problems are, however, very rare if methadone induction is undertaken carefully and with regular clinical review.

Therapeutic drug monitoring

Measuring plasma levels of methadone to determine peaks and troughs may be used in clinical practice, though in practice rarely is. Monitoring of methadone dose is not a necessity in the management of patients, since careful clinical follow-up of objective signs and subjective symptoms is sufficient for dose titration. The clinician might find monitoring useful, however, in selected situations, for example when dosages much in excess of 100 mg/day are prescribed and it is feared that such dosages might lead to very high methadone concentrations and cardiac toxicity.

Injectable preparations

There is a recognised cohort of the treatment population who seem to be resistant to treatment with standard opiate substitution therapy (OST), and who either disengage with treatment altogether or do not make adequate progress (e.g. continue to use high levels of illicit drugs or continue with risk-taking behaviour). Some of these patients would benefit from review and – for example – correction of suboptimal dosing. However, for others there may be a role for the trial of injectable substitute treatment.

Historically, the majority of prescriptions of injectable opioids in the UK were of injectable methadone, which can be prescribed by all prescribers (as opposed to heroin prescribing, which requires a Home Office licence). In recent years, however, there has been a significant reduction in all injectable prescribing, most likely due to improved access to optimised oral OST and in response to clear guidance as to the suitability of such prescribing.[24] The evidence base for inject-able maintenance treatment is weak in many respects, but there has long been a consensus that it may have a potential role in long-term heroin users who appear resistant to standard forms of treatment. Much of the guidance available looks at both injectable methadone and injectable heroin together, but recent research, for example the RIOTT trial,[25] has looked at the use of injectable heroin, and demonstrated its clinical effectiveness in this group. In RIOTT, treatment with supervised injectable heroin led to significantly lower use of street heroin than either supervised injectable methadone or optimised oral methadone, albeit in a selected group of heroin patients unresponsive to orthodox treatment. While these studies show very promising results, at the time of writing injectable opi-oid treatment, and more specifically the use of pharmaceutical heroin (or Heroin Assisted Treatment, HAT), is not available in all specialist services and in all parts of the country. In addition to the logistical issues, there are unresolved issues pertaining to the ethics and sociopolitical factors that are currently holding back this potential treatment option from widespread implementation.

The 2007 Department of Health clinical guidelines describe injectable opi-oid treatment as a 'less established and less accepted form of treatment, which requires greater commitment of time and resources'.[7] Prescribing should be against a background of a long and persistent history of injecting drug use, and with clear goals that are continuously reassessed. Where pharmacy dispensing occurs it should be daily to reduce the risk of diversion, and where evidence of diversion exists daily/supervised dispensing should be re-established.

In the absence of demonstrated significant superior outcomes from this form of treatment, and in the recognition of the greater inherent dangers and the cost burden of such prescriptions, doctors should review and audit outcomes against set performance standards. In all cases the further away from established practice the greater the responsibility of the doctor to ensure prescribing is safe and that mechanisms are in place to minimise risk to the patient. Injectable drugs should be considered only as a possible 'second line' treatment where well-supported oral methadone treatment in appropriate doses is unsuccessful.[25]

Prescribing issues

Supervised consumption

Instalment prescribing for methadone should initially be undertaken under supervised consumption. This enables the pharmacist to check the dose and tolerance, and is recommended always to be used at the start of treatment, as well as at other times if clinically indicated. The Department of Health guidelines[7] recommend three months of supervision at the outset of treatment, though this is a recommendation not a stipulation, and the period of supervision may be reduced if there are good reasons to stop, such as child care, travel difficulties, work or the fact that the patient is adequately and safely stabilised on a stable treatment dose. Usually, however, supervision will continue until 2–3 weeks after final dose titration, by which stage tolerance to the prescribed dose will be established.

The advantages of supervised consumption include:

▶ introduction of a routine as a result of the requirement for daily, personal attendance at the pharmacy

▶ assistance in compliance and avoidance of exceeding a daily dose

▶ daily contact between client and a health professional

▶ the opportunity to increase dosage safely

▶ reduction in diversion onto the illicit market, including where patients are coerced into selling their drug soon after leaving the pharmacist

▶ an opportunity to monitor progress

▶ increased opportunities for communication between other carers.

Before taking a patient off supervision, a clinical review should be undertaken to ensure that the patient is stable enough for this.

There are problems with supervised consumption. At the very least there are cost implications of providing a safe and confidential area for ingestion and fees payable to the pharmacist for providing this service. It has been suggested that strict supervision programmes can discourage people from staying in treatment and that doctors should be allowed to use their clinical judgement so that treatment plans meet the patients' needs rather than adopting a uniform approach for all. Confidentiality can be a problem, particularly in busy small pharmacies, and problems may arise where the pharmacists offer a needle exchange scheme and the patient/client is making use of this. Despite these problems, when used correctly the advantages of supervised ingestion far outweigh the disadvantages and patients can gain considerable benefit from the stabilising influence of daily attendance at a community pharmacist.

Missed doses

Missed doses of methadone will lead to withdrawal symptoms, and – if three successive doses are missed – a potential loss of tolerance that may lead to a requirement for a lower dose of methadone. A clinical review must then be undertaken in order to assess the best approach. If a patient has lapsed back to illicit heroin use following missed doses, then the safest approach may be to begin induction from the start.

Split doses for methadone

There is evidence that some people taking methadone settle better on split doses,[26] particularly during the third trimester of pregnancy. Patients on low doses of methadone may also benefit from splitting the dose (though dose titration should also be considered if there is inadequate clinical effect). Split dosing may also be indicated in patients taking P450 inhibitors such as phenytoin, in whom methadone plasma levels may excessively drop due to the drug interaction. Generally, however, there is usually no clinical benefit derived from splitting the dose. In most cases when a patient is splitting the dose to attempt to counteract withdrawal symptoms, dose titration is the most appropriate solution.

Storage and safety at home

It is crucial that a discussion takes place about the safe storage of methadone at home – this is obviously part of the assessment prior to the removal of supervised consumption, but needs to be considered from the outset of treatment as most pharmacies do not offer seven-day dispensing. Methadone can be fatal to children and opiate-naïve adults in small doses, and the importance of this cannot be overstated.

Tests of compliance / screening

Urine testing

Urine drug testing provides a snapshot of recent drug use and is an essential adjunct for initial assessment. It can also have a useful role in monitoring treatment as it provides an objective means of confirming ongoing methadone use (as well as identifying ongoing illicit use). The recommended frequency of testing would be dictated by clinical progress and the level of stability, and one would expect more frequent testing during induction and periods of instability. It does, however, have the potential to communicate to the patient from the outset that he or she cannot be trusted; it is also expensive and is a method that can be subject to manipulation or sample substitution. Once stable, random testing is recommended about twice a year,[1] and this approach may be helpful, though is not felt to be cost-effective when a patient has declared illicit use. Research studies have shown that – when there is not a threat to the ongoing provision of treatment – there is good concordance between declared drug use and confirmatory urine tests.

Mouth swabs (oral mucosal transudate)

Mouth swab tests provide the same information as urine screens but are less invasive, more convenient and less susceptible to manipulation. They are, however, more time consuming and have a shorter detection window than urine.

Hair analysis

Hair testing can provide a long-term picture of drug use, but is expensive, takes several weeks to attain results, and is primarily used in criminal justice or child custody cases rather than in routine clinical practice.

Using on top

For many patients heroin use does not come to a complete stop when they commence methadone maintenance treatment. A significant number continue to use additional heroin. Many users also 'top up' their prescription with additional methadone acquired through the illicit market, and up to 25% of one sample had taken non-prescribed methadone six months after entering a methadone maintenance programme.[27]

So what influences the individual to continue with illicit drug use, and what should be the response of the primary care practitioner in the further management of the patient? Perhaps the most important factor that determines the frequency and amount of additional use is the dose of methadone being prescribed. Studies have shown a dose-related association, with increasing doses of methadone associated with reducing additional heroin use. Dose, however, is not the whole story; some researchers have failed to find a clear association between methadone dose and reduced heroin use.[28] Factors other than methadone dose are important. Patients who receive psychosocial and behavioural therapies, often as adjunctive treatment to pharmacological treatment, show markedly greater improvements in retention and outcome than those who received methadone alone.[29]

The important message is that successful treatment should not be seen as exclusively related to prescribing a biological substitute, but that its impact on continued heroin use is modified significantly by psychosocial factors such as individual motivation, treatment affiliation, commitment, additional support, education and opportunities for employment.

Given the relatively high prevalence of non-prescribed methadone use and the associated risks, it may be necessary for prescribers to review polices regarding methadone-dispensing management to ensure that patients are neither tempted to sell their prescriptions nor to supplement their prescribed dose through the 'grey' market of diverted methadone.

Drug interactions

The main drug interactions of methadone are associated with its CNS depressant effect and liver metabolism.

Enzyme-inducing drugs, including tobacco and alcohol, can lower methadone levels. Methadone-inhibiting drugs, such as allopurinol, phenytoin, chloramphenicol and ciprofloxacin, can increase methadone plasma levels. Both can have clinical sequelae.

As mentioned earlier, care must also be taken with other drugs that can prolong the QTc interval. These can cumulatively increase the risk of cardiac arrhythmia and resultant clinical issues, including possible sudden death.

Alcohol

Concurrent use of opioids and alcohol is common, and alcohol dependence is more common among drug users than the general population. Many patients continue to use alcohol even after starting methadone replacement. In fact it can become a more prevalent problem as patients stabilise their problematic opioid use. Prevalence rates for the incidence of alcohol abuse in treatment populations have been reported to be between 20% and 50%.[30,31]

Concurrent use of methadone and alcohol provides increased risk as it can negatively affect the process of recovery and increases the risk of serious morbidity and mortality. These patients also have increased levels of anxiety and depression, and are more likely to continue to abuse a range of illicit drugs compared with those without a drinking problem.

Alcohol intake may also increase the CNS depression of methadone, and may result in respiratory depression and hypotension. Additionally, in alcohol-related liver disease, metabolism of methadone may be affected, and this may necessitate a reduction in dose.

Cocaine

There are high rates of cocaine use in patients on methadone, both before admission and during treatment. Patients who use cocaine are more likely to have a negative outcome, are more likely to leave treatment early and are more likely to take part in criminal activities. There is also consistent evidence that methadone treatment reduces the frequency of cocaine use.

The best predictors of reduced cocaine use following methadone treatment initiation are reduced heroin use and reduced injecting. Methadone patients who also use cocaine have greater treatment needs and the treatment objectives may need to be amended to deal with this additional drug problem. At the very least it is important to discuss the negative impact of cocaine on future progress with the patient and to try to reduce this use as much as possible. Cocaine can also accelerate methadone metabolism, and it is associated with cardiac rhythm disturbances, so is ideally avoided in conjunction with methadone, particularly at higher doses.

Benzodiazepines

Benzodiazepines potentiate the effect of methadone, and may cause additive CNS depression, significantly increasing the risk of sedation and death. Large numbers of opioid users also use benzodiazepines, and their use is often implicated in methadone-related deaths.

HIV medications

The concurrent use of HIV medications and methadone may necessitate the adjustment of dose levels, though such adjustments are likely to be minor.[32]

Conclusion

Methadone is considered the gold-standard pharmacological treatment for opioid dependence, based on its clinical effectiveness and significant evidence base.

Its primary function is to reduce illicit opioid use and facilitate a reduction in harm along with improved psychological, physical and social wellbeing. This can be a useful step towards Medically Assisted Recovery. Its use is best undertaken in conjunction with a holistic package of care that involves psychological support.

References

1. RCGP Substance Misuse & Associated Health. *Guidance for the Use of Substitute Prescribing in the Treatment of Opioid Dependence in Primary Care*. London: RCGP, 2011.

2. Rostami-Hodjegan A, Wolff K, Hay A, *et al*. Population pharmacokinetics in opiate users: characterization of time-dependent changes. *British Journal of Clinical Pharmacology* 1999: **47**; 974–86.

3. Humeniuk R, Ali R, White J, *et al*. *Proceedings of Expert Workshop on the Induction and Stabilisation of Patients onto Methadone*. Monograph Series No 39. Adelaide, South Australia: Commonwealth Department of Health and Aged Care, 2000,

4. Borg L. Kreek M J. The pharmacology of opioids. In: Graham A W, Schulz T K, Mayo-Smith M F, *et al*. (eds). *Principles of Addiction Medicine*. Chevy Chase, MD: American Society of Addiction Medicine, 2003, pp. 141–55.

5. Eap C B, Buclin T, Baumann P. Interindividual variability of the clinical pharmacokinetics of methadone: implications for the treatment of opioid dependence. *Clinical Pharmacokinetics* 2002; **41(14)**: 1153–93.

6. Harding-Pink D. Opioid toxicity. *Lancet* 1993; **341(8846)**: 665–6.

7. Department of Health (England) and the devolved administrations. *Drug Misuse and Dependence: UK guidelines on clinical management*. London: Department of Health (England), Scottish Government, Welsh Assembly Government and Northern Ireland Executive, 2007.

8. Bell J, Caplehorn J M, McNeil D R. The effect of intake procedures on performance in methadone maintenance. *Addiction* 1994; **89(4)**: 463–71.

9. National Institute for Health and Clinical Excellence. *Clinical Guideline 52, Drug Misuse: opioid detoxification*. London: NICE, 2007.

10. Modesto-Lowe V, Brooks D, Petry N. Methadone deaths: risk factors in pain and addicted populations. *Journal of General Internal Medicine* 2010; **25(4)**: 305–9.

11. Buster M, van Brussel G. Is methadone more likely to kill you than heroin? *Euro-Methwork* 1996: **9**.

12. Caplehorn J R, Drummer O H. Mortality associated with New South Wales methadone programs in 1994: lives lost and saved. *Medical Journal of Australia* 1999; **170(3)**: 104–9.

13. Ehret G, Desmeules J, Broers B. Methadone-associated long QT syndrome: improving pharmacotherapy for dependence on illegal opioids and lessons learned for pharmacology. *Expert Opinion on Drug Safety* 2007; **6(3)**: 289–303.

14. Karch S B. Stephens B G. Toxicology and the pathology of deaths related to methadone: retrospective review. *Western Journal of Medicine* 2000; **172(1)**: 11–14.

15. Justo D, Gal-Oz A, Paran Y, *et al*. Methadone-associated Torsades de Pointes (polymorphic ventricular tachycardia) in opioid-dependent patients. *Addiction* 2006; **101(9)**: 1333–8.

16. Anchersen K, Clausen T, Gossop M, *et al*. Prevalence and clinical relevance of corrected QT interval prolongation during methadone and buprenorphine treatment: a mortality assessment study. *Addiction* 2009; **104(6)**: 993–9.

17. Medicines and Healthcare products Regulatory Agency. Risk of QT interval prolongation with methadone. *Current Problems in Pharmacovigilance* 2006; **31**: 6.

18. Haigney M C, Alam S, Tebo S, *et al*. Intravenous cocaine and QT variability. *Journal of Cardiovascular Electrophysiology* 2006; **17(6):** 610–16.

19. Schmittner J, Schroeder J R, Epstein D H, *et al*. QT interval increased after single dose of lofexidine. *British Medical Journal* 2004; **329(7474)**: 1075.

20. Wolff K, Sanderson M, Hay A W, *et al*. Methadone concentrations in plasma and their relationship to drug dosage. *Clinical Chemistry* 1991; **37(2)**: 205–9.

21. Kreek M J. Factors modifying the pharmacological effectiveness of methadone, In: Cooper J R, Altman F, Brown B S, *et al*. (eds). *Research on the Treatment of Narcotic Addiction: state of the art*. National Institute of Drug Abuse Research Monograph Series. Washington, DC: Government Printing Office, 1983, pp. 95–114.

22. Leavitt S B. The methadone dose debate continues. *Addiction Treatment Forum* 2003; **12(1)**: 1, 3, http://atforum.com/SiteRoot/pages/current_pastissues/Winter2003.pdf   [accessed November 2012].

23. Ward J, Mattick R, Hall W. The use of methadone during maintenance treatment: pharmacology, dosage and treatment outcome. In J Ward, R Mattick, W Hall (eds). *Methadone Maintenance Treatment and Other Opioid Replacement Therapies*. The Netherlands: Harwood Academic Publishers, 1998, pp. 205–35.

24. National Treatment Agency for Substance Misuse. *Injectable heroin (and Injectable Methadone): potential roles in drug treatment*. London: NTA, 2003, www.nta.nhs.uk/uploads/nta_injectable_heroin_and_methadone_2003_fullguide.pdf   [accessed November 2012].

25. Strang J, Metrebian N, Lintzeris N, *et al*. Supervised injectable heroin or injectable methadone versus optimised oral methadone as treatment for chronic heroin addicts in England after persistent failure in orthodox treatment (RIOTT): a randomised trial. *Lancet* 2010; **375(9729)**: 1885–95.

26. Leavitt S. Methadone dosing and safety in the treatment of opioid addiction. *Addiction Treatment Forum* 2003; **9**: 1–8.

27. Best D, Harris J, Gossop M, *et al*. Use of non-prescribed methadone and other illicit drugs during methadone maintenance treatment. *Drug and Alcohol Review* 2000; **19(1)**: 9–16.

28. Saxon A J, Wells EA, Fleming C, *et al*. Pre-treatment characteristics, program philosophy and levels of ancillary services as predictors of methadone maintenance treatment outcome. *Addiction* 1996; **91(8)**: 1197–209.

29. National Institute for Health and Clinical Excellence. *Clinical Guideline 51, Drug Misuse: psychosocial interventions*. London, NICE, 2007.

30. Hunt D E, Strug D L, Goldsmith D S, *et al*. Alcohol use and abuse: heavy drinking among methadone clients. *American Journal of Drug and Alcohol Abuse* 1986; **12(1–2)**: 147–64.

31. Chatham L R, Rowan-Szal G, Joe G W, *et al*. Heavy drinking in a population of methadone-maintained clients. *Journal of Studies on Alcohol* 1995; **56(4)**: 417–22.

32. McCance-Katz E, Rainey P, Friedland G, *et al*. Effect of opioid dependence pharmacotherapies on zidovudine disposition. *American Journal on Addictions* 2001; **10(4)**: 296–307.

CHAPTER 10

Benzodiazepine use, misuse and management

Susanna Lawrence

IN THIS CHAPTER

Introduction ‖ *Benzodiazepine misuse* ‖ *Dose and route* ‖
Medicopharmacology ‖ *Problems associated with benzodiazepine misuse* ‖
Management of benzodiazepine misuse in illicit drug users ‖ *Future developments
in the management of benzodiazepine dependence* ‖ *Conclusion*

Introduction

Benzodiazepine (BZD) dependence has been widely recognised for over 30
years.[1,2] Twelve million prescriptions per year are produced, somewhere between
0.5 and 1.5 million people in the UK are addicted to prescribed BZDs, and it is
estimated that a further 0.2 million take illicit BZDs.[3] Despite many years of justified concern regarding the long-term adverse effects, and National Institute for
Health and Clinical Excellence (NICE) guidance[4] that reinforces the need to limit
prescribing to four weeks, they remain widely prescribed on a recurrent basis,
principally for the treatment of insomnia and anxiety. They are also prescribed
for the treatment of seizures, skeletal muscle spasticity, alcohol withdrawal, as a
pre-med for surgery and an adjunctive treatment during chemotherapy.

Illicit use of BZDs in the UK and worldwide has increased rapidly over the
last two decades, and is now extremely common among opiate-dependent drug
users. Studies have shown that between 50% and 90% of patients attending opioid substitute programmes have a history of BZD misuse;[5–8] about half injected
their BZDs according to one study.[9] BZDs are now widely and cheaply available.
Historically, prescriptions, mainly by GPs, were diverted to form the bulk of illicit
supplies, but today BZDs are readily available on the internet, and it is likely this
is now the primary source. Internet BZDs are pharmacologically unreliable, but
some pirate preparations are indistinguishable from the legally produced version.

Although pharmacologically distinct, the so called 'Z' drugs (zopiclone, zolpidem and zaleplon) have a similar action to BZDs. NICE guidance[10] does not
recommend their use, as there is a 'lack of compelling evidence' to distinguish
them from BZDs when prescribing short term for insomnia. However, they have

achieved widespread acceptance in primary care, with many GPs viewing them as safer than BZDs. In practice, the Z drugs are abused as much as BZDs, principally for euphoric effect, particularly the short-acting zolpidem and zaleplon.

This chapter will focus on the aetiology and management of illicit BZD use, including indications for prescribing, detoxification and the case for maintenance prescribing. There is some crossover with prescribed groups, as patients develop iatrogenic dependence and may move into the illicit market to manage their symptoms.

Benzodiazepine misuse

Why people use benzodiazepines

There are three reasons why people use BZDs: to prevent withdrawal symptoms once dependent, for symptom control, and for euphoric effect.

Ashton[11] defines three distinct scenarios of dependent BZD use:

1. *Therapeutic dose dependence* – long-term prescribed users developing dependence

2. *Prescribed high-dose dependence* – long-term users, initially prescribed, escalating their dose, eventually via illicit sources

3. *Recreational BZD abuse* – leading to dependence for some users.

Different interpretations of the terms addiction and dependence continue to confuse the literature. The ICD-10[12] definition of dependence, used here, includes evidence of behaviour change as well as the development of tolerance and withdrawal (see pp. 158–9):

Ashton's Group 1 are not considered further in this chapter, although morbidity associated with long-term use applies to this cohort too.

Group 2 are often managed by their GPs, but may also be referred to specialist addiction services. Group 3 behaviour is common, but it is important to note that not all illicit BZD use is recreational; some is therapeutic.

'Simple' use of BZDs, for insomnia or anxiety (with no evidence of abuse or dependence), can occur in illicit drug users just as in the general population. In terms of stability and mental health indicators, this group is no different from non-BZD-using illicit drug users.[7]

However problematic, BZD use (characterised by dependence or misuse) has been associated with a range of mental health problems including psychosis, somatisation, personality disorder and neuroses.[13–15]

Patients who have been prescribed or use illicit BZDs for anxiety symptoms are likely to develop problematic BZD use. Although caution is needed in extrapolating from observations of licit users prescribed BZDs, it is worth noting that Tyler *et al.*[14] have observed that anxiety-related outcomes were less good after withdrawing from BZDs than for the control group; in other words, even short-term BZD use may make symptoms worse. Within the drug-using population, where access to illicit drugs is already established, it is very likely that, should this occur, the patient will seek further illicit supplies to alleviate anxiety symptoms. But they may not need to; BZDs are frequently prescribed to illicit drug users in a mistaken attempt to alleviate symptoms and stabilise other drug use thought to be higher risk, e.g. opioids.

Patients with co-morbidity of illicit drug use and severe mental illness (dual diagnosis) are more likely than those with severe mental illness alone to be prescribed BZDs. This is found across the full range of diagnoses (schizophrenia, bipolar disorder, major depression).[16]

Prolonged BZD use is associated with childhood trauma in patients on opioid substitute programmes. In one study 67% of patients using illicit BZDs reported at least one moderate to severe traumatic event, particularly emotional abuse, emotional neglect and physical neglect.[5]

The association between BZD use and mental health symptoms is complex, and it is often difficult to establish how much BZDs have exacerbated pre-existing problems, or are taken in an attempt to find symptom relief.

Patients using other illicit drugs are likely to use BZDs to counteract the negative effect of other drugs,[17] principally to minimise withdrawal symptoms from opioids, or to 'come down following stimulant use'.

Methadone treatment may trigger the onset, relapse or increase in BZD misuse as a substitute euphoriant once abstinence from heroin is achieved, or in an attempt to increase stability for patients prescribed with an inadequate dose of opioid substitute treatment.[18] BZD consumption within a methadone maintenance treatment (MMT) programme is associated with poorer treatment retention, and increased risk of relapse back to opiate use.[19]

It is not only illicit drug users who misuse BZDs; between 3 and 41% of problematic drinkers report that they also misused BZDs at some time, often to minimise intoxication or withdrawal effects.[20]

BZDs are also widely used for recreational use. Within the illicit drug user population, BZDs are the drugs most frequently used in combination with opioids and are rarely their sole drug of misuse; a potentiated euphoric effect occurs when heroin and BZDs are used together.[13] Recreational use usually leads to problematic use, and will hamper attempts to stabilise opiate treatment.

Current street intelligence states that heroin is frequently contaminated with BZDs. However, it must be recognised that this postulate allows for ongoing illicit BZD use to be obscured behind an explanation that may or may not be valid, should the patient wish to conceal his or her intentional ongoing BZD use from the prescriber.

Table 10.1   **Why people misuse benzodiazepines**

To manage symptoms	As part of polysubstance use
Low mood or depression. Insomnia. Anxiety. Perceived or real BZD withdrawal	Increased 'high', e.g. with alcohol, antihistamines, opioids, particularly methadone.
	To 'come down' from stimulants, e.g. crack cocaine, amphetamines.
	To manage alcohol withdrawal symptoms

In practice, these categories often merge and indications for use in the substance-misusing population is likely to be multifactorial. However, understanding why a patient is using BZDs is important, for clinician, patient and keyworker, in helping the patient move towards reduction and cessation of use.

The literature paints a picture of patients using illicit BZD as part of polysubstance use doing less well than their non-BZD-using counterparts.[15, 21–23]

Patients using illicit BZDs are more likely to have the following characteristics:

▶ chaotic lifestyle, poor quality of life and precariousness

▶ pre-existing anxiety, depression, somatisation and psychotic disorders

▶ more overdoses

▶ childhood trauma

▶ longer years of opioid use

▶ polydrug use

▶ concomitant high-risk/dependent alcohol use

▶ low capacity for introspection, maladaptive coping skills

▶ higher-risk injecting behaviour.

BZDs are used increasingly by younger people as part of a polysubstance use pattern that does not include opiates. Phenazepam, a potent BZD widely available on the internet, is increasingly available in the UK.[24, 25]

Dose and route

For recreational use, an initial oral dose equivalent to diazepam 10–20 mg can produce a euphoric effect. Extremely high doses for recreational purposes have been reported – up to 500 mg daily dose, with plasma concentrations of up to

800% that expected with a therapeutic dose.[26] However, most recreational users will report an illicit daily dose of 20–100 mg.

Most BZDs (apart from midazolam) are poorly water soluble, therefore injecting carries significant risk. There is no up-to-date published information regarding BZD injecting habits. Strang *et al.*'s survey[9] identified the injecting potential of temazepam capsules, which have subsequently been removed from the market, and clinical practice suggests a decline in BZD injecting use since then. Risks include overdose, thromboembolism, amputation and organ damage, in addition to infection; BZD users are more likely to share needles, additionally exposing themselves to the usual risks of blood-borne infection.[19] Interestingly, Seivewright[27] reported BZD withdrawal least likely in BZD injectors, possibly due to the more intermittent nature of injecting misuse.

Some patients have reported a preferred sublingual route (using lorazepam and triazolam) for more rapid effect; others have disclosed increased effectiveness with nasal insufflation (snorting).

Medicopharmacology

A brief exploration of the pharmacology of BZDs assists understanding of their use and misuse; for further reading refer to Nutt and Malizia's review.[28] BZDs have several pharmacological actions. The principal mechanism of action of BZDs is through their interference with the GABA pathway. GABA (gamma aminobutyric acid) is the main central nervous system (CNS) inhibitory neurotransmitter in mammals, acting by modifying the excitability of neurones. BZDs bind to a subset of GABA-a receptors in the brain, locking them into a formation that is more receptive to the GABA neurotransmitter. Thus the inhibitory effect of GABA is increased, leading to hypnotic and anxiolytic effects. Additionally BZDs are thought to act by sensitising the excitatory glutaminergic system. Other effects of BZDs (muscle relaxation, anticonvulsant) may be mediated through peripheral BZD receptors, unrelated to the above. These different modes of activity are reflected by the different therapeutic indications for BZDs, and explain paradoxical effects such as disinhibition, and the phenomenon that tolerance develops at different rates for different pharmacological effects.[29]

BZDs exhibit cross-tolerance with alcohol, hence their utility in alcohol withdrawal. Cross-tolerance has benefits and disadvantages. Short-term maintenance on a BZD can help stabilise a patient post-alcohol withdrawal, but continued BZD use can act as a positive reinforcer, increasing cravings for alcohol.

The Z drugs – zolpidem, zopiclone and zaleplon – are chemically distinct from BZDs, but pharmacologically similar, acting at a subset of the GABA-a receptors.

As potential drugs of abuse, rapid-onset, short-acting BZDs are preferred by illicit drug users (see Table 10.2, overleaf). Non-generic forms and most concentrated formulations tend to have higher street value than generic forms.[30] High-dose formulations are readily available on the internet, including some spurious preparations that are marketed as high-dose BZDs.

Table 10.2   **Equivalence, rates of onset and duration of action for common benzodiazepines and benzodiazepine-like drugs**

Drug	Equivalent dose (mg)	Rate of onset	Duration of clinical action (hours)	Half-life (hours)
Zolpidem	20	Very rapid	2	2
Flunitrazepam	1		6–8	26–8
Diazepam	10	Rapid	4–6	20–100
Nitrazepam	10		6–8	15–38
Zopiclone	15		4	4–6
Lormetazepam	1–2		6–8	10–12
Clonazepam	0.5		10–12	18–50
Temazepam	20	Intermediate	5–6	8–22
Lorazepam	1		4–6	10–20
Chlordiazepoxide	25		6–8	5–30
Promethazine	25		4–6	6–12
Oxazepam	20–30	Slow	4–6	4–15
Loprazolam	1		6–10	6–12

The duration of clinical action is often considerably shorter than the elimination half-life, due to the high fat solubility of most BZDs and consequent rapid re-distribution into fatty tissue. However, the drug and its metabolites continue to exert some effect long after the duration of apparent action, as metabolites leak out of the fatty tissue. This characteristic can be exploited therapeutically, with BZDs with a long half-life, such as diazepam, producing constant plasma levels, thus minimising withdrawal symptoms.

The half-life also increases significantly with increasing age and impaired liver function.

Problems associated with benzodiazepine use

When used alone, BZDs carry an extremely low risk of acute toxicity. However, they are commonly used as part of a habit of polydrug use, and are thought to interact synergistically with other CNS depressants, including alcohol and opioids. Patients using these drugs are at high risk of life-threatening and multiple accidental drug overdose,[6] and fatal overdoses involving BZDs are all too frequent.

Oliver et al.[31] found that BZD use was associated with a 2.5 times increase in risk of fatal heroin overdose in a group of current heroin users, and a near ten times increase in risk of fatal methadone overdose for methadone users. In investigating causality, they concluded that BZDs have the potential to increase the respiratory depressant effect of opioids, but that the behavioural effects of BZDs, or the characteristics of those using BZDs, may also be relevant.

Due to tolerance, doses tend to escalate rapidly. Paradoxical disinhibition may occur in high-dose BZD use, with characteristics of overconfidence, aggression and a sense of invincibility, leading to increased risk taking. Illicit BZD use is linked to a wide range of other increased risk behaviours: needle sharing, higher levels of polydrug use, an increased chance of injecting during methadone maintenance and higher levels of criminality.[32]

Illicit BZD users have been shown to have more chaotic, precarious lifestyles.[15] This, together with high risk taking, also increases the risk of non-overdose-related death.

Depression and emotional blunting can occur with longer-term BZD use.[11] Persistent BZD use to manage stressful situations can lead to a decreased capacity to cope and increased anxiety, as normal psychological adjustment processes are interrupted.

The high prevalence of mental health disorders discussed earlier is reflected by the association of BZD use with suicide. De la Vega Sánchez et al.[33] reported that 38% of suicides within a cohort of substance-misusing patients were associated with BZD use.

Barker et al.[34] conducted a meta-analysis of 13 studies and have reported significant deficits in all 12 cognitive domains tested in long-term BZD users. Only some domains showed improvement on withdrawing from BZDs.

Long-term and high-dose BZD use are associated with negative outcomes. Relapses are more likely and are often characterised by intense cravings.[35,36]

The long-term BZD user is more distressed and chaotic than the intermittent or non-BZD user. It has been suggested that long-term BZD misuse is an indicator of generally more problematic drug use,[37] and as such is a useful proxy indicator to identify the more complex, challenging patients.

Box 10.1 **Complications of problematic benzodiazepine use**

Complications relating to long-term use

✓ Cognitive impairment.

✓ Dependence.

✓ Tolerance.

✓ Withdrawal (including convulsions).

✓ Personality changes: emotional blunting.

✓ Anxiety, depression and suicide.

✓ Abnormal liver function

Complications relating to intermittent high-dose use ('bingeing')

✓ Memory impairment.

✓ Paradoxical inhibition.

✓ Overdose (frequently fatal if used with other CNS depressants, e.g. methadone and/or alcohol).

✓ Psychomotor retardation.

Increased risks of BZD use

✓ Road traffic accidents.

✓ Falls.

✓ Polypharmacy complications.

Dependence

The ICD-10 [12] defines dependence as a maladaptive state characterised by at least three of the following, occurring together for at least one month, or if present for less than one month, have occurred together repeatedly during the previous 12 months:

1. A strong desire or sense of compulsion to take the substance

2. Difficulties in controlling substance-taking behaviour in terms of its onset, termination or levels of use

3. A physiological withdrawal state when substance use has ceased or has been reduced, as evidenced by the characteristic withdrawal syndrome for the substance or use of the same (or closely related) substance with the intention of relieving or avoiding withdrawal symptoms

4. Evidence of tolerance, such that increased doses of the psychoactive substance are required in order to achieve effects originally produced by lower doses

5. Progressive neglect of alternative pleasures or interests because of psychoactive substance use, increased amount of time necessary to obtain or take the substance, or to recover from its effects

6. Persisting with substance use despite clear evidence of overtly harmful consequences.

BZD dependence in the opioid-using population is usually overestimated. Williams *et al.*[38] found, in a detoxification unit, that BZD withdrawal symptoms emerged in only half of opioid-dependent patients using concurrent BZDs. In other reports, prevalence of dependence ranges from 13% to 25%.[39,40] Dependence on BZDs occurs more rapidly with short-acting, high-potency drugs, such as lorazepam.

Tolerance

Tolerance to the different actions of BZDs develops at variable rates and to different degrees. Tolerance to the hypnotic effects tends to develop rapidly, within days or weeks of regular use. Anxiolytic effects will persist for a few months, although without careful monitoring dose escalation does happen in this group, and long-term use may aggravate anxiety.[11] When used to alleviate anxiety, stopping BZDs may exacerbate pre-existing symptoms.[14] However, tolerance does not develop with respect to cognitive impairment.

Withdrawal

The withdrawal syndrome from the abrupt stopping of high-dose use can be severe, including life-threatening delirium.[41] The time frame of the emergence of acute withdrawal symptoms correlates loosely to the half-life of the particular drug taken (there is wide individual variation), and the severity of the withdrawal symptoms increases with dose and length of time that the patient has been taking the medication. Withdrawal symptoms are likely to be more severe if the reduction regime is rapid, and with long-term use. Assessing withdrawal may be difficult, as withdrawal symptoms from therapeutic dosages of BZDs are similar to anxiety symptoms, which may have pre-dated BZD use and re-emerge as the suppressant effect of BZDs is removed.

Table 10.3 categorises symptoms into those common to all anxiety states, and those relatively specific to BZD withdrawal, as a guide to differentiating anxiety symptoms from BZD withdrawal.

Table 10.3 **Benzodiazepine withdrawal symptoms**

Symptoms common to anxiety states and BZD withdrawal	Symptoms relating to distorted perception, usually specific to BZD withdrawal	Major symptoms, rare and usually secondary to abrupt cessation of high dose of BZD
Anxiety, panic attacks, agoraphobia.	Perceptual distortions, sense of movement.	Fits.
Insomnia, nightmares.	Depersonalisation, derealisation.	Delirium.
Depression, dysphoria.	Distortion of body image.	Transient hallucinations.
Excitability, restlessness.	Tingling, numbness, altered sensation.	Psychosis
Poor memory and concentration.	Sensory hypersensitivity (light, sound, taste, smell).	
Dizziness, lightheadedness.	Muscle twitches, jerks, fasciculation.	
Muscle weakness, tremor.	Tinnitus.	
Muscle pain, stiffness.	Psychotic symptoms.	
Sweating, night sweats.	Confusion, delirium.	
Palpitations.	Convulsions	
Blurred or double vision.		
Diarrhoea, constipation.		
Rashes		

A protracted withdrawal syndrome has been described by Ashton,[42] possibly caused by slow reversal of tolerance, and relating to the uneven development of tolerance to the different effects of BZDs. Persistent symptoms last beyond the period expected by the drug's pharmacological activity, into many months, but most are resolved over 6–12 months. Symptoms of the protracted withdrawal syndrome include anxiety, depression, paraesthesia, tinnitus, muscle twitching and diarrhoea.

Management of benzodiazepine misuse in illicit drug users

The evidence base

Adverse effects of long-term use, principally relating to cognitive impairment, are undisputed[34] but literature reviews recurrently identify the lack of published evidence regarding BZD use and dependence in opioid-using patients.[13,17]

In the midst of this paucity of evidence regarding effective treatments, the practice of maintenance BZD is widespread, as clinicians struggle to stabilise this very challenging patient group.

Consensus opinion is that reduction and abstinence are advised for the majority of patients misusing BZDs.[3] There is good evidence that BZD reduction/detox programmes are most effective when the dose is tapered over a significant period of time (months or even years) rather than rapidly over days or weeks.[11,43,44]

Most of the literature on the management of BZD dependence relates to patients prescribed these drugs for psychiatric disorders (mainly anxiety and depression) who tend not to have concurrent drug misuse problems. The advisability of applying standard BZD withdrawal guidelines to illicit drug users is affected not only by clinical criteria but also by the need to avoid abuse and diversion potential of the prescribed medication.

Current management of benzodiazepine prescribing for illicit drug users

In the absence of controlled studies to guide the clinician regarding the co-prescribing of BZDs alongside opioid substitute treatment (OST), the following section summarises the broad consensus of current management from experienced clinicians in the field. Box 10.2 (overleaf) outlines the principles underlying treatment.

For non-dependent patients, supported phased reduction of BZD use without a prescription may be appropriate. For dependent patients exhibiting progress towards stability of illicit drug use, and motivation to stop using BZDs, a reducing prescription of BZDs is indicated. Only in a minority will it be appropriate to consider maintenance prescribing. It is often assumed that this client group will not wish to stop BZDs, but in one study[6] only 19% of those asked said they would not consider stopping if offered effective help.

Phases of treatment

The management of BZD dependence, like other addictions, is best considered in discrete phases. For BZDs these phases are:

▶ assessment

▶ preparation

▶ conversion

▶ dose induction

▶ detoxification

▶ follow-up

▶ maintenance.

Box 10.2   **Principles for managing benzodiazepine misuse in illicit drug users**

Drug use

✓ Abstinence is the aim in managing patients seeking treatment for BZD use.

✓ Only a minority of patients using illicit BZDs are dependent.

✓ 'Bingeing' on BZDs for psychotropic effect is high-risk behaviour and is not evidence of dependence. Therefore a prescription is likely to increase, not reduce, harm.

✓ BZDs should not be initiated for the management of illicit drug use-related symptoms, e.g. insomnia, agitation secondary to stimulant.

✓ Evidence of ongoing illicit opioid or other drugs suggests that the patient is in ongoing contact with a supplier of illicit drugs, and therefore likely to use any prescribed BZDs to enhance psychotropic effect or manage drug-related symptoms.

Before prescribing BZDs

✓ Establish why the patient is using BZDs (e.g. symptomatic use, recreational abuse, managing negative effects of other drugs) and establish the presence or absence of dependence, in order to inform the patient's management plan.

✓ If the indication for prescribing is to prevent withdrawal, dependence must be established before a prescription is initiated.

✓ Patient, prescriber and keyworker need to understand and agree expectations and time scales of prescribing, and agree measurable outcomes

✓ Ensure underlying mental health issues are addressed, e.g. Cognitive Behavioural Theory (CBT) for anxiety disorders.

Prescribing guidance

✓ Long-term prescribing, while widespread, is unlikely to promote stability amongst drug users, particularly those who continue to use illicit opioids and other drugs 'on top' of their prescribed OST. It has adverse consequences.

✓ For managing BZD withdrawal in dependent patients, a regime of gradual dose reduction over weeks or months is advised, alongside structured psychosocial intervention.

Assessment

There is a significant risk that adding a BZD prescription to opiate substitute treatment may increase harm if the patient is not sufficiently stable, motivated or if dependence is not demonstrated. Rigorous assessment of the patient maximises appropriate selection and minimises possibilities for increased harm.

First, the clinician needs to establish the absence of ongoing drug or high-risk alcohol use. Ongoing stimulant use is a contraindication for BZD prescribing, as the patient is likely to use the BZDs to manage stimulant-induced anxiety and paranoia.[39] Prescribing BZDs to a patient with high-risk alcohol use increases the risk of over-sedation and accidental overdose, and at best is unlikely to have a favourable outcome while alcohol use continues uncontrolled.

Ongoing illicit opiate use 'on top' of an opiate substitute prescription raises the likelihood of ongoing BZD abuse, either to manage withdrawal or to increase the euphoriant effect, so initiating a BZD prescription is not advised.

Diversion is a particular risk in the non-dependent patient, and an assessment of the risk of diversion is part of the process prior to initiating a BZD prescription.

Dependence must be established prior to prescribing BZDs, using ICD-10 criteria. A history of daily BZD use for less than three months is unlikely to produce dependence.[38] Where there is doubt about the diagnosis of dependence it may be appropriate to suggest the patient attends for assessment after 48 hours of BZD abstinence, in order to identify presence of BZD withdrawal symptoms. Toxicology tests can be used to confirm ongoing use. Usually two positive toxicology tests within the previous two months is sufficient. If the patient has provided a negative BZD toxicology result within the last four months dependence is unlikely. Some services ask the patient to record BZD use over a two-week period. This process has several purposes: to encourage patients to monitor their intake, take control of the process, and start to regularise their intake.

The clinician must explore previous attempts to stop BZDs, any previous withdrawal symptoms (including fits), underlying or pre-existing symptoms of anxiety, depression or insomnia, and the patient's ability to engage with alternative treatment options for managing these symptoms. Before prescribed BZDs are added, other prescribed medication (usually opiate substitute treatment) must be stabilised.

Prior to commencing a prescription, it is vital that the patient and anyone working with the patient understand why he or she is using illicit BZDs, and explore alternative treatment strategies for symptom control. The patient needs to understand the purpose of the prescription: to assist stabilisation, reduction and detoxification from BZDs.

Detoxification preparation

As with any detoxification process, adequate preparation increases the chances of success.

If the client is on opiate substitute treatment, this must be stabilised prior to commencing BZD prescribing, and should stay at a constant dose during BZD reduction and detoxification.[45]

BZD reduction is likely to be accompanied by an emergence of any pre-existing symptoms of anxiety, therefore an important aspect of detoxification preparation is to identify alternative treatment strategies. CBT, selective serotonin reuptake inhibitors and beta-blockers are possible options, and can be instigated prior to BZD reduction.

Education regarding the nature of BZDs is reported as improving outcomes in managing BZD dependence in non-drug-using populations,[46] although this effect has not been examined amongst illicit drug users. However, general principles of health education require information to be given to all patients regarding BZDs, and it is important not to assume that illicit drug users will be uninterested in such an approach.

Clinicians need to be aware that, once started, the patient may feel uncomfortable with reductions and express a desire to delay reduction, or move to maintenance, as circumstances or health needs change. Understanding withdrawal symptoms that the patient may encounter is the final piece of preparation that may help the transfer and subsequent reduction of BZDs go well. It is particularly important to discuss insomnia, and ensure the patient has alternative strategies in place for managing insomnia.

Psychological support before, during and after withdrawal enhances self-efficacy, supporting the patient in developing alternative coping strategies.[11] Cognitive behavioural interventions have the best evidence for improving detoxification outcomes.[35,44,47] Returning regularly to the benefits of reduction and detoxification will be necessary to support the patient through the process.

Conversion

Department of Health guidelines (the Orange Book)[45] recommend that diazepam is used as the preferred substitute BZD; it has the advantage of being available on an FP10 MDA and thus can be readily prescribed for daily pick-up. However, due to its rapid onset of action it remains widely abused. If there is any concern about diversion a clinician may choose a BZD with a slow onset, such as oxazepam or chlordiazepoxide, which has a low street value. Conversion can be made in one step, and should include Z drugs if they are also being used.

Induction

The dose of diazepam required to stabilise patients who do exhibit withdrawal symptoms is often much lower than claimed use.[26,38] It is not necessary or desirable to match the patient's reported intake with prescribed BZDs. Even patients reporting extremely high doses have been safely transferred to moderate-dose diazepam. Most patients will report current use of between 20 mg and 100 mg diazepam equivalent daily, and conversion to 20–30 mg daily dose is effective for the vast majority of cases.

Even if reported intake is between 100 mg and 200 mg, daily amounts of 30–60 mg are likely to be sufficient.

For high-dose users (between 60 mg and 200 mg) some clinicians advocate an induction phase to a higher dose for stabilisation followed by a two-part reduction: initially reducing to 30 mg, then addressing other issues before recommencing reduction and detoxifying completely from BZDs.

For exceptionally high users, for example over 300 mg per day, initial inpatient treatment may be required.

Box 10.3   **Dose induction**

1. The aim of dose induction is that the patient should be comfortable, but not intoxicated or drowsy during the day.

2. Aim at the lowest dose possible.

3. Start at 10–30 mg daily of diazepam.

4. Higher doses are rarely required, though if illicit use is very high (e.g. 100–200 mg diazepam/day) it may be necessary to prescribe 2 × 10 mg three times/day (60 mg) and reduce to 10 mg three times/day within six weeks.

5. It may be advisable, whatever the daily dose, to suggest the patient takes it in two instalments, reserving a dose for night-time use.

Patients should be reviewed after one or two weeks prescribing, to assess withdrawal symptoms and distinguish from the emergence of pre-existing anxiety prior to medicating with BZDs. If the patient is experiencing withdrawal symptoms then dose can be increased by increments of 5–10 mg, but it is rarely necessary to go above 30 mg.

Detoxification from benzodiazepines

Gradual dose reduction, or tapering, regimes are widely referred to in the literature,[11,43,44] although most are within non-drug-using populations. However, clinical practice supports this approach for illicit drug users. The optimal speed or duration of dose reduction is unknown, but consideration should be given to both the avoidance of withdrawal symptoms, including fits, and minimisation of illicit use.

Patients who do not fit the criteria for prescribed BZDs should be supported intensively in reducing and stopping their BZD use, using the usual tactics: drug diaries, gradual dose reduction, delaying the first dose and extending periods between doses.

If criteria for initiating prescribed BZDs have been met, reduction can begin as soon as the patient is stabilised on the medication, unless there are indications for maintenance, as addressed in a later section.

Most published regimes support a reduction by 5–15% per fortnight. Box 10.4 contains a suggested regime recommended by the Royal College of General Practitioners.

Box 10.4   **Suggested benzodiazepine reduction regime**

1. Reduction by approximately eighth of the daily dose per fortnight, e.g.:

prescribed daily diazepam dose	diazepam reduction per fortnight
60–80 mg	10 mg
30–60 mg	5 mg
20–30 mg	(2 × 2 mg tablets) 4 mg
0–20 mg	2 mg

2. Reduction can be quicker if shorter duration of dependence.

3. When the patient reaches a dose of 20 mg or less, reduce by 2 mg every 1–2 weeks.

4. Many patients will complete the final 4 mg reductions without any withdrawal symptoms.

5. For those experiencing genuine withdrawal once reduced to 4 mg, reductions can be as gradual as 0.5 mg every two weeks, if necessary. (Use a half or quarter of 2 mg tablet or oral solution of diazepam 2 mg/5L or 5 mg/5ml.)

6. Slow down reduction if withdrawal symptoms experienced.

7. Ensure patient is engaging with psychosocial interventions for the entirety of the BZD detoxification.

8. Continue support and relapse prevention after completing detoxification.

Dispensing

Diazepam is the only BZD eligible to be written on an FP10 MDA for instalment dispensing.

GPs should prescribe for daily dispensing at the start of treatment, during the period of stabilisation, and continue daily if on daily prescribing of other substitute prescribing. Discuss dispensing with the pharmacist; some may supervise the first dose of the day if requested on the prescription. Diazepam can be given as a single dose for the purposes of withdrawal avoidance, which may aid compliance.[46]

If a slow-onset BZD is prescribed instead of diazepam, an FP10 MDA cannot be used. Only two days should be issued on any single prescription. Subsequent prescriptions can be post-dated to avoid early use. It is not necessary to review the patient for each prescription. Several can be issued in one consultation.

If prescriptions have been lost or the drugs have been used before the next prescription is due they should not be repeated. The risk of fits is small and it is highly likely that the prescription has been misused or diverted.

Managing symptoms relating to benzodiazepine withdrawal

Once again, the literature largely refers to the use of adjunctive medication used by the general population to support BZD withdrawal. The conclusion of a recent meta-analysis [44] was that there was no significant improvement in overall outcomes for a range of adjunctive medication including melatonin, selective serotonin reuptake inhibitors, beta-blockers and anti-epileptic medication. However, a recent Cochrane Systemic Review (for BZD monodependence only)[43] suggested that carbamazepine may 'have promise' as an adjunctive medication for withdrawal, especially for patients using high-dose BZDs (20 mg diazepam or more).

Carbamazepine has been in use for BZD withdrawal for two decades, and is effective in preventing fits and withdrawal symptoms, particularly for patients on high-dose BZDs.[48] However, as carbamazepine increases methadone metabolism,[49] opiate withdrawal may be precipitated in patients prescribed methadone (one study reporting a 60% decrease in serum methadone levels for patients taking carbamazepine). It is therefore not routinely used in patients prescribed methadone.

Sedating antidepressants should be used only if there is underlying depression and not to treat insomnia, and must be used with extreme care as frequently they feature as part of a polysubstance profile in drug-related deaths. For example, amitriptyline carries additional risk for patients on higher-dose methadone as it prolongs the QT interval on ECG.

A withdrawal symptoms questionnaire, such as the CIWA-B,[50] is useful to benchmark symptoms and monitor progress, and may help distinguish between withdrawal and emerging anxiety. Reduction rates can be reduced to alleviate withdrawal symptoms.

Follow-up

As with other drugs of addiction, BZD dependence has a high risk of relapse,[36] with one review reporting only 25% succeeding in maintaining abstinence in the long term.[51] The National Treatment Outcome Research Study[52] examined the risk of relapse of BZD use in patients on a methadone prescription and found that the rate of use had decreased from 34% at intake into the study to 12% at four to five years follow-up. Rates of relapse can be reduced by ensuring that any other addiction problem is optimally managed.

Protracted withdrawal symptoms may occur, especially if high doses are used and/or there is pre-existing co-morbidity. Patients need to be reassured that these symptoms will resolve in time (anecdotally symptoms are reported to continue for 'one month per year' [of BZD use]) and be actively supported through this time.

Maintenance

Three scenarios face the clinician with respect to BZD maintenance:

1. Indications for short-term maintenance

2. Indications for long-term maintenance

3. Managing patients already maintained on a BZD prescription.

Some patients will move straight to reduction and detoxification once the induction phase is completed and the patient is stabilised; this is the preferred option for patients with no complex needs. However, for many patients a short period of maintenance may be indicated, and for a few patients long-term maintenance.

Maintenance BZD prescribing by default has become widely established within substance misuse services over the last two decades. Clinicians will be faced with the dilemma of managing patients who have been prescribed maintenance BZDs for many years.

The evidence base for BZD maintenance prescribing in illicit drug users is scanty and mixed. Greenwood[53] published results from her clinical treatment service in Edinburgh where dramatic reductions in illicit opioid use and risk behaviour were accomplished by a treatment regime that included maintenance BZD prescribing to methadone-maintained patients. Liebrenz[54] calls for evaluation of the widely practised 'agonist substitution' as a valid treatment for high-dose BZD-dependent patients, citing poor success rates of detoxification regimes, and postulating improved health outcomes for patients maintained on BZDs.

However, others observe that maintenance prescribing of BZDs has not been shown to have any definite medical value (unlike methadone) and in view of the recognised adverse effects (cognitive impairment) is rarely justified.[49,55] Furthermore, there are significant concerns regarding misuse and diversion of any pre-scribed BZD medication.

The clinician should consider maintenance prescribing only if the goals of such prescribing are agreed and measurable, i.e. stabilisation of lifestyle, stabilisation of drug use and evidence of the patient having removed him or herself from the illicit drug market.

Short-term maintenance

Short-term maintenance (usually less than six months) may be considered to allow time to address underlying anxiety issues, e.g. with CBT, or following an alcohol detoxification. Alcohol and BZDs are cross-tolerant, acting at the same GABA-a receptor sites, and therefore maintaining a dose of BZDs following a medically assisted alcohol withdrawal is likely to stabilise the patient and lessen the risk of relapse. The clinician will need to assess the benefits of consolidating abstinence from alcohol against the likely outcome of increasing the severity of BZD dependence by prolonging the BZD prescription. Additional risk factors such as hepatitis C status also need to be considered, tipping the balance in favour of BZD maintenance for patients who are hepatitis C positive. Oxazepam may be the BZD of choice for these patients as it is not metabolised in the liver; it has the additional advantage of slow onset and thus low abuse potential. Lorazepam, although not hepatotoxic, has high abuse liability and should be avoided. BZD prescribing should be stopped if any evidence of alcohol use relapse is observed.

Long-term maintenance

This is only indicated in a small minority of patients. There is no evidence base to support long-term BZD prescribing, but clinical experience suggests that for a very few patients the option of long-term prescribing, taking into account the adverse effects, is preferable to the alternative. A minority of patients with long-term opioid and BZD use do not stabilise on opioid substitution medication alone[56] and are unable to withdraw successfully from BZDs. Additionally, on rare occasions, patients who have identified improved coping skills on regular BZDs may be prescribed BZDs to prevent illicit use.[57] A slow-onset, long-acting BZD is likely to maximise stability and minimise diversion or abuse.

Managing patients already maintained on benzodiazepine prescription

BZDs have been widely prescribed within drug services over the last two decades for a range of reasons. Principally this has been to improve stabilisation on OST and reduce illicit opioid use, and also to assist the patient in avoiding contact with illicit sources.

169

The adverse consequences of long-term BZD use are considerable:

▸ significant impairment of cognitive function

▸ diversion of prescribed medication

▸ abuse of prescribed medication for psychotropic effect

▸ increased risk of accidental overdose

▸ increased severity of dependence and risk of protracted withdrawal syndrome.

For most patients already prescribed BZDs, long-term maintenance prescribing of BZDs is inadvisable. Today it is part of our clinical responsibility to raise with the patient the concerns of long-term maintenance and support the patient in moving towards detoxification. As these prescriptions are now long term for many patients, detoxification may be best achieved by withdrawal over many months or even years.

Future developments in the management of benzodiazepine dependence

The case for more research into the management of BZD dependence amongst illicit drug users has been extensively made. In particular, evidence on management of long-term illicit users and indications for BZD maintenance are needed.

Effective adjunctive medication for use in withdrawal is needed, and antiepileptic medication such as lamotrigine warrants further investigation. Slow infusion of flumazenil for assisted withdrawal from BZDs[58] may be a useful option for very high-dose users but it is unlikely such an intervention will be evaluated in the primary care setting.

A major problem with current regimes is the reliance on diazepam as the preferred substitute medication, supported by FP10 MDA. We know that significant quantities of prescribed diazepam are diverted. Greater exploration of the use of low abuse liability BZDs for substitution and detoxification is needed.

As the drug-using cohort ages, our attention must turn to the different challenges and health concerns of managing BZD misuse in an elderly population. Mortality in drug users can be between 12 and 22 times that of the general population and older illicit drug users are between two and six times more likely to die than younger ones.[59,60] However, there are grounds for optimism – in the only published study by Firoz and Carlson[61] older people do better than their younger counterparts, and may improve still more if services respond to their needs, and society to their marginalisation.

Use of a self-reporting questionnaire[62] may be useful in determining a more differentiated treatment approach for polysubstance use and dependence.

Conclusion

BZD use is a large problem in the illicit drug-using population. Virtually all patients who use BZDs do so as part of a polysubstance use pattern. BZDs are used to reduce anxiety, help sleep, counter the negative effects of other drugs and are also used for enhanced psychotropic effect as part of a polysubstance use pattern. Dependence can and does develop in a minority, but much use is intermittent as part of 'bingeing', and BZDs are commonly subject to abuse and diversion.

Clinicians need to be clear with the patient from the outset as to the indications for prescribed treatment. Treatment goals need to be agreed by patient, clinician and keyworker, with necessary motivational work completed prior to initiating prescribing. Only patients with proven dependence and a motivation to change their lifestyle should be commenced on prescribed BZDs. Assessment and adequate preparation for detoxification are crucial in improving outcomes and achieving abstinence.

Short-term maintenance on BZDs may be appropriate for patients with recent successful alcohol detoxification or with underlying anxiety disorders. Long-term maintenance has significant adverse effects, but may be suitable for a small minority of patients who do not stabilise on opioid substitute treatment alone.

Services need to address mental health symptoms (particularly anxiety and depression, and behaviours relating to personality disorder) alongside drug use in order to improve rates of successful detoxification.

References

1. Tyrer P. Dependence on benzodiazepines. *British Journal of Psychiatry* 1980; **137**: 576–7.

2. Petursson H, Lader M H. Withdrawal from long-term benzodiazepine treatment. *British Medical Journal (Clin Research Ed.)* 1981; **283(6292)**: 643–5.

3. Ford C, Law F, Barjolin J C. *DRAFT Guidance for the Use of Benzodiazepines and Similar Drugs in General Practice*. London: RCGP, 2011.

4. National Institute for Health and Clinical Excellence. *Clinical Guideline 113, Generalised Anxiety Disorder and Panic Disorder (with or without Agoraphobia) in Adults*. London: NICE, 2011.

5. Vogel M, Dürsteler-Macfarland K M, Walter M, *et al.* Prolonged use of benzodiazepines is associated with childhood trauma in opioid-maintained patients. *Drug and Alcohol Dependence* 2011; **119(1–2)**: 93–8.

6. Chen K W, Berger C C, Forde D P, *et al.* Benzodiazepine use and misuse among patients in a methadone program. *BMC Psychiatry* 2011; **11**: 90.

7. Lavie E, Fatséas M, Denis C, *et al.* Benzodiazepine use among opiate-dependent subjects in buprenorphine maintenance treatment: correlates of use, abuse and dependence. *Drug and Alcohol Dependence* 2009; **99(1–3)**: 338–44.

8. Perera K M H, Tulley M, Jenner F A. The use of benzodiazepines among drug addicts. *British Journal of Addiction* 1987; **82(5)**: 511–15.

9. Strang J, Griffiths P, Abbey J, *et al.* Survey of use of injected benzodiazepines among drug users in Britain. *British Medical Journal* 1994; **308(6936)**: 1082.

10. National Institute for Clinical Excellence. *Zaleplon, Zolpidem and Zopiclone for Insomnia.* London: NICE, 2004.

11. Ashton H. The diagnosis and management of benzodiazepine dependence. *Current Opinion in Psychiatry* 2005; **18(3)**: 249–55.

12. World Health Organization: *The ICD-10 Classification of Mental and Behavioural Disorders: clinical descriptions and diagnostic guidelines: 'Dependence'.* Geneva: WHO, 1992.

13. Laqueille X, Launay C, Dervaux A, *et al.* [Abuse of alcohol and benzodiazepine during substitution therapy in heroin addicts: a review of the literature] [Article in French]. *Encephale* 2009; **35(3)**: 220–5.

14. Tyrer P, Seivewright N, Murphy S, *et al.* The Nottingham study of neurotic disorder: comparison of drug and psychological treatments. *Lancet* 1988; **2(8605)**: 235–40.

15. Brands B, Blake J, Marsh D C, *et al.* The impact of benzodiazepine use on methadone maintenance treatment outcomes. *Journal of Addictive Diseases* 2008; **27(3)**: 37–48.

16. Clark R, Xie H, Brunette M. Benzodiazepine prescription practices and substance abuse in persons with severe mental illness. *Journal of Clinical Psychiatry* 2004; **65(2)**: 151–5.

17. Fatséas M, Lavie E, Denis C, *et al.* [Benzodiazepine withdrawal in subjects on opiate substitution treatment] [Article in French]. *Presse médicale* 2006; **35(4 Pt 1)**: 599–606.

18. Heikman P K, Ojanperä I A. Inadequate dose of opioid-agonist medication is related to misuse of benzodiazepines. *Addictive Disorders and Their Treatment* 2009; **8(3)**: 145–53.

19. Specka M, Bonnet U, Heilmann M, *et al.* Longitudinal patterns of benzodiazepine consumption in a German cohort of methadone maintenance treatment patients. *Human Psychopharmacology* 2011; **26**: 404–11.

20. Ciraulo D A, Sands B F, Shader R I. Critical review of the liability for benzodiazepine abuse among alcoholics. *American Journal of Psychiatry* 1988; **145(12)**: 1501–6.

21. Johansson B A, Berglund M, Hanson M, *et al.* Dependence on legal psychotropic drugs among alcoholics. *Alcohol and Alcoholism* 2003; **38(6)**: 613–18.

22. Lintzeris N, Nielsen S. Benzodiazepines, methadone and buprenorphine: interactions and clinical management. *American Journal on Addictions* 2010; **19**: 59–72. doi: 10.1111/j.1521-0391.2009.00007.x.

23. Stark K, Muller R, Bienzle U, *et al.* Methadone maintenance treatment and HIV risk-taking behaviour among injecting drug users in Berlin. *Journal of Epidemiology and Community Health* 1996; **50(5)**: 534–7.

24. Corkery J M, Schifano F, Ghodse A H. Phenazepam abuse in the UK: an emerging problem causing serious adverse health problems, including death. *Human Psychopharmacology* 2012; **27(3)**: 254–61.

25. Gandey A. Young people misusing phenazepam. *Medscape Medical News* 2011, www.medscape.com.

26. Harrison M, Busto U, Naranjo C A, *et al.* Diazepam tapering in detoxification for high-dose benzodiazepine abuse. *Clinical Pharmacology and Therapeutics* 1984; **36(4)**: 527–33.

27. Seivewright N, Dougal W. Withdrawal symptoms from high dose benzodiazepines in polydrug users. *Drug and Alcohol Dependence* 1993; **32(1)**: 15–23.

28. Nutt D J, Malizia A L. New insights into the role of the GABA(A)-benzodiazepine receptor in psychiatric disorder. *British Journal of Psychiatry* 2001; **179**: 390–6.

172

29. Allison C, Pratt JA. Neuroadaptive processes in GABAergic and glutamatergic systems in benzodiazepine dependence. *Pharmacology and Therapeutics* 2003; **98(2)**: 171–95.

30. Parran T, Jr. Prescription drug abuse. A question of balance. *Medical Clinics of North America* 1997; **81(4)**: 967–78.

31. Oliver P, Forrest R, Keen J. *Benzodiazepines and Cocaine as Risk Factors in Fatal Opioid Overdoses.* Research briefing: 31. London: NTA, 2007.

32. Drake S, Swift W, Hall W, *et al.* Drug use, HIV risk-taking, and psychosocial correlates of benzodiazepine use among methadone maintenance patients. *Drug and Alcohol Dependence* 1993; **34(1)**: 67–70.

33. de la Vega Sánchez D, Artieda Urrutia P, Gómez Arnau J, *et al.* Substance abuse is associated with a higher risk of suicide. *European Psychiatry* 2011; **26(1)**: 1–21.

34. Barker M J, Greenwood KM, Jackson M, *et al.* Cognitive effects of long-term benzodiazepine use: a meta-analysis. *CNS Drugs* 2004; **18(1)**: 37–48.

35. Vorma H, Naukkarinen H, Sarna S, *et al.* Long-term outcome after benzodiazepine withdrawal treatment in subjects with complicated dependence. *Drug and Alcohol Dependence* 2003; **70(3)**: 309–14.

36. Mol A J, Oude Voshaar R C, Gorgels W J, *et al.* The role of craving in relapse after discontinuation of long-term benzodiazepine use. *Journal of Clinical Psychiatry* 2007; **68(12)**: 1894–900.

37. Seivewright N. Theory and practice in managing benzodiazepine dependence and misuse. *Journal of Substance Use* 1998; **3(3)**: 170–7.

38. Williams H, Oyefeso A, Ghodse A H. Benzodiazepine misuse and dependence among opiate addicts in treatment. *Irish Journal of Psychological Medicine* 1996; **13**: 62–4.

39. Ciraulo D M, Ciraulo D A. Benzodiazepines: misuse, abuse, dependence. In: H S Smith, S D Passik (eds). *Pain and Chemical Dependency.* Oxford: Oxford University Press, 2008, pp. 137–44.

40. Ross J, Darke S. The nature of benzodiazepine dependence among heroin users in Sydney, Australia. *Addiction* 2000; **95(12)**: 1785–93.

41. Ashton H. Toxicity and adverse consequences of benzodiazepines use. *Psychiatric Annals* 1995; **25(3)**: 158–65.

42. Ashton H. Protracted withdrawal syndromes from benzodiazepines. *Journal of Substance Abuse Treatment* 1991; **8(1–2)**: 19–28.

43. Denis C, Fatseas M, Lavie E, *et al.* Pharmacological interventions for benzodiazepine non-dependence management in outpatient settings. In: *The Cochrane Database of Systematic Reviews.* Issue 3. Chichester: Wiley, 1996.

44. Parr J M, Kavanagh D J, Cahill L, *et al.* Effectiveness of current treatment approaches for benzodiazepine discontinuation: a meta-analysis. *Addiction* 2009; **104(1)**: 13–24.

45. Department of Health. *Drug Misuse and Dependence: UK guidelines on clinical management.* London: DH, 2007.

46. Blunka M, Williams K. Early identification, treatment, and interventions for the prevention of benzodiazepine dependence with anxiety disorders. *Mental Health and Substance Use* 2011; **4(4)**: 277–92.

47. Voshaar R C, Grgels W J, Mol E J, *et al.* Predictors of long-term benzodiazepine abstinence in participants of a randomised controlled benzodiazepine withdrawal program. *Canadian Journal of Psychiatry* 2006; **51(7)**: 445–52.

48. Lingford-Hughes, Welch S, Nutt D J. Evidence-based guidelines for the pharmacological management of substance misuse, addiction and comorbidity: recommendations from the British Association for Psychopharmacology. *Journal of Psychopharmacology* 2004; **18(3)**; 293–335.

49. Kuhn K L, Halikas J A, Kemp K D. Carbamazepine treatment of cocaine dependence in methadone maintenance patients with dual opiate-cocaine addiction. *NIDA Research Monograph* 1989; **95**: 316–17.

50. Busto U E, Sykora K, Sellers E M. A clinical scale to assess benzodiazepine withdrawal. *Journal of Clinical Psychopharmacology* 1989: **9(6)**: 412–16.

51. Soyka M. To substitute or not substitute: optimal tactics for the management of benzodiazepine dependence. *Addiction* 2010; **105(11)**: 1876–7.

52. Gossop M, Marsden J, Stewart D. *NTORS after Five Years. The National Treatment Outcome Research Study; changes in substance use, health and criminal behaviour during the five years after intake.* London: National Addiction Centre, 2001, http://webarchive.nationalarchives.gov.uk/+/ www.dh.gov.uk/en/Publicationsandstatistics/Publications/PublicationsPolicyAndGuidance/ DH_4084908 [accessed February 2013].

53. Greenwood J. Six years' experience of sharing the care of Edinburgh drug users. *Psychiatric Bulletin* 1996; **20**: 8–11.

54. Liebrenz M, Boesch L, Stohler R, *et al.* Agonist substitution: a treatment alternative for high-dose benzodiazepine-dependent patients? *Addiction* 2010; **105(11)**: 1870–4.

55. Darke S, Ross J, Teesson M, *et al.* Health service utilization and benzodiazepine use among heroin users: findings from the Australian Treatment Outcome Study (ATOS). *Addiction* 2003; **98(8)**: 1129–35.

56. Weizman T, Gelkopf M, Melamed Y, *et al.* Treatment of benzodiazepine dependence in methadone maintenance treatment patients: a comparison of two therapeutic modalities and the role of psychiatric comorbidity. *Australian and New Zealand Journal of Psychiatry* 2003; **37(4)**: 458–63.

57. Royal College of Psychiatrists. *Benzodiazepines: risks, benefits or dependence – a re-evaluation.* Council Report CR59. London: RCPsych.

58. Gerra G, Zaimovic A, Giusti F, *et al.* Intravenous flumazenil versus oxazepam tapering in the treatment of benzodiazepine withdrawal: a randomized, placebo-controlled study. *Addiction Biology* 2002; **7(4)**: 385–95.

59. Oppenheimer E, Tobutt C, Taylor C, *et al.* Death and survival in a cohort of heroin addicts from London clinics: a 22-year follow up. *Addiction* 1994; **89(10)**: 1299–308.

60. Bird S, Hutchinson S, Goldberg D. Drug-related deaths by region, sex and age group per 100 injecting drug users in Scotland, 2000–01. *Lancet* 2003; **362(9388)**: 941–4.

61. Firoz S, Carlson G. Characteristics and treatment outcome of older methadone-maintenance patients. *American Journal of Geriatric Psychiatry* 2004; **12(5)**: 539–41.

62. Kan C C, Breteler M M H, van der Ven A H, *et al.* Assessment of benzodiazepine dependence in alcohol and drug dependent outpatients: a research report. *Substance Use and Misuse* 2001; **36(8)**: 1085–90.

CHAPTER 11

Central nervous system stimulants

Jez Thompson

IN THIS CHAPTER

Introduction || Cocaine || Amphetamine || Khat || Ecstasy ||
Gammahydroxybutyrate (GHB) and gammabutyrolactone (GBL) ||
Mephedrone || Piperazines || Looking to the future and new stimulant drugs

Introduction

The term 'stimulant' relates to a diverse group of psychoactive drugs that cause a temporary increase in mental alertness, wakefulness and physical energy together with improvement in mood, self-confidence, sexual arousal and a sense of emotional wellbeing and euphoria. Because of their effects stimulants are sometimes referred to as 'uppers'. Stimulant use is associated with a range of short- and long-term harmful effects.

Stimulants are widely used throughout the world. Some occur naturally in plants and have been used locally in unprocessed forms for centuries. Purified and subsequently synthesised naturally occurring stimulants such as cocaine, and novel compounds such as amphetamine, have formed a major part of worldwide drug cultures since the beginning of the twentieth century.

A development in recent years has been the introduction of a wide range of 'designer' stimulant drugs, sometimes known as 'legal highs' or 'club drugs'. This has included compounds such as ecstasy, piperazines and mephedrone. Some have been entirely newly synthesised compounds, while others have been derivatives or modifications of known psychoactive drugs or plant extracts. They have become part of a powerful, popular and lucrative recreational youth culture, often with innovative means of sale and distribution such as marketing on the internet with delivery next day by post.

New compounds are inevitably unregulated and legal when first developed, and potentially hundreds of new products have appeared in recent years.[1] Controversy about the level of harm associated with the use of new stimulant drugs has fuelled many newspaper column inches, often sensationalist in nature,[2] and has led to conflicting information and advice to users and regulators alike. Diverse branding, the increasingly large number of products available, poor-quality manufacture and the common practice of mixing different active compounds in marketed products mean that it is difficult for consumers to identify exactly what they are taking. This has created further difficulty for those who use these drugs, and for those who attempt to assess their effects or regulate their use. Legal and regulatory systems react as rapidly and as best they can when new substances are found to be harmful (and sometimes in the UK before they are proven to be harmful through Temporary Class Orders under the Police Reform and Social Responsibility Act). However, the confusing stimulant landscape of the early twenty-first century continues to pose a significant challenge to the authorities.[1]

Currently in the UK powder and crack cocaine, ecstasy, 4-methylamphetamine and methamphetamine are regulated as Class A drugs. Amphetamine sulphate and mephedrone are Class B drugs. Piperazines, GHB and GBL are Class C drugs. Khat is not currently an illegal drug in the UK.

Tables 11.1 and 11.2 identify current patterns and trends of use of stimulant drugs in the UK.

Table 11.1   **Proportion of 16–59-year-olds reporting use of drugs (%, England and Wales)**

	Ever taken in lifetime (BCS 2010/11)	Taken in last year (BCS 2009/10)	Taken in last year (BCS 2010/11)	Statistically significant change in use, 'taken in last year', 2009/10 vs. 2010/11
Any cocaine	8.9	2.5	2.2	↓
Powder cocaine	8.8	2.4	2.1	↓
Crack cocaine	1.2	0.2	0.2	n/s
Ecstasy	8.3	1.6	1.4	n/s
Any amphetamine	11.6	1.0	1.1	n/s
Amphetamine	11.4	1.0	1.0	n/s
Methamphetamine	1.0	0.0	0.1	n/s
Benzylpiperazine			0.1	n/a
Khat			0.2	n/a
GBL/GHB			0.0	n/a
Mephedrone			1.4	n/a

Table 11.2 **Proportion of 16–24-year-olds reporting use of drugs (%, England and Wales)**

	Ever taken in lifetime (BCS 2010/11)	Taken in last year (BCS 2009/10)	Taken in last year (BCS 2010/11)	Statistically significant change in use, 'taken in last year', 2009/10 vs. 2010/11
Any cocaine	10.1	5.6	4.5	n/s
Powder cocaine	10.0	5.5	4.4	n/s
Crack cocaine	1.1	0.5	0.3	n/s
Ecstasy	9.5	4.3	3.8	n/s
Any amphetamine	8.9	2.4	2.6	n/s
Amphetamine	8.7	2.4	2.5	n/s
Methamphetamine	0.8	0.0	0.1	n/s
Benzylpiperazine			0.2	n/a
Khat			0.3	n/a
GBL/GHB			0.1	n/a
Mephedrone			4.4	n/a

Source: adapted from Smith K, Flatley J. *Drug Misuse Declared: findings from the 2010/11 British Crime Survey: England and Wales.*[3]

Cocaine

Introduction and pharmacology

Cocaine is a powerful central nervous system (CNS) stimulant. It is an alkaloid obtained originally from the leaves of the coca plant, family Erythroxylaceae, which is native to western South America.

The Inca people revered the coca bush as a plant of divine origin, chewing the leaves to increase their endurance and capacity for work, a cultural practice that persists among Andean Indians. Cocaine hydrochloride was first extracted from coca leaves in pure form in the 1850s, while its chemical structure was identified and the drug first synthesised in the 1890s. Cocaine first appeared on the commercial market in the late nineteenth century in the form of extracts of coca leaf. The best known of these extracts was Vin Mariani, a coca-wine product that was manufactured in France from around 1870. This beverage was closely followed by the development of other products, one of which evolved to become Coca-Cola (originally containing extracts from the caffeine-containing kola nut and coca leaf, the product has not contained cocaine since 1906). By the early 1900s cocaine was the primary stimulant drug used in many commercial tonics and elixirs, and notable users included Sigmund Freud, Robert Louis Stevenson and the fictional detective Sherlock Holmes.

Pharmacologically, once in the CNS, cocaine causes a blockade of the dopamine transporter protein, causing dopamine accumulation in the synaptic cleft and prolonged dopaminergic signalling at the receiving neurone. Cocaine also affects serotonin metabolism by inhibiting the re-uptake of 5-HT3. Potentiation of dopaminergic and serotonergic systems is responsible for the stimulation and euphoria associated with cocaine use. Habitual cocaine use results in down-regulation of dopamine receptors, which may contribute to the reinforcement of cocaine use to counteract this effect and to the depressive mood change when cocaine use is stopped.

Cocaine has a direct action on peripheral nerves, blocking sodium channels and inhibiting normal impulse transmission, resulting in local anaesthesia. Codeine has an additional effect on the noradrenergic system, causing vasoconstriction both locally and systemically together with an increase in blood pressure and pulse rate. Cocaine is metabolised by the liver.

Though the non-medical possession, distribution and sale of cocaine was first made illegal in the UK in the Defence of the Realm Act 1916, cocaine is still available for legal medicinal use and is indicated as a local anaesthetic for some eye, ear and throat procedures.

Cocaine is well absorbed via a number of routes, and may be insufflated into the nose, rubbed directly onto the buccal mucosa (both typically powder cocaine), vaporised and inhaled, or dissolved and injected (typically crack cocaine). After injection or inhalation, peak concentrations are reached within seconds or minutes. This is delayed to around 60 minutes when cocaine is taken intranasally or via the buccal mucosa. Crack therefore produces a faster onset and shorter lasting 'high' than powder cocaine. The stimulant effect of both diminishes after as little as one hour after use, often leading to frequent re-dosing to maintain the stimulant effect.

Patterns of cocaine use

Starting in the USA, cocaine again became a very widespread recreational drug in the 1980s, with the development of 'crack' cocaine in the mid-1980s introducing the substance to a generally poorer, more inner-city market. Within the UK, the BCS has shown the proportion of 16–59-year-olds reporting 'ever' use of cocaine (any type) in their lifetime increasing from 3.1% in 1996, to a peak of 9.4% in 2008/9, and declining slightly to 8.9% in 2010/11. Of these totals, crack cocaine use was 0.7% in 1996, with a slow, generally upward trend, rising to 1.2% in 2010/11 (see Table 11.1 on p. 176).[3]

Table 11.3 **Effects of cocaine use**

Immediate effects (high)	Increased energy.
	Mental alertness.
	Decreased appetite.
	Increased blood pressure.
	Increased pulse rate.
	Increase in core body temperature.
	Dilated pupils.
	Increased activity, talkativeness and restlessness.
	Increased self-confidence
Effects of high doses	Tremor.
	Headache.
	Confusion.
	Occasionally fits.
	Rarely respiratory arrest
Later effects (come down)	Irritability.
	Anxiety.
	Depression.
	Restlessness.
	Persecutory ideas.
	Auditory hallucinations.
	Tactile hallucinations (formication).
	Insomnia.
	Suicidal ideation
Psychological dependence	Tolerance.
	Craving.
	Neglect of other pleasures or interests.
	Continued use despite harmful effects
Tissue damage	Damage to nasal septum (insufflators).
	Damage to lung (smokers).
	Damage to local tissues and DVT (injectors)

Source: adapted from Gerada G, Ford C. Central nervous system stimulants. In C Gerada (ed.). *RCGP Guide to the Management of Substance Misuse in Primary Care*. London: RCGP, 2005, pp. 149–69.

Within the English drug treatment system, 2010 figures show that 6560 clients were identified as crack-only problem drug users (3% of the treatment population) with 64,602 having both opioid and crack use problems.[4] Five percent (10,915) had powder cocaine as their main drug used.

Within illicit drug use cultures, cocaine is used in a variety of forms. In its original powdered form (cocaine hydrochloride, street names 'coke', 'charlie'), cocaine is most commonly used intransasally ('snorting' or 'sniffing'), when it is absorbed through the nasal mucosa. The powder is placed on a very flat surface, such as a mirror, chopped with a razor blade to pulverise any lumps, cut into 'lines', then insufflated via a straw. In some cocaine-using subcultures the straw may be a rolled-up high-denomination bank note. Powder cocaine may alternatively be rubbed directly onto the gums for direct absorption. 'Freebase' is an alkaline powder preparation of cocaine prepared for smoking.

Crack cocaine (also known as 'rock', 'stone', 'white') is a form of freebase cocaine that is usually produced by neutralisation of cocaine hydrochloride with a solution of baking soda and water, to form a brittle, off-white, waxy rock-like material that has a very low point of vaporisation (around 90°C). The name 'crack' refers to the noise made when the 'rocks' are heated in order to be smoked via a crack pipe. To smoke, the rock is typically placed on a bed of cigarette ash on a crack pipe, which may be purpose made or improvised from a tin can or a plastic bottle. Direct heat is then applied to the volatile rock, usually by holding a lighter flame to it, and the vapour is then inhaled through the pipe. Crack cocaine is frequently dissolved and injected, often in combination with heroin (see Table 11.4).

Table 11.4 **Routes of cocaine use**

Nasal insufflation ('sniffing' or 'snorting')	Most common with powder cocaine
Piping	Most common with crack cocaine where direct heat is applied to a rock and the vapour inhaled via a pipe
Injecting	Cocaine powder or crack is dissolved and then injected
Chasing	Like heroin, crack cocaine can be heated on tinfoil and the vapour 'chased' and inhaled
Smoking/chipping	This involves flaking small amounts of cocaine, freebase or crack into the top of a tobacco cigarette to form a 'joint'. Typically less cocaine is absorbed through this route

Source: adapted from Gerada G, Ford C. Central nervous system stimulants. In C Gerada (ed.). *RCGP Guide to the Management of Substance Misuse in Primary Care*. London: RCGP, 2005, pp. 149–69.

The pattern of cocaine use varies considerably (see Table 11.5). 'Recreational' use is relatively common, with individuals taking the drug only occasionally. This is often in association with social activities or parties and includes regular week-end use. Patterns of regular daily use occur, as does heavy and intermittent use or 'bingeing'. Binges take the form of rapidly repeated dosing of the drug as the intensity of each 'high' decreases, often in escalating amounts over a period of hours or days, terminating in a 'crash' with exhaustion and depressive symptoms.

Table 11.5 **Patterns of cocaine use**

Recreational user	Infrequent user, shares with friends and tends not to have a regular pattern of use. May have short-term negative effects after using, but this user tends to run into problems only if use escalates
Binge user	Actively seeks powder or crack cocaine, will re-dose frequently during a session and may use large quantities in one session. Probably experiences several physical or psychological problems including 'come down' or withdrawal phenomena. This person may present for help
Chronic high-dose user (may be associated with psychological dependence)	Likely to consume several times daily and potentially in high quantities. Some users demonstrate life-threatening use. Daily activities and values may centre heavily on acquisition of money, purchase of cocaine and using the drug. Other relationships, activities and work are likely to be affected by cocaine use. The user is very likely to experience significant psychological, social and physical problems relating to cocaine use

Source: adapted from Gerada G, Ford C. Central nervous system stimulants. In C Gerada (ed.). *RCGP Guide to the Management of Substance Misuse in Primary Care*. London: RCGP, 2005, pp. 149–69.

Cocaine may be used in association with other drugs such as amphetamine, alcohol, benzodiazepines or heroin, either to intensify the effect of cocaine, or to manage the symptoms of 'coming down' following use. The injecting of heroin together with cocaine in powder or crack form ('speedballing' or 'snowballing') is a high-risk practice that has become prevalent.

To get from the leaf produced in the highlands of the coca-producing countries to the user in a processed and purified form, cocaine passes through many hands, and is diluted at each stage to increase profit margins. For that reason, the average gram 'wrap' of powder cocaine in the UK is typically between 40 and 60% actual cocaine.[5] The rest is a mixture of bulking agents or other stimulants, including caffeine, glucose, mannitol, cornstarch, vitamin C powder, sugar, talcum powder, baby milk powder and possibly local anaesthetic (to simulate the numbing effect of cocaine). Crack cocaine is typically 60–70% pure, and the purity has fallen considerably in recent years.[5]

In 2010 the price for powder cocaine in the UK was around £40 per gram, whereas crack was more expensive at around £50 per gram, or £10–£20 per rock, with prices depending on purity and the area of the country.[6] A typical recreational powder cocaine user may use 0.5–1g in a session. A single dose of crack is typically one rock, while a heavy crack user on a binge may use tens of rocks over a short period of time.

Harmful effects of cocaine use

Cocaine use has a number of negative physical and mental health effects, some of which can be serious and life threatening.

Because of cocaine's stimulant effects on the noradrenergic system, heavy use carries significant risks of cardiovascular complications, including angina, myocardial infarction and stroke.

Sudden death can occur on the first use of cocaine or unexpectedly thereafter, even with low doses. Deaths may be the result of cardiac arrest or seizures following respiratory depression.

Physical effects from smoking cocaine (with inhalation not only of the drug, but also of elements from the crack pipe including tobacco ash and products of burning paint and plastics when home-made pipes are used) include breathlessness and haemoptysis, chest pain and hoarse voice. The lips may be burnt when a flame is applied to a crack pipe, and this may be potentiated by the local numbing effect of the drug.

Regular intranasal use causes vasoconstriction in the blood supply to the nasal cartilage, which may lead to septal perforation and destruction.

Heavy cocaine use causes tachycardia, and can result in the development of tachyarrhythmias. Cocaine is a constrictor of blood vessels, and leads to a significant rise in blood pressure soon after the drug is taken, with a risk of stroke. In long-term users, surges in blood pressure can contribute to the development of arterial disease, so that a regular cocaine user as young as 25–30 years without any other risk factor may develop coronary artery disease as a result of cocaine use. Reports from the USA suggest that as many as one in four myocardial infarctions in people aged 18–45 are linked to cocaine use[7] and one study has shown that the risk of a heart attack is increased 23-fold in the hour following cocaine use. Dissection of the aorta has also been reported in cocaine users, as has mesenteric ischaemia and infarction.[8, 9]

As with all psychostimulants, cocaine may cause seizures. Brain perfusion deficits and associated neuropsychological compromise (such as problems with attention, concentration, new learning, visual and verbal memory, and word production) may be persistent. Cocaine use can lead to impairments in cognitive function through decreased perfusion and multiple small ischaemic infarcts. Tics, stereotypes of speech or movement, ataxia and disturbed gait may occur, and may disappear after cocaine use is stopped. Some regular users develop tactile hallucinations, likened to the feeling of ants crawling under the skin (formication).

Mental health effects of cocaine use are common. Because of cocaine's direct effects on brain neurotransmitter chemistry, dysphoria, bad dreams, anxiety and depression may follow use. Depression may be severe in heavy users and become associated with suicidal ideation and behaviour. A psychotic episode, especially involving paranoid delusions together with an increase in aggressive and violent behaviour, is a risk of heavy binge use. In some psychotic episodes confusion and aggressive behaviour have developed, and the individual has required restraint prior to treatment. During such restraint, however, sudden deaths have been reported.

The majority of mental health symptoms usually resolve over hours or days after stopping cocaine use but some may be more persistent. Cognitive impairment may be permanent and may affect the ability of the individual to take part in treatment successfully.

Cocaine use is associated with increased risk of autoimmune diseases such as Goodpasture's syndrome and glomerulonephritis.

Cocaine use appears to increase the risk of the transmission of HIV, not only through the potential vectors of shared needles and smoking or snorting paraphernalia, but also through increased sexual activity, loss of sexual inhibition and increased at-risk sexual behaviour while using. Injecting use of cocaine exposes the user to a further range of health effects including local tissue damage (compounded by the local anaesthetic effect and repeated re-dosing) and, for groin injectors, deep-vein thrombosis (DVT).

Crack cocaine has for some time been associated in the press with violent behaviour relating to its marketing and use. However, it is likely that it is the same sociodemographic characteristics, psychiatric variables and non-cocaine substance use disorders that make some individuals more likely to use crack cocaine that are responsible for the increased prevalence of violence observed among crack users, rather than crack itself.[10]

Cocaine use and pregnancy

Miscarriage, premature birth, stillbirth, placental abruption and low birth weight are reported consequences of maternal cocaine use during pregnancy. The mediator for many of these effects is thought to be primarily the vasoconstrictor effects of cocaine on placental vessels.

Many cocaine-using women do not maintain adequate nutrition, do not attend antenatal appointments and use other drugs that could themselves be harmful to the foetus, including alcohol and tobacco. Supporting pregnant women, and cocaine-exposed children and their families, is an important task for all health professionals.

With respect to fears of teratogenic effects on the foetus, numbers of studies over the past decade have indicated that the primary contribution of cocaine has been greatly exaggerated, and that other factors are responsible for many of the long-term effects found in the infants of heavy cocaine users.[11]

Cocaine dependence

There is persisting debate about the presence or otherwise of a cocaine dependence syndrome. Undoubtedly some regular and heavy users become tolerant to the effects of the drug, requiring larger amounts to achieve the required effect. Users may crave using the drug and feel a strong or irresistible compulsion to use. Many may find it difficult to control their cocaine-using behaviour, may neglect other activities or relationships in order to use, and may continue to use the drug despite the clear development of harmful effects. This amounts to a psychological dependence, and although there is a 'come down' from using the drug, including for example anxiety and depression, this is a primary effect of a drug that results in neurotransmitter depletion and receptor down-regulation, and does not amount to a recognised physical withdrawal syndrome.

It is interesting to note that the early media presentation of crack cocaine undoubtedly exaggerated its dependence potential. For example, crack was described in one serious newspaper as 'instantly addictive and undoubtedly deadly'.[12]

Concomitant cocaine and other drug/alcohol use

Cocaine users frequently use cocaine in conjunction with other stimulants, such as amphetamines, in order to maximise the stimulant effect. In addition users often take other sedative drugs to terminate an episode of use and alleviate 'come down' effects. These additional drugs are typically cannabis, alcohol, benzodiazepines and heroin. There is evidence that alcohol and cocaine combine synergistically to cause more harm for the user than the combined effects of either drug taken separately, and thus increase the overall morbidity and mortality associated with cocaine use. The combination increases the euphoriant effects of cocaine through the production in the liver of cocaethylene, a long-acting ethyl homologue of cocaine, which may increase the risk of sudden death.

Treatment for cocaine users

Given the diversity of the cocaine-using population, patterns of use and the differing needs of each user, treatment interventions are ideally provided at a range of levels. Key principles of good service provision include:

184

▸ easy access to services (including opening times, location and timeliness)

▸ multiple points of entry to treatment

▸ person-centred and simple assessment procedures

▸ information, advice and support services

▸ pharmacological and psychosocial interventions when required

▸ effective referral procedures and an integrated approach to providing treatment and care (including specialist mental health and blood-borne virus care)

▸ support for families and children of psychostimulant users when needed

▸ access to social care and accommodation.[13]

Within primary care, potential roles include: identification of problematic cocaine use; brief interventions and other psychosocial interventions designed to help the user control, reduce and stop use; harm reduction advice; mental health and risk assessment; and signposting and referral. They may be most successful if associated with non-judgemental and positive attitudes to working with stimulant users. The National Treatment Agency puts it simply: 'Treating patients with crack dependence is neither extraordinarily difficult nor does it necessarily depend on totally new skills.'[14]

Pharmacological approaches

Though the subject of much study, no proven pharmacological treatment for cocaine misuse exists. There is little evidence to support any prescribed treatment, either to provide symptomatic relief during withdrawal or detoxification or as a substitute medication.

One review of the use of psychostimulant drugs in cocaine use (including drugs metabolised to a psychostimulant) included 16 studies using variously bupropion, dexamphetamine, methylphenidate, modafinil, mazindol, methamphetamine and selegiline. Overall the review found that treatment with psychostimulants did not improve levels of cocaine use, had an unclear beneficial effect in maintaining cocaine abstinence and were not associated with higher retention in treatment.[15]

Another review included 37 studies of antidepressant therapy, namely desipramine, fluoxetine and bupropion, in cocaine use. The review found that any positive results obtained with antidepressants on mood-related outcomes were consistent simply with the primary effect of the antidepressants. Antidepressant treatment was not associated with any positive effect on direct indicators of cocaine misuse or dependence. The study concluded that current evidence from randomised controlled trials does not support the use of antidepressants in the treatment of cocaine use.[16]

Pani *et al.* conducted a review of seven studies that used disulfiram in the treatment of cocaine use. They found a low level of evidence to support the clinical use of disulfiram for the treatment of cocaine use, for example an increased number of weeks of consecutive abstinence when disulfiram was compared with placebo. The authors concluded that larger, randomised investigations are needed to confirm these outcomes.[17]

In another review authors identified 17 randomised controlled trials involving the use of anticonvulsant medication to treat cocaine use. The anticonvulsant drugs studied were carbamazepine, gabapentin, lamotrigine, phenytoin, tiagabine, topiramate and valproate. No significant differences were found between any anticonvulsant and placebo in reducing the number of dropouts from treatment, use of cocaine, craving or severity of dependence, depression or anxiety. The conclusion was there is no current evidence to support the clinical use of anticonvulsant medication in the treatment of cocaine dependence.[18]

A further review considered 23 studies of dopamine agonists (dopamine and amantadine) in the treatment of cocaine use. The authors concluded that current evidence from randomised controlled trials does not support the use of dopamine agonists for treating cocaine dependence.[19]

Naltrexone in combination with relapse prevention therapy has been shown to be of potential help in reducing relapse for cocaine-dependent clients.[20]

Cocaine-related mood problems may require treatment, though the use of antidepressant pharmacotherapies in a client who continues to use cocaine may be relatively ineffective owing to the neurotransmitter effects of the drug, and may increase the risk of serotonin syndrome. MAOI use in conjunction with cocaine may have severe and dangerous complications. Users may request prescribed benzodiazepines or other sedative drugs to manage the symptoms of the withdrawal phase following heavy use, and any consideration of this must be seen in the context of prescribing for short-term and self-limiting symptoms in a known misuser of drugs. There is the potential for even short courses of benzodiazepines to result in worse anxiety when the treatment is stopped, and this may prompt the user to seek out ongoing supplies of benzodiazepines, whether licit or illicit. Cocaine-induced psychosis may require assessment by mental health services and the short-term use of antipsychotic medication.

Pharmacological approaches to cocaine use in opioid dependence

In routine substance misuse treatment adequate maintenance treatment in clients with opioid dependence in addition to cocaine use is associated with reduced cocaine use.[21]

Psychosocial interventions

Simple information and advice is helpful at all stages of the management of the cocaine user. In particular, reassurance during any withdrawal phase that symptoms are self-limiting and short in duration is useful. Brief interventions focused on changing behaviour may be of value[22] and have a potential role in the primary care setting.

Studies have found that an abstinence-based psychotherapeutic approach, which incorporates counselling, formal psychosocial intervention and social support, has the greatest impact on cocaine use.[21] Contingency management, where clients are given rewards such as financial incentives for achieving goals, has been found to be successful in promoting abstinence from cocaine,[23] though has not been widely adopted in the UK. Relaxation and stress-reducing techniques may be useful when clients experience anxiety.

Clients with multiple substance misuse problems may benefit from intensive residential rehabilitation and can potentially have better outcomes than with community-based drug counselling and treatment approaches.[24] However, intensive rehabilitation programmes may potentially be provided equally effectively on a day-care basis.

In 1999, the results from the National Institute on Drug Abuse's Collaborative Cocaine Treatment study were published.[25] This US study aimed to determine the most effective psychosocial therapy for cocaine dependence and compared individual drug counselling therapy plus group drug counselling (GDC), cognitive therapy plus GDC, supportive–expressive counselling plus GDC, and GDC alone over six months. Individual drug counselling plus GDC, which incorporated a 12-step philosophy, was the most effective in reducing cocaine use. The authors proposed that the success of the individual therapy might have been because it focused most strongly on stopping current drug use.

Current national guidance within the UK is that Cognitive Behavioural Therapy (CBT) and psychodynamic therapy should not be offered routinely to people presenting for treatment of cocaine or other stimulant use. However, CBT should be considered for the treatment of co-morbid depression and anxiety disorders in people who misuse stimulants.[23]

Behavioural couples therapy should be considered for people who have a non-drug-misusing partner and who present for treatment of cocaine use.[23]

Mutual aid

Cocaine Anonymous is a mutual self-help group based on the 12-step tradition in which cocaine users are able to share their experiences and hopes, and receive support with the aim of addressing cocaine use (www.cauk.org.uk).

Harm reduction approaches

There are a number of principles of safer drug use that can be discussed with the drug user to reduce the harm associated with powder and crack cocaine use.

For the powder cocaine user advice may include using a nasal spray or water to clean the nostrils after use to reduce the risk of damage or perforation of the nasal septum. Shared straws or rolled-up bank notes may be a transmission vector for HCV or other blood-borne virus (BBV) infection. Users may be advised to avoid bingeing – cocaine users can find themselves taking the drug multiple times in one session. Multiple re-dosing increases the risk of overdose and increases the severity of the 'crash' after a session. A simple measure may be to limit the money taken on a night out and to leave all ATM cards behind. Similarly, using more cocaine to self-medicate the 'come down' will increase the intensity of the withdrawal symptoms in the long run. Good advice is to stop using for as long as possible to allow the body to recover.

Those with more severe depression and/or anxiety associated with use should be advised to cease use. A simple explanation of the neurobiological effects of cocaine use may help the user to make an informed choice about the risks of continued use. Users should be aware of the danger of precipitating acute mental health problems including acute psychosis while using cocaine.

Recreational users should be given safer-sex advice and encouraged to take condoms with them when planning to use cocaine. Users should be given information about the harmful effects of using cocaine with other drugs, including alcohol.

Harm reduction advice for crack users includes the above. In addition crack users need to be careful not to burn their face when using crack pipes and to hold lighters as far away as possible. Sharing pipes is a known vector for transmission of HCV and other BBV infections, and should be avoided. Use of Pyrex pipes is safer than glass pipes, and the use of home-made crack pipes made from drink cans or plastic bottles is particularly dangerous because of the inhalation of various products of combustion when the pipe is heated. To make a pipe safer, a screen can protect from inhalation of particles such as cigarette ash, and wrapping the pipe end in paper can reduce burning of the lips.

Injecting users need to be aware of the increased risks of BBV transmission, and the dangers of DVT if groin injecting. BBV testing and immunisation may be appropriate harm reduction interventions.

Female cocaine and crack users should be advised about the risks of using during pregnancy.

Liaison with social agencies may reduce harm for families in highly problematic users.

Complementary therapy approaches

A number of complementary approaches have been suggested, though most have not been subject to study. Seven studies were included in a review of auricular acupuncture for cocaine dependence. All were of generally low methodological quality. No differences between acupuncture and sham acupuncture or acupuncture and no acupuncture were found for any measure of cocaine or other drug use. The authors concluded there is currently no evidence that auricular acupuncture is effective for the treatment of cocaine dependence.[26]

Cocaine vaccine

A 'cocaine vaccine' could be a promising immunotherapeutic approach to managing cocaine use. It induces the immune system to form antibodies that prevent cocaine from crossing the blood–brain barrier to act on receptor sites in the brain. Preliminary studies in rats have shown that cocaine antibodies can block cocaine from reaching the brain and prevent reinstatement of cocaine self-administration. A successful phase 1 trial of a human cocaine vaccine has been reported.[27] The most promising application of a vaccine may be to prevent relapse to use or dependence in abstinent users who voluntarily enter treatment. Any potential use of a vaccine to treat cocaine addicts under legal coercion raises major ethical issues.[28]

Amphetamine

Introduction and pharmacology

The term amphetamine is used for a range of stimulant drugs including amphetamine sulphate (a racemic mixture of both levoamphetamine and dextroamphetamine, street names 'billy', 'whiz', 'speed', 'bennies', and trade name Benzedrine) and dextroamphetamine (or dexamphetamine, also known as 'dexies', trade name Dexedrine). Both the above types of amphetamine may be marketed as a paste, a crystalline white powder or in tablet form, and are taken orally, nasally or injected. As with other psychostimulants amphetamine boosts energy, increases alertness and wakefulness, improves mood and decreases appetite in the short term. The related compound methamphetamine, another crystalline white powder, has stronger and longer-lasting effects than amphetamine, and is most commonly smoked as larger crystals known as 'crystal meth', 'ice' or 'glass'. Crystal meth may also be used orally, intranasally or by injection, and produces a particularly intense high lasting 4–12 hours. Along with a more marked stimulant effect methamphetamine is associated with a greater tendency to produce tolerance and escalating use, a more severe 'crash' after use and a greater prevalence of mood disturbance with regular use.

Amphetamine was first synthesised in the 1880s as a derivative of ephedrine, a naturally occurring adrenergic and stimulant compound that is found in a variety of plant sources. However, it wasn't until the 1930s that amphetamine was marketed as a medical product under the trade name Benzedrine, initially as an inhaler to relieve bronchospasm and nasal congestion, and later in tablet form in the management of narcolepsy and a range of other conditions. Amphetamines have more recently been used in the treatment of attention deficit disorder in children, where it can produce a paradoxical reduction in hyperactivity. Amphetamine derivatives have for many years been used, and misused, as 'diet pills' because of their appetite-suppressant effects.

Soon recognised as a potent stimulant, amphetamine was given to soldiers to combat fatigue and improve alertness during the Second World War, and by the 1950s amphetamine was being used outside the forces as a recreational stimulant. From the 1960s, amphetamine use has been popular within a number of youth subcultures in Britain, including mods and punks, and is used to increase energy at parties and all-night dances. Amphetamines have been used within sports, particularly cycling, to improve performance, where their use has been associated with sudden death.[29] They may be used on a 'one-off' basis by those wanting to stay awake for prolonged periods, for example cramming for exams or driving through the night.

Amphetamine exerts its central stimulant effects by modulating neurotransmitter activity in specific areas of the brain, in particular dopamine- and serotonin-based systems. Amphetamine has been shown to increase the concentrations of both these transmitters in the synaptic cleft, primarily by triggering presynaptic leakage, thereby heightening the response of the post-synaptic neurone, and producing a stimulant effect.

In the rest of the body amphetamine has a sympathomimetic effect, causing tachycardia, arrhythmias, vasoconstriction and raised blood pressure. Amphetamine may increase intraocular pressure and aggravate glaucoma.

Amphetamines may have a serious harmful reaction if used together with MAOI antidepressant tablets.

Patterns of amphetamine use

Amphetamines have been misused almost continually since their introduction into medical practice. The ease of synthesis from inexpensive and readily available chemicals makes widespread illicit amphetamine production possible. Of 180 million people worldwide consuming illicit drugs in the late 1990s, 29 million were taking amphetamine-type stimulants.[30] This figure was larger than the number of people consuming cocaine and opioids combined. An Australian multi-city study looking at injecting drug users found that amphetamines were the drugs most commonly first injected (45.8%) and almost half of the 872 study sample had used amphetamines in the month prior to the interview (94.4% of whom had injected them).[31] More recent figures from the UK show almost 12% of adults and almost 9% of young adults have used amphetamine at some time during their lifetime (see Table 11.1 on p. 176 and Table 11.2 on p. 177).[3] For people in drug treatment in England in 2009/10, amphetamine was the main drug for 3858 clients and an adjunctive drug for 7259, out of around 200,000 clients in total.[4]

Routes and patterns of amphetamine use are complex and changeable, and vary between users, geographical regions and socioeconomic groups. Amphetamine can be taken orally (as tablets or a paste or powder wrapped in a cigarette paper and swallowed, or the powder added to a soft drink), injected (dissolved powder, crushed tablets or methamphetamine crystals), intranasally (as a powder that is prepared in a similar way to powder cocaine) or smoked (as amphetamine base or crystal methamphetamine).

A number of regular amphetamine users make the transition from oral or intranasal to injecting use, and for many this occurs after about two years of use.[32] Once users begin injecting they may be reluctant to return to snorting or swallowing. Taken intravenously, the abuse potential of amphetamines has been said to be comparable to that of heroin or cocaine.[33] Injecting amphetamine use is associated with more frequent use, higher risk of tolerance, poorer social function and greater psychological morbidity.

The World Health Organization has classified the patterns of amphetamine use as: [34]

1. *Instrumental use* – amphetamines are exploited by the users to achieve desired goals, such as to improve concentration and ward off fatigue

2. *Subcultural/recreational use* – amphetamine stimulant properties are exploited to allow the user to remain active for longer periods in social/recreational settings, such as at music and dance events

3. *Chronic use* – for several reasons, such as craving, tolerance and withdrawal, some amphetamine users turn into chronic users to relieve unwanted effects of abstinence.

The purity of amphetamine powder seizures has remained fairly stable over the years at around 8.6%, with caffeine and glucose the most common adulterants found in amphetamine powder. Other substances found in marketed amphetamine include methamphetamine, MDMA, cocaine, ketamine, ephedrine, phenacetin and selegiline.[35] UK street prices of amphetamine in 2010 were around £11 per gram and £23 per gram for methamphetamine.[6]

Harmful effects of amphetamine use

The Diagnostic and Statistical Manual of Mental Disorders, Fourth Edition (DSM IV) describes the following ten psychiatric-related disorders linked to amphetamine use:[36]

1. Amphetamine-induced anxiety disorder

2. Amphetamine-induced mood disorder

3. Amphetamine-induced psychotic disorder with delusions

4. Amphetamine-induced psychotic disorder with hallucinations

5. Amphetamine-induced sexual dysfunction

6. Amphetamine-induced sleep disorder

7. Amphetamine intoxication

8. Amphetamine intoxication with delirium

9. Amphetamine withdrawal

10. Amphetamine-related disorder not otherwise specified.

Common negative effects associated with amphetamine use include headache, hyperactivity and short-term difficulty in sleeping. Users may experience palpitations and tremor. Bruxism (teeth grinding) may occur in users of amphetamines and related stimulants.

Following a period of amphetamine use the 'come down' can last several days, with subjective feelings of tiredness, lethargy, excessive sleep and poor concentration. Regular users may be predisposed to catching viral illnesses and colds. In the longer term, regular amphetamine use can lead to chronic anxiety and depression. Short- and long-term heavy use is associated with irritability, aggression and potentially suicidal behaviour, and may result in persecutory ideas, irrational fear and acute psychosis with visual, auditory and tactile hallucinations. These symptoms are short lived and resolve over a short number of days when use of the drug is stopped. Injecting use may be associated with damage to veins and skin ulceration, and with viral hepatitis and HIV infection.

Death in amphetamine users is rare but, where it has occurred, it is usually attributable to accidents, cerebrovascular haemorrhages, acute cardiac failure and suicide.[37]

Dependence

The potential for an amphetamine dependence syndrome has been the subject of debate.

There is no doubt that some users crave the drug, feel compelled to use it and continue to use it despite the presence of harm. Tolerance to the stimulant effect is clear for some users, but not all. For the regular user, stopping use may result in an unpleasant rebound effect, characterised by nocturnal insomnia and paradoxical daytime drowsiness, lethargy, low mood, irritability and anxiety. These features are likely to be due to the neurotransmitter depletion caused by regular amphetamine use and do not represent a true physical withdrawal state or syndrome. Thus a psychological dependence to amphetamine may be a feature for some heavy and regular users, though this is likely to represent a small minority, and a physical dependence syndrome does not occur.

Treatment for amphetamine users

Despite the prevalence of its use, information from the BCS and National Treatment Agency for Substance Misuse (NTA) annual reports show that amphetamine users in the UK infrequently access formal treatment services.[3, 4] Three-quarters of amphetamine users surveyed in an Australian study had tried to reduce their use without professional assistance. Of these, 93% successfully reduced their amphetamine use and 83% were satisfied with the outcome.[38]

The management of amphetamine use has similarities to that of cocaine, with a focus on harm reduction, psychosocial treatments and the management of complications of use. Pharmacological treatments have generally not been shown to be effective in the management of amphetamine use, and therefore psychosocial interventions form the mainstay of treatment.

Pharmacological approaches

Although the number of amphetamine users worldwide is large, very few controlled trials in the pharmacological management of amphetamine use have been conducted. The limited evidence available suggests that no treatment has been demonstrated to be effective in the treatment of amphetamine misuse.

One review study focused on potential pharmacological treatment modalities for amphetamine use including fluoxetine, amlodipine, imipramine and desipramine. Four trials were considered. The authors concluded that the studied medications have limited benefits in the treatment of amphetamine dependence and abuse. Fluoxetine may decrease craving in short-term treatment and imipramine may increase the duration of adherence to treatment in medium-term treatment. However, apart from these, no other benefits were found.[39]

Shoptaw et al. reviewed four randomised controlled trials that studied the management of amphetamine withdrawal supported with amineptine or mirtazapine.[40] Amineptine significantly reduced treatment drop-out rates and improved overall clinical presentation, but did not reduce withdrawal symptoms or craving compared with placebo. Amineptine is not available for use due to concerns over abuse potential. The benefits of mirtazapine over placebo for reducing amphetamine withdrawal symptoms were not clear. One study suggested that mirtazapine may reduce the hyperarousal and anxiety symptoms associated with amphetamine withdrawal but a second study failed to find any benefit of mirtazapine over placebo on rates of retention in treatment or on the severity of amphetamine withdrawal symptoms. The authors concluded that there is no medication that has been shown to be effective for the treatment of amphetamine withdrawal.

Another review considered the management of amphetamine-related psychosis, but found only one eligible study. Outcomes from this trial indicated that antipsychotic medications effectively reduced the symptoms of amphetamine psychosis. The newer generation and more expensive antipsychotic medication, olanzapine, demonstrated significantly better tolerability than haloperidol.[41]

Health professionals may be asked to prescribe for depressive symptoms related to amphetamine use. Prescribers must balance the likely limited effectiveness of antidepressant treatment, and the risk of causing serotonin syndrome as long as amphetamine use continues, against the client's need for assistance. Additionally, withdrawal from amphetamines may be accompanied by requests for benzodiazepines or other hypnotics to help manage resultant sleeplessness or anxiety. Again, the potential benefits for the client must be seen against the risks of diversion of prescribed medication and the addition of a potential benzodiazepine misuse problem on top of an already complicated situation.

Amphetamine substitute treatment

Dextroamphetamine sulphate (trade name Dexedrine) is the most frequently studied substitute drug for amphetamine users and is currently prescribed in England and Wales for the treatment of primary amphetamine use and dependence. It was estimated in 1995 that there were between 900 and 1000 people in the UK being prescribed amphetamine.[42]

Proponents of oral amphetamine substitution therapy argue that:

1. There is a need for an appropriate and effective intervention for amphetamine users, and that current treatment modalities for illicit drug users are irrelevant to their needs, in that they are oriented primarily to opioid users or to symptomatic relief on abrupt amphetamine withdrawal[43]

2. Oral amphetamine substitution can allow patients to stabilise on a dose of prescribed medication that causes neither withdrawal nor craving, and thereafter facilitate a subsequent gradual dose reduction and eventual cessation of amphetamine use

3. Needle sharing by amphetamine users makes substitute amphetamine prescribing an important public health and harm reduction approach in the prevention of BBV transmission, a potential for good that may outweigh the risks associated with prescribing.

However, there are a number of counter-arguments why amphetamines should not be prescribed, including risks of toxicity of prescribed dextroamphetamine, the risk of precipitating acute psychosis, the potential for diversion of prescribed medication, difficulties with monitoring illicit use and the lack of a strong evidence base for its effectiveness. In addition, many amphetamine users are not regular or dependent users, and therefore there is a significant risk of increasing drug use, tolerance, psychological dependence and contributing to further instability when prescribing substitute medication.

The 2007 Clinical Guidelines sum up: 'Even though there may be individual patients for whom existing treatment should be continued for the time being, substitute stimulant prescribing does not have demonstrated effectiveness and, accordingly, should not ordinarily be provided.'[21]

Psychosocial interventions

As in the management of cocaine use, simple information and advice is helpful at all stages of the management of the amphetamine user. Brief interventions that focus on changing behaviour may be of value in helping clients to reduce use.[44]

Current UK guidance is that CBT and psychodynamic therapy should not be offered routinely to people presenting for treatment of amphetamine or other stimulant use, but CBT should be considered for the treatment of co-morbid depression and anxiety disorders for people who misuse stimulants.[23]

Behavioural couples therapy should be considered for people who have a non-drug-misusing partner and who present for treatment of amphetamine use.[23]

Contingency management has been shown to be effective in facilitating the short-term achievement of abstinence or reduction of amphetamine use in a number of studies.[23]

Reassurance during any withdrawal phase that symptoms are self-limiting and short in duration is useful. However, in a small percentage of cases amphetamine use and withdrawal may precipitate significant psychological symptoms such as anxiety, low mood, depression, self-harm and suicide, violence, agitation and depression, and these may require a full mental health assessment, treatment (which may include short-term antipsychotic medication) and careful monitoring. For younger users this may include close liaison with suitable child and adolescent mental health teams.

Harm reduction approaches

Amphetamine users are at risk of harm from their drug-using behaviour, and brief interventions focusing on information and advice may be of value in reducing harm to the individual.

Harm reduction advice to the amphetamine user may include advising on the low purity and presence of contaminants in all street drugs, and the particular risks of toxicity with injecting use. If injecting, advice should be given on safer injecting practices to reduce the physical harm and BBV transmission associated with injecting.

If the user has problems with difficult come downs following amphetamine use, the answer is to use less, and use less often. This advice may be supported by an explanation of the neurotransmitter effects of amphetamine use and the symptoms of dopamine depletion, which may help the user to make an informed choice about continued use.

It is important to advise the user to stop if pregnant or breast feeding, and to stop or use less if there are any signs of cardiovascular problems.

If the user is sexually active while using amphetamine, safer-sex advice should be offered regarding protection from sexually transmitted diseases and unintended pregnancy. Injecting users should be offered BBV immunisation and testing.

Khat

Introduction and pharmacology

Khat (sometimes known as chat or qat) has been known and used as a stimulant plant drug for centuries across the Horn of Africa and the Arabian Peninsula. The chewing of fresh khat leaf remains a cultural tradition in Ethiopia, Somalia and Yemen. Often done in large social groups, generally consisting of adult males, khat is chewed while topics of interest are discussed, local music and poetry are performed, and disputes or conflicts resolved. Sometimes dried khat leaves are infused to make a tea, though khat's potency is partially lost in the drying process.

The development of air transportation has increased the availability of fresh khat leaves outside its indigenous area, and within the UK khat is frequently used within North/East African immigrant communities. Its use is becoming more common outside its traditional domains.

The khat plant contains the psychotropic substances cathine and cathinone, which are chemically similar to ephedrine and amphetamines. When absorbed from chewed leaves, these substances have stimulating properties, acting as releasing agents for dopamine and other neurotransmitters. The effects are similar to, but less powerful than, those of amphetamine. Increased alertness, a sense of wellbeing, appetite suppression and euphoria are all features of khat use.

As a plant drug, khat is not subjected to international control and is regarded and handled as a fresh product when transported. It is not an illegal drug in the UK though other countries including the USA have placed khat under domestic drug control.

Patterns of khat use

Elderly khat users may adhere to and observe traditional patterns of use following migration to the UK. New trends and patterns of khat use are developing among both women and younger male users within immigrant communities, and this may be associated with the social problems associated with migrant status, including unemployment, poverty, boredom, isolation and cultural alienation, though for some women it may represent greater social freedom.[45] The 2010/11 BCS showed that 0.2% of the adult population had used khat within the study year 2010/11.[3] Use was slightly more common in younger adults (see Table 11.1 on p. 176 and Table 11.2 on p. 177).

Harmful effects of khat use

Heavier and more regular khat use is associated with sleeplessness, loss of appetite, short-term confusion, raised blood pressure, palpitations, inflammation and soreness of the oral mucosa, anxiety, irritability, loss of libido and panic attacks. Khat chewing is not thought to be physically addictive, but, similar to other drugs of the amphetamine family, psychological dependence may be a potential risk. Excessive and prolonged chewing use may lead to more serious health risks including oral cancer.[46]

As with other stimulants, khat users may encounter problems through the use of sleeping pills or alcohol to help sleep at the end of a session.

Treatment for khat use

Treatment follows the principles given above of harm reduction advice and motivational approaches to support the user to reduce or stop use.

Ecstasy

Introduction and pharmacology

Though first synthesised in the 1910s, and largely forgotten for 70 years, ecstasy may be considered the original 'designer dance drug', with high-profile links to the music culture of the late 1980s and early 1990s. Ecstasy (also known as 3,4-methylenedioxymethamphetamine, MDMA, 'brownies', 'crystal', 'E', 'mandy', 'pills',

'XTC') produces the subjective effects of increased energy, alertness and wakeful-ness, and is used by clubbers to help them dance through the night. It may have mild hallucinogenic effects and users report experiencing colours and sounds as intensified. Ecstasy is a so-called 'empathogen', a group of stimulant drugs sup-posed to have distinct emotional and social effects. The mild sense of euphoria and lowered levels of anxiety associated with ecstasy use are claimed to result in a sense of greater intimacy, love and empathy for others. Effects start around 30–60 minutes after taking ecstasy, plateau for 2–3 hours, and some hours later there may be a 'come down' accompanied by fatigue, depression and irritability.

Chemically ecstasy is an amphetamine derivative synthesised from safrole, an oil that is extracted from parts of the sassafras tree. MDMA exerts its stimulant effect through its action as a CNS-releasing agent for serotonin, noradrenaline and dopamine.

Patterns of ecstasy use

MDMA was being used recreationally in the USA by 1970 and by the 1980s its use was prevalent in the UK dance/rave scene. It rapidly became notorious through newspaper coverage of a number of high-profile deaths that were possibly related to its use. Ecstasy use in the UK has remained stable over the last decade, with 1.4% of adults reporting use of the drug in the last year in the 2010/11 BCS (see Table 11.1 on p. 176).[3] Out of around 200,000 drug users in treatment in England in 2009/10, 273 identified ecstasy as their main drug and 2263 as an adjunctive drug.[4]

Ecstasy is typically taken in tablet form, or less commonly powder, and is used orally. It is commonly taken in combination with a range of other drugs, includ-ing amphetamine, LSD and cannabis. In 2010, the price of a single ecstasy tablet was around £4.[6]

Harmful effects of ecstasy use

Immediate negative effects of use can include raised body temperature, dehydra-tion, excessive thirst and tachycardia, with all of these potentially complicated by prolonged, energetic dancing in hot environments. Other short-term effects, partic-ularly when 'coming down', include anxiety, panic attacks, problems with concen-tration, confusion and disorientation, and problems with paranoid and suspicious thoughts. A slang term given to the period of low mood following weekend MDMA consumption is 'Tuesday Blues', most likely related to depleted CNS serotonin lev-els. More serious consequences of ecstasy overdose include the potentially serious serotonin syndrome, stimulant-related psychosis and/or hypertensive crisis. Like amphetamine, problematic bruxism (teeth grinding) can occur in ecstasy users.

Over 100 deaths related solely to ecstasy were identified in the UK between 1997 and 2007. There were a greater number when ecstasy was used in combination with other drugs, particularly amphetamine and methlyamphetamine.[47]

Treatment for ecstasy users

Treatment of ecstasy use includes harm reduction advice, brief interventions and motivational approaches to support reducing, controlling and stopping use, together with the management of uncommon though serious mental health effects, and the potentially fatal physical health complications of dehydration and hyperpyrexia.

Harm reduction approaches

Harm reduction advice to a user may include the following.

Be careful what you take and how much you take. When taking an illicit drug, it is impossible to be certain of the actual content or the dose. Many ecstasy tablets contain potentially dangerous mixtures of drugs. Limiting the number of tablets taken and increasing the interval between tablets reduces a wide variety of risks.

In particular, be aware of the relatively long interval between taking a tablet and the onset of stimulant effects (up to 60 minutes), and avoid taking a second or third tablet because the first 'hasn't worked'. This can result in overdose. Because of the development of tolerance, taking fewer tablets and having gaps between sessions may actually maximise the quality of each individual experience.

Reduce the risks of overheating, dehydration and over-hydration. Dancers should take regular breaks to 'cool off' when using ecstasy. Drinking too much or too fast can be as dangerous as drinking too little. Good advice is to sip between half and one pint of water or other non-alcoholic drink every hour while taking a rest from dancing.

Those with heart problems, hypertension, epilepsy or asthma should avoid using ecstasy.

Those experiencing prolonged or deep depression or anxiety following use should be advised to take a long break or stop using the drug. An explanation of the cause and effects of serotonin depletion may be helpful for the user and motivate change in drug-using behaviour.

Gammahydroxybutyrate (GHB) and gammabutyrolactone (GBL)

Introduction and pharmacology

GHB (a.k.a. 'liquid ecstasy', 'liquid X') is a naturally occurring substance found in small quantities in the human CNS, as well as in wine, beef and some citrus fruits. GBL is a synthetic compound with a number of industrial uses, for example as a solvent. GBL acts as a precursor for GHB, being rapidly converted in the body into GHB by lactonase enzymes found in the blood. GHB has a short half-life (approximately 30 minutes), with effects peaking at between 30 and 60 minutes. Patterns of use that include frequent re-dosing are common.

GHB has a complex mixture of direct and indirect CNS actions leading to both stimulatory and sedative effects. The results of taking GHB (and GBL) include euphoria, reduction of social inhibitions and increased sexual arousal, and both GHB and GBL are used as stimulants to enhance the experience of clubs and parties. At higher doses GHB can cause acute intoxication, amnesia and unconsciousness, and it is these properties that have led to the compound being used in the medical setting as a general anaesthetic, and illegally as a 'date rape' drug. There is a narrow margin between euphoria and overdose, particularly when GHB is taken with alcohol,[48] and significant overdose is associated with the rapid onset of respiratory depression and profound unconsciousness. Overdose is most often self-limiting, though deaths have been reported.

GHB and GBL have also been used by body builders to improve sleep and in the belief they develop body mass. There is no evidence that either is the case.

Patterns of GHB/GBL use

GHB usually appears as an odourless, colourless, tasteless liquid, but can also be found as a powder or capsule. GBL is a colourless liquid. Both are taken orally and, when liquid preparations are taken, doses are measured by volume. Insecurity about the potency of liquid preparations contributes to the risk of overdose.

Though seemingly prevalent in the rave party scene, the 2010/11 BCS[3] shows GHB/GBL use to be relatively uncommon in the UK. GHB/GBL use is most prevalent in young adults (see Table 11.1 on p. 176 and Table 11.2 on p. 177). It is possible that the national statistics underestimate GHB/GBL use and 'hide' pockets of much more prevalent use.

Most users take the drug on an occasional and recreational basis, though some become regular and frequent users.

Harmful effects of GHB/GBL use

Even at low doses the use of GHB or GBL has been associated with high-risk sexual behaviour, agitation, accidents and injury. At higher doses, GHB may cause nausea, dizziness, drowsiness, agitation, visual disturbances, depressed breathing, amnesia, unconsciousness and ultimately death. Consuming GHB with alcohol is thought to be particularly dangerous as it may lead to vomiting together with unrouseable sleep, a potentially fatal combination.

Tolerance to the euphoric effects, loss of control of use and craving may be features for some heavy and regular users, and some may re-dose up to two-hourly through the day.[1] Physical dependence and documented withdrawal syndromes have been described. The symptoms of acute withdrawal are unpredictable, may be complicated by confusion, delirium and fits, and can be life-threatening.[49, 50] Withdrawal may be followed by insomnia, anxiety and depression that may last for several weeks.

Tolerance to the effects of overdose does not occur.

Treatment for GHB/GBL users

As with other stimulants treatment of GHB/GBL use includes harm reduction advice, brief interventions and motivational approaches to support reducing and stopping use.

Both intoxication and withdrawal may be potentially fatal, and must be treated as medical emergencies, with the likely need for hospital assessment and admission.

Pharmacological approaches

In some areas very heavy and dependent use has been managed with formal medically assisted withdrawal as an inpatient. Benzodiazepine medication has been prescribed along lines similar to medically assisted alcohol withdrawal to limit symptoms and reduce the risk of withdrawal fits.[48, 50]

Baclofen, a $GABA_B$ agonist, has been successfully used in isolated cases of life-threatening acute GHB withdrawal in addition to benzodiazepines to reduce the risk of delirium and fits.[51]

Within the context of GHB dependence one study has explored the approach of tapering GHB doses in an inpatient setting to facilitate withdrawal.[49]

Harm reduction approaches

Because of their association with disinhibited sexual behaviour, users should be given advice about the associated risks of sexually transmitted diseases and unplanned pregnancy.

Because of the small gap between euphoria and intoxication, users must take extreme care with dosing, and in particular with early re-dosing. Users should be made aware of the risk of potentially fatal intoxication, and that, if a friend shows signs of intoxication or impaired consciousness following GHB/GBL use, medical advice should be sought. They must not be left simply to 'sleep it off'.

Users should be alerted to the risk of dependence in heavy and regular use.

Mephedrone

Introduction and pharmacology

Mephedrone (also called 'meph', 'meow meow', '4 MMC', 'miaow', 'bounce', 'bubble', 'M-cat') is a synthetic stimulant that is chemically related to cathinone, the psychoactive substance found in the khat plant, which itself is related to the amphetamine group of compounds. Mephedrone was first synthesised in the 1920s, using cathinone extracted from khat as the initial substrate. Its potential for use as a stimulant remained untapped until the early part of this century when it hit drug markets amidst a flurry of free publicity in the popular press. Alongside its new-found popularity, new techniques for mass synthesis have been developed, including an oxidative process involving ephedrine analogues.

Though not yet studied as closely as other stimulants that have been in use for longer periods, mephedrone is likely to have similar neurochemical effects to its related compounds. The reported stimulant effects of mephedrone are dose related and include euphoria, elevated mood and self-confidence, increased energy and increased libido. In a similar way to ecstasy, mephedrone is reported as having an 'empathogenic' effect – inducing a strong sense of empathy and a temporary affection for those who may be around the user. Less welcomed effects are anxiety, sweating, headache, nausea, vomiting, teeth grinding, reduced appetite and tachycardia.

Patterns of mephedrone use

Mephedrone is a new addition to drug cultures. Between 2009 and 2010 its use increased dramatically in the UK, and questions about its use first appeared in the BCS only in the 2010/11 questionnaire.[3] This survey showed that during 2010/11 1.4% of those aged 16–59 had used mephedrone (the third most used stimulant within this age group). For those aged 16–24, mephedrone use (4.4%) was higher, being the second most used stimulant drug amongst young people.

The most recent NTA report gives no information on how many mephedrone users have accessed treatment in England, though anecdotal evidence is that numbers are small. This has prompted one author to question why this might be and to identify three possible explanations: Is the use of mephedrone and other 'club drugs' overestimated? Are they relatively harmless? Or are users of mephedrone and other 'club drugs' simply not presenting for treatment, whether because services do not meet their needs or for other reasons?[52]

Mephedrone comes in the form of a tablet or a fine white powder, and is most commonly taken intranasally or orally. Mephedrone is less frequently injected or smoked.

The typical dose for a single use is around 0.5 g and the cost around £20 per gram.

Harmful effects of mephedrone use

Commonly reported negative effects of mephedrone use include anxiety and agitation, sweating, loss of appetite, sleep problems, palpitations and grinding of teeth. If snorted mephedrone is known to cause nose bleeds. Mephedrone may contribute to overheating, especially when taken with ecstasy. The potential for tolerance and dependence is not clear, but mephedrone is likely to follow the pattern for amphetamines, with the risk of psychological but not physical dependence.

A small number of deaths have been reported in mephedrone users, though in most cases there were other physical health issues, or additional drug use, as complicating factors.[53]

Treatment for mephedrone users

Like other stimulant drugs, treatment focuses on harm reduction, motivational approaches to supporting reduction and cessation of use, and the management of complications.

Harm reduction approaches

General harm reduction advice would include: use the drug only occasionally (allowing a week to recover after each 'session') and use only small doses (no more than 0.5 g/session). Oral use is safest and avoids the risks of injecting. Snorting is relatively safe but has the risk of producing nose bleeds. If the user does inject, advise on safer injecting practice. If dancing for prolonged periods, the user should drink water in reasonable amounts to prevent dehydration and take regular breaks to avoid overheating. The risks of taking mephedrone appear to be increased by concomitant use of alcohol or other drugs, and this should be avoided.

Piperazines

Introduction and pharmacology

Piperazines (a.k.a. 'A2', 'blast', 'bolts extra strength', 'BZP', 'cosmic kelly', 'ESP', 'euphoria', 'exodus', 'fast lane', 'frenzy', 'happy pills', 'legal E', 'legal X', 'nemesis', 'party pills', 'pep', 'pep love', 'pep stoned', 'pep twisted', 'rapture', 'silver bullet', 'smiley's', 'the good stuff') are members of a broad class of chemical compounds with a wide range of industrial applications including the manufacture of plastics and brake fluid. Within medicine they have been used for many years as an anthelmintic, or worming tablet. In recent years they have been used as stimulants that mimic the effects of ecstasy. The best known piperazines are BZP (benzylpiperazine), TFMPP, DBZP and mCPP. Piperazines probably have a direct effect on serotonin receptors and produce feelings of arousal, alertness, euphoria, wakefulness and wellbeing. The effects can last for six to eight hours.

Patterns of piperazine use

Piperazines are generally taken intermittently and recreationally by users. The most common piperazine is benzylpiperazine, presented as a tablet and used within a 70–150 mg dose range. The 2010/11 BCS shows a relatively low level of benzylpiperazine use in the UK,[3] though use is more common in young adults (see Table 11.1 on p. 176 and Table 11.2 on p. 177).

Harmful effects of piperazine use

Piperazine use may be characterised by difficulty getting to sleep and an unpleasant hangover-like reaction that can last for up to 24 hours after use. Other reported effects have been agitation, vomiting, reduced appetite, stomach pain, palpitations and diarrhoea. Allergic reactions and fever have also been reported.

In rare cases users may develop 'serotonin syndrome'. This can result in dangerously high blood pressure, tachycardia and overheating, and may be fatal.

Treatment for piperazine use

The focus is on harm reduction advice. Piperazine drugs may be particularly risky if taken by anyone with high blood pressure or heart problems. It is thought that mixing piperazines with alcohol may be particularly dangerous, and this should be avoided. Users should be advised of the small risk of developing serotonin syndrome.

Looking to the future and new stimulant drugs

It is almost certain that as the twenty-first century progresses new stimulants will be introduced into drug markets. It is probable that these new drugs will be derivatives or modifications of current ones, though there may be some entirely new compounds. Each new drug will be legal initially, but many, if not all, will eventually be placed under drug control legislation. Given the experience with other stimulant drugs, including crack, ecstasy and mephedrone, there is a good chance that criminalisation will follow a period of sensationalist reporting in the press, where the risks and problems of use will be exaggerated. With time a more realistic appreciation of the harm associated with use will develop and the drug will feature less prominently in the mass media. As with the majority of currently available stimulant drugs, full physical dependence syndromes are unlikely, though this may occur with some new drugs. Treatment approaches are likely to focus on harm reduction advice, brief and more in-depth psychosocial approaches to help users to control and stop use, and the management of any complications of use. Some new stimulants will assume a regular place within drug use repertoires. Others will fall by the wayside, and either not be used or be used by small minorities.

Health professionals through their contact with users can play a role in the identification of new stimulant drugs and patterns of use, can contribute to a measured debate on the risks associated with use, and can assist in the development of a rational approach to the management of new stimulant use and users.

References

1. Winstock A, Mitcheson L. New recreational drugs and the primary care approach to patients who use them. *British Medical Journal* 2012; **344**: e288. doi: 10.1136/bmj.e288.

2. Measham F, Moore K, Newcombe R, *et al.* Tweaking, bombing, dabbing and stockpiling: the emergence of mephedrone and the perversity of prohibition. *Drugs and Alcohol Today* 2010; **10(1)**: 14–21.

3. Smith K, Flatley J. *Drug Misuse Declared: findings from the 2010/11 British Crime Survey: England and Wales.* London: Home Office, 2011.

4. National Treatment Agency for Substance Misuse/Department of Health. *Statistics from the National Drug Treatment Monitoring System (NDTMS) 1 April 2009–31 March 2010,* 7 October 2010.

5. Independent Drug Monitoring Unit Submission to the House of Commons Select Committee, June 2009,

6. Independent Drug Monitoring Unit, www.idmu.co.uk/ [accessed November 2012].

7. Mittleman M A, Mintzer D, Maclure M, *et al.* Triggering of myocardial infarction by cocaine. *Circulation* 1999; **99(21)**: 2737–41.

8. Edgecombe A, Milroy C. Sudden death from superior mesenteric artery thrombosis in a cocaine user. *Forensic Science, Medicine, and Pathology* 2012; **8(1)**: 48–51. Epub 18 May 2011.

9. Qureshi A I, Suri M F, Guterman L R, *et al*. Cocaine use and the likelihood of nonfatal myocardial infarction and stroke: data from the Third National Health And Nutrition Examination Survey. *Circulation* 2001; **103(4)**: 502–6.

10. Vaughn M G, Fu Q, Perron B E, *et al*. Is crack cocaine use associated with greater violence than powdered cocaine use? Results from a national sample. *American Journal of Drug and Alcohol Abuse* 2010; **36(4)**: 181–6.

11. Buehler B A. Cocaine: how dangerous is it during pregnancy? *Nebraska Medical Journal* 1995; **80(5)**: 116–17.

12. Gossop M. *Living with Drugs* (5th edn). Aldershot: Ashgate.

13. Scottish Advisory Committee on Drug Misuse. *Psychostimulant Working Group Report 10/06/02*. Edinburgh: Scottish Government, www.scotland.gov.uk/library5/health/pwgr-02.asp [accessed November 2012].

14. National Treatment Agency for Substance Misuse. *Research into Practice no. 1a. Drug services' briefing, treating cocaine/crack dependence*. London: NTA, 2002, www.nta.nhs.uk/uploads/nta_treating_crack_cocaine_2002_rip1a.pdf   [accessed November 2012].

15. Castells X, Casas M, Pérez-Mañá C, *et al*. Efficacy of psychostimulant drugs for cocaine dependence. Cochrane Drugs and Alcohol Group. Published online: 17 March 2010.

16. Pani P P, Trogu E, Vecchi S, *et al*. Antidepressants for cocaine dependence and problematic cocaine use. Cochrane Drugs and Alcohol Group. Published online: 7 December 2011.

17. Pani P P, Trogu E, Vacca R, *et al*. Disulfiram for the treatment of cocaine dependence. Cochrane Drugs and Alcohol Group. Published online: 20 January 2010.

18. Minozzi S, Amato L, Davoli M, *et al*. Anticonvulsants for cocaine dependence. Cochrane Drugs and Alcohol Group. Published online: 21 January 2009.

19. Amato L, Minozzi S, Pani P P, *et al*. Dopamine agonists for the treatment of cocaine dependence. Cochrane Drugs and Alcohol Group. Published online: 7 December 2011.

20. Schmitz J M, Stotts A L, Rhoades H M, *et al*. Naltrexone and relapse prevention treatment for cocaine-dependent patients. *Addictive Behaviors* 2001; **26(2)**: 167–80.

21. Department of Health (England) and the devolved administrations. *Drug Misuse and Dependence: UK guidelines on clinical management*. London: Department of Health (England), the Scottish Government, Welsh Assembly Government and Northern Ireland Executive, 2007.

22. Bernstein J, Bernstein E, Tassiopoulos K, *et al*. Brief motivational intervention at a clinic visit reduces cocaine and heroin use. *Drug and Alcohol Dependence* 2005; **77(1)**: 49–59.

23. National Institute for Health and Clinical Excellence. *Clinical Guideline 51, Drug Misuse: psychosocial interventions*. London: NICE, 2007.

24. Simpson D, Joe G W, Broome K M. A national 5-year follow-up of treatment outcomes for cocaine dependence. *Archives of General Psychiatry* 2002; **59(6)**: 538–44.

25. Crits-Christoph P, Siqueland L, Blaine J, *et al*. Psychosocial treatments for cocaine dependence: National Institute on Drug Abuse Collaborative Cocaine Treatment Study. *Archives of General Psychiatry* 1999; **56(6)**: 493–502.

26. Gates S, Smith L A, Foxcroft D. Auricular acupuncture for cocaine dependence. Cochrane Drugs and Alcohol Group. Published online: 16 July 2008.

27. Hall W, Carter L. Ethical issues in using a cocaine vaccine to treat and prevent cocaine abuse and dependence. *Journal of Medical Ethics* 2004; **30(4)**: 337–40.

28. Hall W, Gartner C. Ethical and policy issues in using vaccines to treat and prevent cocaine and nicotine dependence. *Current Opinion in Psychiatry* 2011; **24(3)**: 191–6.

29. Manning J L. Simpson was killed by drug, *Daily Mail*, UK, 31 July 1967.

30. United Nations Office for Drug Control and Crime Prevention. *World Drug Report 2000*. Oxford: Oxford University Press, 2000.

31. Loxley W, Carruthers S, Bevan J. *In the Same Vein: first report of the Australian Study of HIV and Injecting Drug Use*. Perth: NCRPDA, Curtin University of Technology, 1995.

32. Darke S, Cohen J, Ross J, *et al.* Transitions between routes of administration of regular amphetamine users. *Addiction* 1994; **89(9)**: 1077–83.

33. Kramer J C, Fischman V S, Littlefield D C. Amphetamine abuse: pattern and effects of high doses taken intravenously. *Journal of the American Medical Association* 1967; **201(5)**: 305–9.

34. World Health Organization. *Amphetamine-Type Stimulants*. Geneva: WHO, 1997.

35. The Forensic Science Service. Drugs Intelligence Unit. *Drug Abuse Trends* 27, April–June 2004.

36. American Psychiatric Association. *Diagnostic and Statistical Manual of Mental Disorders* (4th edn). Washington, DC: APA, 2000.

37. Kalant H, Kalant O J. Death in amphetamine users: causes and rates. *Canadian Medical Association Journal* 1975; **112(3)**: 299–304.

38. Hando J, Topp L, Hall W. Amphetamine-related harms and treatment preferences of regular amphetamine users in Sydney, Australia. *Drug and Alcohol Dependence* 1997; **46(1–1)**: 105–13.

39. Srisurapanont M, Jarusuraisin N, Kittirattanapaiboon P. Treatment for amphetamine dependence and abuse. Cochrane Drugs and Alcohol Group. Published online: 16 July 2008.

40. Shoptaw S J, Kao U, Heinzerling K, *et al.* Treatment for amphetamine withdrawal. Cochrane Drugs and Alcohol Group. Published online: 15 April 2009.

41. Shoptaw S J, Kao U, Ling W. Treatment for amphetamine psychosis. Cochrane Drugs and Alcohol Group. Published online: 21 January 2009.

42. Strang J, Sheridan J. Prescribing amphetamines to drug misusers: data from the 1995 national survey of community pharmacies in England and Wales. *Addiction* 1997; **92(12)**: 833–8.

43. Mattick R, Darke S. Drug replacement treatments: is amphetamine substitution a horse of a different colour? *Drug and Alcohol Review* 1995; **14(4)**: 389–4.

44. Baker A, Lee N K, Claire M, *et al.* Brief cognitive behavioural interventions for regular amphetamine users: a step in the right direction. *Addiction* 2005; **100(3)**: 367–78.

45. Harris H. *The Somali Community in the UK: what we know and how we know it*. London: ICAR, 2004.

46. Soufi H E, Kameswaran M, Malatani T. Khat and oral cancer. *Journal of Laryngology and Otology* 1991; **105(8)**: 643–5.

47. Schifano F, Corkery J, Naidoo V, *et al.* Overview of amphetamine-type stimulant mortality data – UK, 1997–2007. *Neuropsychobiology* 2010; **61(3)**: 122–30. Epub 29 January 2010.

48. Munir V L, Hutton J E, Harney J P, *et al.* Gamma-hydroxybutyrate: a 30 month emergency department review. *Emergency Medicine Australasia* 2008; **20(6)**: 521–30.

49. de Jong C A, Kamal R, Dijkstra B A, *et al.* Gamma-hydroxybutyrate detoxification by titration and tapering. *European Addiction Research* 2012; **18(1)**: 40–5. Epub 3 December 2011.

50. van Noorden M S, Kamal R, de Jong C A, *et al.* Gamma-hydroxybutyric acid (GHB) dependence and the GHB withdrawal syndrome: diagnosis and treatment. *Nederlands tijdschrift voor geneeskunde* 2010; **154**: A1286.

51. LeTourneau J L, Hagg D S, Smith S M. Baclofen and gamma-hydroxybutyrate withdrawal. *Neurocritical Care* 2008; **8(3)**: 430–3.

52. Bowden-Jones O. New generation, new drugs: the rise and rise of club drugs. *Network 34,* April 2012: 3–4.

53. Maskell P D, De Paoli G, Seneviratne C, *et al.* Mephedrone (4-methylmethcathinone)-related deaths. *Journal of Analytical Toxicology* 2011; **35(3)**: 188–91.

CHAPTER 12

Alcohol

Jack Leach and Clare Gerada

IN THIS CHAPTER

*Introduction ‖ Alcohol consumption ‖ The costs and harms from drinking ‖
Identification of problem drinking ‖ Treatment ‖ Special groups ‖ Conclusion*

Introduction

Alcohol is part of our culture and forms the basis of much of our social life. Most
adults will drink alcohol either regularly or at some time of the year. Moderate
intake of alcohol in people over 40 years of age can reduce risks of heart and kidney disease. Overall, however, alcohol creates far more harm than benefit because
excessive drinking leads to a considerable and wide range of health and social
problems, as well as to premature death. This is for two reasons. First, a significant proportion of our population drinks sufficiently for it to be harmful to their
health and social wellbeing. Second, harm from alcohol exponentially increases
with increasing alcohol consumption.

Across the UK every GP, practice nurse and pharmacist will encounter at least
two patients per day who drink sufficient amounts of alcohol to either affect their
health or to affect their future health. About one in five individuals consulting
primary care drink more than the recommended amount. Problem drinkers are
twice as likely to consult their GP than the average patient.

In recognising the major public health impact of alcohol the UK government in
2004 published an alcohol strategy.[1] This has been followed by clinical and public health guidelines from the National Institute for Health and Clinical Excellence (NICE) and the National Treatment Agency review of the effectiveness of
treatment for alcohol problems.[2–7] However, many social determinants of alcohol
dependence such as price, availability, social acceptability and the responsibility
of the alcohol industry remain largely unaddressed.

This chapter in the following four sections discusses some of the key contextual
and clinical issues of tackling alcohol problems. Health and social care professionals are not good at recognising problem drinking and its consequences. Many
health professionals are put off from tackling problem drinking because they feel
insufficiently skilled and that nothing can be done to help problem drinkers and
their families. We hope this chapter will change this view and convince professionals that identifying problem drinking is worthwhile and that much can be
done to help reduce the consequences of problem drinking.

Alcohol consumption

Harm from alcohol is related to the amount and frequency of drinking, the duration of drinking excessively and the susceptibility of the individual to alcohol-related harm. Table 12.1 summarises the definitions and behaviours associated with different levels of drinking.

Table 12.1   **Definitions used for alcohol consumption**

	Men	**Women**
Light	1–14 units/week	1–10 units/week
Moderate	15–21 units/week	11–14 units/week
Heavy	35–50 units/week	22–35 units/week
Very heavy	>50 units/week	>35 units/week
Sensible	<21 units/week 3–4 units/day with two drink-free days per week	<14 units/week 2–3 units/day with two drink-free days per week
Hazardous	Very heavy and binge drinkers whose drinking poses a considerable risk to their own or others' health (Royal College of Physicians, RCP)	
Harmful or problem drinking	Clear evidence that alcohol is responsible for or substantially contributes to physical or psychological harm, including impaired judgement or dysfunctional behaviour that may lead to disability or have adverse consequences for interpersonal relationships	
Binge or heavy episodic	**Adults** 10+ units on a single occasion (RCP) 8+ units (Health Education Authority, HEA) **Young** Five drinks in a row on three+ occasions in past 30 days	**Adults** 7+ units in a single sitting (RCP) 6+ units (HEA) **Young** Five drinks in a row on three+ occasions in past 30 days
Alcohol dependence	Three or more of the following present at some time during the previous year: a strong desire or compulsion to drink; difficulty controlling drinking; a physiological withdrawal state on stopping or reducing alcohol use; evidence of tolerance; progressive neglect of other pleasures or interests; persisting use of alcohol despite clear evidence of harm (ICD-10) (see Chapter 1)	

The amount of alcohol consumed is measured in units. A unit of alcohol in the UK is 10 ml of pure alcohol or 8 g. All alcoholic drinks must carry the amount contained (in litres) and the amount of alcohol they contain in percentage alcohol by volume (%ABV). For example, 10%ABV means a tenth of the volume is pure alcohol. Figure 12.1 shows the amount of alcohol present in some commonly available drinks. Beer and ciders vary from 2 to 9%ABV, wines from 7 to 13%, fortified wines and sherry from 15 to 20%, and spirits from 35 to 55%.

Figure 12.1   **Common amounts of alcohol**

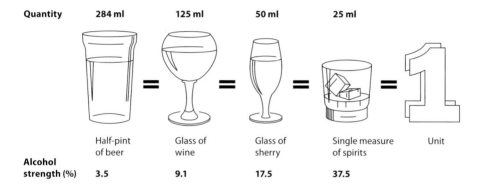

Quantity	284 ml	125 ml	50 ml	25 ml	
	Half-pint of beer	Glass of wine	Glass of sherry	Single measure of spirits	Unit
Alcohol strength (%)	3.5	9.1	17.5	37.5	

How much do we drink?

Current drinking levels

Regular statistics about the amount we drink, drinking patterns and consequences of problem drinking are published on the NHS Information Centre for Health and Social Care (www.ic.nhs.uk, search on 'alcohol'). Alcohol consumption is estimated from two main sources. First, the amount of alcohol consumed in the country based on duty paid divided by the adult population gives the per capita consumption level. Household expenditure survey estimated how much individuals and families spend on alcoholic drinks and what types of drinks they consume. There are also special surveys looking at particular aspects of alcohol and its consequences. Figure 12.2 (overleaf) summarises data from the Office for National Statistics.

A significant proportion drink more than the recommended safer limits, as shown in Figures 12.3 (overleaf) and 12.4 (on p. 213).

Figure 12.2   **Proportion of adults who drank in the last week by age and gender**

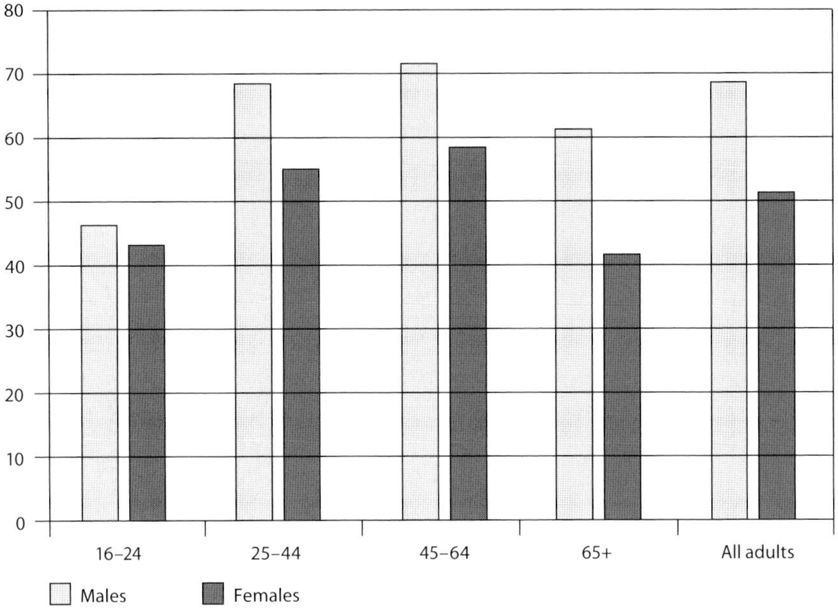

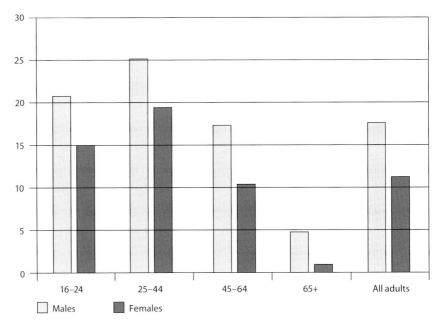

Source: Copyright © NHS Information Centre for Health and Social Care.[8]

Figure 12.3   **Proportion of adults who exceeded daily recommended limits on one day of the proceeding week (males more than 8 units, females more than 6 units) by age and gender**

Source: Copyright © NHS Information Centre for Health and Social Care.[8]

Figure 12.4 **Proportion of adults drinking more than 50 units per week (males) and 35 units (females) by age and gender**

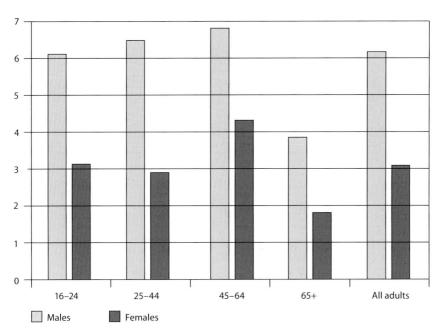

Historical trends

Although there has been an increase in alcohol consumption in this country since the 1950s, as a nation this is at a lower level that during the eighteenth and nineteenth centuries when relatively cheap alcohol was widely available to a large proportion of the population, was unregulated and there was a culture of acceptable excessive drinking. Figure 12.5 (overleaf) shows the trends in per capita consumption of alcohol from 1900 to the present.

International

Figure 12.6 on p. 215 shows the variation in alcohol consumption in different countries. Babor *et al.* identifies two broad patterns of drinking: chronic and binge drinking.[9] Britain is infamous for its binge drinking culture. Binge drinking is particularly associated with intoxication and antisocial behaviour.

Figure 12.5 **Per capita (litres per head per year) consumption of pure alcohol in the UK population, 1900–2005**

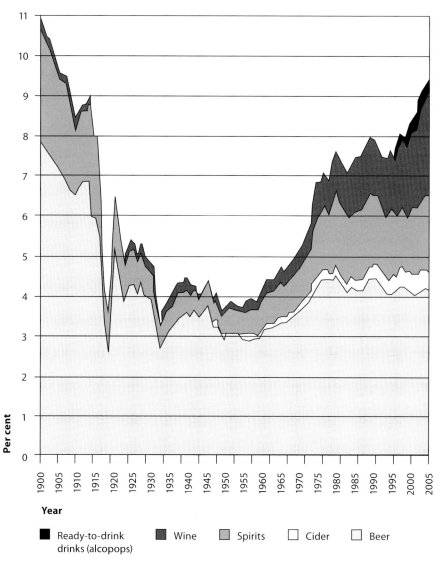

Source: British Medical Association Board of Science. *Alcohol Misuse: tackling the UK epidemic*. London: BMA, 2008.[10]
Copyright © British Medical Association. Used with permission.

Figure 12.6 **Total adult (15+) per capita consumption, in litres of pure alcohol, 2005***

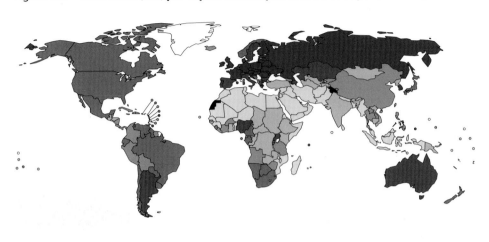

Per capita consumption (litres)

| | <2.50 | | 2.50–4.99 | | 5.00–7.49 | | 7.50–9.99 |
| | 10.00–12.49 | | ≥12.50 | | Data not available | | Not applicable |

* Best estimates of 2005 using average recorded alcohol consumption 2003–2005 and unrecorded alcohol consumption 2005.

Source: Copyright © World Health Organization.[11]

The costs and harms from drinking

The economic benefits from the revenue from alcohol sales, and employment of people in the alcohol industry, is fair exceeded by the costs to society of dealing with alcohol problems. In 2003 the Cabinet Office produced the report *Alcohol Misuse: how much does it cost?*[12] The estimated costs in England, based on 2001 prices, are:

1. A cost to the NHS of £1.7 billion

2. A cost of alcohol-related crime and antisocial behaviour of £7.3 billion

3. A cost to the workplace or reduced productivity of £6.4 billion.

In 2008 the Cabinet Office produced a further report *The Cost of Alcohol Harm to the NHS*.[13] Using similar methodology based on 2006/7 prices the cost was estimated at £2.7 billion. The gross domestic product for that year was £2283 billion.

Figure 12.7 (overleaf) shows national estimates of the wide range of harms from alcohol.

Figure 12.7   **Alcohol-related harm**

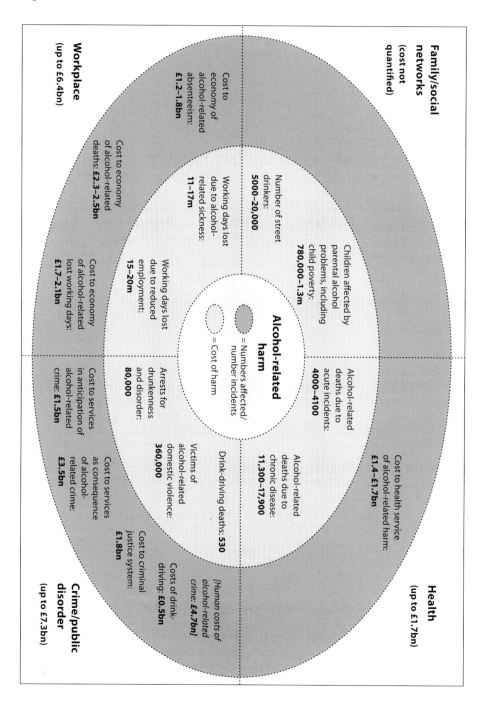

Alcohol and offending

The annual cost of crime and antisocial behaviour associated with alcohol misuse is estimated as £8–13 billion. This has increased more than inflation since 2004. Of this:

▶ 1.8 billion is attributed to the criminal justice system, including the costs of prison custody

▶ 3.5 billion is attributed to services as a consequence of alcohol-related crime

▶ 1.5 billion is attributed to services in anticipation of alcohol-related crime

▶ 4.7 billion is the estimated human costs of alcohol-related crime problems.

Approximately 20% of alcohol-related arrestees have four or more previous convictions. Individuals with mental illness and impairment, and associated alcohol misuse, are much more likely to commit criminal offences that the general population.

There is a higher prevalence of harmful and dependent drinkers in prison than amongst the general population (18–30% of men and 10–24% of women prisoners). There is an over-representation of intellectually impaired people in the prison system, through mental illness, learning difficulties or impairment development.

Health harms from drinking

Alcohol may cause harm to health from intoxication, chronic tissue damage, withdrawal syndromes and dependence. Based on answers to the AUDIT questionnaire from survey data, it is estimated that in England: [8]

▶ 33% of males and 16% of females over 16 years of age are drinking hazardously

▶ 6% of males and 2% of females over 16 years of age are drinking harmfully.

Based on answers to the severity of alcohol dependence questionnaire from survey data it is estimated that 9.3% of males and 3.6% of females between 16 and 74 years of age are dependent on alcohol.

Intoxication

Alcohol initially inhibits the inhibitor parts of the brain, causing disinhibition. However, then increasing drinking causes sedation with impaired psychomotor functioning, and eventually unconsciousness and respiratory depression. Intoxication may result in disturbed reckless behaviours including violent behaviour. It is associated with an increased risk of accidents and injury to the drinker and to others, and with alcohol poisoning. Excessive drinking may be associated with illicit drug use, such as cocaine and cannabis, enhancing the adverse effects of alcohol. Intoxicated states are associated with increased immediate and longer-term consequences of injury, and increased likelihood of A&E and hospital admission.

There has been considerable concern about binge drinking by young people and public violence, especially in inner-city night-time entertainment areas, encouraged by cheap alcohol sales such as 'Happy Hour'. Binge drinking is defined as drinking twice or more of the daily recommended alcohol limit in one sitting associated with alcohol intoxication. Binge drinkers are more likely to be men and under 25 years of age, although women's drinking has risen considerably over the past ten years. The impacts on society are visible in, for example, high levels of attendance at A&E departments related to alcohol. Over 6 million people drink more than twice the daily recommended amount weekly. Binge drinking has been 'blamed' on women, where women, with their increasing participation in heavy drinking, now no longer act as a restraint on men.

Chronic tissue damage

Excessive drinking may affect every system and part of the body. Chronic exposure to alcohol damages the body tissues over time and is a major cause of chronic illness and premature death. Periods of reduced drinking or abstinence may enable recovery for some of this tissue damage. Alcohol is a potent carcinogen. The extent of tissue damage is related to the level and duration of drinking and to the vulnerability of the individual to the damaging effects of alcohol. Excessive drinking may aggravate a range of pre-existing acute and chronic illnesses, for example hypertension, heart disease and stroke, diabetes, chronic obstructive airways disease, renal disease, depression, anxiety and schizophrenia. Table 12.2 illustrates the proportion of deaths attributable to alcohol for various conditions.

When assessing a patient for excessive drinking, particularly if he or she is older and has been drinking excessively for a long time, consider the following health complications:

1. *Liver disease* – the main stated cause of death to alcohol-dependent people. There are three stages of severity: fatty liver (abnormal liver function tests, no specific symptoms or clinical signs); alcoholic hepatitis (may be acute, with the patient ill and requiring hospital admission, or chronic, where there are abnormal liver function tests as associated with early symptoms and signs of liver disease); and cirrhosis, where there are symptoms and signs of liver cell failure and portal hypertension

2. *Acute and chronic pancreatitis* – there may be associated diabetes and gallstones, and biliary tract disease

Table 12.2 **Estimates of proportion of deaths attributable to alcohol from various conditions**

Condition	Attributable death (%)
Cancer, oesophagus	14–75
Cancer, liver	15–29
Cancer, female breast	3–4
Hypertension	5–11
Chronic pancreatitis	60–84
Acute pancreatitis	24–35
Falls	23–35
Drowning	30–38
Fire injuries	38–45
Suicide	27–41
Assault	27–47

Source: Greenfield TK. Individual risk of alcohol related disease and problems.[14]

3. *Gastrointestinal disease* – with gastritis, peptic ulcer, oesophageal varices, if portal hypertension, weight loss and diarrhoea, associated with poor nutrition and enteropathy

4. *Cardiovascular* – with increased risk of cardiomyopathy, ischaemic heart disease, myocardial infarction and stroke

5. *Neurological* – alcoholic dementia from Wernicke–Korsakoff syndrome, cerebellar syndrome, peripheral neuropathy and proximal myopathy

6. *Cancers* – particularly gastrointestinal cancers.

In addition, alcohol as a drug interacts with many other prescribed, over-the-counter and illicit drugs. It can do this in two ways. First, it can affect how the body organs, particularly the liver and kidney, metabolise other drugs (pharmacokinetic). Second, it can inhibit or enhance the effect of other drugs on target organs, such as the brain, reducing the drug's effectiveness or increasing the risk of overdose (pharmacodynamic).

There is some evidence that moderate drinking can reduce the risk of cardio-vascular and renal disease. This is mainly believed to apply to middle-aged men. However, with increasing consumption the harms of alcohol quickly exceed any benefits.

Alcohol withdrawal states

If a dependent drinker suddenly stops drinking he or she can become severely ill, even requiring hospital admission. There is a small risk of death. The main severe withdrawal states are withdrawal seizures, alcoholic hallucinations, delirium tremens and Wernicke's syndrome.

Alcoholic hallucinations

Alcohol withdrawal hallucinations are noted as early as 24 hours after the last drink and last approximately as long. They occur in about a quarter of cases and are usually visual but less frequently will be auditory or combined auditory and visual.[15]

Delirium tremens

Delirium tremens is a severe and perhaps life-threatening complication of alcohol withdrawal. It is characterised by increasingly pronounced disorientation, agita-tion and autonomic stimulation, with hypertension, tachycardia, hyperthermia and profound diaphoresis. Mortality rates of up to 20% have been noted in the past but have improved gradually with better recognition and treatment. Onset typically occurs approximately 48 hours after cessation of drinking. The mild tremor and lucid hallucinations of early withdrawal give way to delirium and agitation. The patient begins to pull at imaginary objects or at his or her clothing and sheets. Death can occur through hyperthermia and dehydration.

Alcohol withdrawal seizure

Alcohol is a common cause of adult convulsions. Alcohol itself may also exacer-bate other existing conditions, such as epilepsy. Chronic alcohol dependence is associated with structural brain abnormalities either due to chronic tissue dam-age from drinking or head injury trauma.[16,17]

Wernicke's syndrome

Wernicke's is a severe alcohol withdrawal syndrome with confusion, ataxia and ophthalmoplegia, though not all features need to be present for the diagnosis. It is associated with vitamin deficiencies, in particular thiamine (vitamin B1). It is believed to be due to, first, chronic excessive drinking reducing the body stores of B vitamins and, second, the hyper-metabolic state of alcohol withdrawal putting additional demands on the depleted stores, resulting in the acute brain dysfunction of the syndrome. Not only is there an immediate risk of severe illness and death but also longer-term consequences from the damage to the brain, known as Korsakoff's syndrome. Ideally, it should be prevented by good preparation for detoxification. However, once it develops the patient should be admitted to hospital and high-dose intravenous thiamine, B and C vitamins given.

Identification of problem drinking

The identification of problem drinking by health and social care professionals can be improved. The Omnibus survey found only 10% of male and 7% of female drinkers had been asked about their drinking by a GP or other healthcare professional in the previous year.[8]

1. Assess the quantity and frequency of alcohol consumption. The more a person drinks and more frequently, the more likely he or she is to have problems.

2. Use structured questions such as the AUDIT: consumption, problems and dependence.

3. The results of investigations, though not good for screening, may indicate the extent of alcohol-related harm.

4. Clinically assess for alcohol-related harm.

5. Assess for alcohol dependence.

Alcohol consumption

Alcohol consumption is the quantity and frequency of alcohol drunk. The quantity is calculated using standardised units of alcohol. In the UK a unit is 10 ml or 8 g of alcohol, while other countries use different amounts. The frequency of drinking is best estimated by asking the patient to keep a drink diary. They record what they drink and when.

The number of units a person consumed is calculated by:

volume in litres multiplied by concentration in percentage alcohol by volume (%ABV)

For example, a woman drinks a bottle of 12% wine (a bottle is 750 ml), three 330 ml bottles of 5% cider and two large vodkas with lime (a large measure is 50 ml, her vodka is 40% ABV) each day except Sunday. What is her weekly consumption? And what is her average daily consumption?

▸ *Daily consumption* $= (12 \times 0.75) + (5 \times 1) + (40 \times 0.1) =$ **18 units**.

▸ *Weekly consumption* $= 6 \times 18 =$ **108 units**.

▸ *Average daily consumption* $= 108/7 =$ **15.4 units**.

The more alcohol a person consumes and the more frequently he or she consumes at this level, the more problems he or she is likely to have and the greater the risk of future harm. The Department of Health suggests that men who drink more than 4 units daily and women more than 3 units daily are at risk of alcohol-related harm.[16]

Screening for alcohol problems

A number of screening tools are available to identify current or potential alcohol problems among patients.[17] The most widely used and extensively validated, including in primary care, is the Alcohol Use Disorders Identification Test (AUDIT),[18] with its shorter forms, AUDIT-PC, AUDIT-C, FAST and SASQ. AUDIT is an alcohol screening questionnaire developed by the World Health Organization to identify patients whose alcohol consumption is or may be hazardous to their health (see Box 12.1).

Most recent data suggest that the first three questions of the AUDIT provide a sensitive measure of problem use. Each item is scored on a 0 to 4 scale with never = 0 and daily or almost daily scored 4. A score of 5 or less suggests that alcohol use is not a problem at this point in time. A score of 6–7 suggests hazardous or harmful levels of drinking while a score of 8 or more indicates significant alcohol problems/abuse/dependence. It is important to emphasise that current recommendations are that women who are pregnant do not drink any alcohol at all.

Box 12.1 **Alcohol Use Disorders Identification Test (AUDIT)**

FOR EACH QUESTION SELECT YOUR ANSWER AND FILL IN THE SCORE GIVEN IN THE BRACKETS [ ]

One unit of alcohol is: half a pint of average-strength beer/lager **OR** one glass of wine **OR** one single measure of spirits. *Note*: a can of high-strength beer or lager may contain 3–4 units.

1. How often do you have a drink containing alcohol?

[0] Never

[1] Monthly or less

[2] 2–4 times a month

[3] 2–3 times a week

[4] 4 or more times a week

SCORE = ...

2. How many units of alcohol do you drink on a typical day when you are drinking?

[0] 1 or 2

[1] 3 or 4

[2] 5 or 6

[3] 7, 8 or 9

[4] 10 or more

SCORE = ...

3. How often do you have six or more units of alcohol on one occasion?

[0] Never

[1] Less than monthly

[2] Monthly

[3] Weekly

[4] Daily or almost daily

SCORE = ...

4. How often during the last year have you found that you were not able to stop drinking once you had started?

[0] Never

[1] Less than monthly

[2] Monthly

[3] Weekly

[4] Daily or almost daily

SCORE = ...

5. How often during the last year have you failed to do what was normally expected from you because of drinking?

[0] Never

[1] Less than monthly

[2] Monthly

[3] Weekly

[4] Daily or almost daily

SCORE = ...

6. How often during the last year have you needed a first drink in the morning to get yourself going after a heavy drinking session?

[0] Never

[1] Less than monthly

[2] Monthly

[3] Weekly

[4] Daily or almost daily

SCORE = ...

7. How often during the last year have you had a feeling of guilt or remorse after drinking?

[0] Never

[1] Less than monthly

[2] Monthly

[3] Weekly

[4] Daily or almost daily

SCORE = ...

8. How often during the last year have you been unable to remember what happened the night before because you had been drinking?

[0] Never

[1] Less than monthly

[2] Monthly

[3] Weekly

[4] Daily or almost daily

SCORE = ...

9. Have you or someone else been injured as a result of your drinking?

[0] No

[2] Yes but not in the last year

[4] Yes, during the last year

SCORE = ...

10. Has a relative or friend or doctor or another health worker been concerned about your drinking or suggested you cut down?

[0] No

[2] Yes but not in the last year

[4] Yes, during the last year

SCORE = ...

TOTAL SCORE (out of total of 40) = ...

INTERPRETING THE QUESTIONNAIRE SCORE

    0–7 Lower risk

    8–15 Increasing risk (hazardous drinking)

    16–19 Higher risk (harmful drinking)

20 or over Possible dependence

Source: Copyright © World Health Organization.[18]

Table 12.3   **AUDIT 3**

Thinking about your drinking in the last six months, please circle the answer that is correct for you.				
1. How often do you have a drink containing alcohol?				
Never	Monthly or less	2–4 times a month	2–3 times a week	4+ times a week
2. How many drinks containing alcohol do you have on a typical day when you are drinking?				
1 or 2	3 or 4	5 or 6	7 to 9	10 or more
3. How often do you have six or more drinks on one occasion?				
Never	Less than monthly	Monthly	Weekly	Daily or almost daily

Source: Meneses-Gaya *et al.*[19] Copyright © Wiley. Used with permission.

Alcohol-related harm and dependence

GPs should carry out a full history for alcohol-related diseases with appropriate examination and investigations. Table 12.4 shows some of the investigations that may indicate alcohol-related tissue damage, although there are other causes for the abnormality.

Assessment of alcohol dependence

The international classification of disease version 10 (ICD-10) sets out criteria for diagnosing dependence (see Box 12.2 on p. 228).

Alcohol dependence can also be assessed using a standardised questionnaire, such as the Severity of Alcohol Dependence Questionnaire (SADQ), set out in Table 12.4.

Treatment

Psychological and brief interventions

Over the past decade there has been considerable emphasis on brief and minimal interventions (less than five-minute sessions) in the treatment of non-dependent and dependent drinkers. Brief interventions have been found effective for helping non-alcohol-dependent patients reduce or stop drinking, for motivating alcohol-dependent patients to enter long-term alcohol treatment, and for treating some

Table 12.4 **Investigations indicating tissue damage from excessive drinking**

Test	Findings
Full blood count	Low haemoglobin level from GIT bleeding. Enlarged red cell volume (MCV). Reduced platelets
Liver function tests	Raised liver enzymes from inflammation (GGT, ALT). Reduced albumen, and raised bilirubin from liver cell failure. Prolonged prothrombin time
Electrolytes and renal function	Disturbed electrolytes from vomiting and diarrhoea. Raised creatinine from hepato-renal syndrome
Liver ultrasound	Fatty liver and inflammation. Fibrosis and disturbed architecture from cirrhosis
Chest X-ray	Enlarged heart from cardiomyopathy
ECG	Various abnormalities from cardiomyopathy and ischaemic heart disease
EEG, CT and MRI brain scans, nerve conduction studies and EMG	Abnormalities from associated brain, peripheral nerve and muscular disease

alcohol-dependent patients. Research indicates that brief intervention for alcohol problems is more effective than no intervention [20-23] and is often as effective as more extensive intervention.[24]

Brief interventions are designed to be carried out in general healthcare settings – including general practice and A&E departments – and generally restricted to four or fewer sessions. Each session lasts from a few minutes to one hour, and is delivered by health professionals who do not specialise in addictions treatment. It is most often used with patients who are not alcohol dependent, and its goal may be moderate drinking rather than abstinence.[25,26]

The content and approach of brief intervention vary depending on the severity of the patient's alcohol problem. Although the approaches used in brief intervention are similar for alcohol-dependent and non-alcohol-dependent patients, the goal of brief intervention for alcohol-dependent patients is abstinence.

The governments's alcohol strategy contains a commitment to improve early identification of alcohol problems.[1] It also announced the development of a number of pilot schemes to test how best to use a variety of models of targeted screening and brief intervention in primary and secondary care. The strategy also acknowledges the importance of training for medical and nursing staff.

Box 12.2   **Criteria for diagnosing substance dependence (ICD-10)**

Three or more of the following manifestations should have occurred together for at least one month or, if persisting for periods of less than one month, should have occurred together repeatedly within a 12-month period:

---

1. A strong desire or sense of compulsion to take the substance

2. Impaired capacity to control substance-taking behaviour in terms of its onset, termination or levels of use, as evidenced by the substance being often taken in large amounts or over a longer period than intended, or by persistent desire or unsuccessful efforts to reduce or control substance use

3. A physiological withdrawal state when substance use is reduced or ceased, as evidenced by the characteristic withdrawal syndrome for the substance or the use of the same (or closely related) substance with the intention of relieving or avoiding withdrawal symptoms

4. Evidence of tolerance to the effects of the substance, such that there is need for significant increased amounts of the substance to achieve intoxication or the desired effect, or a marked diminished effect with continued use of the same amount of the substance

5. Preoccupation with substance use, as manifested by important alternative pleasures or interests being given up or reduced because of substance use, or a great deal of time being spent in activities necessary to obtain, take or recover from the effects of the substance

6. Persistent substance use despite clear evidence of harmful consequences, as evidenced by continued use when the individual is actually aware , or may be expected to be aware of, the nature and extent of harm.

The GMS contract provides an opportunity to improve the care of people with alcohol misuse problems through an enhanced service. Whereas some areas may choose to implement the National Enhanced Service it is felt that most localities will look to a locally enhanced scheme to increase the quality and range of alcohol interventions provided in primary care settings, including developing some GPs with a special interest in the field.

As little as five minutes of advice from a health professional can significantly reduce drinking six months later in a non-dependent drinker. Brief intervention involves the following elements:

- ▸ **F**eedback – assessment and evaluation of the problem
- ▸ **R**esponsibility – emphasising that drinking is their choice
- ▸ **A**dvice – explicit advice on changing drinking behaviour
- ▸ **M**enu – offering alternative goals and strategies
- ▸ **E**mpathy – the role of the counsellor is vital.

Follow-up

The healthcare professional continues to follow up on the patient's progress and provide ongoing support. Follow-up may take the form of telephone calls from office staff, repeat office visits or repeat physical examinations or laboratory tests.

Timing

Much of the research investigating the relationship between an individual's readiness to change and actual behaviour change is based on studies of smoking cessation. Research findings have been applied to reducing drinking.[27] Individuals are most likely to make behaviour changes when they perceive that they have a problem and when they feel they can change. Some patients may not be ready to change when brief intervention begins, but may be ready when they experience an alcohol-related illness or injury. Because a patient's readiness to change appears to be a significant predictor of changes in drinking behaviour it is important to assess patients' readiness to change when beginning a brief intervention. For patients with little motivation to change, Heather and colleagues found that Motivational Interviewing was more effective than specific instructions.[28]

Motivational Interviewing with problem drinkers

Miller has described an alternative approach to dealing with problem drinkers who are not ready to change their addictive behaviour.[29] The traditional approach is to assume that the patient is not motivated and 'in denial'. This usually results in the adoption of a confrontational approach by the counsellor or clinician; such confrontation might be characterised by an attempt on the part of the counsellor to label the drinker and to prescribe the best course of action. If the patient has not yet decided to embark on any course of action the natural response will be to resist such exhortation.

Motivational Interviewing gives an alternative strategy for the clinician, which addresses the motivational balance of the patient. Behaviour continues when the perceived advantages of changing are outweighed by the perceived disadvantages.

Table 12.5   **Severity of Alcohol Dependence Questionnaire (SADQ)**

INSTRUCTIONS *The following questions cover a wide range of topics to do with drinking. Please read each question carefully but do not think too much about exact meaning. Think about your **MOST RECENT** drinking habits and answer each question by placing a tick (✓) under the **MOST APPROPRIATE** heading. If you have any difficulties **ASK FOR HELP**.*

	Nearly never (0)	Sometimes (1)	Often (2)	Always (3)
1. Do you find difficulty in getting the thought of drinking out of your mind?				
2. Is getting drunk more important than your next meal?				
3. Do you plan your day around when and where you can drink?				
4. Do you drink in the morning, afternoon and evening?				
5. Do you drink for the effect of alcohol without caring what the drink is?				
6. Do you drink as much as you want irrespective of what you are doing the next day?				
7. Given that many problems might be caused by alcohol do you still drink too much?				
8. Do you know that you won't be able to stop drinking once you start?				
9. Do you try to control your drinking by giving it up completely for days or weeks at a time?				
10. The morning after a heavy drinking session do you need your first drink to get yourself going?				
11. The morning after a heavy drinking session do you wake up with a definite shakiness of your hands?				

	Nearly never (0)	Sometimes (1)	Often (2)	Always (3)
12. After a heavy drinking session do you wake up and retch or vomit?				
13. The morning after a heavy drinking session do you go out of your way to avoid people?				
14. After a heavy drinking session do you see frightening things that later you realise were imaginary?				
15. Do you go drinking and the next day find you have forgotten what happened the night before?				
SCORING *The 15 items summed for a total score that can range from 0 to 45. Scale totals are interpreted as follows: 1–9 low dependence, 10–19 medium dependence, and 20 or greater high dependence*				

Source: reprinted with permission from D. Raistrick and Alcohol Concern.

Success happens when the clinician is able to shift this balance and this is best done, according to Miller, through the use of a series of self-motivational statements so that there is a recognition that their behaviour causes problems, that they are able to express concerns about this behaviour and its consequences, and they expressed an intention to change their behaviour and have an optimistic belief about such change. The key principles of Motivational Interviewing are described as:

▶ de-emphasising labelling, or using such terms as alcoholic or addict

▶ assertion that the definition of the problem and a decision to change rest with the patient

▶ that responsibility for any course of action rests with the patient

▶ that identification of a discrepancy between where the patient is and where they want to be, or between what they are doing now and how they perceive themselves, is an uncomfortable state likely to result in change.

The goals of Motivational Interviewing are: to increase self-esteem and self-efficacy, as these are associated with positive changes; and to increase dissonance and direct it towards behaviour change. The strategies likely to enable the clinician to reach these goals are: reflective listening, the expression of accurate empathy, affirmation of the patient's difficulties and achievements, and identification of how the patient perceives and can solve his or her problems through the use of open questions.

The practice of Motivational Interviewing has been the subject of several studies and clinical trials. It has been shown to be associated with reductions in drinking when compared with a confrontational approach, greater compliance with treatment than a standard approach, and similarly improved drinking outcomes (reduced levels of consumption) when compared with Cognitive Behavioural Therapy and 12-step treatment programmes. It can equally be used with opioid users.

Planned reduction in drinking to achieve controlled drinking

This approach is useful either as a treatment in itself or in preparation for assisted alcohol detoxification. However, it may not be appropriate for the following type of patients, who:

▶ are severely dependent

▶ have severe physical and mental complications of their drinking

▶ have diseases aggravated by any level of drinking

▶ need to aim at abstinence. If the patient is unwilling or unable to have an assisted detoxification or is waiting, then it could be beneficial to work with the patient to reduce the drinking and gain more control over his or her drinking.

The principles for reducing drinking to sensible levels are:

▶ reduce at a rate that avoids moderate to severe withdrawal symptoms and any withdrawal syndromes by ensuring you accurately assess level of dependence and likelihood of severe withdrawal symptoms and syndromes

▶ reduce at a rate that the patient can not only physically but also psychologically cope with

▶ reduce at a rate that does not aggravate any current physical or mental disease

▶ ensure the patient is supported, e.g. ensure family member drinking does not make the processes more difficult

▶ ensure the home and or/work and/or leisure environment supports the patient's reduction, including good verbal and written advice.

Generally, a reduction of 10% of the daily consumption per week is likely to be achievable and not result in severe withdrawal symptoms.

Assisted alcohol detoxification

The purpose of an assisted community alcohol detoxification is to ensure safely that the patient stops drinking, prevent severe withdrawal symptoms and ensure that the patient is given the best chance of remaining abstinent after completion of the detoxification. The patient should be carefully assessed to ensure that the treatment and setting are appropriate for them. The patient should be carefully prepared for the detoxification so that the patient and carer are clear about what is being done, why it is being done, and what to do if problems arise. The preparation must include plans for the patient to remain abstinent after the detoxification.

Assessment

You should assess the patient's level of alcohol dependence as outlined above in the section of identification of alcohol problems. You should ask about previous alcohol detoxification or stopping drinking and what happened. You should assess for the presence of diseases consequent of drinking and the presence of any other significant acute or chronic physical or mental illness.

You should ensure that the patient is dependent on alcohol and that this is more appropriate for him or her than gradual reduction in consumption. You should ensure that this is the most appropriate setting for his or her detoxification. You should also ensure that the patient:

▶ agrees to the programme

▶ has the support of carers, who will be with the patient throughout the programme

▶ is not or is at minimal risk of severe withdrawal syndromes

▶ can be closely monitored by a healthcare professional, at least daily physical contact and ready telephone access.

You should avoid carrying out an assisted community alcohol detoxification on the following types of patients:

▶ an older patient with a long history of heavy regular drinking without any periods of sobriety

▶ a patient with severe alcohol withdrawal symptoms who feels that he or she can not go more than four hours without a drink and needs to drink during the night

▶ a patient with any history of severe alcohol withdrawal syndromes, such as seizures, delirium tremens and confusional states, Wernicke's syndrome and acute alcoholic hepatitis

▶ a patient with severe physical health complications of drinking, such as loss of weight, severe liver disease, marked peripheral neuropathy and proximal myopathy.

Conduct of the alcohol detoxification

Many alcohol withdrawal episodes take place without any medical or pharmacological treatment and are self-managed. In those patients where detoxification is a planned medical or nursing intervention, the balance between giving medication unnecessarily and giving sufficient to minimise withdrawal symptoms appropriately has to be struck.

With appropriate shared care and support GPs can safely provide alcohol detoxification to patients in community settings, and perhaps this can be part of an enhanced service offered (as defined in the GMS contract) by the practice. Appropriate patients for community detoxification are those with good support at home, where there are no serious concomitant physical or psychological problems, where there is no previous history of severe alcohol withdrawal, in particular delirium tremens, and where the patient is committed to attending for frequent reviews, certainly daily at the start of treatment.

The clinician must be prepared to review the patient daily for at least the first seven days (once stable this can be by telephone review) and should be available during the detoxification should complications arise.

Partnership with a local pharmacist and support through a shared-care or community alcohol nurse are also important aspects for successful treatment.

The specific regimen used will differ for individual patients, but is based on a rapidly reducing dose of benzodiazepines, together with the administration of thiamine and symptomatic treatment for muscle pains, insomnia and where necessary prophylactic antiepileptic medication. NICE has published guidelines for alcohol detoxifications in different settings.[2–7] Its recommendations for community-assisted alcohol detoxification are set out below. In a hospital setting NICE suggests symptoms-triggered chlordiazepoxide administration based on a standardised assessment of withdrawal signs and symptoms, such as the Clinical Institute Withdrawal Assessment for Alcohol revised chart (CIWA-Ar) with, where appropriate, high-potency intravenous thiamine.[3]

It is important to advise the patient to maintain his or her fluid intake. If severe vomiting is experienced or if the carer is concerned as to the level of confusion or consciousness, the detoxification programme should be terminated and medical assistance sought.

What detoxification treatment to use

Benzodiazepines

Benzodiazepines are the drug of choice for the treatment of acute alcohol withdrawal. The most important consideration is not which benzodiazepine to use, but to ensure that adequate doses are administered early in the course of withdrawal. Early treatment coupled with close and regular monitoring appear to be effective in avoiding prolonged withdrawal, sedation-related morbidity and extra resource utilisation.

The British Association for Psychopharmacology has recently reviewed the use of benzodiazepines in alcohol withdrawal and concludes that they all appear to be equally efficacious in reducing signs and symptoms of withdrawal.[30] Particular drugs can be used to suit different circumstances, for example lorazepam or oxazepam in liver failure. Longer-acting benzodiazepines, such as diazepam, may be more effective in preventing seizures and delirium, but this needs to be weighed against their accumulation in the elderly and in those with marked liver disease.

Medication is typically given for seven days. Alcohol withdrawal severity varies widely and the amount of benzodiazepine required for symptom amelioration can also vary. There is no fixed standardised dose for all patients, but a typical regimen for covering uncomplicated withdrawal is a reduction of Librium 80–120 mg in four divided doses during the first 24 hours, reducing in a linear fashion to stop over seven days. You should be aware of local community alcohol detoxification guidelines and medication programmes.

Vitamins

Oral thiamine and B vitamins are recommended for all patients undergoing community alcohol detoxification. Ideally these should be started when the patient has been assessed as appropriate for detoxification before the detoxification starts. They should be continued for 6–8 weeks after detoxification when the patient's appetite has returned and is eating a normal diet.

For higher-risk assisted detoxifications parenteral thiamine and B vitamins should also be given. This is because in more severely dependent patients there is a greater risk of thiamine deficiency and Wernicke's syndrome, and they are more likely to have vitamin deficiencies from poor diet and malabsorption for alcohol-induced enteropathy. In particular they should be given to patients who have been losing weight and show other evidence of physical disease from their drinking. Pabrinex, containing thiamine, B and C vitamins, is available as intramuscular and intravenous formulations. The risk of severe adverse effects such as anaphylaxis is extremely low, estimated as around 1 in 5 million doses for intramuscular administration. For prophylaxis of Wernicke's syndrome where the patient is seen as a higher risk based on his or her age, duration of drinking, level of dependence and reduced nutritional level, but without history of previous severe withdrawal syndromes, then one pair of Pabrinex ampoules daily for three days during the week before or from the start of the detoxification is appropriate.

Neural protection

Research suggests that stopping drinking whether this is assisted or not can lead to two important central nervous system problems:

1. Detoxification leads to death of brain cells, and benzodiazepines and vitamins alone do not appear to reduce or stop this death. It is likely that accumulation of brain cell death leads to alcoholic dementia and the cerebellar syndrome

2. Kindling is a sensitisation of the brain to more severe withdrawal symptoms and syndromes from repeat unassisted or assisted detoxifications, in addition to the duration of alcohol exposure causing tissue damage.

Certain drugs have been found to reduce the neural damage and sensitisation. These include acamprosate and anticonvulsants such as carbamazepine. Consequently, it may be worth considering starting acamprosate either before or at the commencement of the assisted detoxification.

Relapse prevention

Reducing the risk of relapse is best achieved through a combination of psychological therapies, social interventions and medication.

Psychological

Psychological therapies are based on constant reminders and reinforcement of the benefits of staying abstinent and the adverse consequences of restarting drinking. They involve learning social skills to manage drinking cues.[31]

Social

The social environment should be changed, either by encouraging alternative activities to drinking such as exercise or by education programmes. There are approaches that seek to change drinking behaviour through altering relationships in the family and significant people in the life of the patient (family therapy and community reinforcement).

Medication

There is a range of drugs that have been found to alter drinking behaviour, though their affects are only marginal.[32,33] They should be combined with psychological support and social interventions.

Disulfiram

Disulfiram when taken with alcohol causes an accumulation of acetaldehyde, and hence flushing, nausea and vomiting, palpitations, and difficulty in breathing. This drug was popular in the treatment of alcohol dependence around 20 years ago and it was claimed that it worked through negative reinforcement: reducing the pleasure from drinking and producing an unpleasant effect soon after drinking. However, research has generally failed to find a significant effect from disulfiram when compared with placebo in double-blind trials. It may have an effect when combined with psychosocial treatment, family involvement, supervision or coercion. There is no evidence to support the efficacy of disulfiram implants.[34]

Naltrexone

Naltrexone is an opioid agonist that is licensed for use in relapse prevention from alcohol dependence in the USA and some European countries. In July 2012 it was licensed for use in the UK. Like acamprosate, naltrexone is used to maintain abstinence as an adjunct to psychosocial intervention.

The evidence for effectiveness is mixed. Although there is some evidence of a reduction in alcohol consumption and relapse in naltrexone-treated subjects, compliance is a problem, with high drop-out rates. Nausea appears to be the main problem and seems to be related to the frequency and level of alcohol consumption. Naltrexone also has adverse effects on liver function and has limited value in patients with severe liver disease.[35,36] The principal contraindication is coexisting opiate addiction, which therefore rules it out as a treatment of choice in patients with dual addictions. As for acamprosate, it is not clear how long to prescribe naltrexone for, and the trials tend to be short in duration, for example 12 weeks.

Acamprosate

A national review of the large number of randomised controlled trials into the effectiveness of acamprosate concluded that it had a small but potentially important effect, was cost effective, had a low frequency of side effects and no major drug interactions.[7]

Acamprosate does not have hypnotic, anxiolytic or antidepressant effects. It is metabolised and excreted by the kidneys and so is relatively safe to use in liver disease. Side effects are infrequent but include diarrhoea, headache, nausea and pruritus. Compliance may be an issue as the dose is generally two tablets (333 mg each) three times a day. In view of the fact that not everyone benefits from acamprosate, there have been several attempts to define the characteristics of a 'responsive' alcohol-dependent patient. As yet there is no clear evidence to suggest which type of patient may benefit although it has been suggested that a classical, primary type of alcohol-dependent patient appears more likely to benefit than one with a psychiatric or organic disorder, with social problems or one who is an episodic drinker.[37]

Special groups

Women and drinking

The levels of drinking in women are rapidly increasing in almost all Westernised societies. Young women and women working in male-dominated environments are more likely to drink heavily and to have drinking problems. Women appear to be more influenced by the drinking patterns of their partners than by their peer group, although women who drink heavily are likely to mix with men who drink heavily and be more tolerant of their partners' drinking patterns. Women who have multiple roles (family, marriage, employment) appear to have a lower risk of problem drinking, as though it would be difficult to juggle different roles if alcohol were a significant part of the woman's life.

Risk factors associated with problem drinking in women

The risk factors are:

▶ strong family history

▶ behavioural disorder in childhood

▶ early use of illicit drugs

▶ depression

▶ divorced/separated

▶ heavy-drinking partners

▶ working in a male-dominated environment.

Sex differences

The ways in which women and men metabolise alcohol differ significantly. After consuming a given dose of alcohol adjusted according to body weight, women have higher blood alcohol levels than men. The higher proportion of body fat in women, changes in alcohol absorption with the menstrual cycle, and differences in the relative amount of gastric alcohol dehydrogenase contribute to this disparity.[38]

These differences may explain the 'telescoping' phenomenon of alcohol use disorders in women. Women experience a more rapid progression to alcoholism and its medical complications than men despite lower levels of consumption.[39]

Pregnancy

It is estimated that over 20% of pregnant women worldwide consume alcohol.[40] Current research suggests that alcohol intake of seven or more standard drinks (one standard drink = 13.6 g of absolute alcohol) a week during pregnancy poses a significant risk to the foetus.[41] Risks to the foetus include, in early pregnancy, miscarriage, small for dates, preterm delivery, death *in utero* and neonatal death, and foetal abnormality. Foetal abnormality at its extreme is described as the foetal alcohol syndrome. Problem drinking by the mother can adversely affect long-term health and development of her children.

Alcoholic liver disease

The telescoping phenomenon is most evident in the rates of alcoholic liver disease in women compared with men. A prospective study over 12 years of more than 13,000 men and women found that women have a higher risk of liver disease for any given level of alcohol intake compared with men.[42] This study estimated the relative risk of cirrhosis in women who consumed 28 to 41 drinks a week to be 16 times higher than that of non-drinking women. For the same level of alcohol consumption, men were estimated to have one-third the risk of cirrhosis of women.

Breast cancer

A recent meta-analysis of six large, prospective cohort studies demonstrated a correlation between alcohol use and breast cancer risk.[43] Women who consumed, on average, two and a half to five drinks a day had a 40% higher incidence of breast cancer than non-drinkers. Importantly, this study also found a dose–response relationship between alcohol consumption and breast cancer risk. The risk was elevated by 9% for each 10 g increase in alcohol intake a day for increases of up to 60 g a day; this effect persisted even when adjusting for possible confounders such as age, diet, smoking, menarche, parity and menopause.

Osteoporosis

Alcohol consumption influences the incidence of hip fractures among women. One study showed that women younger than 60 years who consumed two to six drinks per day had an increased risk of hip and forearm fracture.[44] This increased risk may be due to a greater incidence of falling and to alcohol's inhibitory effect on bone remodelling, which has been demonstrated in men. Several recent large studies have suggested that moderate alcohol consumption may lead to increased bone mineral density in postmenopausal women.[45] Whether increased bone mineral density leads to a reduced fracture risk has yet to be determined.

Psychiatric disorders

All psychiatric diagnoses are more prevalent in alcohol-abusing women than in either non-alcohol-abusing women or alcohol-abusing men. Only antisocial personality disorder is more prevalent in male alcoholics. Studies indicate that the prevalence of depression is 30–40% in alcohol-abusing women. Interestingly, women with alcohol problems seem to have a much higher rate of 'dual' diagnoses, in which a primary affective disorder pre-dated their chemical dependence, than men with alcohol problems.

In the Epidemiologic Catchment Area Study,[46] depression was primary and alcoholism was secondary in 66% of alcohol-abusing women. In contrast, alcoholism was primary and depression was secondary in 78% of alcohol-abusing men. Many women cite worsening depressive symptoms as their main reason for entering an alcohol treatment programme. This information may help primary care physicians target their preventive efforts and tailor their treatment recommendations.

Alcohol-abusing women attempt suicide four times more often than women who do not have alcoholic problems.[47] Among adults with alcohol use disorders, the suicide rate in women equals that in men, but women attempt suicide more often than men. Anorexia and bulimia are also more prevalent in alcohol-abusing women (15–32%), significantly higher than the prevalence in the general population (anorexia 1.5%; bulimia 7%).[48]

Psychosocial consequences

Women experience significant psychosocial consequences from their alcohol use disorder. Family and marital problems are more common among women, whereas job and legal problems occur more often in men. Women are more likely to be divorced after entering treatment; they often report a fear of losing custody of their children as an important motivating factor for treatment. Women with alcohol problems are more likely to be victims of alcohol-related aggression, such as domestic violence and rape. Women who misuse alcohol often have a male partner with alcohol problems, and alcohol use in men is highly linked with partner abuse.

The elderly and drinking

Although the prevalence of alcohol dependence and problem drinking in the elderly is lower than in the young, it is nevertheless common and associated with considerable morbidity and mortality. Problem drinking in this age group often goes undetected. One primary care study identified 10% of older patients as having current evidence of alcoholism, yet fewer than half had this documented in their medical records.[49]

Elderly people are less likely to disclose their problem and health professionals have a lower degree of suspicion when assessing them for medical, psychiatric or social problems. The presentation of older people differs from that of their younger counterparts. They may for example present with falls, confusion or depression.[50] Sensible drinking limits do not apply to the elderly population, who, like adolescents, have lower tolerance to alcohol and suffer increased sensitivity to the effects at lower blood alcohol levels.[51]

Elderly people have been shown to be as likely to benefit from treatment as younger people although pharmacological interventions can be more hazardous because of coexisting medical problems. It is probably wise for elderly patients to be admitted to hospital for detoxification because of the increased risk of fluid and electrolyte problems, and confusion. Benzodiazepine-associated detoxification should be undertaken with care owing to increased sensitivity to adverse effects and altered pharmacokinetics.

Conclusion

Excessive drinking is a major cause of illness and premature death, not just among dependent drinkers. Problem drinking affects individuals, their families, their community and our society.

There is much as a society we can do to reduce problem drinking and to promote health and social wellbeing. There is much too that health professionals can do to reduce problem drinking and its consequences.

Further reading and online resources

Alcohol Concern. *Factsheet: putting brief interventions into practice*, 2006, www.alcoholconcern.org.uk/publications/factsheets   [accessed November 2012].

Civitas. *Alcohol and Crime*. Civitas Crime Factsheet, 2010.

Cooper D. *Alcohol Home Detoxification and Assessment*. Oxford: Radcliffe Medical Press, 1994.

Department of Health (England) and the devolved administrations. *Drug Misuse and Dependence: UK guidelines on clinical management*. London: Department of Health (England), the Scottish Government, Welsh Assembly Government and Northern Ireland Executive, 2007.

Heather N, Peters T J, Stockwell T. *International Handbook of Alcohol Dependence and Problems*. Chichester: Wiley, 2001.

Marlatt G A, Donovan D M. *Relapse Prevention: maintenance strategies in the treatment of addictive behaviours*. New York: Guilford Press, 2005.

Marshall E J, Humphreys K, Ball D M, *et al. The Treatment of Drinking Problems: a guide to the helping professions* (4th edn). Cambridge: Cambridge University Press, 2010.

Office for National Statistics, www.statistics.gov.uk.

Ritson B, Morgan M. *Alcohol and Health* (5th edn). London: Medical Council on Alcohol, 2010.

Royal College of General Practitioners. Assessment and Brief Interventions in Alcohol Misuse. Training for Primary Care Professionals 2002/3.

Royal College of General Practitioners. Certificate in the Management of Alcohol Problems in Primary Care. See details and other training resources at www.rcgp.org.uk.

Royal College of Physicians. *Alcohol: can the NHS afford it? Recommendations for a coherent alcohol strategy for hospitals. A report of a Working Party of the Royal College of Physicians*. London: RCP, 2001.

Substance Misuse Management in General Practice, www.smmgp.org.uk.

References

1. Cabinet Office, Prime Minister's Strategy Unit. *Alcohol Harm Reduction Strategy for England*. London: Strategy Unit, 2004.

2. National Institute for Health and Clinical Excellence. *Public Health Guidance 24, Alcohol-Use Disorders: preventing the development of hazardous and harmful drinking*. London: NICE, 2010, http://guidance.nice.org.uk/PH24   [accessed November 2012].

3. National Institute for Health and Clinical Excellence. *Clinical Guidance 100, Alcohol-Use Disorders: diagnosis and clinical management of alcohol-related physical complications*. London: NICE, 2010, http://guidance.nice.org.uk/CG100. http://guidance.nice.org.uk/CG100   [accessed November 2012].

4. National Institute for Health and Clinical Excellence. *Clinical Guideline 115, Alcohol-Use Disorders: diagnosis, assessment and management of harmful drinking and alcohol dependence*. London: NICE, 2011, http://guidance.nice.org.uk/CG115   [accessed November 2012].

5. National Institute for Health and Clinical Excellence. *Quality Standard 11, Alcohol Dependence and Harmful Alcohol Use*. London: NICE, 2011, http://publications.nice.org.uk/alcohol-dependence-and-harmful-alcohol-use-quality-standard-qs11   [accessed November 2012].

6. National Institute for Health and Clinical Excellence. *Alcohol Use Disorders Pathway*. London: NICE, 2011, http://pathways.nice.org.uk/pathways/alcohol-use-disorders   [accessed November 2012].

7. Raistrick D, Heather N, Godfrey C. *Review of the Effectiveness of Treatment for Alcohol Problems*. London: NTA.

8. Health and Social Care Information Centre. *Statistics on Alcohol: England, 2012*. Leeds: Information Centre, www.ic.nhs.uk/webfiles/publications/003_Health_Lifestyles/Alcohol_2012/Statistics_on_Alcohol_England_2012.pdf   [accessed November 2012].

9. Babor T, Caetano R, Casswell S, *et al. Alcohol: no ordinary commodity* (2nd edn). Oxford: Oxford Medical Publications, 2010.

10. British Medical Association Board of Science. *Alcohol Misuse: tackling the UK epidemic*. London: BMA, 2008.

11. World Health Organization. Alcohol statistics. www.who.int/gho/alcohol/consumption_levels/adult_recorded_percapita/en/index.html   [accessed November 2012].

12. Cabinet Office. *Alcohol Misuse: how much does it cost?* London: Cabinet Office, 2003.

13. Cabinet Office. *The Cost of Alcohol Harm to the NHS*. London: Cabinet Office, 2008.

14. Greenfield T K. Individual risk of alcohol related disease and problems. In: N Heather, T J Peters, T Stockwell (eds). *International Handbook of Alcohol Dependence and Problems*. London: Wiley, 2001, pp. 413–37.

15. Victor M, Brausch C. The role of abstinence in the genesis of alcoholic epilepsy. *Epilepsia* 1967; **8(1)**: 1–20.

16. Department of Health. *Sensible Drinking: the report of an inter-departmental working group*. London: HMSO, 2005.

17. National Institute on Alcohol Abuse and Alcoholism. *Screening for Alcoholism. Alcohol Alert No. 8*. Rockville, MD: NIAAA, 1990.

18. Babor T F, De La Fuente J R, Saunders J, *et al. AUDIT: the Alcohol Use Disorders Identification Test: guidelines for use in primary health care*. Geneva: WHO, 1989.

19. Meneses-Gaya C, Zuardi A W, Loureiro S R, *et al.* Is the full version of the AUDIT really necessary? Study of the validity and internal construct of its abbreviated versions. *Alcoholism: clinical and experimental research* 2010; **34(8)**: 1417–24.

20. World Health Organization. WHO Brief Intervention Study Group. A cross-national trial of brief interventions with heavy drinkers. *American Journal of Public Health* 1996; **86(7)**: 948–55.

21. Wallace P, Cutler S, Haines A. Randomised controlled trial of general practitioner intervention in patients with excessive alcohol consumption. *British Medical Journal* 1988; **297(6649)**: 663–8.

22. Kristenson H, Öhlin H, Hultén-Nosslin M B, *et al.* Identification and intervention of heavy drinking in middle-aged men: results and follow-up of 24–60 months of long-term study with randomized controls. *Alcoholism: Clinical and Experimental Research* 1983; **7(2)**: 203–9.

23. Fleming M F, Barry K L, Manwell L B, *et al.* Brief physician advice for problem alcohol drinkers: a randomized trial in community-based primary care practices. *Journal of the American Medical Association* 1997; **277(13)**: 1039–45.

24. Edwards G, Orford J, Egert S, *et al.* Alcoholism: a controlled trial of 'treatment' and 'advice'. *Journal of Studies on Alcohol* 1977; **38(5)**: 1004–31.

25. Bien T H, Miller W R, Tonigan J S. Brief interventions for alcohol problems: a review. *Addiction* 1993; **88(3)**: 315–36.

26. Graham A W, Fleming M S. Brief interventions. In: A W Graham, T K Schultz, B B Wilford (eds). *Principles of Addiction Medicine* (2nd edn). Chevy Chase, MD: American Society of Addiction Medicine, 1998, pp. 615–30.

27. O'Connor P G, Schottenfeld R S. Patients with alcohol problems. *New England Journal of Medicine* 1998; **338(9)**: 592–602.

28. Heather N, Rollnick S, Bell A. Predictive validity of the Readiness to Change Questionnaire. *Addiction* 1993; **88(12)**: 1667–77.

29. Miller W. Motivational interviewing with problem drinkers. *Behavioural Psychotherapy* 1983; **11**: 147–72.

30. Lingford-Hughes A R, Welch S, Nutt D J. Evidence-based guidelines for the pharmacological management of substance misuse, addiction and comorbidity: recommendations from the British Association for Psychopharmacology. *Journal of Psychopharmacology* (Oxford) 2004; **18(3)**: 293–335.

31. Marlatt G A, Donovan D M. *Relapse Prevention: maintenance strategies in the treatment of addictive behaviours.* New York: Guilford Press, 2005.

32. Drummond C. Pharmacological approaches to the treatment of excessive drinking and alcohol dependence. *Expert Review of Neurotherapeutics* 2002; **2(1)**: 119–25.

33. Agency for Healthcare Research and Quality. *Pharmacotherapy for Alcohol Dependence*. Rockville, MD: AHRQ, 1999.

34. O'Farrell T J, Fals-Stewart W. Family-involved alcoholism treatment: an update. *Recent Developments in Alcoholism* 2001; **15**: 329–56.

35. Maxwell S, Shinderman M S. Use of naltrexone in the treatment of alcohol use disorders in patients with concomitant major mental illness. *Journal of Addictive Disease* 2000; **19(3)**: 61–9.

36. Srisuraponont M, Jarusuraisin N. Opioid antagonists for alcohol dependence. In: *The Cochrane Database of Systematic Reviews* CD001867. Chichester: Wiley, 2000.

37. Fox G C, Loughlin P, Cook C C H. Acamprosate for alcohol dependence (Protocol for a Cochrane Review). In: *The Cochrane Library*. Issue 3. Chichester: Wiley, 2004.

38. Frezza M, di Padova C, Pozzato G, *et al*. High blood alcohol levels in women: the role of decreased gastric alcohol dehydrogenase activity and first-pass metabolism. *New England Journal of Medicine* 1990; **322(2)**: 95–9.

39. Randall C L, Roberts J S, Del Boca F K, *et al*. Telescoping of landmark events associated with drinking: a gender comparison. *Journal of Studies on Alcohol* 1999; **60(2)**: 252–60.

40. Chang G, Goetz M A, Wilkins-Haug L, *et al*. A brief intervention for prenatal alcohol use: an in-depth look. *Journal of Substance Abuse Treatment* 2000; **18(4)**: 365–9.

41. Abel E L, Hannigan J H. Maternal risk factors in fetal alcohol syndrome: provocative and permissive influences. *Neurotoxicology and Teratology* 1995; **17(4)**: 445–62.

42. Becker U, Deis A, Sørensen T I, *et al*. Prediction of risk of liver disease by alcohol intake, sex, and age: a prospective population study. *Hepatology* 1996; **23(5)**: 1025–9.

43. Smith-Warner S A, Spiegelman D, Yaun S S, *et al*. Alcohol and breast cancer in women: a pooled analysis of cohort studies. *Journal of the American Medical Association* 1998; **279(7)**: 535–40.

44. Hernandez-Avila M, Colditz G A, Stampfer M J, *et al*. Caffeine, moderate alcohol intake, and risk of fractures of the hip and forearm in middle-aged women. *American Journal of Clinical Nutrition* 1991; **54(1)**: 157–63.

45. Ganry O, Baudoin C, Fardellone P. Effect of alcohol intake on bone mineral density in elderly women: the EPIDOS Study. Epidémiologie de l'Ostéoporose. *American Journal of Epidemiology* 2000; **151(8)**: 773–80.

46. Regier D A, Farmer M E, Rae D S, *et al*. Comorbidity of mental disorders with alcohol and other drug abuse. Results from the Epidemiologic Catchment Area (ECA) Study. *Journal of the American Medical Association* 1990; **264(19)**: 2511–18.

47. Gomberg E S. Suicide risk among women with alcohol problems. *American Journal of Public Health* 1989; **79(10)**: 1363–5.

48. Lilenfeld L R, Kaye W H. The link between alcoholism and eating disorders. *Alcohol Health and Research World* 1996; **20(2)**: 94–9.

49. Callahan C M, Tierney W M, Health services use and mortality among older primary care patients with alcoholism. *Journal of the American Geriatrics Society* 1995; **43(12)**: 1378–83.

50. Reid M C, Anderson P A. Geriatric substance use disorders. *Medical Clinics of North America* 1997; **81(4)**: 999–1016.

51. O'Connell H, Chin A V, Cunningham C, *et al*. Alcohol use disorders in elderly people: redefining an age old problem in old age. *British Medical Journal* 2003; **327(7416)**: 664–7.

CHAPTER 13

Cannabis

Adam Winstock

IN THIS CHAPTER

Introduction || *Prevalence* || *Preparations and constituents of cannabis* ||
Routes of use || *Acute sought-after effects and harms* || *Cannabis, mental
health and cognition* || *Cannabis and pregnancy* || *Dependence* ||
Is withdrawal a problem and how do you manage it? || *Therapeutic uses
of cannabis* || *Conclusions following reclassification*

Introduction

Following the downgrading of all forms of cannabis in 2004 from Class B to Class
C, the prevalence of cannabis use across the UK fell. With no new scientific evidence but on the back of concerted media and political pressure, cannabis was
then returned to its Class B classification in 2009. The change in classification
appears overall to have had no impact on this downward trajectory of use in the
UK. Apart from these legislative changes and greater awareness of issues related
to the impact of the early onset of use of cannabis on cognitive development, cannabis dependence and withdrawal, little has changed regarding policy and treatment pertaining to cannabis since this chapter was first drafted seven years ago.
Although GPs are the likely first point of contact for people using cannabis, the
general psychiatrist in a community mental health team is more likely to see cannabis users than many in specialist addiction teams. For most people cannabis
use does not pose a serious health risk. As with other drugs the risks of harm are
associated with level and duration of use, and the presence of discrete vulnerability factors. Those most vulnerable to the adverse effects of cannabis are the young,
the pregnant and those with underlying serious mental health problems where
use is associated with poorer treatment response and higher rates of violence, suicide and imprisonment. Cannabis psychosis, so often spoken about, is in reality
a mythical beast that contributes to the delayed diagnosis of schizophrenia. In
reality, too, the greatest mental harms from cannabis use will be in exacerbating
illness in those already diagnosed with a severe mental illness.

Prevalence

Cannabis remains the most commonly used illicit drug in the UK. The most recent British Crime Survey, published by the Home Office, indicated 6.8% of the UK population had used cannabis in the last 12 months.[1] These figures represent 2.3 million 16–59-year-olds having used cannabis in the last year, with around 1.3 million people having done so in the past month. An interesting study from a national survey published in 2012 also highlighted the growing use of cannabis among those aged over 50, with 1.8% reporting use in the last year. This represents a ten-fold increase since 1993 among 50- to 64-year-olds. However, use remains most common in the 16–29-year-old age group. Compared with the rest of the EU, the UK has one the highest rates of cannabis use but has overall lower levels of treatment seeking – a situation that compounds the high rates of use. Low levels of treatment seeking may reflect a lack of awareness of harms among users or a perception that services are poorly equipped (or motivated/funded) to address the needs of those with cannabis use-related harms. Although the new drugs strategy explicitly directs providers to consider drug use problems beyond Class A drugs, in the current financial climate it is unlikely that new funds will be made available to address the needs of those who use cannabis.

Its status as the most commonly used illicit drug in the UK is reflected by its relatively easy availability and cost, and although the latter is increasing it remains affordable to many young people (1 g of skunk grass costs about £10, with resin cheaper). Supplying cannabis remains a serious offence and, although many caught in possession of small amounts will be given a caution, dealing carries a penalty of up to 14 years in jail. With a thriving home production market and use that transcends culture, ages and geography, it is also impossible to effectively curtail the UK's 'cannabis economy' (worth £5 billion/year). Whether or not the calls for a full-scale revision of the existing Misuse of Drugs Act occurs, it does seems likely that the way society addresses cannabis-related harm will entail both supply reduction and harm reduction approaches. It is too early to say whether or not the appearance of synthetic cannabis products will pose a real challenge to traditional cannabis products, but early indicators suggest that the 'real thing' is both more desirable and associated with fewer unwanted effects.[2]

Preparations and constituents of cannabis

Cannabis contains over 400 chemicals, about 60 of which are cannabinoids. These are compounds with a chemical structure related to delta-9-tetrahydrocannabinol (THC) – the main active ingredient that is most responsible for the euphoric effect commonly referred to as being 'stoned'.[3] An endogenous cannabinoid receptor ligand 'anandamide' was identified in 1988. Like THC (a partial receptor agonist) it acts upon central CB1 and peripheral CB2 receptors. The endogenous cannabinoid system has numerous interconnections with a variety of brain structures modulating mood, memory, cognition, sleep and appetite. Other active ingredients within cannabis include cannabidiol (CBD), which is responsible for the slightly more sedating/calming effects that some people report when they use cannabis. There are three major preparations of cannabis in widespread use in the UK today, though terminology and precise delineation between herbal forms can be tricky to the uninitiated. Currently, most herbal preparations tend to contain virtually no CBD due to selective breeding and cropping of homozygote THC-containing plants and CBD is now almost only found in resinous preparations made from a combination of all types of plants. Other constituents such as the terpenes are responsible for the characteristic smell that is given off when cannabis is smoked. Most users of cannabis get between 2–10 joints from one gram of cannabis (a mean of 4).

The average THC of cannabis resin and herbal cannabis has been in the range of 4–5% for many years. A review by the European Monitoring Centre for Drugs and Drug Addiction in 2004 has concluded that over the last three decades there have been modest changes in THC levels and these are largely confined to the relatively recent appearance on the market of intensively cultivated domestically produced cannabis.[4] Cannabis of this type, commonly referred to as skunk or hydro in the UK, has on average 14% THC and virtually no CBD.[5,6] The impact of no CBD on the effect may be more important than the higher potency of the THC, with unopposed psychogenetic effects of THC perhaps explaining the higher levels of paranoia that are reported by users of skunk as opposed to other cannabis preparation. How significant the impact of higher-potency forms of cannabis are upon health is uncertain. Much will be dependent upon whether users are willing or able to titrate their consumption when using higher-potency forms. Many just might end up smoking more!

In terms of detection the inactive fat-soluble metabolites of cannabis, THC-11-oic acid (which are detected in routine urine drug screens), are slowly released from fat stores. Chronic daily users may remain positive for up to 7–8 weeks after last use. In less regular users the detection window is much shorter. For example, a single exposure may only be detectable for a few days or up to one week. Heavy smokers may continue to be positive for up to six weeks after their last use.[7] Cessation of use can be monitored by taking serial urine measures over several weeks. Before collection it is advisable to have an advance discussion with local laboratories, which may vary in their ability to provide this additional information. Recent advances in forensic toxicology mean that recent use can now be detected on oral fluids. These have relevance for roadside drug testing, which may make inroads in the UK in the coming years.

Routes of use

Although cannabis can be consumed orally (baked into cakes or biscuits or as tea/alcohol infusion), by far and away the most common method of use is through the smoking route, with or without tobacco. Cannabis smoke is usually (and very unnecessarily) inhaled deeply and kept in the lungs for a few seconds in the belief that this increases absorption of psychoactive substance. In fact, most of the THC is absorbed in the upper airways; deep inhalation is not required and combined with prolonged inhalation simply increases the deposition of tar and carcinogens. Tobacco is used as a bulking agent and can facilitate burning of cannabis. It can also be used as a path into tobacco dependence with many tobacco users first smoking tobacco in combination with cannabis. Do not forget co-morbid tobacco dependence in those who use cannabis.

In the UK 85% of users mix their herbal or resinous cannabis with tobacco in cannabis cigarettes commonly known as 'joints' or 'spliffs'. Other methods for smoking include pipes and bongs (smoked through water). Compared with tobacco smoking, cannabis is associated with a nearly five-fold greater increment in the blood carboxyhaemoglobin level, an approximately three-fold greater increase in the amount of tar inhaled, and retention in the respiratory tract of one-third more inhaled tar. The smoke from cannabis contains the same constituents (apart from nicotine) as tobacco smoke, including bronchial irritants, tumour initiators (mutagens), tumour promoters and carcinogens. Also, compared with the tar in tobacco smoke, the tar from cannabis smoke also contains greater concentrations of benzanthracenes and benzopyrenes, both of which are carcinogens.[8] See the section on pulmonary harm below.

Assessing use

GPs ask about illicit drug use less often than about alcohol and tobacco, and patients' responses are less honest with many denying use. Fear of judgement or uncertainties about the limits of confidentiality may play a part. Framing screening with the assessment of other lifestyle questions about tobacco and alcohol use is helpful (see Box 13.1). Although experimental use is often non-problematic, there is no absolute level of cannabis use below which problems do not arise. Problems and cannabis use disorders are more likely to arise in long-term, heavy, daily users than more casual, infrequent users but those with severe mental illness may be very sensitive to even small amounts. Use may be specifically asked about in consultations related to smoking, mental health, sleep disturbances and accidents. Box 13.2 shows possible problems that cannabis users might present with in primary care.

Box 13.1 Asking about use in current cannabis users and identifying problems including withdrawal

✓ Quantify amount – how long does a gram last (an eighth of an ounce = 3.5 g). How many joints a day do you smoke? How many joints from a gram?

✓ Quantify frequency – how many days per week or per month do you smoke?

✓ Do you mix it with tobacco? Do you smoke cigarettes as well?

✓ Does your cannabis use cause you any problems such as anxiety, cough, interference with your sleep or appetite?

✓ Does your smoking ever interfere with what you want to do or what you have to do such as work or studying?

✓ Have you ever thought about cutting down or stopping?

✓ Have you ever tried to cut down or stop?

✓ What happened? Were you able to sleep? Do you get irritable or moody?

✓ If you managed to stop for a while how did you feel afterwards?

Source: Winstock *et al*.[9]

Box 13.2 Problems of cannabis users presenting in primary care

✓ Respiratory problems – exacerbation of asthma, chronic obstructive airways disease, wheeze or prolonged cough or other chest symptoms.

✓ Mental health symptoms – anxiety, depression, paranoia, panic, depersonalisation, exacerbation of underlying condition.

✓ Problems with concentration, studying, or employment and relationships.

✓ Difficulties stopping cannabis use.

✓ Legal or employment consequences.

Source: Winstock *et al*.[9]

Acute sought-after effects and harms

Cannabis is used by most people for its ability to induce euphoria and relaxation.[10] It can enhance sensory perception and at higher doses can produce sensory distortion, only rarely causing frank hallucinations, most commonly following oral consumption or in those with underlying mental health conditions. Excessive use in non-tolerant users or use in combination with alcohol can lead to users (often novices) feeling nauseous, dizzy and faint. Oral consumption of hash cookies is unpredictable and can result in intense prolonged effects due to a bimodal kinetic profile and metabolic breakdown products. Spotting cannabis use can be hard beyond bloodshot eyes, glassy conjunctiva and empty pizza boxes (see Box 13.3 for effects). A dry mouth, sedation, the smell of the drug, inappropriate affect (giggling) and excessive appetite (the 'munchies') may be giveaways in naïve smokers. When smoked, effects are felt after a few minutes, peaking 30–60 minutes after use, with a duration of 2–4 hours. Table 13.1 lists the physiological and psychological effects.

Box 13.3 **Effects of cannabis use**

✓ Red eyes, conjunctival suffusion.

✓ Short-term memory loss.

✓ Heightened sensory awareness.

✓ Changes in time and spatial awareness.

✓ Impaired psychomotor coordination (especially with alcohol).

✓ Sedation/occasionally increased arousal.

✓ Increased appetite.

✓ Slight hypotension.

✓ Analgesia.

Effects are more intense, prolonged and more likely to be adverse among inexperienced (non-tolerant users) and those who have consumed the drug orally, which can result in unpredictable effects. For most users occasional consumption of cannabis will not cause any significant harms beyond the risks associated with acute intoxication with any drugs. Compared with other commonly used drugs including alcohol the acute toxicity of cannabis is very low, with most short-term harms being self-limiting and confined to adverse psychological responses, most commonly panic attacks, paranoia, depersonalisation and derealisation. True hallucinations are rare and there is little evidence to support a cannabis psychosis

Table 13.1   **Physiological and psychological effects of cannabis (peak after 30 minutes and last for 2–4 hours)**

Psychological (mood/perceptual)	Physiological
A sense of euphoria and relaxation	Increase in appetite
Perceptual distortions, time distortion and the intensification of sensory experiences	Increase in heart rate and decrease in blood pressure
Impairment of attention, concentration, short-term memory, information processing and reaction time	Conjunctival injection and suffusion
Feelings of greater emotional and physical sensitivity	Dry mouth
Anxiety, panic and paranoia	Impaired psychomotor coordination and sedation

Source: Winstock et al.[9]

syndrome. Most adverse psychological effects will fade rapidly within hours or days. Persistence of psychopathology beyond a few weeks strongly suggests an underlying condition. Many studies have shown that cannabis also impairs balance, tracking ability, hand–eye coordination, reaction time and physical strength.[11] Sedation and impaired coordination especially at higher dose and in combination with alcohol can lead to accidents including a doubling of the risk of fatal car accidents.[12]

Longer-term harms

Both age of onset and duration of use appear to be the key factors mediating the risk for longer-term harm. There is consistently strong evidence from serial epidemiological studies that earlier age of first use (which may be a marker for other psychosocial problems) is associated with a greater risk of dependence, other substance use problems, mental health problems and a more negative impact on emotional, academic and social development.[13] See Table 13.2 (overleaf) for a summary of short- and longer-term harms.

On a population basis the three most significant longer-term health consequences of cannabis use are lung damage (already alluded to above), cognition and mental health including dependence. We will briefly review each of these in turn. In summary the key information to impart to users is that, although people vary in their susceptibility to these harms, they are predictably higher in those who smoke more for longer. Any reduction in risk, reversal or halting of progression of disability occurs the sooner they stop or cut down. The one irreversible risk

Table 13.2   **Harms and risks associated with cannabis use**

Acute intoxication risks	Impaired attention, memory and psychomotor performance while intoxicated
	Increased risk of motor vehicle accidents, especially if mixed with alcohol
	Psychotic symptoms at high doses
Most probable chronic effects	Dependence (1 in 10 users)
	Subtle cognitive impairment in attention, verbal memory, and the organisation and integration of complex information in chronic daily user (> 10 years), especially in those who start young. Some evidence of reversibility with prolonged abstinence but not in those who start before the age of 18 years old
	Pulmonary disease and respiratory symptoms such as COPD and chronic cough (synergistic harm with tobacco)
	Malignancy of the oropharynx
Possible chronic effects	Xerostomia and consequent dental health problems
	Some evidence that cannabis may affect female fertility
	In utero exposure to cannabis may lead to low-for-weight babies and later behavioural, problem-solving and attentional difficulties
	Increased rate of lung cancer
Probable risks amongst specific populations	Impaired personal and educational attainment
	Adolescent cannabis use is associated with: • higher rates of truancy, delinquency and criminality • higher rates of other problematic substance use including alcohol • poorer academic achievement and educational attainment with more unemployment • lower levels of relationship satisfaction. Mental health problems such as depression, anxiety and psychotic conditions may be exacerbated
Limited or no evidence	Birth defects (except low birth weight)

Source: adapted from Winstock *et al*. 2010[9] (from National Cannabis Prevention and Information Centre Guidelines 2009, www.ncpic.org.au) and Hall and Degenhardt 2009.[13]

254

factor is age of onset, with a younger age associated with longer cannabis-related career with a consequence of greater risk of cannabis-related harm. A useful tool to allow people to reflect on their personal vulnerability to cannabis-associated harms and to highlight the need for reduction in or change in use is the drugs meter self-assessment tool, which is available both online (at www.drugsmeter.com) and for the smart phone.

Cannabis and pulmonary harms (including malignancy)

In many cultures, especially in the UK, for many people cannabis use acts as a gateway to subsequent tobacco smoking. Tobacco smokers who use cannabis have poorer tobacco quit rates than those who do not use cannabis. Tobacco use is a predictor of poorer outcome for those undergoing treatment for their cannabis use than sole cannabis users.

Treatment and dependence aside, it is the synergistic harms that tobacco and cannabis have upon pulmonary health that represents the most potent cannabis-related public health harm. While it is true that most cannabis users do not become daily users and do not usually smoke for as long as cigarette smokers, cannabis smoking shows a dose–response relationship with pulmonary risk in the same way tobacco does. Smoking cannabis is associated with a weakened immune system with use adversely affecting the functioning of T cells, natural killer cells and macrophages.[14] A longitudinal study of young cannabis smokers demonstrated that regular heavy use can result in symptoms of chronic bronchitis such as coughing, shortness of breath and production of sputum due to chronic inflammatory changes in the respiratory tract.[15] Highlighting the respiratory harms of inhaling smoke to a generation who have the lowest tobacco use levels in history may be thus a smart individual and public health approach to encouraging young people to reduce their exposure to cannabis-related harm.

With an ageing population of cannabis smokers and with cannabis smoking likely to precipitate airway disease in the vulnerable, GPs should think about the use of cannabis in those presenting with COPD in their thirties and forties. In terms of cigarette–joint equivalence a study comparing pulmonary function tests and CT scans between different smoking groups estimated that one cannabis joint caused the equivalent airflow obstruction of 2.5–5 cigarettes.[16] A recent cross-sectional study reported that concurrent smoking of cannabis and tobacco leads to synergistic respiratory harm with elevated rates of COPD.[17] Heavy cannabis use should be specifically enquired about in those presenting with early-onset airways disease.

In terms of cancer, case series of cannabis-only smokers strongly suggest that cannabis may be implicated in the development of a range of oropharyngeal cancers.[18] More recent studies suggest heavy chronic use of cannabis use is also an independent risk factor for lung cancer, increasing rates more than five-fold even accounting for age, tobacco use and family history of lung cancer.[19] Cannabis use may also exacerbate the risk of coronary events in those with pre-existing cardiovascular disease.

So what is the safest way to smoke?

Without tobacco is the simple answer (or eat it, which avoids smoking and consequent carcinogen production). The evidence for using water pipes or bongs that cool and filter smoke as harm reduction methods is not there, and such approaches may in fact increase tar delivery to the lungs. The safest methods of smoking are either using an unfiltered joint without tobacco or a vapouriser that heats the plant material, releasing the THC as a vapour but avoiding combustion. While early models were large and injected smoke into jars or roasting bags, technology and demand mean they are now available as pocket-sized devices that cost between £40 and £100. Evidence for the use of vaporisers as a harm reduction recommendation is not that strong at present but their use is preferred compared with continued smoking in someone with COPD.[20] Box 13.4 lists harm reduction tips for those who insist on continuing to smoke.

Cannabis, mental health and cognition

People are most likely to achieve their optimal mental health if they don't use cannabis, especially when they are young. Saying that, most people use cannabis without experiencing significant mental harms and many who smoke cannabis would say that its use is associated with a range of positive psychosocial effects. Many of course do realise that long-term use may also be associated with negative effects. In a recent large online survey of 2000 non-treatment-seeking cannabis users (www.globaldrugsurvey.com), effects on memory, mental health, motivation and the ability to work and study were identified as the most significant health concerns.

People of course vary in their vulnerability to experiencing such harms, with those having a family history of serious mental illness being at elevated risk. There is a clear link between early use and the development of psychotic disorders, particularly schizophrenia (especially in males and in those under the age of 16 years old). Early cannabis use approximately doubles the risk of schizophrenia from 0.7 per 1000 population to 1.4 per 1000 population.[21,22] Predisposition to elevated risk appears to be genetic, with both a family history of a psychotic illness and a personal history of unusual personal experiences increasing cannabis-related risk.[23] Despite plausible biological theories causality has yet to be confirmed, with residual confounding bias and reverse causation both remaining as possible explanatory models.[24] It is thought that the overall population percentage of schizophrenia attributable to cannabis is around 8%.

Box 13.4   **Harm reduction for cannabis smokers**

✓ Do not mix with tobacco.

✓ Avoid daily and binge use.

✓ Do not use a cigarette filter – will reduce cannabis/tar ratio 30% less cannabis, 60% more tar.

✓ Do not hold smoke in lungs –will not get more stoned but will increase tar and carcinogens in contact with lungs.

✓ Do not inhale too deeply – most THC is absorbed from the upper airways.

✓ Do not mix with alcohol and/or other drugs such as cocaine.

✓ Remove stalks, leaves, etc.

✓ Do not use too many papers.

✓ Clean bong (water pipe)/pipes thoroughly.

✓ Avoid bongs/water pipes – pulling on a bong or using a bucket may cool smoke but will also force smoke deeper into lungs and may filter more THC out than tar.

✓ Avoid plastic bottles/pipes/aluminium foil etc. as they can increase toxic fumes.

✓ Avoid use if there is a history of significant mental illness.

✓ Do not drive while intoxicated, especially when mixed with alcohol.

Source: adapted from © 1999–2005 HIT UK Ltd.

Regardless of its possible role in precipitating psychotic illness or causing it *de novo*, a recent systematic review highlighted that cannabis use amongst those with psychotic disorders was consistently associated with increased relapse and non-adherence.[25] Addressing use within this group is of course more difficult than in otherwise healthy populations, with studies suggesting that routine Cognitive Behavioural Therapy (CBT) and Motivational Interviewing (MI) are less effective in those with concurrent illness.[26] However, it should not be forgotten that, for those patients with serious mental health problems, effective pharmacological and psychosocial treatment of the underlying condition can help reduce the use of cannabis and other substances.

The link between cannabis use and depression is less clear. Although studies report increased levels of depressive and anxiety symptoms amongst cannabis users,[27] no causal relationship has been consistently found between the two, with shared common aetiological factors being the most likely explanation.[28, 29] There also appears to be little evidence to support the idea of self-medication of depression with cannabis though recent work suggest that social anxiety may be more common premorbidly in regular cannabis smokers.[30] Regarding anxiety disorders, although higher rates of cannabis use are found among those with anxiety disorders and heavy cannabis users have higher levels of anxiety, the nature of the relationship is not clear. In the author's experience chronic cannabis use and intoxication can sometimes appear like depression (lethargy, sleep and appetite disturbance, social withdrawal, problems at work or at home, cognitive impairment) or anxiety/social phobia (motor restlessness, rumination, palpitations, increased self-monitoring and low-level paranoia with avoidance of social situations). Thus it is essential when assessing psychiatric symptoms in substance users to differentiate between acute and chronic intoxication and symptoms of mental illness. If mental health symptoms were present before the onset of use there is a greater likelihood of a psychiatric disorder being present. If symptoms resolve on cessation of use the likelihood of a primary psychiatric diagnosis diminishes. In many heavy cannabis users depressive symptoms resolve with abstinence.[31] Clinicians should thus avoid diagnosing affective disorders and commencing antidepressants in current smokers, instead reviewing their mental state at 2–4 weeks following cessation (see Figure 13.1).[9]

Cognition

People don't function at their smartest when they are stoned, with short-term memory loss and impaired recall being common complaints. Acute cannabis-related impairments in learning ability can be a serious problem for some young people who smoke cannabis. Impairments in some aspects of attention, memory, learning and organising can be present for more than 24 hours after use. Concerns over longer-term cognitive impairment in chronic smokers have been increasingly reported. Although there are many confounders, studies have shown that students who smoke cannabis regularly attain lower grades than those who do not.[32] In addition, early opinion that cannabis did not cause the same sort of gross structural changes seen in long-term drinkers has been replaced by evidence from more recent imaging studies. These have identified exposure-related reductions in the volumes of cannabinoid receptor-rich areas including the amygdale and hippocampus in heavy cannabis smokers.[33] These findings may explain studies that identify duration of use and dose-related impairments in memory and attention in long-term heavy cannabis users.[34] Recent studies have confirmed the

Figure 13.1   **Identifying and responding to cannabis use disorders**

```
┌─────────────────────────────────────────┐
│  Cannabis use identified at interview    │
└─────────────────────────────────────────┘
```

Infrequent/non-problematic use – give information on related health risks and highlight tobacco-related harms and harm reduction advice

Regular weekly/daily screen for dependent/problematic use – with brief intervention framework, e.g. FRAMES

Motivated to stop/cut down? Is there evidence of dependence?

If yes, provide advice on gradual dose reduction, withdrawal symptoms, sleep hygiene and NRT if appropriate

If no, conduct brief intervention and inform of dose-related health risk and encourage the patient to consider what would prompt him or her to think about cutting down/stopping

If patient successfully cuts down – provide positive feedback and discuss simple relapse prevention techniques.

Provide follow-up assessment of any baseline psychological symptoms

If the patient is unable to reduce, consider referral for extended psychological intervention, e.g. group, 1:1 CBT, MI

Provide harm reduction and advice

If withdrawal is barrier to abstinence, consider brief periods of symptomatic relief

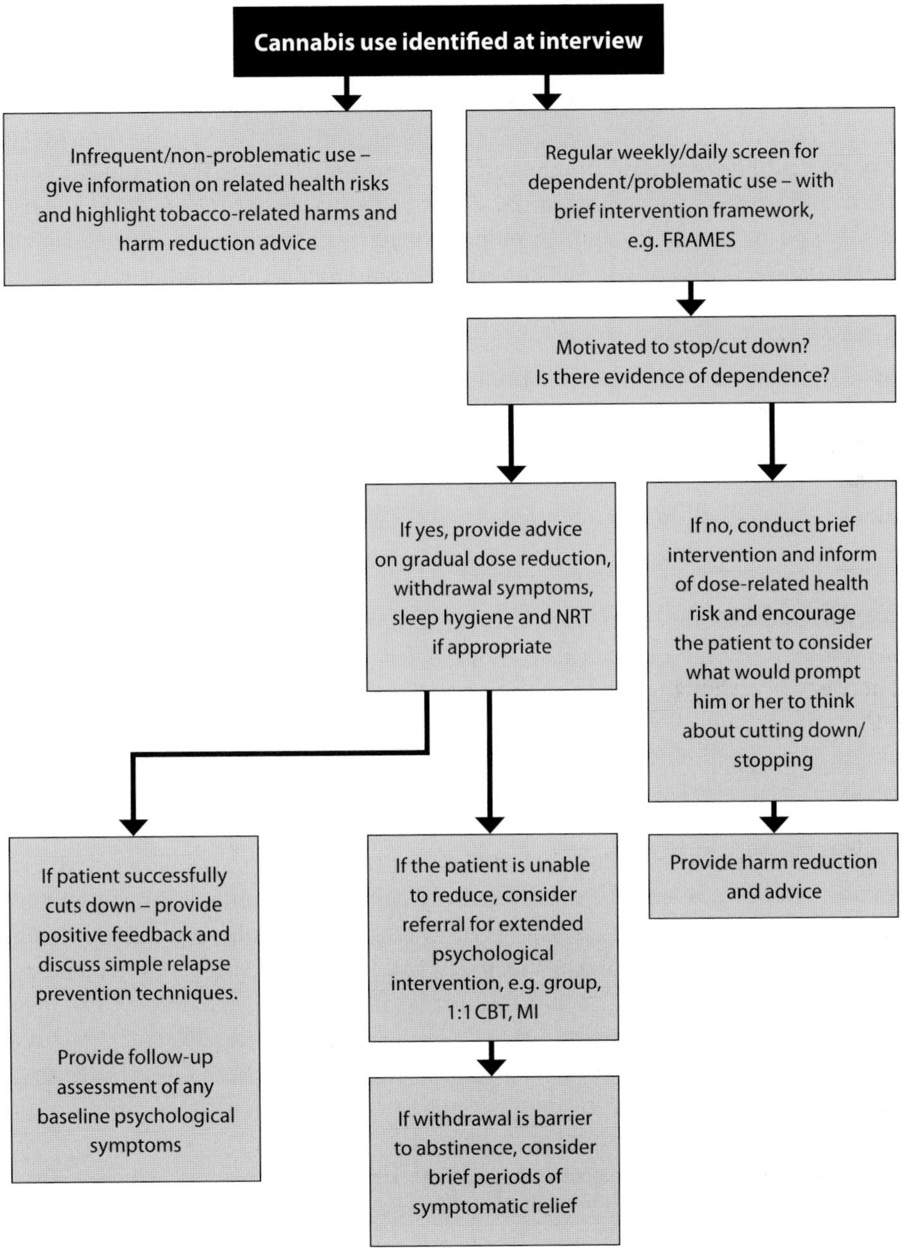

Source: reproduced from Winstock AR, Ford C, Witton J. Assessment and management of cannabis use disorders in primary care. *British Medical Journal* 2010; **340**: c1571 with permission from BMJ Publishing Group Ltd.

importance of delaying the onset of cannabis until adulthood with use commencing before the age of 18 being associated with an irreversible cognitive decline.[35]

Cannabis and pregnancy

The effects of cannabis on pregnancy and neurodevelopmental outcome are not clear, and research is confounded by a host of factors. In theory the effects of prenatal exposure could be significant given that the cannabinoid receptor system is the first one to develop in the foetus and is among the most numerous. Like all substances, any potential harm effect will be mediated by a host of other maternal behavioural (diet, other substance use including alcohol and tobacco) and social factors. The likelihood of concurrent tobacco use makes some of the effects predictable and thus cessation of use should strongly be encouraged for both substances given the well-documented adverse effects of prenatal tobacco exposure. From small uncontrolled studies prenatal exposure to cannabis has been associated with low birth weight and prematurity.[36]

Dependence

There are probably more people dependent upon cannabis in the UK than any other illicit drug. Around 10–15% of regular users are likely to meet DSM-IV criteria for dependence, and dependence on cannabis is the most common but most under-recognised consequence of regular cannabis use. Vulnerability to both experiencing reinforcing positive effects and dependence have a heritable component[37] as well as environmental ones that predispose to any problematic substance use disorder.[38] Across the EU and many other countries drug treatment monitoring systems have recorded steady increases in the number of people seeking help for cannabis-related problems including dependence, especially among younger people. Dependence upon cannabis often coexists with other substance use disorders – most commonly tobacco. Concurrent cannabis use/dependence is often ignored among those dependent upon other substances in the same way tobacco use is. Yet the impact upon the individual can be marked, with cessation often bringing new enthusiasm and energy.

Effective treatments include CBT, MI, contingency management and relapse prevention.[39–41] Online interventions show promise[26] and a range of other as yet untested approaches to encouraging reduction and adoption of healthier use are now available (e.g. www.drugsmeter.com). Concurrent tobacco smoking, which is prevalent in cannabis smokers, is a predictor of poor outcome, so nicotine replacement therapy (NRT) should be encouraged. As noted above, the concurrent use of cannabis and tobacco makes it harder to quit either substance,[42] and combined withdrawal from tobacco and cannabis is more severe than from either alone. NRT should be considered a central component in those who also use tobacco. While younger people may present with concerns over mental health and memory, older users may appear with concerns about lung health, personal relationships and employment issues.

Until recently the idea that cannabis users may experience withdrawal significant enough to be a barrier to achieving abstinence was, at least in the UK, given little thought. However, despite its absence from previous DSM iterations evidence for its existence as a clinical entity is strong and it is likely to find its way into the DSM-V. Community studies of treatment seekers suggest over three-quarters of daily users report withdrawal symptoms on cessation (peaking at day 2–3, with most symptoms over by day 7–10), as outlined in Box 13.5.[31,43] As with other substance use disorders, a stepped approach to treatment provision is advised, with longer periods of more intensive interventions being given to those with more severe problems and those who do not respond to initial brief interventions (see Figure 13.2, overleaf).

Box 13.5 **Cannabis withdrawal symptoms**

✓ Irritability, restlessness.

✓ Insomnia with weird dreams (take off NRT patches at night).

✓ Appetite disturbance (drop in weight).

✓ Craving.

✓ Depression.

✓ Aggression, violence (especially in those with premorbid aggression).

✓ Sweating, chills, stuffy nose.

✓ Muscular aches/pains.

✓ Fatigue, yawning.

✓ Nausea/GI symptoms, hyperemesis in a minority.

✓ Tremor, shakiness.

✓ Exacerbation of underlying psychotic illness.

Figure 13.2   **A decision pathway for assessing affective symptoms in cannabis users**

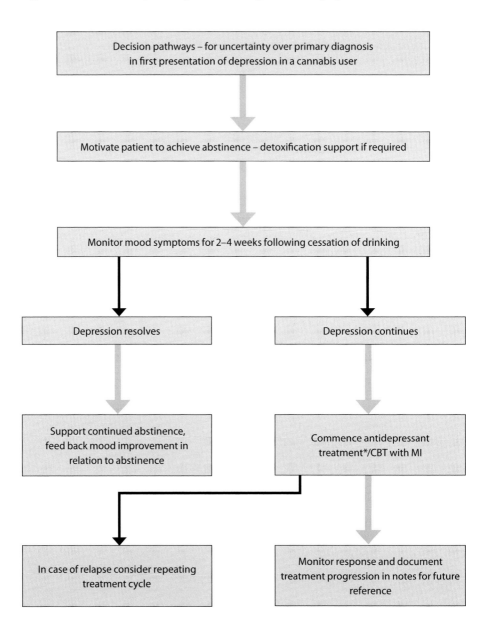

Source: reproduced from Winstock AR, Ford C, Witton J. Assessment and management of cannabis use disorders in primary care. *British Medical Journal* 2010; **340**: c1571 with permission from BMJ Publishing Group Ltd.

Note: * antidepressants should not typically be commenced during the early period of withdrawal since early side effects especially of SSRIs may make withdrawal worse.

Is withdrawal a problem and how do you manage it?

Withdrawal from cannabis among dependent users is reported by 75% of treatment seekers. For some, its severity, especially the insomnia and irritability, can be a barrier to abstinence. It tends to be more severe in those who are heavy smokers, who stop suddenly without planning, among concurrent tobacco users and those with mental illness. Psycho-education regarding the nature, severity and duration of common withdrawal effects can be useful to help users and their families understand and prepare. Common symptoms peak on day 2 or 3 and, for most, any major distress is over by day 7. Sleep problems, mood lability and vivid dreams can continue for 2–3 weeks.[43] There is no evidence-based pharmacological intervention to manage cannabis withdrawal,[31,44] although some small studies exploring the utility of oral THC show promise in reducing withdrawal and craving.[45] The essential components outlined in Box 13.6 (overleaf) are a reduction in use if possible before cessation, provision of NRT if appropriate, good sleep hygiene with caffeine avoidance or reduction (caffeine level can double on cessation of tobacco consumption) and the provision of a few days of night sedation and occasionally low-dose daytime anxiolytics. A typical regime might be diazepam 5 mg b.d. and zopiclone 7.5 mg at night for 4–7 days. Bupropion if used for nicotine dependence must begin at least one week before cessation of both substances, since commencing treatment on day one of cannabis cessation can exacerbate withdrawal symptoms.[46] There is no evidence to support the use of antidepressants in the management of cannabis withdrawal or dependence. The initiation of some classes such as SSRI during withdrawal may in fact worsen symptoms. It is far better to wait and see if the mood improves with cessation to support a motivational attribution to cessation than to a medication that many not have been needed (see Figure 13.2).

Therapeutic uses of cannabis

Medicinal cannabis may have a role in the management of a wide range of conditions from chemotherapy-induced nausea, to multiple sclerosis, AIDS and pain syndromes.[47] While oral preparations have been used for some years, more recent administration devices utilise aerosol technology.[48]

Conclusions following reclassification

The reclassification of cannabis as a Class B drug in 2009 after five years as Class C in the UK did not seem to be driven by any new scientific evidence. Use continued to fall and has currently levelled out with about 1.5–2 million last-year users in the

Box 13.6   **Management of withdrawal**

✓ Advise gradual reduction in amount used prior to cessation.

✓ Suggest delaying first use till later in the day.

✓ Suggest patient considers use of NRT if planning to stop independent tobacco use at same time.

✓ Advice on good sleep hygiene with avoidance of caffeine that may exacerbate irritability, restlessness and insomnia.

✓ Relaxation, progressive muscular relaxation, distraction.

✓ Psycho-education for user and family members as to nature, duration and severity of withdrawal.

✓ Cue and trigger avoidance.

✓ Symptomatic short-term medication provision of analgesia and sedation if required.

✓ If irritability and restlessness marked consider limited provision of very low-dose diazepam for 3–4 days.

UK. Use has fallen since its peak but may become a serious public health issue as older smokers face the reality of unmet treatment for dependence and chronic pulmonary harms. The long-term impact of chronic exposure and dependence upon health, wellbeing and relationships is probably under-recognised and under-disclosed. Forgetting to assess and manage cannabis use among those with chronic mental health problems will mean that an important potential site for intervention that would bring improvements in mental health outcome and physical health will be missed. GPs will remain the most important point for initial assessment and in many cases a suitable site for intervention.

Good sources of information for users and practitioners

Self-help sites such as www.knowcannabis.org.uk and www.drugsmeter.com provide objective, comparative feedback on a person's use of cannabis and other drugs. They also provide harm reduction tips and tips on cutting down, as well as assessment of dependence.

▶ www.talktofrank.com and www.youngminds.org.uk.

▶ Join a support group, for instance the online www.marijuana-anonymous.org.

▶ www.homeoffice.gov.uk/materials/kc-stop.pdf.

▶ Find local providers from www.drugscope.org.uk.

Competing interests

Adam Winstock is the creator of Drugs Meter (www.drugsmeter.com).

Further reading

Budney A J, Hughes J R, Moore B A, *et al*. Review of the validity and significance of cannabis withdrawal syndrome. *American Journal of Psychiatry* 2004; **161(11)**: 1967–77.

Copeland J, Frewen A, Elkins K. *Management of Cannabis Use Disorder and Related Issues. A clinician's guide*. Sydney: National Cannabis Prevention and Information Centre, 2009.

Hall W, Pacula R L. *Cannabis Use and Dependence: public health and public policy*. Cambridge: Cambridge University Press, 2003.

Miller W R, Rollnick S. *Motivational Interviewing: preparing people for change*. New York: Guilford Press, 2002.

References

1. Home Office. *Drug Misuse Declared: findings from the 2010/11 British Crime Survey*, www. homeoffice.gov.uk/publications/science-research-statistics/research-statistics/crime-research/hosb1211/ [accessed November 2012].

2. Winstock A, Barratt M. Synthetic cannabis: a comparison of patterns of use and effect profile with natural cannabis in a large global sample. *Drug and Alcohol Dependence*. In press.

3. McLaren J, Swift W, Dillon P, *et al*. Cannabis potency and contamination: a review of the literature. *Addiction* 2008; **103(7)**: 1100–9.

4. European Monitoring Centre for Drugs and Drug Addiction. *EMCDDA Insights. An overview of cannabis potency in Europe*. Luxembourg: Office for Official Publications of the European Communities, 2004.

5. Potter D J, Clark P, Brown M B. Potency of delta 9-THC and other cannabinoids in cannabis in England in 2005: implications for psychoactivity and pharmacology. *Journal of Forensic Sciences* 2008; **53(1)**: 90–4. doi: 10.1111/j.1556-4029.2007.00603.x.

6. Hall W, Swift W. The THC content of cannabis in Australia: evidence and implications. *Australian and New Zealand Journal of Public Health* 2000; **24(5)**: 503–8.

7. Huestis M A, Cone E J. Differentiating new marijuana use from residual drug excretion in occasional marijuana users. *Journal of Analytical Toxicology* 1998; **22(6)**: 445–54.

8. Henry J A, Oldfield W L, Kon O M. Comparing cannabis with tobacco. *British Medical Journal* 2003; **326(7396)**: 942–3.

9. Winstock A R, Ford C, Witton J. Assessment and management of cannabis use disorders in primary care. *British Medical Journal* 2010; **340**: c1571.

10. Gold M S. Marijuana. In: N S Miller (ed.). *Comprehensive Handbook of Alcohol and Drug Addiction*. New York: Marcel Dekker Inc., 1991, pp. 353–76.

11. Golding J F. Cannabis. In: Jones D M, Smith A P (eds). *Handbook of Human Performance: health and performance*. Vol. 2. New York: Academic Press, 1992, p. 175.

12. Ashbridge A, Hayden J A, Cartwright J. Acute cannabis consumption and motor vehicle collision risk: systematic review of observational studies and meta-analysis. *British Medical Journal* 2012; **344**: e536.

13. Hall W, Degenhardt L. Adverse health effects on non-medicinal cannabis use. *Lancet* 2009; **374(9698)**: 1383–91

14. Baldwin G C, Buckley D M, Roth M D, *et al.* Alveolar macrophages derived from the lungs of tobacco, marijuana and cocaine users are functionally compromised. In: L S Harris (ed.). *Problems of Drug Dependence. Proceedings of the 57th Annual Scientific Meeting of the College on problems of drug dependence*. NIDA Research Monograph Series 162. Rockville, M D: USDHHS, 1996, p. 192.

15. Taylor D R, Fergusson D M, Milne B J, *et al.* A longitudinal study of the effects of tobacco and cannabis exposure on lung function in young adults. *Addiction* 2002; **97(8)**: 1055–61.

16. Aldington S, Williams M, Nowitz M, *et al.* Effects of cannabis on pulmonary structure, function and symptoms. *Thorax* 2007; **62(12)**: 1058–63.

17. Tan W C, Lo C, Jong A, *et al.* Marijuana and chronic obstructive lung disease: a population-based study. *Canadian Medical Association Journal* 2009; **180(8)**: 814–20.

18. Donald P J. Marijuana and upper aerodigestive tract malignancy in young patients. In: G G Nahas, C Latour, N Hardy, *et al.* (eds) *Physiopathology of Illicit Drugs: cannabis, cocaine and opiates*. Oxford: Pergamon Press, 1991, pp. 39–54.

19. Aldington S, Harwood M, Cox B, *et al.* Cannabis use and risk of lung cancer: a case-control study. *European Respiratory Journal* 2008; **31(2)**: 280–6.

20. Earleywine M, Barnwell S S. Decreased respiratory symptoms in cannabis users who vaporize. *Harm Reduction Journal* 2007; **4**: 11.

21. Sugranyes G, Flamarique I, Parellada E, *et al.* Cannabis use and age of diagnosis of schizophrenia. *European Psychiatry* 2009; **24(5)**: 282–6.

22. Hall W. Is cannabis use psychotogenic? *Lancet* 2006; **367(9506)**: 193–5.

23. Verdoux H, Ginde C, Sorbara F, *et al.* Effects of cannabis and psychosis vulnerability in daily life: an experience sampling test study. *Psychological Medicine* 2003; **33(1)**: 23–32.

24. Macleod J, Davey Smith G, Hickman M. Does cannabis use cause schizophrenia? *Lancet* 2006; **367(9516)**: 1055.

25. Zammit S, Moore T H, Lingford-Hughes A, *et al.* Effects of cannabis use on outcomes of psychotic disorders: systematic review. *British Journal of Psychiatry* 2008; **193(5)**: 357–63.

26. Kay-Lambkin F J, Baker A L, Lewin T J, *et al*. Computer-based psychological treatment for comorbid depression and problematic alcohol and/or cannabis use: a randomized controlled trial of clinical efficacy. *Addiction* 2009; **104(3)**: 378–88

27. Degenhardt L, Hall W, Lynskey M. Exploring the association between cannabis use and depression. *Addiction* 2003; **98(11)**: 1493–504.

28. Crippa J A, Zuardi A W, Martín-Santos R, *et al*. Cannabis and anxiety: a critical review of the evidence. *Human Psychopharmacology* 2009; **24(7)**: 515–23.

29. Moore T H M, Zammit S, Lingford-Hughes A, *et al*. Cannabis use and risk of psychotic or affective mental health outcomes: a systematic review. *Lancet* 2007; **370(9584)**: 319–28.

30. Buckner J D, Crosby R D, Wonderlich S A, *et al*. Social anxiety and cannabis use: an analysis from ecological momentary assessment. *Journal of Anxiety Disorders* 2012; **26(2)**: 297–304.

31. Winstock A R, Lea T, Copeland J. Lithium carbonate in the management of cannabis withdrawal *Journal of Psychopharmacology* (Oxford) 2009; **23(1)**: 84–93.

32. Lynskey M, Hall W. The effects of adolescent cannabis use on educational attainment. *Addiction* 2000; **95(11)**: 1621–30.

33. Yücel M, Nadia Solowij N, Colleen Respondek C, *et al*. Regional brain abnormalities associated with long-term heavy cannabis use. *Archives of General Psychiatry* 2008; **65(6)**: 694–701.

34. Solowij N, Stephens R S, Roffman R A, *et al*., Marijuana Treatment Project Research Group. Cognitive functioning of long-term heavy cannabis users seeking treatment [published correction appears in *Journal of the American Medical Association* 2002; **287(13)**: 1651]. *Journal of the American Medical Association* 2002; **287(9)**: 1123–31.

35. Meier M H, Caspi A, Ambler A, *et al*. Persistent cannabis users show neuropsychological decline from childhood to midlife. *Proceedings of the National Academy of Sciences* 2012; **109(40)**: E2657–64.

36. Linn S, Schoenbaum S C, Monson R R, *et al*. The association of marijuana use with outcome of pregnancy. *American Journal of Public Health* 1983; **73(10)**: 1161–4.

37. Scherrer J F, Grant J D, Duncan A E, *et al*. Subjective effects to cannabis are associated with use, abuse and dependence after adjusting for genetic and environmental influences. *Drug and Alcohol Dependence* 2009; **105(1–2)**: 76–82.

38. Lloyd C. Risk factors for problem drug use: identifying vulnerable groups. *Drugs: education, prevention and policy* 1998; **5**: 217–32.

39. Litt M D, Kadden R M, Kabela-Cormier E, *et al*. Coping skills training and contingency management treatments for marijuana dependence: exploring mechanisms of behaviour change. *Addiction* 2008; **103(4)**: 638–48.

40. McCambridge J, Strang J. The efficacy of single-session motivational interviewing in reducing drug consumption and perceptions of drug-related risk and harm among young people: results from a multi-site cluster randomized trial. *Addiction* 2004; **99(1)**: 39–52.

41. Copeland J, Frewen A, Elkins K. *Management of Cannabis Use Disorder and Related Issues. A clinician's guide*. Sydney: National Cannabis Prevention and Information Centre, 2009.

42. Moore B A, Budney A J. Tobacco smoking in marijuana dependent outpatients. *Journal of Substance Abuse* 2001; **13(4)**: 583–96.

43. Budney A J, Hughes J R, Moore B A, *et al*. Review of the validity and significance of cannabis withdrawal syndrome. *American Journal of Psychiatry* 2004; **161(11)**: 1967–77.

44. Vandrey R, Haney M. Pharmacotherapy for cannabis dependence: how close are we? *CNS Drugs* 2009; **23(7)**: 543–53.

45. Budney A J, Vandrey R G, Hughes J R, *et al*. Oral delta-9-tetrahydrocannabinol suppresses cannabis withdrawal symptoms. *Drug and Alcohol Dependence* 2007; **86**: 22–9

46. Haney M, Ward AS, Comer S D, *et al*. Bupropion SR worsens mood during marijuana withdrawal in humans. *Psychopharmacology* 2001; **155(2)**: 171–9.

47. Seamon M J, Fass J A, Maniscalco-Feichtl M, *et al*. Medical marijuana and the developing role of the pharmacist. *American Journal of Health-System Pharmacy* 2007; **64(10)**: 1037–44.

48. Robson P. Therapeutic aspects of cannabis and cannabinoids. *British Journal of Psychiatry* 2001; **178**: 107–15.

CHAPTER 14

Tobacco use

Deborah Arnott, Melanie McIlvar and Andy McEwen

IN THIS CHAPTER

Introduction

Smoking remains the biggest single cause of preventable illness and premature death, killing around 100,000 people in the UK each year, more than the next six causes put together, including alcohol, obesity and illegal drug use.[1] For every death caused by smoking, approximately 20 smokers are suffering from a smoking-related disease.[2,3] Improving the nation's health requires a significant reduction in the number of people who smoke. Population-level measures are crucial and effective, but healthcare professionals also have a key role to play in supporting smokers to quit. GPs will in future have an even more crucial role to play not only as primary care physicians but also as commissioners for secondary care.

It is inconceivable that today's health professionals are not well aware of the risks of smoking. The original studies defining many of these risks were conducted on British GPs and as the initial results began to be disclosed doctors were amongst the first to give up smoking. In 2004, the 50-year follow-up of smokers in this study found that smokers died on average about ten years younger than lifetime non-smokers, and stopping smoking at age 60, 50, 40 or 30 years gained, respectively, about 3, 6, 9 or 10 years of life expectancy.[4]

The health professional's role is not an easy one. Although more than two-thirds of smokers want to give up[5] and regret having started, less than one in twenty succeed each year, rising to nearly one in five with counselling and medication.[6] But because smoking is so harmful, interventions with low levels of successful outcome are still highly cost-effective. All stop-smoking interventions provide excellent value for money, costing less than £1000 per life year saved, better than most other interventions in medicine,[7,8] and far better than the £20,000 benchmark for cost-effectiveness recognised by the National Institute for Health and Clinical Excellence (NICE).[9]

However, despite this, identification and referral of smokers into evidence-based stop-smoking support, although much more effective in reducing disease risk than most other current routine medical practices, is still not routine and systematic. In fact, over a third (35%) of patients when asked reported that during a GP consultation smoking was either not mentioned or, where mentioned, support was not offered.[10]

Policy context

There is a great deal of evidence about the most effective measures to reduce uptake and encourage smokers to quit. The most cost-effective measures are at population level and include reducing affordability by increasing the price through taxation and mass media campaigns to discourage smoking. However, smoking cessation treatments are essential to help smokers unable to quit unaided and are highly cost-effective compared with other healthcare interventions.

The first international health treaty, the World Health Organization (WHO) Framework Convention on Tobacco Control (FCTC), codifies the most effective tobacco control measures, including cessation treatment. Adopted in 2003 it is one of the most rapidly ratified treaties ever and now has 174 parties, including the UK, covering over 80% of the world population, over 70% of world cigarette consumption and over 70% of the world's cigarette producers.

The UK, and, as appropriate, the devolved administrations, have in place comprehensive tobacco control strategies in line with the WHO FCTC and its guidelines. The UK is acknowledged as leading Europe on tobacco control.[11] Key policies currently in place, under the six-strand approach set out by the World Bank, include:

1. **Stopping the promotion of tobacco**

   ▸ a comprehensive ban on advertising, promotion and sponsorship of tobacco

   ▸ a ban on tobacco displays is currently in the process of being implemented

2. **Making tobacco less affordable**

   ▸ high taxes, with annual budget increases above inflation

   ▸ a strong anti-smuggling strategy, which has led to year-on-year declines in the size of the illicit market

3. **Effective regulation of tobacco products**

   ▸ sale of tobacco products to minors prohibited (below 18)

   ▸ ban on the sale of tobacco from vending machines

   ▸ large health warnings on packs, including picture warnings

4. **Helping tobacco users to quit**

   ▸ stop-smoking services free at the point of delivery available to all smokers

5. **Reducing exposure to secondhand smoke**

   ▸ comprehensive smokefree laws including enclosed public places, public transport and work vehicles.

   ▸ smokefree homes and cars campaigns

6. **Effective communications for tobacco control**

   ▸ mass media campaigns to encourage quitting and discourage uptake.

The UK government consulted on the implementation of plain, standardised packaging of tobacco products in 2012. Australia was the first government to introduce such a policy in December 2012.

Health harms caused by smoking

Most smoking-related deaths are from one of three types of disease: lung cancer, chronic obstructive pulmonary disease and coronary heart disease. Smoking is estimated to be the causal factor in 35% of all respiratory deaths, 29% of all cancer deaths and 14% of all cardiovascular disease deaths. Estimates of the cost of smoking to the NHS in England alone range from £2.7 bn [12] to £5.2 bn a year.[13]

Table 14.1 **Estimated percentages and numbers of deaths attributable to smoking in England by cause, 2010**

| | Deaths estimated to be caused by smoking | | | | | |
| | Number of deaths | | | | % of deaths | |
	All deaths	Men	Women	Total	Men	Women
CANCER						
Lung, trachea and bronchus	28,044	13,800	9200	23,100	88	75
Oesophagus	6199	2900	1300	4200	71	62
Bladder	4131	1300	400	1700	46	31
Pancreas	6587	800	900	1700	24	27
Upper respiratory sites	1818	900	300	1200	74	51
Stomach	4041	700	200	900	27	13
Kidney	3357	700	100	800	36	9
Larynx	601	400	100	500	82	76
Myeloid leukaemia	2268	300	100	400	23	10
Cervical	699		100	100		12
Unspecified site	8075	2100	1000	3000	55	23
All cancer	**65,820**			**37,500**		
RESPIRATORY						
Chronic obstructive lung disease*	22,346	9400	8400	17,800	85	80
Pneumonia	23,565	2400	2100	4500	24	15
All respiratory	**45,911**			**22,300**		

Deaths estimated to be caused by smoking						
Number of deaths				**% of deaths**		
All deaths	Men	Women	Total	Men	Women	
CIRCULATORY						
Ischaemic heart disease	65,128	6200	3100	9400	16	11
Aortic aneurysm	6456	2500	1500	4000	64	58
Cerebrovascular disease	40,374	1900	1400	3400	12	6
Other heart disease	23,593	1900	1500	3400	19	11
Other arterial disease	2511	200	300	500	18	19
Atherosclerosis	374	0	0	100	29	13
All circulatory	**138,436**			**20,600**		
DIGESTIVE						
Stomach and duodenal ulcer	2340	600	600	1200	54	47
All deaths	**255,801**					
Total caused by smoking		**49,000**	**32,700**	**81,700**		

Source: adapted from NHS Information Centre for Health and Social Care.[14]

Note: * ICD codes J40–J44, which includes bronchitis, emphysema and other chronic obstructive lung disease. The proportion of deaths attributable to smoking is the median (midpoint) between the highest and lowest estimates for this group of diseases.

Reproductive functions are affected by smoking.[15] Female fertility is significantly reduced and smoking also increases the likelihood of early menopause. For men smoking can lead to reduced sperm count and motility, sperm being less able to penetrate the ovum and increased shape abnormalities, as well of course as an increased likelihood of impotence. There are many other medical conditions associated with or aggravated by smoking, which may not be fatal but still cause years of debilitating illness (see Box 14.1, overleaf).[1]

Box 14.1   **Medical conditions associated with smoking**

Heart and circulation

✓ Angina.

✓ Buerger's disease (severe circulatory disease).

✓ Peripheral vascular disease.

Diseases of the gums and teeth

✓ Acute necrotising ulcerative gingivitis (gum disease).

✓ Tooth loss.

✓ Tooth discolouration.

Stomach/digestive system

✓ Colon polyps.

✓ Crohn's disease (chronic inflamed bowel).

✓ Duodenal ulcer.

✓ Stomach ulcer.

Ligaments, muscles and bones

✓ Ligament, tendon and muscle injuries.

✓ Neck and back pain.

✓ Osteoporosis (in both sexes).

✓ Rheumatoid arthritis (in heavy smokers).

Eyes

✓ Cataract.

✓ Macular degeneration.

✓ Nystagmus (abnormal eye movements).

✓ Optic neuropathy (loss of vision).

✓ Ocular histoplasmosis (fungal eye infection).

✓ Tobacco amblyopia (loss of vision).

Skin

✓ Psoriasis.

✓ Skin wrinkling.

Other

✓ Depression.

✓ Hearing loss.

✓ Type 2 diabetes.

Health harms caused by secondhand smoke

While the relative health risks from secondhand smoke (SHS) are small in comparison with risks from active smoking, the overall health impact is large because the diseases are common.

SHS can have a particularly damaging effect on cardiovascular health and studies in the USA, Scotland and elsewhere have shown that smokefree laws have reduced hospital admissions for heart attacks.[16] Smokefree legislation has had a significant impact in reducing the levels of exposure to secondhand smoke, particularly among adults,[16] and exposure now is largely confined to private spaces, in particular homes and cars.

It has been estimated that domestic exposure to secondhand smoke in the UK causes around 2700 deaths in people aged 20–63 and a further 8000 deaths a year among people aged 65 years and older.[17]

Children are particularly vulnerable to passive smoke exposure in the home. About 2 million children currently live in a household where they are exposed to cigarette smoke. Passive smoking amongst children in the UK[18] is responsible each year for:

- over 20,000 cases of lower respiratory tract infection

- 120,000 cases of middle-ear disease

- at least 22,000 new cases of wheeze and asthma

- 200 cases of bacterial meningitis

- 40 sudden infant deaths (SIDs) – one in five of all SIDs.

These cases generate over 300,000 UK GP consultations and about 9500 hospital admissions, and cost the NHS about £23.3 million.

Relative to children in non-smoking families, passive smoke exposure is around three times higher if the father smokes, over six times higher if the mother smokes, and nearly nine times higher if both parents smoke. Children growing up with parents or siblings who smoke are also 90% more likely to become smokers themselves. The most effective means of protecting children from passive smoking is to reduce the prevalence of smoking in their parents and carers.[18]

Benefits of smoking cessation

Stopping smoking is the single most important thing a smoker can do to improve his or her current and future health. Stopping smoking halves the risk of recurrence of myocardial infarction, a much greater and more cost-effective impact than that achieved by other routine interventions such as therapy with aspirin, beta-blockers, ACE inhibitors or statins, but in clinical practice is the least likely intervention to be applied.

Smoking cessation is the only intervention that halts the development of chronic obstructive airways disease or reduces the risk of lung cancer, but only half of all UK chest specialists have direct access to a smoking cessation counsellor.[19]

Smoking rates are similar for diabetics and non-diabetics, but smoking increases the risk of serious disease and death in diabetics from 4 to 11 times. Stopping smoking before surgery can have a dramatic impact on outcome. In hip and knee operations it reduces postoperative complications by two-thirds and duration of stay in hospital by 15%.[20]

Epidemiology of smoking

The UK historically had amongst the highest smoking rates in the world, peaking at 82% of men in 1948 and 45% of women in the 1960s. The rate of smoking was continuing to increase amongst women as it declined amongst men and over time overall smoking rates for men and women have converged. The rate of decline reached a plateau in the 1990s and then began to fall again following the introduction of the government's first comprehensive tobacco control strategy in 1998. Smoking rates fell by a half amongst children (aged 11–15) and a quarter amongst adults between 1998 and 2008, but since then rates of decline have slowed.[21]

Between 2007 and 2009, overall smoking prevalence among adults in the UK remained the same at 21%, dropping to 20% in 2010 (21% of men and 20% of women).[21] Smoking prevalence is highest in the 20–24 age group among women (29%) and in the 25–34 age group among men (28%) but thereafter in older age groups the proportion of smokers declines due to a combination of quitting and death from smoking-related diseases.

The prevalence of regular smoking among children aged 11–15 remained stable at between 9% and 11% from 1998 until 2006. However, in 2007 there was a fall in overall prevalence from 9% to 6%, the lowest rate recorded since surveys of pupils' smoking began in 1982. There was a further decline in 2010 to 5% overall and to 12% among 15-year-olds. However, it is still the case that over 200,000 11–15-year-olds take up smoking each year. Smoking uptake starts earlier amongst girls such that 14% of 15-year-old girls smoke compared with only 10% of boys,[22] but by the time they reach adulthood smoking rates are very similar amongst men and women.

Smoking and health inequalities

Fifty years ago smoking rates were very similar across the classes, but since then they have declined most rapidly amongst the most affluent in society and differential smoking rates are now the single largest reason for the differences in life expectancy between the richest and poorest in society.[23] Smoking is independently linked with every indicator of disadvantage, but there is a particularly strong link between any type of mental illness or substance use disorder and high rates of smoking prevalence (see Table 14.2, overleaf).

Patients diagnosed with mental illness or substance use disorder are not only more likely to be smokers but also are more likely to smoke heavily, which is not only more harmful to health but also is costly, a critical factor for a group of people already often financially disadvantaged because of the potentially incapacitating effects of their disorders. Inpatient smokers in the UK, for example, were almost five times more likely to be classified as heavy smokers (defined as smoking more than 20 cigarettes a day) than the general population.[24]

Amongst those diagnosed with schizophrenia, rates of cancer, cardiovascular disease and respiratory diseases have been shown to be double those of people of similar age in the general population [25] and it is estimated that most of the excess mortality observed in those diagnosed with schizophrenia is due to smoking and not to schizophrenia itself.[26] More people with serious alcohol problems die from smoking-related diseases than from alcohol-related diseases and the impact of alcohol and tobacco use combined significantly increases the risk of many diseases such as mouth and throat cancers, and cirrhosis of the liver.[27]

Smokers with schizophrenia also require higher levels of medication, experience increased psychiatric symptoms and a higher number of admissions to hospital compared with non-smokers. It is not the nicotine in the tobacco but the smoke that affects the serum level of some medications, such as antipsychotic drugs, antidepressants and several other over-the-counter and prescribed medications.[26] If patients were to use nicotine replacement therapy (NRT) rather than smoke tobacco the amount of drugs they need to take could be substantially reduced. For example, to achieve the same blood concentration of clozapine, an antipsychotic drug, requires an increase in dose of up to 50% for smokers, which can be reduced after quitting.[27]

Smoking increases the risk of developing some mental illnesses,[28] and is associated with higher suicide rates.[29] Stopping smoking has been shown to improve not just physical but also psychological wellbeing.[30] Although, as with other addictive disorders, there can be weight gain after quitting, there is little evidence of worsening of psychiatric symptoms and no significant increase in levels of aggression,[31] despite the fears often expressed about this by many mental health workers. There is a strong relationship between tobacco use and depressive/anxiety symptoms both in people with and without mental health problems. However, symptoms

Table 14.2   **Smoking rate by mental disorder (age-standardised rates)**

	Number of cases	**Prevalence of disorder in the population**	**Proportion who are 'regular smokers'**
Total sample	7393		22%
Type of mental disorder			
CIS-R assessed disorders			
Depressive episode	255	3%	37%
Phobias	160	2%	37%
Generalised anxiety disorder	363	4%	36%
Obsessive-compulsive disorder	86	1%	34%
Panic disorder	83	1%	31%
Mixed anxiety and depression	639	8%	29%
Any common mental disorder (CIS-R)	**1275**	**16%**	**32%**
Illicit drug dependence [a]	200	3%	69%
Alcohol problem (AUDIT 8+)	1600	24%	30%
Alcohol dependence [c]	367	6%	46%
Probable psychosis	40	1%	40%
Problem gambling	41	1%	38%[b]
PTSD screen	215	3%	37%
ADHD screen	39	1%	31%[d]
Eating disorder screen	108	2%	20%[d]
Attempted suicide [a]	51	1%	57%
Any mental disorder	**1690**	**23%**	**33%**

Source: McManus S, Meltzer H, Campion J. *Cigarette Smoking and Mental Health in England.*[32] Reproduced with permission from the National Centre for Social Research.

Notes: [a] It was not possible to age-standardise for these categories. [b] Despite the high rate of smoking identified among people with problem gambling, this was not found to be significantly higher than the prevalence of smoking in the general population. This is likely to be because of the small number of people identified in the survey sample with problem gambling. Other studies have found smoking rates to be elevated in this group. [c] Alcohol dependence was used rather than the more inclusive 'alcohol problem' variable. Borderline personality disorder and antisocial personality disorder are included in this composite variable but are not shown separately due to the small number of cases identified in the survey sample (16 and 9 respectively). [d] The smoking rate for these disorders was not significantly different from that of the general population as a whole.

reduce rapidly, and wellbeing improves, with levels of anxiety declining as soon as one week after quitting.[31]

Nicotine dependence

Nicotine dependence is recognised in the ICD-10 and DSM-IV as a psychiatric disorder in which long-term cessation is in part dependent upon motivation, as evidenced by the number of smokers who want to quit, make an attempt but who can't maintain abstinence.[33] The defining features include failed attempts to abstain, powerful urges to use nicotine and withdrawal symptoms on cessation. An estimated 80% of cigarette smokers are classifiable as dependent by DSM-IV criteria. Tobacco in smoked form is as highly addictive a drug as heroin or cocaine.[34] It is an addiction of young people with over 80% of regular smokers starting smoking before they are 19 and two-thirds by the age of 18.[5]

Prevention

As most smokers begin in their late teens it might seem a sensible policy to commence prevention strategies with pre-teens. Research shows, however, that unless this is part of a comprehensive programme of personal health and social education, youth smoking prevention policies are largely ineffectual. At best they may delay the onset of smoking but they have little impact on overall smoking prevalence.[35]

Effectively supporting smokers to stop

The provision of effective interventions and pathways to support smokers to stop is an important part of any comprehensive tobacco control strategy.[36]

However, the fact that less than 2% of smokers making a quit attempt currently do so with medication and behavioural support (the most effective combination) [10] means that stop-smoking services have only been able to demonstrate a limited impact upon smoking prevalence. This also suggests that other tobacco control interventions should not only prompt quit attempts, but also should encourage those quit attempts to take place with the support of stop-smoking services and using effective medication.

There are a number of evidence-based stop-smoking interventions that vary in intensity and content. These include: very brief advice, brief interventions and pharmacological support only, as well as more intensive interventions that include both pharmacological and behavioural support.

Very brief advice

Every healthcare professional has a vital role to play in effectively support-ing smokers to stop. This begins with the routine delivery of very brief advice (VBA) (see Figure 14.1, overleaf), which, especially when delivered by a physician, can double the likelihood of a smoker attempting to stop.[10] To have the greatest impact, however, it is particularly important that both treatment and support is recommended. For example, when compared with no advice to smokers, the odds of quitting are 68% higher if stop-smoking medication is offered and 370% higher following an offer of support such as that provided by in-house or local stop-smoking services.[37]

Routine identification of smokers and offer of support are also promoted by a number of national initiatives designed to encourage the effective delivery of healthcare services to patients. These include the Quality and Outcomes Frame-work (QOF) within which a number of smoking-related indicators are included with respect to recording smoking status, provision of information and the offer of support and treatment.

Figure 14.1   **Very brief advice on smoking**

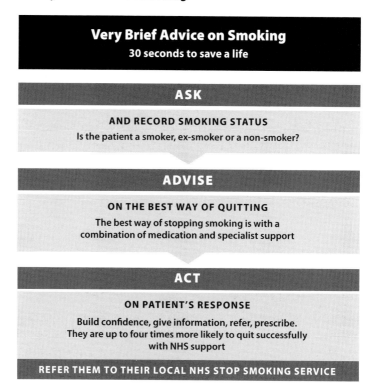

Source: National Centre for Smoking Cessation and Training. Used with permission.

Intensive stop-smoking interventions

Structured stop-smoking interventions that combine pharmacological and behavioural support are the most effective and roughly quadruple a smoker's chances of stopping.[6, 10] Since 1999 local stop-smoking services have been available across the UK; since their inception, services in England have supported just under 3 million smokers to stop.[38] However, services continue to be dramatically under-used, which both decreases an individual smoker's chances of stopping and reduces the impact services could have on smoking prevalence.

In the main, services follow the abrupt model of support, which focuses on a smoker setting a quit date, after which he or she aims to stop smoking completely and adhere to the 'not a puff rule'. While there is an emerging evidence base regarding reduction approaches to quitting involving NRT, the abrupt model remains the most effective and widely used.

In order to be as accessible as possible, services commonly offer a range of intervention types including one-to-one, group and drop-in support in a variety of settings. Findings from randomised controlled trials were further supported by a recent review of data from 24 stop-smoking services (126,890 treatment episodes). It showed that smokers receiving stop-smoking support from specialist clinics, treatment in groups and using varenicline or combination NRT were more likely to succeed than those receiving treatment in primary care, one-to-one and single-product NRT.[39]

Training to support stop-smoking interventions

Since 2010 national training has been available to practitioners involved in the delivery of intensive stop-smoking interventions via the National Centre for Smoking Cessation and Training (www.ncsct.co.uk). More recently a short VBA module has also become available via BMJ e-learning.

Pharmacotherapy

Currently there are three stop-smoking medications recommended by NICE: NRT, bupropion and varenicline.

Nicotine replacement therapy

NRT products can be prescribed to patients on FP10s but many local areas now also have voucher or alternative pathways in place to make NRT more easily available for the cost of a prescription. NRT is also available to buy over the counter or on general sale; however, only NRT provided via a healthcare professional such as a practitioner or pharmacist is known to have any added benefit.[10]

In terms of effectiveness, no single NRT product is more effective than others. However, for highly dependent smokers the 4 mg gum is more effective than 2 mg gum and higher-dose patches are more effective than lower-dose patches. There is no clear evidence that the 24-hour patch is more effective than the 16-hour patch and no evidence that tapering patch dose after eight weeks improves effectiveness.[40]

A range of NRT products exists:

- transdermal patch (varying doses, 16-hour and 24-hour duration)

- gum (2 mg and 4 mg)

- inhalator

- mouth spray

- nasal spray (0.5 mg per dose)

- sublingual tablet (2 mg)

- lozenge (1 mg, 2 mg and 4 mg)

- mini-lozenge (1.5 mg and 4 mg).

NRT increases the chance of achieving abstinence for at least six months. These figures arise from many high-quality randomised controlled trials with biochemical verification of smoking status at follow-up (usually from expired air carbon monoxide). There is also evidence that combinations of NRT products are more effective overall than single products, and that combinations are safe. NRT delivers pure nicotine that, while highly addictive when smoked (and to a slightly lesser extent chewed), does not pose a cancer risk, or a risk of COPD or other respiratory disease. NRT use is safe in patients with stable coronary heart disease; the risks of using NRT during pregnancy are slightly less clear, however. Since 2005 NRT products have been licensed for use during pregnancy and, where it is not possible for a woman to stop without pharmacological support, their use is also recommended by NICE. This is based upon analysis that any risks associated with the use of NRT are far outweighed by the risks of the mother continuing to smoke.

Although patients may be concerned about becoming dependent upon NRT ('swapping one addiction for another'), this is not common. The biggest problem with NRT is that people do not use enough of it for long enough. So if a patient is using NRT long term they should probably continue rather than risk returning to smoking. A minority of smokers transfer dependence from cigarettes to NRT. Such patients would probably resume smoking if they could not continue NRT use.

Varenicline

Varenicline (trade name Champix), a prescription-only medication, is the latest type of stop-smoking medication to be recommended by NICE (approval received in 2007). It works by reducing urges to smoke and the reinforcing effects of smoking while lessening any withdrawal symptoms experienced after stopping.

A Cochrane Review consisting of trials that compared the use of varenicline with placebo concluded that varenicline approximately trebles a smoker's chance of stopping long term compared with stopping without pharmacological support.[41]

In comparison with the other stop-smoking medications, varenicline has been shown to be superior to bupropion.[42, 43] Comparison with NRT is less clear although there is evidence to show that smokers using varenicline have a greater chance of success in the short term, although this is not necessarily sustained for longer-term abstinence.[44]

There are few contraindications associated with varenicline. However, smokers who have had a previous adverse reaction to the medication, who are pregnant and/or under the age of 18 should not use it. Varenicline is also not recommended for patients with end-stage renal failure.

Despite a number of initial reports in the media linking varenicline with a number of suicide deaths, further reviews have found no evidence to suggest a causal link between the use of varenicline and the occurrence of suicide-related events, suicidal ideation or depressive disorders. Depression can however be a symptom of nicotine withdrawal.

The findings of a meta-analysis published in 2011,[45] which looked at the number of cardiovascular events seen in 8216 clients taking either varenicline or placebo, indicated that it may be worth investigating the link between cardiovascular events and varenicline further. However, there is currently little reason to avoid this medication on these grounds. This view is in line with the European Medicines Agency, which confirmed a positive benefit–risk balance for varenicline and concluded that its benefits as a smoking cessation medicine outweigh any slight increase in cardiovascular events.[46]

Bupropion

The atypical antidepressant bupropion (trade name Zyban) is also marketed for use when stopping smoking and can also double the chances of long-term abstinence.[47] There is inconclusive evidence as to whether bupropion is less or more effective than NRT, although randomised controlled trials have shown it to be less effective than varenicline,[43] and it does have a more serious side effect profile than the other medications.

Bupropion is contraindicated in people with a past history of seizures, depression, suicide ideation or bipolar affective disorder, and its safety has not been well established in pregnancy and young people under 18 years old. The use of bupropion in combination with other stop-smoking medicines is also not recommended.

Effect of stopping smoking on medications

As cigarette smoke stimulates a liver enzyme responsible for metabolising some medicines in the body, the metabolism of certain medications can be affected when a patient stops smoking and may require monitoring and/or adjustment. Medicines affected in this way include theophylline, insulin, paracetamol, propranolol, tamoxifen, verapamil and warfarin-R, as well as some mental health medications.

Summary of treatment for smoking

▶ Supporting smokers to stop is an essential element of any comprehensive tobacco control strategy.

▶ All healthcare professionals should routinely deliver VBA to identify and refer patients who want to quit to local stop-smoking services.

▶ Patients who decline referral for intensive stop-smoking support should be offered a form of pharmacological support on prescription as an alternative.

▶ Those patients not ready to quit should be told that this is fine and that you will be available to help them in the future when they do want to stop smoking.

▶ Stop-smoking interventions that combine pharmacological and behavioural support are the most effective, quadrupling the likelihood of quitting.

▶ NRT, bupropion and varenicline are the three stop-smoking medications currently available to smokers in the UK.

▶ Combining two NRT products (combination NRT) is more effective than using just one product (single NRT). Varenicline appears to be more effective than bupropion and single NRT although there is less evidence regarding a comparison with combination NRT.

Tobacco harm reduction

The public health goal in relation to smoking tobacco must be to reduce the death and disease it causes. Reducing tobacco or nicotine consumption is not an end in itself. There is now substantial experience with medicinal nicotine taken in the form of smoking cessation products. Although addictive, the main harm from nicotine is related to the method of use: inhaling hot smoke. Where smokers cannot give up their nicotine habit, converting to forms of nicotine other than smoked tobacco will reduce their risks of morbidity and premature mortality to levels similar to non-smokers. It is for this reason that the MHRA has licensed NRT for long-term use and is currently looking at how it should regulate nicotine-containing products, such as e-cigarettes, as an alternative to smoking and not just as a cessation aid. NICE is currently developing guidelines for tobacco harm reduction. (Both initiatives are due for publication in spring 2013.) There is enormous potential to narrow health inequalities and dramatically cut the numbers dying from smoking by substituting safer forms of nicotine for smoked tobacco for longer-term use, not just to help cessation in the very short term.

Conclusion

Smoking amongst professional groups is seen as an embarrassment and becoming less and less common (even in private). The same cannot be said for other socioeconomic groups. It is worrying that young people are continuing to take up the habit, many of them to become lifelong smokers. Targeting our interventions at young people seems a sensible way forward but has not been proven effective. The evidence is that if smoking is to become the exception rather than the norm it requires government policies to encourage behaviour change at population level. The health professional's role is perhaps to effectively support existing smokers to access help in quitting, while informing political leaders of the risks that the population of tomorrow face if smoking prevalence does not continue to significantly decline.

References

1. Action on Smoking and Health. ASH Factsheet. Smoking statistics: illness & death, 2011.

2. US Department of Health and Human Services. *How Tobacco Smoke Causes Disease: the biology and behavioral basis for smoking-attributable disease: a report of the Surgeon General*. Atlanta, GA: US Department of Health and Human Services, 2010.

3. Cigarette smoking-attributable morbidity: United States, 2000. *Morbidity and Mortality Weekly Report*, 5 September 2003.

4. Doll R, Peto R, Boreham J, *et al.* Mortality in relation to smoking: 50 years' observations on male British doctors. *British Medical Journal* 2004; **328(7455)**: 1519.

5. Dunstan S. *The 2010 General Lifestyle Survey*. Newport: Office for National Statistics, 2012.

6. Bauld L, Bell K, McCullough L, *et al.* The effectiveness of NHS smoking cessation services: a systematic review. *Journal of Public Health* (Oxford). 2010; **32(1)**: 71–82.

7. Flack S, Taylor M, Trueman P. *Cost-Effectiveness of Interventions for Smoking Cessation*. York: NICE, 2007.

8. Godfrey C, Parrott S, Coleman T, *et al.* The cost-effectiveness of the English smoking treatment services: evidence from practice. *Addiction* 2005; **100(Suppl 2)**: 70–83.

9. National Institute for Health and Clinical Excellence. *The Guidelines Manual.* London: NICE, 2009.

10. Smoking Toolkit Study, www.smokinginengland.info.

11. Joossens L, Raw M. *The Tobacco Control Scale 2010 in Europe.* Brussels: Association of European Cancer Leagues, 2010.

12. Callum C, Boyle S, Sandford A. Estimating the cost of smoking to the NHS in England and the impact of declining prevalence. *Health Economics, Policy and Law* 2010. doi: 10.1017/S1744133110000241.

13. Allender S, Balakrishnan R, Scarborough P, *et al.* The burden of smoking-related ill health in the UK. *Tobacco Control* 2009; **18(4)**: 262–7.

14. NHS Information Centre for Health and Social Care. Statistics on smoking: England, 2011, www.ic.nhs.uk/pubs/smoking11 [accessed November 2012].

15. Action on Smoking and Health. ASH Factsheet. Smoking and reproduction, 2011.

16. Bauld L. *The Impact of Smokefree Legislation in England: evidence review.* Bath: University of Bath, 2011.

17. Jamrozik K Estimate of deaths among adults in the United Kingdom attributable to passive smoking: database analysis. *British Medical Journal* 2005; **330(7495)**: 812.

18. Royal College of Physicians. *Passive Smoking and Children: a report of the Tobacco Advisory Group of the Royal College of Physicians.* London: RCP, 2010.

19. Campbell I A, Lewis K E, Preston L A. Surveys and assessment of secondary care smoking cessation services in the UK, 2001–2003 (abstract). *Thorax* 2003; **53(Suppl III)**: iii42–iii43.

20. Møller A M, Villebro N, Pedersen T, *et al.* Effect of preoperative smoking intervention on postoperative complications: a randomised clinical trial. *Lancet* 2002; **359(9301)**: 114–17.

21. Action on Smoking and Health. ASH Factsheet. Smoking statistics: who smokes and how much, 2012.

22. Information Centre for Health and Social Care. *Smoking, Drinking and Drug Use among Young People in England in 2010.* London: National Centre for Social Research, 2011.

23. Jarvis M J, Wardle J. Social patterning of health behaviours: the case of cigarette smoking. In: M Marmot, R Wilkinson (eds). *Social Determinants of Health* (2nd edn). Oxford: Oxford University Press, 2005, pp. 240–55.

24. Farrell M, Howes S, Taylor C, *et al.* Substance misuse and psychiatric comorbidity: an overview of the OPCS National Psychiatric Morbidity Survey. *Addictive Behaviors* 1998; **23(6)**: 909–18.

25. Williams J M, Ziedonis D M, Abanyie F, *et al.* Increased nicotine and cotinine levels in smokers with schizophrenia and schizoaffective disorder is not a metabolic effect. *Schizophrenia Research* 2005; **79(2–3)**: 323–35.

26. Brown S, Inskip H, Barraclough B. Causes of the excess mortality of schizophrenia. *British Journal of Psychiatry* 2000; **177(3)**: 212–17.

27. Olivier D, Lubman D I, Fraser R. Tobacco smoking within psychiatric inpatient settings: biopsychosocial perspective. *Australian and New Zealand Journal of Psychiatry* 2007; **41(7)**: 572–80.

28. Cuijpers P, Smit F, ten Have M, *et al.* Smoking is associated with first-ever incidence of mental disorders: a prospective population-based study. *Addiction* 2007; **102(8)**: 1303–9.

29. Malone K M, Waternaux C, Haas G L, *et al.* Cigarette smoking, suicidal behavior, and serotonin function in major psychiatric disorders. *American Journal of Psychiatry* 2003; **160(4)**: 773–9.

30. Ratschen E, Britton J, Doody G A, *et al*. Tobacco dependence, treatment and smoke-free policies: a survey of mental health professionals' knowledge and attitudes. *General Hospital Psychiatry* 2009; **31(6)**: 576–82.

31. Campion J, Checinski K, Nurse J, *et al*. Smoking by people with mental illness and benefits of smoke-free mental health services. *Advances in Psychiatric Treatment* 2008; **14**: 217–28.

32. McManus S, Meltzer H, Campion J. *Cigarette Smoking and Mental Health in England: data from the Adult Psychiatric Morbidity Survey 2007*. London: National Centre for Social Research, 2010.

33. West R. *Theory of Addiction*. Chichester: Wiley, 2006.

34. Balfour D, Bates C, Benowitz N, *et al*. *Nicotine Addiction in Britain. A report of the Tobacco Advisory Group of the Royal College of Physicians*. London: RCP, 2000.

35. Reid D, McNeill A D, Glynn T J. Reducing the prevalence of smoking in youth in Western countries: an international review. *Tobacco Control* 1995; **4(3)**: 266–77.

36. World Bank. *Tobacco Control at a Glance*, 2003, www1.worldbank.org/tobacco.

37. Aveyard P, Begh R, Parsons A, *et al*. Brief opportunistic smoking cessation interventions: a systematic review and meta-analysis to compare advice to quit and offer of assistance. *Addiction* 2011. doi: 10.1111/j.1360-0443.2011.03770.x.

38. NHS Information Centre. *Statistics on NHS Stop Smoking Services: England, April 2010–March 2011*. Leeds: NHS IC, 2011, www.ic.nhs.uk/statistics-and-data-collections/health-and-lifestyles/nhs-stop-smoking-services/statistics-on-nhs-stop-smoking-services-england-april-2010-march-2011 [accessed November 2012].

39. Brose L, West R. McDermott M, *et al*. What makes an effective stop smoking service? *Thorax* 2011. doi:10.1136/thoraxjnl-2011-200251

40. Silagy C, Ketteridge S. The effectiveness of physician advice to aid smoking cessation. In: *The Cochrane Library*. Issue 2. Chichester: Wiley, 1998.

41. Cahill K, Stead L F, Lancaster T. Nicotine receptor partial agonists for smoking cessation. In: *The Cochrane Database of Systematic Reviews*. Issue 3. Chichester: Wiley, 2008.

42. Jorenby D E, Hays J T, Rigotti N A, *et al*. Efficacy of varenicline, an α4β2 nicotinic acetylcholine receptor partial agonist, vs placebo or sustained-release bupropion for smoking cessation. *Journal of the American Medical Association* 2006; **296(1)**: 56–63.

43. Gonzales D, Rennard S I, Nides M, *et al*. Varenicline, an α4β2 nicotinic acetylcholine receptor partial agonist, vs placebo or sustained-release bupropion for smoking cessation. Presented at 12th SRNT, 15–18 February 2006, Orlando, Florida. Abstract PA9-2.

44. Aubin H, Bobak A, Britton J R, *et al*. Varenicline versus transdermal patch for smoking cessation: results from a randomized open-label trial. *Thorax* 2008; **63(8)**: 717–24.

45. Singh S, Loke Y K, Spangler J G, *et al*. Risk of serious adverse cardiovascular events associated with varenicline: a systematic review and meta-analysis. *Canadian Medical Association Journal* 2011. doi: 10.1503/cmaj.110218.

46. European Medicines Agency. Press release: European Medicines Agency confirms positive benefit–risk balance for Champix. 21 July 2011. www.ema.europa.eu/.

47. Hughes J R, Stead L F, Lancaster T. Antidepressants for smoking cessation. *The Cochrane Database of Systematic Reviews*. Issue 1. Chichester: Wiley, 2007.

CHAPTER 15

Injecting drug use: reducing the harm

Jon Derricott, Emer Coffey and David Young

Harm reduction and recovery

Since the mid-1980s, in response to the threat of HIV, UK drug policy has been largely one of harm reduction. Harm reduction is best described as a pragmatic, public health-oriented approach that focuses on optimising health and wellbeing, minimising the disease and mortality associated with higher-risk behaviours, while recognising that there are many reasons why people engage in higher-risk behaviour and that the behaviour may continue despite the risks.

More recently, UK drug policy has been driven by the concept of recovery. Recovery is perhaps most usefully described as a sustainable lifestyle engaged in by someone who has been or continues to be dependent on drugs. This definition would, for example, include someone who is stable on an opiate substitution prescription (although there is a lack of consensus about what constitutes recovery, with some equating recovery with abstinence). Recovery and harm reduction should be entirely compatible, with each having roles to play at different stages in a drug-using 'career'. Harm reduction has a huge part to play in maintaining and improving the health of people who inject drugs (PWID).

Injecting drug use

It is important for doctors, nurses and pharmacists to be able to engage effectively with PWID. To do this, they need to have knowledge of the drugs injected, the injecting equipment used, the risks associated with each stage of the injecting process and how those risks can be lowered.

Injecting drug use became a medically popular form of administration following the invention of the hypodermic syringe in the nineteenth century. Illicit injecting began to take hold after the First World War, with the first reports of disease transmission (malaria) via this route coming in the 1920s.[1]

Prevalence

The prevalence of injecting in England has been falling for several years. The numbers of people entering treatment who have never injected, or who no longer inject, have both increased. In 2009/10, 47% of those entering drug treatment were current or former PWID (with 27% being former and 20% current PWID). The consensus view is that we are now past the peak of the heroin epidemic of the 1980s, with fewer under-25s entering treatment for heroin problems and the largest proportion of PWID entering treatment being between the ages of 30 and 34. The number of former PWID over 40 entering treatment after many years of injecting and resulting health problems is rising.[2] These changes are encouraging for the future public health. The causes for the changes are likely to include: successful harm reduction-based treatment strategies, changes in fashion and culture, and the declining quality of street heroin.

Injecting

The vast majority of PWID do so intravenously, as it maximises the effects (and many dangers) of drugs. Subcutaneous injection ('skin-popping') is less common, but still occurs. Intramuscular injection is similarly infrequent and may be intentional, or happen accidentally when the individual misses the vein or the subcutaneous space.

The most commonly injected drugs are heroin, cocaine and anabolic steroids. Street heroin usually comes as a brown powder, and cocaine either in the form of crack or as a white powder. Brown heroin and crack cocaine are both in base form and require the addition of an acid to make them soluble in water. Any water-soluble drug may be injected, including amphetamines, buprenorphine, methadone[3] and benzodiazepines.[4,5] Recently there have been reports of injecting of the former 'legal high' mephedrone associated with significant physical harm.[6] Street drugs may be 'cut' with other substances to increase bulk: glucose powder, flour, talcum powder or even chalk. Injecting these intravenously can cause granulomas in the lungs, while injecting them under the skin can increase the likelihood of abscesses and other infections.

When a drug is injected, the time to the onset of maximum effect is about 15–30 seconds for the intravenous route, and 3–5 minutes for the intramuscular or subcutaneous route. Drug effects from inhaling a drug begin in 7–10 seconds, and drug effects from intranasal use begin in 3–5 minutes.

Injecting sites

PWID often have 'favourite' injecting sites. These mostly depend on the ease of finding a viable vein and therefore these preferred sites can be subject to frequent change. The results from a sample of 200 PWID interviewed about their bodily injection sites found that the mean number of injection sites ever used by subjects was 3.1, with a mean of 2.0 sites used in the previous six months. Sixteen per cent of subjects had injected in five or more sites. Almost all (99%) had injected in the cubital fossa. The next most popular site was the forearm (71%). Other sites included the hand (53%), foot (19%), leg (18%), neck (10%) and groin (6%). There was a clear progression in sites used, from the cubital fossa at initial injection to the use of sites such as the groin after ten years of injecting. Female intravenous drug misusers used significantly more injection sites than men and reported more injection-related problems. The use of more injection sites was independently associated with a greater number of injection-related problems and a greater number of drug classes ever injected.[7]

Problems associated with injecting

The main problems associated with injecting drug use are overdose and local or systemic infections (due to equipment sharing, poor injecting technique and unsafe sexual behaviour).

Mortality

Drug users are at substantially greater risk of premature death than their non-drug-using peers. Longitudinal studies indicate yearly mortality rates of between 1% and 3% among heroin users. The excessive mortality rates among heroin users have been variously estimated to be between 6 and 20 times those experienced among others of the same age and gender. The causes of death are many, including HIV/AIDS, hepatitis, violence and overdose.[8]

An Australian study showed that the mortality rate for people regularly using illicit opiates was more than 13 times greater than that observed for the general community. It is estimated that 9.4% of total mortality in Australians aged 15–39 years of age can be attributed to regular use of illicit opiates.[9] Death from the direct toxic effects of a heroin overdose is usually associated with respiratory depression, coma and pulmonary oedema. Death from direct effects of cocaine is often associated with cardiac dysrhythmias and conduction disturbances, leading to myocardial infarction and stroke. The 'typical' heroin overdose death is of an older, heroin-dependent male who is not currently in drug treatment and is an experienced user. This contrasts with the popular view that it is naïve or recreational users that are most at risk of overdose death. A fatal overdose is likely to involve the use of other central nervous depressant drugs, such as benzodiazepines and alcohol, in conjunction with heroin. 'True' heroin overdose, involving only heroin, appears to be comparatively rare.[8] (See also Chapter 2.)

Equipment sharing

Recent data suggest that about 20% of PWID directly share needles and syringes, and this rises to about 35% for indirect sharing (filters, spoons, water). However, these figures represent a significant fall from 1999 to 2009, with direct sharing falling by 10% and indirect sharing falling by 20%.[10]

Sharing of injecting equipment is not uniformly found. Stimulant users are more likely to share injecting equipment than users of other drugs and women are more likely to share than men.[11, 12] The risk of blood-borne virus transmission amongst steroid injectors is probably lower because of a greater likelihood of hygienic use of injecting equipment and lower levels of sharing.[13]

Overdose

Overdose of heroin following injection is a common, sometimes fatal, experience. Thirty-eight per cent of a South London sample of PWID self-reported that they had experienced an overdose. The majority (54%) had witnessed someone else overdose. Overdosing is not usually a solitary experience; over 80% of subjects who had overdosed had done so in the presence of someone else, but only 27% reported ambulances having been called, probably because of fears that the police might routinely attend (something that is usually no longer the case). Factors found to be associated with overdose were: age at which injecting began; gender (women being more likely to experience overdose); use of alcohol; and polydrug injection.[14] Different batches can have different strengths and overwhelm users; PWID therefore should be advised to try a small amount first to gauge the strength. In 2012, the Advisory Council on the Misuse of Drugs (ACMD) concluded that the supply of take-home naloxone to PWID is evidence based and can save lives.[15]

Bacterial infections

Injecting drug use causes medical problems by introducing pathogens and other contaminants into the body via shared needles, a lack of sterile preparation, poor injecting technique and drug contamination. The resulting infections can be either local or systemic. Local damage to veins occurs for a number of reasons including: infection, repeated injections over the same site, re-using blunt and/ or dirty needles, and severe chemical irritation caused by the drugs themselves or by adulterants. Injecting cocaine is often associated with more tissue damage than other substances; probably because of its local anaesthetic effects, combined with 'binge' injecting, the user may be less likely to be aware of any local injury or infection.

Injecting site infections (often *Staphylococcus aureus* or group A streptococcal infections) are common. In 2010 37% of participants in the Unlinked Anonymous Monitoring survey (UAM),[16] who had injected in the last four weeks, reported experiencing an abscess, sore or open wound in the preceding year. These people were more likely to have injected into the veins in the hands, legs and feet, and to have injected crack cocaine or cocaine in the last four weeks.

Systemic infections are less common but often serious and include endocarditis, clostridial infections and anthrax. Between 2000 and 2010 there were 163 suspected cases of wound botulism, 93 cases of *Clostridium novyi* and 34 cases of tetanus in the UK. The strong suspicion is that, where clusters of cases occur, these are likely to be due to contamination with bacterial spores during drug preparation or transit. Sporadic cases may be due to contamination at the point of use.[10]

Blood-borne viral infections

The infections discussed below are usually transmitted via the blood-to-blood route, with the exception of hepatitis A, where the virus is likely to be spread via the faecal/oral route. However, blood-to-blood spread through needle sharing during viraemia is also possible.

Hepatitis B

Transmission of hepatitis B is still continuing amongst PWID, but appears to have declined over the decade from 2001 to 2011 amongst those taking part in the UAM, from 28% to 16%. In the same period, self-reported uptake of hepatitis B vaccination (which means receiving at least one dose of vaccine) has increased from 37% to 76%.[17]

Proactive provision of hepatitis B virus (HBV) vaccination through widely available services is critical for protecting this difficult-to-reach target group and should be delivered in, and form an important part of, primary care.

The presence in the blood of antibodies to a virus indicates that a person has at one time been infected with or been vaccinated against the virus. In contrast to other blood-borne viruses that commonly affect intravenous PWID (HIV, hepatitis C) there is an effective vaccine against HBV. Thus, in the case of HBV, the proportion of PWID who do not have antibodies (anti-HBs or anti-HBc) against the virus constitutes the potential vaccination population and is an important indicator of the need for a vaccination programme. Current HBV infection is indicated by the presence in the blood of HBsAg, and can be an indication of either recent or chronic infection. High levels of current infection suggest a high future level of severe, long-term complications and a high transmission risk to others through high-risk injecting behaviour or unsafe sex.

Vaccination

Hepatitis B vaccination should be considered an essential component of the care offered to drug users in primary care. Practices who opt to provide a National Enhanced Service to drug users under the GMS contract will be expected to undertake six-monthly audits of hepatitis B screening and immunisation data of this patient population (www.nhsemployers.org/SiteCollectionDocuments/nes_drugs_cd_130209.pdf).

Poor patient attendance is often reported as a major barrier. To address this issue, vaccination needs to be carried out opportunistically at the time when the drug user makes contact with the practice, for example at the time of methadone prescribing. Practices should keep a stock of HBV vaccine.

Pre-vaccination testing

Current expert advice has been to shift the emphasis away from testing and towards protection of the drug user by vaccination. Pre-testing should never act as a barrier or delay to vaccination. Drug users should have access to vaccination without testing. If a drug user wishes to be tested, the first dose of vaccine should be offered at the same time.[18] Delaying vaccination can do harm because a drug user may become infected before the next visit or may not return.

Primary vaccination schedule

A pragmatic approach to vaccination schedule is recommended. Emphasis needs to be placed on giving as many doses as possible. Even incomplete vaccination schedules offer some protection.[19] Accelerated schedules (0, 1 and 2 months or 0, 7 and 21 days) are now widely recognised as the most appropriate for people at high risk including drug users. A study of homeless drug users at an inner-city primary care centre found a seven-fold higher completion rate with the 0, 7 and 21-day schedule compared with the conventional six-month schedule.[20] The 0, 7 and 21-day schedule is being promoted by the Department of Health for prisons and is the most strongly recommended regimen.[21] In addition, services need to ensure that there is a robust system for recall.

Booster doses and post-vaccination testing

Current best practice is to give a booster at 12 months if an accelerated schedule is used. Follow-up of PWID for booster doses can be difficult. It seems sensible to recommend that resources would be better invested in improving uptake and completion of three-dose schedules than in seroconversion testing or boosters.

Post-vaccination testing for seroconversion is not generally recommended unless the drug user is known to be immunodeficient, for example because of HIV infection.

Promotion of vaccination

Prominent display of posters and use of leaflets promoting HBV vaccination may be helpful. Promotion of vaccination is dependent on motivated, knowledgeable staff. In drugs services, uptake rates have been found to be higher where staff training and confidence were better.[22] GPs and practice nurses may also need training and awareness sessions to ensure greater uptake of vaccination.

Vaccination of partners and children of drug users

Hepatitis B can be transmitted through sexual contact and non-sexual intimate contact. Children infected with HBV have a higher risk of chronic infection than adults. Drug users should be advised about the risk of transmission of HBV to their partners and children. Partners and children should be routinely offered vaccination.

Organising the vaccination of families may not be straightforward. Families may not be registered with the same practice as the drug user. Some drug users may be reluctant to disclose the risk to their partners. Healthcare workers need to work with drug users to advise them of the risks and promote the routine offering of vaccination to partners and children.

Monitoring/audit of vaccination

Local information on vaccine uptake and completion is crucial in order to judge the quality of the service and plan achievable improvements. The minimum standard for monitoring recommended by the National Treatment Agency is the number of vaccinations received by a drug user.[23] A simple recording system is required.

Criteria for audit should be kept straightforward. The minimum criteria should be the number and percentage of drug users who have received one, two and three doses of hepatitis B vaccine.

Treatment

In 2004, the National Institute for Health and Clinical Excellence (NICE) recommended combination therapy with pegylated interferon and ribavirin for six months to one year. Treatment is successful in clearing the infection, with no detectable virus in the blood six months after treatment has ceased in up to 55% of patients. This needs expert referral and assessment at a tertiary referral centre. NICE has also issued guidance stating that entecavir and tenofovir are options for the treatment of chronic HBV. The NICE guidelines suggest that patients with current injecting drug use and those with alcohol problems could still receive this treatment.

Hepatitis A

PWID can be at high risk of hepatitis A virus (HAV) infection owing to poor living conditions.

Hepatitis A vaccination of PWID infected with HCV and/or with chronic liver disease has been recommended for many years because of the risk of more serious illness if they became infected.[24] The 2007 UK clinical guidelines document recommends that PWID are vaccinated against hepatitis A and hepatitis B. The guidance states that the benefits of hepatitis A vaccination are modest and the benefits of hepatitis B vaccination are substantial and so recommends prioritising hepatitis B vaccination when necessary.[25]

Hepatitis A vaccine can be given as a two-dose schedule over six to 12 months when using the single-component vaccine (usually the preferred option), or as a three-dose schedule over three weeks to six months when using the combined hepatitis A/B vaccine.

As with hepatitis B, there is no need to blood test for viral status prior to vaccination.

Criteria for audit should again be kept simple, being the percentage of drug users who have received one and two doses of HAV vaccine.

Table 15.1 **Licensed schedules of hepatitis A and B vaccines**

Hepatitis vaccines	Schedule
Single A	Two doses with second dose after 6–12 months. Second dose may be delayed for up to three years
Combined A and B	Routine: 0, 1, 6 months Accelerated: 0, 7, 21 days with booster ideally at 12 months

Hepatitis C

Prevalence

Around 0.4% of the general population and equating to 218,000 people are infected by hepatitis C virus (HCV). Overall prevalence of antibodies to HCV amongst PWID in England who participated in the UAM survey was 39% in 2000 and 49% in 2010. There are major differences between regions, with prevalence being much higher in London and the northwest of England than elsewhere. Prevalence of anti-HCV is lower among more recent initiates to injecting. Prevalence in England and Wales in people who began injecting in the past three years has been stable at around 20% from 2001 to 2010,[26] increasing from around 9% in the last three years of the previous decade.

HCV is far more infectious than HIV and can be transmitted more easily through injecting materials other than syringes, such as filters, spoons and water (but is far less readily transmitted sexually).

Routes of transmission

The major route of HCV transmission in the UK is by sharing injecting equipment, usually by blood-contaminated needles and syringes, though if contaminated with infected blood other equipment can also spread the infection. Mother-to-baby transmission is very uncommon, with upper estimates of around 6%. This rate is increased to around 14–17% where there is co-infection with HIV. Hepatitis C does not spread through breast milk. Sexual transmission is very rare, with studies suggesting that less than 5% of the regular sexual partners of people with HCV infection become infected.

Natural history

The majority of people infected with HCV suffer no symptoms when they become infected; some may feel slightly unwell and in rare cases become jaundiced. About 60–80% of people who acquire the infection become chronically infected; the remainder clear the infection spontaneously. Chronic infection may be asymptomatic for many years and the majority of these have a normal life expectancy. Around 1 in 5 to 1 in 20 of those chronically infected may develop serious liver disease after 20 years. A small proportion may develop liver cancers. Certain factors are associated with more rapid progression to severe liver disease. These are:

▶ over 40 years old at the time of infection

▶ alcohol consumption

▶ male

▸ co-infected with hepatitis B or HIV

▸ on immunosuppressive therapy.

Who should be tested? [27] Antibody testing should be considered for:

▸ anyone who has ever injected drugs

▸ current PWID

▸ recipients of blood (before September 1991) or blood products (before 1986 in the UK) – if not already tested

▸ regular sexual partners of those with HCV (risk of sexual transmission low at approximately 5%)

▸ children born to mothers with HCV (risk of transmission 6%; may be higher if co-infected with HIV [NB test result may be difficult to interpret in children under 18 months old, owing to the presence of maternal antibodies])

▸ people who may have had unsterile medical treatment abroad

▸ people who may have had ear piercing, body piercing, tattooing or acupuncture with unsterile equipment.

The reasons to be tested are:

▸ allaying anxiety even if result is positive

▸ positive test allowing early monitoring and intervention by a specialist if required

▸ opportunity to immunise against hepatitis B and A (co-infection significantly worsens prognosis)

▸ encouraging the patient to change patterns of behaviour such as injecting drug use or excessive drinking whether the result is positive or negative.

Life insurance and mortgage issues

A negative HCV test has no impact on ability to get life insurance or a mortgage. A positive test may make it more difficult to get life insurance policy or a mortgage linked to a life policy.

HIV / AIDS

By the end of 2010, an estimated 91,500 HIV infected people are alive in the UK; about a quarter of these have undiagnosed infections. People living with diagnosed HIV in the UK have a near-normal life expectancy, particularly if diagnosed early. In 2010 6660 people were diagnosed with HIV. The number of infections acquired in the UK (3640, almost exclusively through sexual transmission) exceeds those acquired abroad (3020).[28]

Although the potential still exists for HIV transmission through injecting drug use there is no evidence of significant current HIV spread amongst PWID in the UK. It was the threat of HIV/AIDS amongst drug users that spurred the move away from abstinence-based treatment into one of harm reduction. The ACMD stated in its *AIDS and Drug Misuse Update* report that awareness of the HIV-related risks of injecting drug use has grown significantly and has provided a focus for harm reduction activities. It stated that greater efforts are now needed to reduce the extent of drug use itself, particularly drug-injecting behaviour. It also asserted the need for a wider recognition that all interventions to discourage drug misuse will contribute to HIV prevention.[29]

The ACMD recommended a series of actions directed towards:

▶ encouraging cessation of drug use

▶ discouraging new recruitment into experimentation with drugs

▶ discouraging regular drug use among experimental drug users

▶ discouraging drug injecting among potential PWID

▶ discouraging sharing of injecting equipment

▶ encouraging current PWID to switch to safer practices or oral use

▶ ensuring all drug users have access to advice on safer sexual and injecting practices as well as access to clean injecting equipment.

Through the foresight of the ACMD and the implementation of its recommendations, the spread of HIV by needle and syringe sharing was largely averted. This was largely achieved by the establishment of needle exchange schemes and widespread opiate substitution treatment. This has helped the UK to have lower HIV and HCV prevalence rates than other countries. GPs cannot be complacent though, and should always give and reinforce appropriate harm reduction messages to patients.

Safer injecting

Route transitions

The best way of reducing the harm associated with injecting is to stop injecting. For many PWID this will not be an immediate option, but for some it is, and a sensitive discussion about possible alternatives to injecting should be undertaken at some point. Alternatives to injecting include prescribed oral medication or changing the route of use, for example from injecting to smoking their drug of choice.

Drug preparation

It's not possible to talk here about the preparation of all drugs for injection, but it makes sense to discuss the two most commonly injected street drugs, heroin and crack cocaine.

Street heroin comes as a brown powder that was originally formulated for smoking and so it needs to be chemically altered from a base to a salt to render it water-soluble. An acid (typically citric or ascorbic) is used to do this. Heroin powder is combined in a spoon or 'cooker' with water and acid. The mixture is heated to speed the reaction and the resulting solution is filtered to avoid blockages when drawing up into a syringe.

The process for preparing crack cocaine (also a base) for injection is very similar to the above process, but crack is much more sensitive to heating. Overheating the solution causes the crack to coagulate and solidify.

When the two drugs are prepared together in a 'speedball' the heroin is dissolved first and the crack added to the warm solution.

Factors to be taken into account when considering drug preparation are:

▶ *the drug* – What is it? Did it come from a trusted source? What is its purity?

▶ *the environment* – factors include privacy, lighting, warmth and a clean area on which to prepare

▶ *equipment* – syringe/needle/cooker/filter/acid/water. Ideally all equipment directly involved with preparation should be sterile and previously unused. Where re-use of equipment is unavoidable, people should re-use their own and sterilise first with bleach. Group injecting situations may make accidental mix-ups of syringes more likely. Using colour-coded syringes or uniquely marking syringes makes accidental sharing less likely.

All equipment listed above, apart from tourniquets and water (see below), are usually available from needle exchange schemes as sterile items. The acid most commonly available is citric acid in 100 mg sachets. It is important to note that 100 mg of citric acid is sufficient to acidify over 1 g of heroin at average street purity. It is likely that many people will habitually use too much acid when preparing injections and they should be cautioned to use the smallest possible amount to avoid unnecessary tissue irritation and damage. Water for injections (WFI) is sometimes available from needle exchanges, but often not. Where WFI is not available, people should be advised to use boiled water or, failing that, water from the cold tap.

Injecting technique

The 'safest' injecting sites are found in the antecubital fossa and in the superficial veins in the forearm. Users should be encouraged to rotate these sites. Watching a patient run through his or her injecting technique can be very informative. Consider giving advice on identifying superficial veins (particularly to women, who often find it harder to easily access superficial veins) to help avoid progression to more dangerous sites such as the groin and neck. If patients are intent on groin injecting, showing them the simple technique of how to avoid the femoral artery, by feeling for the pulse and placing their fingers protectively on top of it, can be life saving. It is important that patients use appropriate equipment for their injecting site. Where patients are accessing surface veins, it is usually best to use the smallest appropriate needle and syringe, usually a fixed 1 ml insulin-type syringe. Where people are using deeper veins, longer, separate needles are likely to be more suitable.

When injecting, patients should:

▸ ensure that all the equipment they need is easily to hand and where possible is sterile

▸ have adequate light to clearly see what they are doing

▸ be warm, comfortable and relaxed as this will make surface veins easier to locate

▸ wash their hands and the injecting site with soap and water

▸ use an appropriate tourniquet to apply light pressure to the upper arm and raise surface veins

▸ confidently puncture the identified vein at a shallow angle and draw back venous blood to check that they are in the vein

▸ release the tourniquet

▸ keep the syringe still during the process to ensure that it remains in the vein. Releasing some tourniquets may require letting go of the syringe – this is why PWID often improvise tourniquets that they can control with their mouth

▸ inject slowly.

On completing the injection, before withdrawing the needle many PWID draw more blood into the syringe and inject again. Often called flushing or booting, this is usually done to ensure that none of the drug is left in the syringe. If it is done, it should only be done once and not repeatedly, as this can cause more local tissue damage and irritation than is necessary.

After withdrawing the syringe, light pressure should be applied to the injecting site using a blood-proof sterile pad (usually supplied by needle exchanges). This helps to prevent contamination of the injecting site and fingers, and also makes bruising of the injecting site less likely.

Storage and disposal of used equipment

Used injecting equipment should be immediately stored in a sharps container (supplied by all needle exchanges) and regularly returned to the needle exchange scheme for safe disposal. If needles and syringes are stored for later re-use (not advised, but it does happen, often due to lack of enough equipment), they should be clearly marked, stored in a place that cannot easily be accessed by others or children and sterilised with bleach before re-use. A video showing a quick and effective bleaching technique is available via the Harm Reduction Works You-Tube channel (www.youtube.com/user/HarmReductionWorks?feature=watch).

Useful resources

The Harm Reduction Works campaign was funded by the Department of Health and the National Treatment Agency between 2008 and 2012. It produced a variety of very useful print and film resources around:

▶ HIV

▶ hepatitis C

▶ hepatitis B

▶ overdose

▶ crack cocaine

▶ safer injecting

▶ femoral injecting.

Some of the resources are aimed at professionals and others at drug users. Funding for the free distribution of the campaign materials has now ceased, but many of the print publications are available for free download via the campaign website or can be bought. See www.harmreductionworks.org.uk.

Further reading

Royal College of General Practitioners. *Guidance for the Prevention, Testing, Treatment and Management of Hepatitis C in Primary Care*. London: RCGP, 2007 [includes appendices on hepatitis A and B vaccination guidance, hepatitis B and HIV].

References

1. Biggam A G. Malignant malaria associated with the administration of heroin intravenously. *Transactions of the Royal Society of Tropical Medicine and Hygiene* 1929; **23(2)**: 147–53.

2. National Treatment Agency. *Injecting Drug Use in England: a declining trend*, London: NTA. 2010, www.nta.nhs.uk/uploads/injectingreportnov2010finala.pdf   [accessed November 2012].

3. Lintzeris N, Lenne M, Ritter A. Methadone injecting in Australia: a tale of two cities. *Addiction* 1999; **94(8)**: 1175–8.

4. Darke S, Topp L, Ross J. The injection of methadone and benzodiazepines among Sydney PWID 1996–2000: 5-year monitoring of trends from the Illicit Drug Reporting System. *Drug and Alcohol Review* 2002; **21(1)**: 27–32.

5. Fry C L, Bruno R B. Recent trends in benzodiazepine use by PWID in Victoria and Tasmania. *Drug and Alcohol Review* 2002; **21(4)**: 363–7.

6. Van Hout M C, Bingham T. 'A costly turn on': patterns of use and perceived consequences of mephedrone based head shop products amongst Irish PWID. *International Journal on Drug Policy* 2012; **23(3)**: 188–97.

7. Darke S, Ross J, Kaye S. Physical injecting sites among PWID in Sydney, Australia. *Drug and Alcohol Dependence* 2001; **62(1)**: 77–82.

8. Darke S, Zador D. Fatal heroin 'overdose': a review. *Addiction* 1996; **91(12)**: 1765–72.

9. Hulse G K, English D R, Milne E, *et al*. The quantification of mortality resulting from the regular use of illicit opiates. *Addiction* 1999; **94(2)**: 221–9.

10. Health Protection Agency. *Shooting Up: infections among drug users in the UK 2009. An update: November 2010*. London: HPA, 2010, www.hpa.org.uk/webc/HPAwebFile/HPAweb_C/1287143384395   [accessed November 2012].

11. Tyndall M W, Currie S, Spittal P, *et al*. Intensive injection cocaine use as the primary risk factor in the Vancouver HIV-1 epidemic. *AIDS* 2003; **17(6)**: 887–93.

12. Bennett G A, Velleman R D, Barter G, *et al*. Gender differences in sharing injecting equipment by drug users in England. *AIDS Care* 2000; **12(1)**: 77–87.

13. Crampin A C, Lamagni T L, Hope V D, *et al*. The risk of infection with HIV and hepatitis B in individuals who inject steroids in England and Wales. *Epidemiology and Infection* 1998; **121(2)**: 381–6.

14. Powis B, Strang J, Griffiths P, *et al*. Self-reported overdose among PWID in London: extent and nature of the problem. *Addiction* 1999; **94(11)**: 1745–6.

15. Advisory Council on the Misuse of Drugs. *Consideration of Naloxone*. London: Home Office, 2012, www.homeoffice.gov.uk/publications/agencies-public-bodies/acmd1/consideration-of-naloxone?view=Binary   [accessed November 2012].

16. Health Protection Agency, Health Protection Services and Microbiology Services. *Unlinked Anonymous Monitoring Survey of Injecting Drug Users in Contact with Specialist Services: data tables*. London, HPA, 2011.

17. Health Protection Agency. *Data Tables of the Anonymous Monitoring Survey of HIV of HIV and Hepatitis in People Who Inject Drugs. Surveillance update: July 2012*. London: HPA, www.hpa.org.uk/webc/HPAwebFile/HPAweb_C/1317135226434 [accessed November 2012].

18. Heptonstall J. Strategies to ensure delivery of hepatitis B vaccine to PWID. *Communicable Disease and Public Health* 1999; **2(3)**: 154–6.

19. Lamden K H, Kennedy N, Beeching N J, *et al*. Hepatitis B and hepatitis C virus infections: risk factors among drug users in Northwest England. *Journal of Infection* 1998; **37(3)**: 260–9.

20. Wright N, Campbell T, Tompkins C. Comparison of conventional and accelerated hepatitis B immunisation schedules for homeless drug users. *Communicable Disease and Public Health* 2002; **5(4)**: 324–6.

21. Piper M. Senior Prison Health Adviser, Department of Health (personal communication), 2003.

22. Morrison D, Gilchrist G, Ahmed A. Potential of specialist drug services to deliver hepatitis B vaccination. *Communicable Disease and Public Health* 2002; **5(4)**: 321–3.

23. National Treatment Agency for Substance Misuse. *Models of Care for the Treatment of Drug Misusers. Part 2: full reference report 159*. London: NTA, 2002.

24. Salisbury D M, Begg N T (eds). *Immunisation against Infectious Disease*. Ed. Edward Jenner. Bicentenary edition. London: HMSO, 1996.

25. Department of Health (England) and the devolved administrations. *Drug Misuse and Dependence: UK guidelines on clinical management*. London: DH, 2007.

26. Health Protection Agency. *Hepatitis C in the UK: 2011 report*. London: HPA, 2011.

27. Department of Health. *Hepatitis C: essential information for professionals and guidance on testing*. London: HMSO, 2004.

28. Health Protection Agency. *HIV in the United Kingdom: 2011 report*. London: HPA, 2011.

29. Advisory Council on the Misuse of Drugs. *AIDS and Drug Misuse Update. Report by the Advisory Council on the Misuse of Drugs*. London: ACMD, 1993.

CHAPTER 16

Beyond pharmaceutical treatments

Gordon Morse and Jan Hernen

IN THIS CHAPTER

Introduction ‖ *Social support* ‖ *Psychological therapies* ‖ *Conclusion*

Introduction

Despite the very evident legal and health consequences of self-administered psychoactive drug use, it has been a very popular pursuit ever since (and almost certainly before) Genesis 9, in which Noah 'planted a vineyard and became drunken'. And so in helping individuals to address their drug use, we would do well to reflect on what their motivation might be – why, indeed, they would want to recklessly endanger their health? It is manifestly obvious that these chemicals are rewarding in a recreational sense, use can become habitual, and in some people (perhaps with some sort of genetic or other weakness) this can escalate into an addiction – this is certainly the case in the vast majority of tobacco addicts. However, most people who become dependent on heroin have to a greater or lesser extent (and usually greater) psychological or social morbidities that they are attempting to self-medicate. And for the few in whom their addiction did not have some serious psychosocial pre-morbid state, then the years of dependency very soon create psychosocial damage from which further drug use will afford short-term escape.

When a person who is self-medicating asks a doctor for help, his or her fundamental need therefore is for help with a psychosocial morbidity. The pharmaceutical issues are secondary. However, as doctors, and because drugs are our 'stock in trade', we are easily distracted by what are in effect the symptoms rather than the underlying condition. Doctors are trained to relieve suffering, and the tools that GPs use most frequently are prescribed drugs. We feel comfortable prescribing – it is what we know a lot about, the patients appreciate the implied care and kindness and, broadly, prescribed treatment is effective.

In the case of prescribed opioid substitution therapy (OST) GPs can be particularly confident as there is a very large evidence base of effectiveness of reducing harm from continued use of illicit drugs. Indeed, to withdraw OST even at the explicit request of the patient entertains the possibility of facilitating harm. However, we need to remember that OST does little more than afford a stable state of avoidance of the opiate withdrawal syndrome (OWS). Yes, the pain and craving of withdrawal is a huge motivator to use heroin, and to eliminate OWS is therefore a very valuable thing to achieve, but there is a great deal more to drug addiction than the simple matter of tolerance and dependence on a chemical.

Many of our patients began misusing drugs because of mental illness and/or the enduring emotional distress that can arise from severely traumatised childhoods. Drug use often starts early in life, education is subsequently impeded and years may be spent acquiring skills of resourcing a drug habit that then becomes a very demanding yet purposeful activity in itself. Heroin and other illicit psychoactive drugs are immensely powerful palliatives of psychological distress. Resourcing a drug habit gives those with little education or employment skills the opportunity to become highly proficient and very busy – and on occasions even relatively wealthy. So while OST very effectively addresses the painful but transient issue of OWS, and could be reduced over a period of time to withdraw dependence on the *chemical* dimension of heroin addiction, it does nothing to address the resurgent psychological distress, the lack of social, educational or interpersonal skills, and the lost decade or more of work experience.

This is painting a worst-case scenario of course. Not all patients are entirely lacking in 'social capital', but most are affected to a greater or lesser extent. Meaningful treatment therefore requires much more than just prescribing. While we congratulate ourselves on all the harm that we are undoubtedly reducing through well-delivered OST, we must keep remembering the greater ambition – to help our patients to achieve an independent and more satisfying life.

Most heroin addicts when they present for treatment are surfing a wave of very powerful motivation: exhaustion, debts, ill health and disintegration of family and social functioning. All of these harms are immensely powerful external motivators that demand life change to something different, something better. In reducing that harm with prescribed OST, what we actually achieve is a transfer of dependence from a 'fence', a dealer and one drug, to dependence on a doctor, a treatment system, and a much more boring drug. At the same time much of the impetus to change is removed. That is not an argument against harm reduction – far from it: harm reduction prescribing has undoubtedly spared the individual, his or her family and the wider society enormous amounts of cost in the quality and quantity of life, as well as in financial terms – but harm reduction prescribing *is not an end in itself*. It should be seen as the stable platform from which the patient can start to rebuild his or her life, and, wherever possible, achieve *independence*.

Social support

Human relationships

The family for most of us is a source of enduring support from cradle to grave. It is where we learn the skills of how to behave in civilised society, experience the ultimate altruism and spiritual reward of loving and being loved and of sharing some of the staples necessary to living, such as secure accommodation, food, warmth and safety. How our children take all this for granted! In contrast, many of our patients have lost, or never had, this vital life resource, and some have even been brought up in a home life that is the antithesis of positive support. Here they have known pain, exploitation and abuse, and learned nothing but unhealthy behaviours in response to a hostile and frightening environment. Education has been sabotaged and personalities have become shaped in dysfunctional ways. Patients lack the skills necessary to integrate into society and become self-supporting, and all the while carry a huge burden of emotional pain.

Many of our patients find proxy 'families' amongst those with similar upbringings, where they find validation from those with similar dysfunctional behaviours, and share the use of drugs that afford a degree of comfort and acceptability within their peer group. Gregory Roberts, himself a former user of heroin, once wrote: [1]

> Heroin is a sensory deprivation tank for the soul. Floating on the dead sea of the drug, there is no sense of pain, no regret or shame, no feelings of guilt or grief, no depression and no desire. The sleeping universe enters and envelops every atom of existence. Insensible stillness and peace disperse fear and suffering.

These words amply demonstrate the power of the drug to those who carry a burden of emotional pain.

Essential to recovery from such an early life therefore is the support and role modelling from healthy others – loneliness and isolation are well known to be very poor prognostic factors in those with addictions. [2] Sometimes families can be brought together, support given and relationships restored to a better state of health. At times others within a person's social network can be recruited in a formal way to aid the recovery process, as can those in wider society – employers, neighbours, friends, charitable organisations, clubs and self-help groups. This is a social support network that has come to be known as 'mutual aid'.

12-Step or Minnesota method

These groups have been an extraordinary phenomenon since their inception in the 1930s. The original groups set themselves up with no professional input to address their alcohol dependence and became known as Alcoholics Anonymous

(AA). As the years have passed, the same philosophy has been extended to all addictive drugs (Narcotics Anonymous), specific drugs such as cocaine (CA), and also sex (SA), gambling (GA) and other behaviours that are banded together as 'addictions'. 12-Step groups are available in most cities in the world and many smaller rural areas as well. There is no trained or professional input, and each group will behave in slightly different ways, reflecting the different personalities within it.

Contrary to the widely held belief, they are not faith based. Membership does not require a religious belief, but the 'Steps' (towards recovery) become a sort of faith in themselves – that if you admit your powerlessness over your addiction to the group and ask for help, and if you keep to the programme, you will achieve sustained abstinence. The language employed can be arcane and off-putting to some, but there are a number of studies showing a close correlation between 12-Step meeting attendances and duration of abstinence, as well as being highly cost-effective.[3,4]

Much research has been devoted to identifying the key triggers for relapse, most of which can be boiled down to the two biggest pre-determinants – demoralisation and isolation.[2] 12-Step groups address these by lending real, first-hand optimism to the newcomer by being made up of those already recovering from addictions. They address the isolation by offering a new peer group of those with healthier behaviours. Within these groups new relationships are often formed and employment can be found. Many people believe that they would not be alive today were it not for their involvement in the 'Steps'.

Therapeutic relationships

The relationship between patient and GP is often a remarkably powerful tool in and of itself. Very often a GP will have known his or her patient for many years, perhaps even from birth – the GP will know the family and the circumstances of the upbringing. This well-established and trusting relationship is the product of numerous consultations and treatment episodes over the years, but these consultations tend to be brief. However, when issues of addiction need to be addressed, interventions may frequently demand time that a GP would struggle to give. In 'shared care' arrangements, the relationship with the patient's drugs worker from the community drug team will augment the time spent with the patient and can also be invaluable. These relationships between patient and professional are inconsistent, unmeasurable and poorly defined – yet many studies have shown that the continuing role of care and advocacy with a trusted individual is as beneficial to treatment outcomes as almost any measurable and discrete psychological intervention.[5,6]

Finally and perhaps obviously, having stable accommodation and purposeful activities to fill the day are no less important. Low self-esteem is very common amongst the socially marginalised, so having a home of their own and some sense of daily achievement are enormously beneficial. Training, voluntary and paid work are all essential components of planning a package of care to help the patient recover from his or her addiction.

Psychological therapies

Psychosocial and psychological interventions

Alcohol misuse

Motivational interventions

In any process of change and decision making, some degree of ambivalence is a natural part of that process. If we side-step this ambivalence and jump into *how* to change, we risk imposing our own desire for the patient to change and leaving them struggling with the ambivalence.

Motivational Enhancement Therapy (MET) is a fairly brief and very effective intervention that is typically offered on an individual basis for three to four sessions of 50 minutes over a 12-week period.[7] It is based on Motivational Interviewing (MI) and includes giving personalised normative feedback to the patient in a non-confrontational manner. The aim is to help patients to explore their ambivalence about change using an empathic but directive approach, eliciting reasons for change from the patient him or herself. Natural resistance to change is responded to in a neutral way rather than by contradicting the patient or giving unsolicited advice. Motivational interventions should be available within the local drug and alcohol treatment service.

Skills-based interventions

Drinking patterns are determined at least in part by one's learning history and current environmental circumstances. Hence the focus here is on skills acquisition and altering relevant aspects of the person's environment.

In Behavioural Self Control Training (BSCT),[8] the patient is taught to monitor his or her drinking, use defined strategies to reduce alcohol intake, reward successes in achieving goals, analyse and learn from unsuccessful efforts, and develop alternative coping skills for high-risk situations. While BSCT has been found to be effective for non-dependent drinkers with a controlled drinking goal,[9] a longer-term study has shown that even people meeting criteria for alcohol abuse or dependence revealed more modest, but still clinically significant, outcomes.[10]

BSCT is typically offered in a group format of eight sessions with periodic follow-ups. Elements are often integrated into relapse prevention interventions offered by drug and alcohol treatment services.

Social-behavioural interventions

Given the importance of social influences on our behaviour, it is not surprising that effective interventions should take into account the support networks of people misusing alcohol. What is perhaps more surprising is that treatment services have for so long been based on individual or group interventions that largely ignore the existence or lack of these networks.

Social Behaviour and Network Therapy (SBNT) is a welcome advance in this regard. In the recent United Kingdom Alcohol Treatment Trial [11] it has been shown to be as effective as the well-researched Motivational Enhancement Therapy and equally as cost-effective. The core principle of SBNT is to enhance positive social support for change by inviting family members and concerned others in to the treatment process with the person misusing alcohol. The focal person and network members meet for eight treatment sessions to agree a treatment goal (abstinence or controlled use), discuss relapse management, work on communication skills, build positive alternative activities to drinking and choose from a range of other skills-based topics.

As we increasingly recognise the value of mutual aid and community approaches, it is likely that treatment services will need to modify traditional individual ways of working and embrace socially based interventions.

Drug misuse

The NICE guidelines for drug misuse (2007) [12] refer to a range of evidence-based interventions for clients misusing a variety of substances. The British Psychological Society Toolkit [13] divides these into low- and high-intensity interventions. Low-intensity interventions can be delivered by key workers in drug and alcohol treatment centres, whereas high-intensity interventions should be delivered by mental health professionals specifically trained in these approaches. As mentioned earlier in this chapter, drug misuse often masks other mental health problems that manifest as substance misuse reduces. Therefore drug-specific interventions are differentiated from those designed to target mental health problems.

Interventions for drug misuse

The aim for these lower-intensity interventions is to engage patients in treatment, achieve harm reduction objectives and support early changes in drug-using behaviour. They should be used in the context of coordinated and care-planned treatment journeys with identification of a recovery goal beyond treatment (for example in relation to family, meaningful activity or social activities).

Motivational Interviewing

MI is a form of collaborative conversation for strengthening a person's own motivation and commitment to change. It is a person-centred counselling style that explores ambivalence about change within an atmosphere of acceptance and compassion. It can help those who misuse cannabis or stimulants, increasing rates of abstinence and deceasing drug use, and for people who misuse opiates and are not in formal drug treatment.[12] The key elements of MI are also contained in much briefer interventions of 5–30 minutes and distilled into the **FRAMES** model:

▸ **F**eedback on patterns of use

▸ **R**esponsibility for change being with the patient

▸ **A**dvice on how to change

▸ **M**enu of treatment options

▸ **E**mpathy

▸ **S**elf-efficacy or increasing confidence.[14]

Contingency management

Contingency management (CM) is an approach that encourages positive behaviour change (for example abstinence) by providing positive consequences when patients meet treatment goals and by withholding those consequences when treatment goals are not met. The intervention is clearly based on principles that govern many of our behaviours. It tends to be used most for engagement in treatment when prolonged drug use is likely to have reduced the reinforcement potential of natural reinforcers such as social attention, praise and physical wellbeing.

Commonly used incentives are vouchers of monetary value that can be exchanged for goods, prize draw entries or clinic privileges such as take-home doses of prescribed medications. CM has been found to enhance compliance with a range of harm reduction interventions, such as vaccinations for hepatitis B.[12] It is also more likely to promote abstinence in stimulant misusers than standard care.[15] A further use of CM has been in reducing the illicit drug use of those on methadone maintenance programs.[16]

Currently, CM is most often used in the context of dose dispensing frequency but use of monetary vouchers is being tested in some UK treatment centres.[17]

A higher-intensity intervention is indicated where lower intensity has not been effective and for clients with a number of unsuccessful attempts at change. NICE guidelines suggest that the most effective intervention has both social and behavioural elements, just as we have seen for alcohol misuse.

Behavioural Couples Therapy

This is a behavioural couples-based intervention focused on promoting absti-nence or decreasing illicit drug misuse in the drug-using member of the couple.[18] Behavioural Couples Therapy (BCT) consists of up to 20 sessions with the couple and contains these elements: a daily structured verbal commitment to change, teaching effective communication skills and increasing positive behavioural exchanges between the couple. It is most effective for clients with a non drug-using partner but can also be used where both partners misuse drugs if there is at least a temporary commitment to abstinence from both people.

Interventions for common mental health problems

There is a high prevalence of mental health problems, particularly depression and anxiety, in the drug-using population, whether as a pre-existing problem or as a result of the substance misuse and lifestyle itself. One estimate of prevalence of depression and anxiety is of 30–60% in substance misuse populations.[19] Both guided self-help and behavioural activation are evidence based for these prob-lems where the healthcare professional facilitates use of the material by monitor-ing and reviewing outcomes. Typically health workers will offer one assessment session and three to six further sessions of 20–30 minutes, with some of these sessions offered by telephone.

Guided self-help

Guided self-help is for clients with mild to moderate anxiety problems. It consists of working through self-help manuals or computer-assisted programmes based on a cognitive-behavioural model. Attention is paid to the relationship between thoughts, behaviour and feelings. Regular goals are set that incorporate use of coping strategies and decreasing avoidance of feared situations in a graded way.

Behavioural activation

Behavioural activation is for clients with mild to moderate depression where depression is seen in terms of a low rate of positively rewarded and rewardable behaviour. The intervention focuses on helping clients to monitor their daily life for rewarding and/or pleasurable behaviours, then to encourage development of more task-focused and rewarding behaviours. There have been some positive results for behavioural activation in substance misuse populations.[20]

For clients who have not benefited from low-intensity intervention or for those where risk/severity of problems indicates a greater need, a higher-intensity inter-vention will be indicated. This will be of longer duration (up to 20 sessions of

50–60 minutes) and delivered by mental health professionals specifically trained in this intervention.

Cognitive behavioural therapy

Cognitive behavioural therapy (CBT) is the only intervention with a good evidence base across a range of common mental disorders including depression, generalised anxiety disorder, panic disorder, obsessive-compulsive disorder and post-traumatic stress disorder.[21-24] Therapy is a collaborative venture, based on a formulation of development of the problem and its current maintaining factors made up of thought, behaviour and feeling patterns. Therapy is based on an active approach to decreasing behavioural avoidance, learning coping skills and challenging unhelpful thinking patterns. The NICE guidelines for drug misuse suggest that drug misuse does not preclude use of CBT for a coexisting mental health problem as long as the frequency and amount of that use allows the client to actively engage in therapy and between-session homework tasks.

Conclusion

Treating a 'drug addict' creates challenging role reversals for the doctor. Normally the doctor is the expert in his or her subject and is comfortable in imparting education and expertise to the grateful patient. But in the case of drug users, the patient is usually far more expert. Patients can use a language that is often not understood and an array of drugs in quantities and mixtures that are a very long way outside the sort of conventional pharmaceutical therapeutics that doctors are taught. Then there is the role reversal of 'Who is treating who?' Drug-using patients are very often treating their own morbidity, albeit in a flawed and damaging way – and in trying to confront and change that behaviour the doctor will inevitably discomfort the patient, the opposite of our role with most patients. Finally there is the paradox of drugs themselves. While as doctors we see them as a force for good with which to help people, in the user who treats him or herself we can instinctively think of drugs as negative forces that need to be taken away.

It is particularly important that this latter prejudice is set aside: that drug use is somehow 'bad'. How can it be when the medical profession itself inflicts its own drugs on the rest of the population almost every time that a patient presents? Drug use is simply a behaviour that serves varying needs and has varying health consequences. What is certain is that both doctors and the consumers of prescribed and illicit drugs place an unreasonable expectation on the ability of drugs to deliver comfort and happiness.

Doctors in training today are prevailed upon to consider all conditions presenting to them in three dimensions – the physical, the psychological and the social. Surely there can be no condition quite like drug misuse that is both deeply rooted in all three dimensions and impacts so deeply on each dimension of a person's health? Therefore, by implication, there is no condition that needs so much more than a narrow physical response?

In treatment, as in life itself, there is a lot more to offer than drugs.

References

1. Roberts G D. *Shantaram*. Melbourne: Scribe Publications, 2003.

2. Miller W, Harris R. A simple scale of Gorski's warning signs for relapse. *Journal of Studies on Alcohol* 2000; **61(5)**: 759–65.

3. McKellar J, Stewart E, Humphreys K. Alcoholics Anonymous involvement and positive alcohol-related outcomes: cause, consequence or just a correlate? *Journal of Consulting and Clinical Psychology* 2003; **71(2)**: 302–8.

4. Moos R H, Moos B S. Long-term influence of duration and frequency of participation in Alcoholics Anonymous on individuals with alcohol use disorders. *Journal of Consulting and Clinical Psychology* 2004; **72(1)**: 81–90.

5. Ball J C, Ross A. *The Effectiveness of Methadone Maintenance Treatment: patients, programs, services and outcome*. New York: Springer-Verlag, 1991.

6. Meier P S, Barrowclough C, Donnall M C. The role of the therapeutic alliance in the treatment of substance misuse: a critical review of the literature. *Addiction* 2005; **100(3)**: 304–16.

7. Project MATCH Research Group. Project MATCH (Matching Alcoholism Treatment to Client Heterogeneity): rationale and methods for a multisite clinical trial matching patients to alcoholism treatment. *Alcoholism: clinical and experimental research* 1993; **17(6)**: 1130–45.

8. Sanchez-Craig M. *A Therapist's Manual: secondary prevention of alcohol problems*. Toronto: Addiction Research Foundation, 1996.

9. Walters G D. BSCT for problem drinkers: a meta-analysis of randomised controlled studies. *Behavior Therapy* 2000; **31(1)**: 135–49.

10. Miller W R, Leckman A L, Delaney H D, *et al*. Long-term follow-up of behavioural self-control training. *Journal of Studies on Alcohol* 1992; **53(3)**: 249–61.

11. UKATT Research Team. Effectiveness of treatment for alcohol problems: findings of the randomised UK Alcohol Treatment Trial (UKATT). *British Medical Journal* 2005; **331(7516)**: 541.

12. National Institute for Health and Clinical Excellence. *Clinical Guideline 51, Drug Misuse: psychosocial interventions*. London: NICE, 2007.

13. Pilling S, Hesketh K, Mitcheson L. *Psychosocial Interventions in Drug Misuse: a framework and toolkit for implementing NICE-recommended treatment interventions*. London: NTA/BPS, 2010.

14. Hester R K, Miller W R. *Handbook of Alcoholism Treatment Approaches* (2nd edn). Boston, MA: Allyn & Bacon, 1995.

15. Higgins S T, Silverman K. *Motivating Illicit Drug Abusers to Change Their Behaviour: research on contingency management interventions*. Washington, DC: APA, 1999.

16. Rawson R A, Huber A, McCann M, *et al*. A comparison of contingency management and cognitive-behavioural approaches during methadone maintenance treatment for cocaine dependence. *Archives of General Psychiatry* 2002; **59(9)**: 817–24.

17. Mitcheson L. Bridging the gap between guidelines and practice. Presentation at Pompidou Group, Cyprus, 2009, www.nta.nhs.uk.

18. Fals-Stewart W, O'Farrell T J, Birchler G R. Behavioural Couples Therapy for male substance-abusing patients: a cost-outcome analysis. *Journal of Consulting and Clinical Psychology* 1997; **65(5)**: 789–802.

19. Weaver T, Madden P, Charles V, *et al.* Co-morbidity of substance misuse and mental illness in community mental health and substance misuse services. *British Journal of Psychiatry* 2003; **183**: 304–13.

20. Daughters S B, Braun A R, Sargeant M N, *et al.* Effectiveness of a brief behavioural treatment for inner-city illicit drug users with elevated depressive symptoms: the life enhancement treatment for substance use (LETS Act!). *Journal of Clinical Psychiatry* 2008; **69(1)**: 122–9.

21. National Institute for Health and Clinical Excellence. *Clinical Guideline 113, Generalised Anxiety Disorder and Panic Disorder (with or without Agoraphobia) in Adults.* London: NICE, 2011, www.nice.org.uk/guidance/CG113 [accessed November 2012].

22. National Institute for Health and Clinical Excellence. *Clinical Guideline 91, Depression in Adults with a Chronic Physical Health Problem: treatment and management.* London: NICE, 2009, www.nice.org.uk/guidance/CG91 [accessed November 2012].

23. National Institute for Health and Clinical Excellence. *Clinical Guideline 31, Obsessive-Compulsive Disorder: core interventions in the treatment of obsessive-compulsive disorder and body dysmorphic disorder.* London: NICE, 2005, www.nice.org.uk/guidance/CG31 [accessed November 2012].

24. National Institute for Health and Clinical Excellence. *Clinical Guideline 26, Post-Traumatic Stress Disorder (PTSD): the management of PTSD in adults and children in primary and secondary care.* London: NICE, 2005, www.nice.org.uk/guidance/CG26 [accessed November 2012].

CHAPTER 17

Young people and substance use

Daphne Rumball and Dickon Bevington

IN THIS CHAPTER

Introduction || Definitions: distinguishing child from adult substance use || The developmental context || The safeguarding context || The legal framework || Preparatory work || Epidemiology || Complexity, risk and resilience || Natural history || Gateway theory || Identification of need/engagement and assessment || Presentations in primary care and special circumstances || Special situations || Interventions in primary care || When to refer || Conclusion

Introduction

This chapter considers the needs of children and young people who use substances problematically. The age range considered in reference material varies greatly and for the purpose of this chapter we will mainly consider those of 18 years or under. We refer to under-13-year-olds as children, and those of 13–18 years as young people.

The structure of this chapter is pragmatic, employing a framework that describes common problems, and opportunities to intervene with young people *as they present in primary care*. The material is underpinned by research litera-ture but also draws on experience, basic principles and established guidelines. Research in this field is in an early stage of development, hampered by changing patterns of substance use, complex ethical issues and limited resources.

Primary care teams are in a unique position, having good knowledge of local population norms, resources and needs, with trans-generational knowledge of families and young people. Many GPs with the confidence of young people and parents will be the first port of call for complex problems. While some will pres-ent with direct requests for specialist help with substance use, others present opportunities for primary or secondary prevention. The health promotion role of primary care teams is of particular importance regarding the establishment of appropriate help-seeking behaviours in this patient group.

A fundamental goal is to encourage primary care practitioners *to ask* about substance use, including alcohol. Young people are frequently reticent about offering such information, or may have little sense of the problematic nature of their use. There is a range of practical interventions available in the event that substance use is revealed. Primary care staff may feel ill equipped for these roles, out of touch with ever-changing jargon, and believing they lack information or skills to open up opportunities for intervention. The chapter begins with preparatory work to equip a primary care team with information to support this role, before going on to consider the presenting problems, their assessment and possible intervention in the primary care context, and advises on when to consider referral to secondary services.

Definitions: distinguishing child from adult substance use

Substance use in children and young people is multifaceted and heterogeneous in nature so that evidence-based practice has been slow to accumulate. However, the growing literature does support a range of key components of effective practice.

A key point arising from research literature is the necessity of making clear distinctions between child and adolescent substance use and its adult equivalents. Although *existing definitions* of harmful or dependent use (ICD or DSM) are relevant, *additional factors* need to be borne in mind when considering children and young people, particularly the developmental context and the safeguarding framework. Thresholds for concern need to be lower than in the adult population.

The developmental context

Children or young people who start using substances do so at a crucially sensitive point in their developmental trajectory: when key biological processes are still unfolding, particularly the 'synaptic refinement' of brain pathways (which preserves those neural pathways in active use, but 'prunes out' ones that are not). This supports the brain to adapt to the functions that it is being 'asked' to perform. The (dopaminergic) reward circuits that encode for pleasure and the motivation to repeat experiences identified as pleasurable are powerfully influenced during this phase of life, too, with lasting influences into adulthood. There is also strong emerging evidence that early exposure to substances induces lasting change at the cellular level, especially in these reward circuits.

Also, other significant developmental tasks in the interpersonal, social and educational spheres are scheduled at this age, e.g. exams and learning, the development of intimate relationships, individuation and the beginnings of independent living. The loss of such 'time-critical' developmental stages (to chronic intoxication or other sequelae of substance use) is akin to the effects of physical insults on other time-critical developmental processes – in many respects the deficits sustained may never entirely 'catch up'. In contrast, the adult who has achieved a reasonable educational status, has developed social skills and has non-substance-using friends may suffer some 'lost years' from drink or drugs, but has very much more to build on in recovery than the young person who has left school prematurely, has poor educational attainments, has limited social skills and has no non-substance-using friends. The majority of severe and chronic adult substance use disorders have their onset in adolescence.

The safeguarding context

The practitioner must consider young people's explicit vulnerability and the potential applicability of safeguarding or other legal considerations. Because of the obvious differences in power and status, the child or adolescent who uses substances is significantly more vulnerable to exploitation than most adults. The practitioner has a duty to consider the effectiveness of any adults in caring roles to protect children in their care from significant harm.

The legal framework

Concerns about legal requirements and pitfalls can cause reluctance to proceed. However, the frameworks are familiar to primary care teams, being the same as those that apply in sexual health, mental health and all other encounters with young people. It is important to know how the acts and principles apply and where to seek further advice.

Children Act 1989 and Fraser Guidelines (confidentiality and competency)

The Children Act[1] is the legislative framework governing all young people in England and Wales. Similar legislation exists for Scotland and Northern Ireland, but is not covered separately here. The major principles of the act are that the welfare of the child is paramount, and the child's wishes and views must be considered, alongside requirements for interagency collaboration and action if risks are identified.

The implications of this act for the primary care practitioner are that early discussion of confidentiality and its limits is crucial. Confidentiality, which is in the interest of the therapeutic relationship, may sometimes be over-ridden by a need to safeguard the child. In reality, shared understanding of this duty of care can make it easier to decide how to proceed and emphasises to the young person that his or her problems are being taken very seriously.

Situations that require disclosure may include the role of the young person as a parent him or herself, the consideration of an unborn baby during a young person's pregnancy, exploitation by older substance users or others, involvement in violence, sex working or the presence of severe self-neglect.

The Family Law Reform Act 1969 gives the right to consent to treatment to anyone aged 16 to 18 years. Children under the age of 16 years can consent to medical treatment if they have sufficient maturity and judgement to enable them fully to understand what is proposed. The Fraser guidelines[2] state that, in order for a practitioner to offer treatment to a young person under 16 years without parental consent, some requirements should be fulfilled (see Box 17.1).

Box 17.1   **Requirements for treating a young person under 16 without parental consent**

✓ The young person will understand the professional's advice.

✓ The young person cannot be persuaded to inform his or her parents.

✓ The young person is likely to begin, or to continue having, sexual intercourse with or without contraceptive treatment.

✓ Unless the young person receives contraceptive treatment, his or her physical or mental health, or both, are likely to suffer.

✓ The young person's best interests require him or her to receive contraceptive advice or treatment with or without parental consent.

Although in law these criteria specifically refer to contraception, the principles are deemed to apply to other treatments, and are generally applied to engaging a young person in treatment of substance use, including prescribing of medication for substitution or withdrawal.

The Fraser guidelines referred specifically to doctors but are considered to apply to other health professionals, including nurses. They may also be interpreted as covering youth workers and health promotion workers who may be giving advice to young people under 16, but this has not been tested in court.

Mental Health Act 1983 and 2007[3]

Mental health legislation provides powers of assessment and detention for reasons of mental disorder in the interests of the health and safety of the patient, and the prevention of serious risk to others. The act can apply to any situation where mental disorder is present and includes mental disorder arising from the effects of substance use or withdrawal. However, *the act cannot be used for compulsory treatment of substance misuse itself,* which means that a young person cannot be detained solely to remove him or her from a risky pattern of substance use or to enforce detoxification, no matter how risky the scenario may be, unless there is a mental disorder that falls within the criteria of the act.

Assessment of mental capacity[4] is also relevant to decisions to proceed with interventions and treatment. It includes assessment of temporary impairment due to intoxication as well as inherent capacity.

Preparatory work

Performing a local service inventory

When starting to develop a practice interest in substance use of young people, it is important to know where to turn for further advice, either for professional consultation or referral of a young person or a concerned parent or carer.

Once contact with local services has been established it will also be possible to obtain useful posters, leaflets and, most importantly, named person contacts and referral pathways.

What services are there in your area?

The structure of specialist services for young substance users varies widely from one area to another and can change rapidly with changes in commissioning and national requirements. It is essential to keep this knowledge updated.

Resources drawn from the wider context

It can also be helpful to know about web-based resources with useful information for professionals, young people or parents. See Box 17.3 on p. 323 for a list.

How it should all come together: specialist treatment service principles

Government reports and advice have laid out recommendations for how services should be configured. All stress the need for collaborative multi-agency working[5–8]

Box 17.2　**Specialist services commissioned for young substance users**

✓ **Child and Adolescent Mental Health Services (CAMHs)** – a minority of CAMHs act as the lead agency for provision of substance misuse services. Most do not. Essential information concerns any specialist interest in substance use within CAMHs teams and the division of labour between them, other specialist substance use services and primary care.

✓ **Specialist services for parents or adults using substances** – knowledge of transitional pathways to adult services are important. Knowledge about adult services can also be valuable for addressing needs of parents or carers.

✓ **Specialist midwifery services** – for young people and/or substance-using women.

✓ **Local Education Authority resources** – resources for education and training.

✓ **Early Intervention in Psychosis teams** – there is an increased incidence and prevalence of psychosis associated with substance use.[9] This pathway is very important.

Epidemiology

Substance use in children and young people is extremely common: 39% of 11–15-year-olds have smoked tobacco, of whom 9% regularly, while 55% have used alcohol and 24% have used illicit drugs.[10] Recent surveys have shown some encouraging reverses in trends of usage over the past ten years, with recent significant falls in the use of heroin and cocaine, and small reductions in cannabis use. Conversely, there is evidence that those young people who *do* start using substances are using *larger quantities and more varied types* of substances, in particular the newer designer drugs. These latter drugs, which are often referred to as 'powders' as most are snorted, carry largely unknown risks. Some are 'legal' though completely untested. The problem over time is becoming more concentrated and entrenched in a smaller group of much more vulnerable and complex young people.

Complexity, risk and resilience

Young people with problematic use of substances often have families where one or more parent uses substances or has mental health problems, or experience other problems including poverty, educational failure and social exclusion.[11] Presentations of substance use in adolescence should prompt enquiry about mental health and other vulnerabilities, and vice versa.[12] A wide range of risk and resilience, or protective factors, are known to operate, and these are summarised in Table 17.1 (overleaf) and Box 17.4.

Box 17.3   **Web-based resources**

For professionals

✓ DrugScope is a national charity and membership organisation (www. drugscope.org.uk/resources/goodpractice/treatment/youngpeople).

For young people

✓ FRANK (www.talktofrank.com) is a Department of Health-led web information service with advice and information on substances, harms and treatments.

✓ YouthHealthTalk (www.youthhealthtalk.org) provides advice and first-hand accounts of experiences of a range of health issues (including substances).

For parents

✓ FRANK (www.talktofrank.com).

✓ DrugScope (www.drugscope.org.uk/resources/posters/info-for-parents).

Table 17.1   **Risk factors for persistent and problematic drug use**

Risk factors	Examples
Drug factors	Ability to produce mind-altering, pleasurable effects.
	Dependence potential (tolerance and withdrawal syndrome).
	Price.
	Availability
Environmental factors	Social deprivation.
	Poor housing.
	Neighbourhood crime.
	Lack of community support.
	Acceptance of drug use
Personal factors	Sex M > F.
	Adolescent.
	Scholastic failure.
	Unemployment.
	Conduct disorder.
	Friends who use.
	ADHD.
	Family attitudes, e.g. tolerance of use, approval of smoking and drinking

Resilience factors

Preventive interventions that have shown benefit largely relate to the enhancement of resiliencies. This is similar to research on young people at risk of psychological illness.[13]

Box 17.4   **Protective/resilience factors**

✓ A consistent, caring adult, not necessarily a parent.

✓ Engagement in a constructive interest or hobby.

✓ Academic or career achievement.

✓ A positive (pro-social) peer group.

✓ Clear parental/carer values and expectations.

Primary care staff have a key role in encouraging and supporting these protective factors. The engagement of families with risk factors in treatment may be supported by a focus on supporting and enhancing existing resiliencies (a 'strengths-focused' approach) as much as by intervening to change risk factors.

Natural history

Most young people who use substances do not go on to develop lifelong substance use disorders. Many, perhaps the majority, pass through a period of substance use with no apparent long-term effects. Adolescence is characterised by increased exploration and a certain amount of risk-taking and boundary-testing. It is young people with other vulnerabilities – especially multiple and complex needs – who are at particular risk of progression from initiation to harmful use. The challenge for the primary care practitioner is the *early identification* of at-risk youth and the *provision of effective services* that are acceptable to such hard-to-reach young people. Some commentators have referred to adult substance use disorders as 'paediatric illnesses with lifelong consequences'[14] and, viewed from that perspective, work with children and young people who are using substances is a good example of early intervention.

Gateway theory

This theory postulates that the use of less harmful drugs, such as cannabis, introduces people to a criminal subculture where they meet other drug users and dealers who encourage them to experiment with other, often more harmful, drugs.

It is difficult to untangle the evidence that is often presented to serve political purposes. Certainly most heroin users have used cannabis, but very few cannabis users progress to heroin use. In one study, 96% of opioid users had used cannabis in the previous year but only 7% of cannabis users had ever taken heroin.

An alternative theory is that progression from cannabis to more harmful drugs is more about individual vulnerability,[15] and thus cannabis use is a consequence not a causal factor in predicting future drug use. If there are gateway substances, then early tobacco and alcohol use are most powerfully evidenced as the main risks, and are thus pointers to opportunities for early intervention. The risk of early cannabis use as a trigger for psychosis in previously vulnerable individuals is well established.[5]

Identification of need / engagement and assessment

Modes of presentation

There are two main areas in which identification is relevant: those at risk of initiation into regular use, for whom primary prevention interventions should be considered, and those currently using substances in a risky or harmful way, which requires advice or treatment.

Identifying at-risk youth (primary prevention)

For young people with known increased risk factors of developing substance use problems, opportunistic screening should be undertaken whenever possible. Screening may involve specific instruments. CRAFFT is one such tool that is validated for use in young people and asks 'true to life' questions [16] and uses careful engagement in discussion (see Box 17.5).

Box 17.5   **The CRAFFT tool**

CRAFFT is a mnemonic acronym of first letters of key words in the six screening questions. The questions should be asked exactly as written.

C – Have you ever ridden in a **CAR** driven by someone (including yourself) who was 'high' or had been using alcohol or drugs?

R – Do you ever use alcohol or drugs to **RELAX**, feel better about yourself or fit in?

A – Do you ever use alcohol or drugs while you are by yourself, or **ALONE**?

F – Do you ever **FORGET** things you did while using alcohol or drugs?

F – Do your family or **FRIENDS** ever tell you that you should cut down on your drinking or drug use?

T – Have you ever got into **TROUBLE** while you were using alcohol or drugs?

Enquiry should be made in a routine and appreciative manner with terms such as 'I am asking you because I like to ask everyone, and because there are things that I and others can do to support you.' If two or more questions are answered affirmatively, then further assessment and possible referral is warranted.

Identifying using youth

Assessment of substance use in a young person – especially by an authority figure such as a GP – is a powerful intervention in its own right. It communicates the significance (and potential harms) of substance use, and is an opportunity for engagement that may define the subsequent course of treatment.

Again, it can be helpful to enquire in an appreciative manner with terms such as 'I would like to consider this with you because there are things that I and others can do.' Areas to explore will be the age at first use, and age when regular use started, levels of current use, and current understandings of the risks and harms, and thoughts about change (covered below).

As well as the presenting substance, each young person should also be asked about alcohol, smoking, cannabis and other drugs. Enquiry should be made about illicit drugs, drugs/substances obtained from friends or family, prescription drugs and over-the-counter substances. This approach will open the way to exploring the *context* of use of each substance: who with, how often, the route of use (swallowing, smoking, snorting or injecting) and for how long it's been occurring.

Engagement

Engagement is essential for successful treatment for substance use. In the primary care setting this implies the need for rapid recognition of the incidental or context-specific anxieties that an adolescent attending a health setting may experience. Anxieties about the extraordinary intimacy of a health-related interview, about questions of confidentiality, about the potential for stigma or disapproval to trigger hostility from the professional may overwhelm the adolescent's capacity to concentrate, believe or take in suggestions. Additional prefacing remarks that acknowledge and empathise with this predicament and explicitly work to reduce the level of affect in the room are important: 'This is an odd kind of conversation, isn't it? But do remember that I am only being this "nosey" to get a better understanding, so I can be more helpful – and I have strict rules about confidentiality that I can explain to you.'

Another challenge is the constantly varying 'street language' about drugs, which can leave the practitioner feeling uncertain, naïve or even incompetent. Aside from the increasingly frequent arrival of new designer drugs, the names for specific substances or practices vary from region to region, and change frequently; this is reminiscent of the re-branding of tired retail products. The practitioner is advised to use this uncertainty about drug names confidently, in ways that support engagement with the young person:

'Look, I'm sure you know the names of drugs are changing all the time; you will know a whole lot more about the names in use right now than I ever will – so you need to help me here, please.'

'Tell me what you mean when you talk about this "X"?'

'Does it have other names?'

'What does it look like? How much does it cost?'

'How do you take X?'

By taking this 'one-down stance' the practitioner emphasises respect for the competency and expertise of the young person, but can also 'cross-reference' the young person's answers against his or her own knowledge base (the young person who explains that his 'cocaine' is a sticky black substance is unlikely to be taking cocaine!).

Consider culture

Careful enabling of disclosure of problems and concerns will help avoid assumptions about values and norms. Substance problems are known to be under-recognised in social groups where use is prohibited, in females and Asian populations.[17]

Thinking and talking about change

Assessing the *stage of change*[18] is important (see Figure 1.1 on p. 11).

1. *Pre-contemplation* describes the state of holding tacit beliefs that 'the sums add up in favour of my continuing these behaviours, despite what others may say'.

2. *Contemplation* is where a tentative balancing of *pros and cons* has begun.

3. *Planning or preparation* is most commonly passed over directly, in favour of …

4. *Action*, in which plans (well-formed or barely identified) are enacted.

Having clarified the stage of change, the practitioner must then *adapt the mode of discourse*, to fit that particular stage. Addressing a young person who is in a 'pre-contemplative' state of mind in the language of 'planning' is highly likely to result in that young person disengaging from further care.

Managing complexity as a tool of engagement

Addressing a complex condition affecting multiple domains (biological, psychological, relational, legal) and risks requires expertise to pursue parallel work streams, clarifying the physical health status of the young person, as well as their care environment. However, it does provide more than one area through which to approach the issue of substance use.

The literature on Motivational Interviewing encourages practitioners to 'roll with resistance' and strenuously avoid argumentation about the merits/demerits of the young person's views. The practitioner who practises 'side-stepping' potential confrontations to address *other* areas (such as physical health) will find it easier to hold a stance towards his or her patient that sustains explicitly the intention to be helpful, which in turn sustains engagement.

Discussing risk

For each substance, first exploring the *subjective* effects and *extent of intoxication* will enable discussion of risky behaviours and prevention of accidental overdose. Those effects are usually the desired outcome; although the worker avoids ever colluding with substance use, it is equally important to avoid denying the subjective pleasure and perceived benefits of use – which will be driving ongoing use. The potential toxic risk of combining substances, or of overdose, is often underestimated. This is an important aspect to cover for the safety of the young person. For the determined user at risk there is real value in giving information such as the early signs of overdose, or harm minimisation advice such as avoiding using while alone, or the use of the recovery position for friends who are stricken, and to record this for medico-legal purposes. Any such risks should carefully be considered in the context of the young person's mental state, too. Depressive ideas or suicidal ambivalence are common in the context of substance use [19] and can lead to heightened risk taking, requiring more intensive and specialist psychosocial approaches.

Presentations in primary care and special circumstances

Drug/alcohol crisis with help-seeking behaviour

A young person, or a parent or other on his or her behalf, may present seeking urgent advice or intervention. There are several possible reasons, of which a new discovery or revelation that the young person is using drugs is the most common.

The situation may be complicated by a recent arrest or an event at school or college. Usually such situations are not actually an emergency, but require a calm approach and empathy while making further assessment and, if necessary, referral for additional help.

Physical dependence

The situation may be apparently more urgent if *physical dependence* on a substance is present and there is a risk of acute withdrawal, particularly in respect of alcohol. It is essential not to be rushed into undertakings, such as prescribing, or to undertake interventions beyond the expertise of the practitioner, before adequate assessment. At such times, knowledge of local resources and information ready to hand will pay dividends. Symptomatic treatment of withdrawal symptoms, though perhaps not what the patient may be requesting, will offer realistic support while further action is undertaken.

Acute withdrawal

A route of supply may have suddenly become unavailable following police activity, the young person may have become unable to fund their use, or they may have spent time in hospital or in custody, emerging unwell and seeking help. Again it is essential to take time to assess, provide interim care and make referral as needed.

Acute intoxication

Intoxication with altered level of consciousness requires transfer to hospital for assessment. This is particularly so because of the likely association of other substance effects and the unpredictable nature of drug and alcohol effects in young people. With lower levels of intoxication, perhaps only producing an altered emotional state, it is advisable to enlist a responsible adult if the young person intends to leave the safe environment. Overdose advice and monitoring should be given with clearly advised emergency actions.

Non-urgent help seeking

Fortunately this is the most usual. The young person, alone or with concerned others, seeks help for him or herself. This is the time to elicit concerns and build a picture of the patient's need. Very commonly there will be an underlying emotional, physical health or social need.

Psychological

Any substance use presentation in primary care should prompt enquiry into emotional health. Co-occurrence of mental illness or emotional distress with problematic substance use has a raised prevalence, either as trigger or consequence of the substance itself or underlying social risks.

Anxiety

This is the first symptom of withdrawal of any sedating substance such as opiates. If that substance is used repeatedly, anxiety will be experienced repeatedly until it can seem that the substance is needed to relieve the anxiety. This would be referred to as drug-provoked anxiety. Repeated use of benzodiazepines can produce such paradoxical anxiety. It is also likely that an underlying tendency to be anxious is linked to adverse past or current experience, which itself can predispose to substance use. This is known as the common factors model. Cocaine, amphetamine, other stimulant substances and cannabis can produce anxiety as a direct effect, and may escalate to paranoid states.

Depression

This can occur through similar mechanisms and is a withdrawal state following repeated use of stimulants, ketamine and ecstasy. Most commonly, depression is present due to common factors in personal history or current environment.

Other psychological states with increased association include obsessive-compulsive disorder (OCD) and eating disorders. Substance use can begin for facilitation of weight loss, control of appetite or management of distress and can escalate to dependent use very quickly.

Early psychosis

This can be difficult to distinguish from substance effects. Both are prevalent in adolescence. In practice it may be necessary to keep an open assessment, particularly if potentially provocative substance use continues. Expert help from an early interventions team should be useful.

Other presentations and notes of caution

▸ Adolescent exaggeration of reported drug use can relate to status seeking, particularly in young people with poor self-esteem.

▸ Attempts at obtaining excessive amounts of medication may be recognised, typically seeking benzodiazepines or methadone. If so, thought should be given to the possibility of a manipulative older person seeking to obtain drugs by proxy, and the potential need for a safeguarding assessment.

▸ Prescription drugs such as hypnotics and anxiolytics can be sought for misuse, or for self-management of symptoms of other drug effects such as stimulant come down or opiate withdrawal anxiety. Thought should be given to the possibility of more serious underlying substance use.

Box 17.6   **Physical presentations that might suggest substance use**

Weight loss

This is a general outcome of most substance use. It occurs through reduction of appetite with opiates and stimulants, increase in metabolic rate with stimulant use, or from dietary neglect through indifference or lack of money. Although cannabis typically provokes cravings for sweet food, weight gain is unusual because of apathy at other times. Alcohol is an exception due to its calorific content, though in regular use gastric irritation can cause anorexia and vomiting. Anabolic steroids are taken as part of body building for the purpose of muscular weight gain.

Abdominal pain

This occurs in response to various drugs and in withdrawal states from opiates. Most striking pain occurs with ketamine use, often called K-cramps. These are intense, persistent pains due either to effects on the gut or from bladder and urinary tract inflammation. It can be mistaken for acute abdominal conditions of surgical nature.

Other gastrointestinal symptoms

These include constipation of opiate use, vomiting in opiate withdrawal, vomiting in alcohol toxicity and withdrawal, and sub-costal pain from inflammation of the liver, typically in response to alcohol.

Bladder and urinary tract symptoms

These are due to ketamine and are increasingly common. The drug causes interstitial inflammation of the bladder wall, and presents resembling severe, acute urinary tract infection that is unresponsive to antibiotics. Direct enquiry about ketamine use should be routine. Cessation of ketamine may allow gradual recovery but the damage to urinary tract may progress. Early referral to urology is recommended.[20]

Sexual health

Drugs and alcohol typically alter sexual libido. Sedating drugs reduce, and stimulant drugs increase, libido. The latter may lead to inappropriate sexual activity, as can the disinhibiting effects of alcohol and ecstasy, and the depersonalising effects of benzodiazepines, ketamine and various recreational or party drugs. Psychosexual presentations and sexually transmitted infections should prompt a drug enquiry and harm reduction advice.

Special situations

In keeping with our emphasis on the importance of identifying and engaging particularly high-risk children and young people who are using substances, the following section provides brief notes on a range of special situations that refer to young people from identified risk populations, or whose substance use carries with it more specific risks or recommended actions and interventions. In most of these 'Red Flag' cases referral on to specialist services would be an appropriate response, though there is value in understanding some of the key issues at stake.

Injecting

The child or young person who is injecting (regardless of the substance) is considered to be at the highest end of the spectrum of clinical risk, just short of life threatening. This is not simply because of the wide range of serious associated physical health risks (accidental overdose, local infections, systemic infections including blood-borne viruses) associated with injecting but also because of the unique *contextual* questions that are raised in relation to the young age of the user. For instance, there are significant *safeguarding* issues in play.

▸ How is the injecting equipment being accessed?

▸ Most injecting behaviour begins with being taught, or being injected by others. Who has taught the young person or may be actively helping with the techniques required for successful injecting?

▸ Is there coercion or exploitation involved?

Exploitation

Adults are commonly involved in young people's substance use, either in the supply or in shared use. Concerns may include exploitation of the young person *while he or she is intoxicated* such as inappropriate or abusive sexual contact, or encouragement to commit crimes or other high-risk activities, or the exploitation of the young person in relation to the *provision of substances*.

Questioning about exploitation needs to be done sensitively, avoiding the risk of reinforcing stigmatising views. Early explanation about patient confidentiality and its limits is helpful, as a young person can be reminded about these realities. A helpful technique is to normalise the problems:

'Some of the young people I have worked with before have spoken about feeling that along with the things they have liked, *they have also begun to get themselves into relationships or activities that leave them feeling uncomfortable. If*

I gave you some examples of the kinds of difficulties other young people have spoken about, do you think you could say if you recognise any of them in your own experience?'

If identified, then safeguarding protocols may be required to guide the most appropriate response.

Pregnancy

Pregnancy may occur unplanned but this may be an incorrect assumption. Advice about contraception for harm reduction purposes should be preceded by exploring intentions and wishes.

The identification and treatment of substance use in pregnancy are covered in more detail in Chapter 18. In the case of a young person's pregnancy, key areas for consideration are shown in Box 17.7.

Young people in custody

Young people held in police cells may complain or show signs or symptoms of acute intoxication or withdrawal, or may reveal substance use disorder in relation to the alleged offence (stealing alcohol, for instance). A GP may be asked to assess them in his or her role as Forensic Medical Examiner.

This may be the first time substance use has come to light, or the young person may already be well known to services. Either way, there are important networking aspects to bear in mind that will maximise the likelihood of improved outcomes. The value of proactive attempts to identify and alert any existing therapeutic relationships (CAMHS, specialist substance use services, the Local Authority) cannot be underestimated. Communication between penal institutions and local health and social care facilities is historically difficult, as release from custody may be at short notice and custody cannot be prolonged pending such information exchange. Protocols do exist, and are usually part of service commissioning protocols, the onus being on the custody-setting service to seek continuity of care by referral.

The arrest and incarceration may provide a window of opportunity for referral to existing young people's substance use services – if only because the negative consequences of their substance use are harder to deny in that setting.

Medical management of withdrawal (from opiates or alcohol in particular) or acute intoxication is covered elsewhere, but the risks attached to a young person in custody, particularly self-harm, suicide and accidental overdose following release, are potentially higher due to the coincident stressors, isolation, negative emotional states during withdrawal, and difficulties in ensuring monitoring of physical and psychological states.

Box 17.7   **Areas to consider for young people and pregnancy**

Safeguarding

The primary care practitioner has a duty of care to the foetus *as well as the mother*, who may herself still fit the legal definition of a child. Urgent and assertive liaison with colleagues in Social Services, and an urgent planning meeting to address this, are required. In giving advice about potential harms of substance use in pregnancy it is important to recognise that the young person, or her partner, may be ambivalent about continuation of the pregnancy. Such advice may paradoxically escalate risky use. It is essential to explore wishes about continuation of pregnancy at the earliest stage possible.

   Liaison and communication between the multiple specialists in such cases (the unborn child would highly likely be subject to a child protection plan) are crucial, and the GP may be in a unique position, holding both a holistic understanding of the case and having the authority to encourage or insist that such integration takes place. Most UK obstetric services have a member of staff, usually a midwife, with special expertise in working with drug-using pregnant women, working in close collaboration with specialist substance use services.

Stimulant and other drug use

These can threaten the viability of pregnancy. The effects of many substances commonly used by young people are largely unknown.

Alcohol

This has known teratogenicity, particularly in high doses such as binge use common among young people. Withdrawal from dependent use is particularly important and should be achieved with expert help because of the risk of miscarriage. Benzodiazepine use probably has similar risks and management.

Opiate dependence

Sudden withdrawal of opiates carries a recognised risk of miscarriage and premature labour, and is likely to exacerbate morning sickness. Pregnant women should be advised against suddenly stopping opiate use or reducing without supervision. Expert assessment and care needs to be accessed as a matter of urgency.

   Pregnancy can be very motivating for change, and many women wish to become drug free. Although early intervention with substitute opiate treatment is usually an important starting point, stable maintenance is not necessarily appropriate, especially for young people whose dependence may be only recent. Withdrawal during pregnancy can therefore be considered once full assessment of the balance of risks has taken place in the context of motivation and individual resources. Methadone has been better trialled, but buprenorphine may be the drug of choice, especially if vomiting is a problem (sublingual absorption). Neither is licensed in pregnancy.

Children of substance-using parents

The risk of substance use in children is greatly increased if there is a history of parental substance use.

Engaging the parents in their own treatment is an effective intervention for children, both in terms of prevention and treatment of the child's own substance use.

Some local adult services will have facilities for family therapy, while others will not. Young person's substance use services should all provide family-based interventions, and the GP may have an important role to play in ensuring or insisting that these services integrate their work around the needs of the child.

Safeguarding issues will be central in planning care, in respect of potential parental neglect or the emotional abuse implicit in exposing children to their own intoxication. Early liaison with the Local Authority in this respect is advised.

Children in care

Children or young people who are looked after away from their family of origin are known to be at significantly higher risk of substance use disorders.

The statutory medical assessments that the Local Authorities with responsibility for such children are obliged to arrange offer a valuable opportunity for screening.

Without the consistency and permanency that placement in a family setting offers, efforts to develop a sensitive, well-informed, watchful and protective network around a young person are considerably more challenging.

Early identification of any key caring figures who are explicitly *acknowledged in the young person's mind* is of value. Ideally these may be the allocated social worker or keyworker, but they may be workers with less explicit responsibilities towards the young person, or less formal training, such as another care worker in a shared home or a local youth worker. Encouraging and supporting liaison between a worker who has a lot of contact and other more remote experts may offer an additional portal through whom education and therapy can be delivered. Crucially, this liaison may ensure that such figures remain 'on message' with more specialised work as it gets under way.

Children with mental health or serious behaviour problems

Children with complex mental health needs, who may have suffered abuse, neglect or trauma, and who may have conduct disorders, or other emerging personality disorders (particularly with difficulties in the arena of affect-regulation) are at higher risk of substance use than the general population.[21]

Risks may be associated with:

▸ *extrinsic factors* such as the tendency to mix with other substance-using peers so as to have substances easily available to them, or

▸ *intrinsic factors* such as the use of substances to 'self-medicate' distressing states of mind (such as depression or anxiety) or a 'sensation-seeking' temperament.

Identification of such risk factors in an individual, and then being able to reflect sensitively upon this in understandable language with that young person, and to formulate simple plans with them to address their own specific vulnerabilities, has been shown to be an effective early intervention.[22]

Conduct disorders have an especially high risk of co-occurrence with substance use disorders, and this should be borne in mind during assessment.

The treatment of affective or psychotic disorders should not be delayed if there is co-occurring substance use disorder, not least because these conditions are often reciprocally synergistic in their effects upon each other.

▸ *Psychological approaches* are addressed briefly below, and should be the mainstay of most treatment plans.

▸ *Prescribing* in such conditions is more difficult (and should normally be assessed and initiated by specialists), but conduct disorder is certainly not an absolute contraindication.

Prescribing may, in addition to any intrinsic effectiveness, offer routes to engagement in treatment for a young person whose attitude to the mental world is highly materialistic ('a pill [or other substance] for every ill'). Measures to ensure that prescribed medication is carefully tended, and is not available to be misused by the young person, usually require the presence of a responsible adult. Avoiding prescribing large amounts of any medication at one time is a vital precaution.

Two groups with clear co-morbid difficulties who are over-represented in surveys of young people using substances are:

Attention deficit hyperactivity disorder

Children with attention deficit hyperactivity disorder (ADHD) tend to score more highly on measures of sensation seeking, and are at higher risk of later conduct disorder and substance use disorders.

Large treatment studies have shown that the risk of later substance use disorders is significantly reduced by effective treatment of ADHD, and that this outweighs the putative risks associated with introducing vulnerable youth to stimulant drugs. However, it should be borne in mind that stimulant medication is still a controlled drug and has its own street value, so that active parental support and involvement is essential. Long-acting (modified-release) preparations of stimulants tend to reduce the risk of misuse, and non-stimulant treatments (such as atomoxetine) are also available.

Learning difficulties

Young people with mild or moderate learning difficulties or disabilities are at higher risk, perhaps because of their more limited repertoire of responses to peer pressure, a desire to integrate while being less able to assess risks, and having greater vulnerability to exploitation.

Clinical experience suggests that they are more likely to use solvents regularly, which are more dangerous, but more easily available, substances. They can be sourced (often by theft from hardware shops) without the level of social skills that are required to form relationships with dealers of illicit drugs.

Adjustments may be required to the language used in psycho-educational and motivational approaches with such young people.

Work with parents and carers is highly important in this sub-group as the core deficits that produce risk may be less amenable to treatment and change than the surrounding care network.

Children and young people out of formal education

Young people who are excluded, refusing or truanting from school are at higher risk, not least because this implies greater periods of time during which they are subject to lower levels of adult monitoring.

While specific psycho-education on the risks and harms attributable to substance use (and if necessary specific interventions) will of course be no less important for this group, there are two important additional factors to bear in mind:

▶ first, conventional psycho-educational approaches that echo the school settings that these young people have opted out of are likely to be less than successful. The health professional who chooses to offer a learned treatise is unlikely to see his or her seeds take root; instead, techniques that employ playfulness, interaction and role reversal should be used. ('So if I was a young person that needed to know what was what about cannabis so I didn't come across as an amateur, what would you be telling me?')

▶ second, this group illustrates a more general point. Efforts to support re-engagement in meaningful activities that are perceived to have value *by the young person* (as opposed to just the adults around him or her) may be at least as important as more specialised and explicitly therapeutic interventions.

Interventions in primary care

Harm reduction

This refers to advice-giving predicated on an understanding that, despite best intentions, and notwithstanding safeguarding concerns, a particular risky behaviour is highly likely to continue in the present circumstances. The practitioner may thus need to decide whether he or she should give the young person information that will at least minimise the most serious risks, even though this could potentially be seen as condoning or accepting the behaviour. As regards the latter point, any harm reduction intervention with a young person should be both prefaced and closed with clear 'signposting' that 'this is far from ideal', and that there is a preferable outcome (such as abstinence). One technique that can be helpful is to refer to 'amateurs' and 'experts' – emphasising that the real experts (who have 'been there, done that') move on, stop doing that, and live to tell the tale. Very few young people will consciously choose to be an amateur rather than an expert at whatever it is they are doing.

Examples of harm reduction would include suggesting that:

▸ heroin is far safer smoked than injected

▸ buying ready-rolled cannabis cigarettes (joints) is less safe than rolling one's own, as ready-made joints may be adulterated (cut) with other more addictive drugs such as crack cocaine, and thus complicate risk and addiction potential (much as supermarkets offer new brands as 'loss leaders').

Single-session 'there and then' interventions

In addition to opportunities for appropriate referral for more specialist treatment, the primary care practitioner is in an ideal position to deliver 'single session' (very brief) interventions involving psycho-education and motivational techniques. There is evidence to support the effectiveness (over the short term) of such interventions, especially for higher-risk youth.[23] Moreover, if such brief interventions address the way vulnerabilities that are specific to the patient might affect substance use, then this appears to add further value.[22] For example, children with a *stimulus-seeking temperament* or *impulsivity* (both common in ADHD) are at risk by virtue of their 'exploratory' or thrill-seeking nature, whereas children with proneness to anxiety are at risk of using substances to self-medicate.

Motivational Interviewing

Motivational Interviewing [24] proposes a style of relating to the patient that helps to articulate and clarify existing motivations, rather than 'injecting' motivation into the subject. It emphasises four key aspects.

▸ *Express empathy* refers to the need to understand the issue from the young person's perspective.

▸ *Develop discrepancy* is a cognitive technique, whereby enquiry about long-term goals and wishes 'makes space for' growing awareness of the discrepancy between present behaviours and these long-term goals. It is important to recognise that many young people – especially those at most risk of serious substance use problems – find it hard to articulate long-term goals, and the practitioner will take pains to avoid such enquiry being received as 'inquisitorial'. It is also important to emphasise that this technique is most effective only if it is the young person who ultimately identifies the discrepancy, rather than this being imposed.

▸ *Roll with resistance* refers to the importance of avoiding arguments about using or not-using, which are 'un-winnable' from the practitioner's point of view. The worker adopts a style that fluidly side-steps confrontation, changing the subject to areas that both parties can more actively collaborate over.

▸ *Support self-efficacy* refers to the way the practitioner constantly defers to the patient's autonomy, and seeks to support the patient's own motivation to carry through his or her choices rather than taking responsibility for this. Of course, in working with children or young people, this principle may require *modification* in so far as young people's competency may be more limited, and safeguarding concerns may overrule the level of autonomy that an adult would rightly expect.

Psycho-education

Psycho-education about the risks and potential harms of substances works better if efforts are made to avoid the 'lecture' in favour of a more playful, interactive style, perhaps starting by acknowledging the young person's expertise about local names for substances, and then asking him or her if there are any questions he or she would be interested to get answers for. A helpful technique is to promise that 'I certainly don't know all the answers, but we could look them up together on the internet if you ask a really difficult question.' A good website that can then be demonstrated live is the UK drug information site www.talktofrank.com. Many young people will be much faster at navigating a site like this than their doctor, and this is another opportunity to let them demonstrate mastery. Asking a young person to help compile a list of all the information a younger person thinking about using a substance ought to know is another way to avoid didactic teaching.

Planned work in the primary care setting

Although referral on to specialist services may be considered at an early stage, there may also be circumstances where planned work in primary care can and should be considered – especially if this is something the young person is requesting. Many young people's substance use services in the UK are able to provide consultation to support such locally based solutions, and there may be advantages to this solution.

▸ It avoids the multiplication (and potential duplication) of allocated workers that young people with complex difficulties often attract, so reducing the likelihood of 'dis-integrated' practices being delivered by different parts of a complex multi-agency network.

▸ Consultation with a primary care worker builds on an existing (and, one hopes, trusting) relationship that is liable to be longer term than a specialist service would sustain, and which can address a wider range of health needs more directly than a specialist substance use service.

Cognitive behavioural interventions have also been shown to be effective, especially in combination with motivational approaches and family interventions. Such work may well be delivered by specialist services, in which case it is useful for the primary care practitioner to understand the basic principles, though versions of these techniques may also be applied in primary care settings With a young person a first step is to encourage simple *diary keeping* to assess a baseline of usage over, say, two weeks. This allows the introduction of the idea of 'ABC' (antecedents, behaviour, consequences) so as to emphasise that substance use happens in certain (potentially predictable) circumstances. A second step is to introduce '*decisional balance*', which is better known as 'pros and cons', drawing these out on a large piece of paper, perhaps on a see-saw or set of scales. It is helpful to *start* by asking about the 'pros' of substance use; this allows for explicit expression of empathy as the rationale for substance use is explored, and it is not uncommon for the young person to be the one to introduce the 'cons' to usage. This is highly preferable from a motivational point of view, rather than the practitioner being the one to raise the negative aspects of substance use.

There is some evidence to support the use of regular *urine screening*, as part of a structured, rewards-based programme, though this may not be available to GP practices. Reward can range from positive reinforcement for progress (screens with no drug use showing) to formal 'contingency management' with pecuniary rewards. If used constructively, many patients welcome the boundaries of objective tests in conjunction with positive reinforcement. Evidence suggests it is the structure and positive regard that matters more than pecuniary reward. Conversely, there is a risk that if motivation is low and there is no legal mandate, i.e. a Court Order requiring treatment, a great deal of energy may be spent testing and counteracting attempts to subvert the testing process that could be spent more productively in other activities. For those in substitute prescribing programmes testing gives some assurance that the prescribed substance is being taken, though this is largely obviated by provision, stipulated on prescription, requiring witnessing by the pharmacist of consumption of opiate replacement medication.

Family work is strongly associated with improved outcomes in adolescent substance use disorder,[25] but it is not unusual for a young person to be reticent to involve his or her parents, or in some cases for parents to be reticent about joining therapy. If it is possible to engage the parents early on, they may support the young person's attendance at subsequent sessions, and agree ground-rules with their child about use at home. A focus on increasing positive interactions in the family, which proactively de-focuses attention from confrontations about substance use and instead offers incentives for improving relationships and mutual understanding, is helpful.

The identification and promotion of *resilience factors* or normative meaningful structured activity are vital.

Implicit in this work is the need for *proactive liaison with other professionals and agencies*, which can be time consuming but is seldom wasted.

When to refer

Specialist services for young substance users vary widely in structure, lead agency and lead professional roles. National standards set out commissioning goals. All will have tiers of provision from generic advice to highly specialised interventions including substitute prescribing and detoxification. Inpatient units are very rare, as are residential rehabilitation resources specifically for young people.

The tiers of service will be integrated in a manner that enables referral requesting interventions ranging from basic to complex levels. Self-referrals are also commonly accepted and encouraged. The wide variation in skill level of those who make referrals is well recognised. Therefore, the decision to refer must be based on an assessment of when additional assistance or resources are needed, rather than on specified agency criteria. It is the role of the specialist agency tiers to assess and arrange care according to the needs of the young person. Most also offer professional advice and consultancy. It is always better to hold back and refer than to attempt interventions beyond confidence or competency, both of which will develop with interest, advice, training and experience.

Box 17.8 **Prescribing – do's and don'ts**

Do's

✓ Do make proper assessment first, including objective tests (urine screen and physical signs) of reported use of substances.

✓ Do assess risks and benefits; substitute prescribing is not necessarily harm reduction and may add to risk.

✓ Do try to engage a parent or supportive adult.

✓ Do record your assessment of Fraser guideline competency.

✓ Do record your assessment of risks and advice given to reduce risk.

✓ Do make sure to provide advice and information on overdose prevention and management.

Don'ts

✓ Don't be rushed into prescribing; symptomatic treatments or supportive withholding are also important.

✓ Don't act beyond training and expertise.

✓ Don't go it alone; all guidelines emphasise a multidisciplinary/ multi-agency approach.

Conclusion

Addressing the needs of young people at risk or currently using substances is a challenging, but worthwhile, area of work that can have helpful outcomes and promote new and pleasing collaborations. We have highlighted a range of effective early measures that primary care services can take to clarify screening and assessment procedures, increase early recognition of problems, and improve outcomes through timely brief interventions. Consideration of when and how to refer for specialist care, and the need for proactive liaison with other workers and agencies in the field, will help minimise the risk of 'dis-integrated' interventions.

Acknowledgements

The authors wish to thank Dr Clare Gerada and Dr Beate Becker for their work in the first edition of Chapter 17, and Dr Ruth Bastable, Dr Kate Last and Dr Shobhana Nagraj for their helpful comments on drafts of this work.

Further reading

Crome I, Ghodse H, Gilvarry E, *et al.* (eds). *Young People and Substance Misuse*. London: Gaskell, 2004.

References

1. Children Act 1989, www.legislation.gov.uk/ukpga/1989/enacted.   [accessed May 2013].

2. Lord Fraser. House of Lords' ruling in the case of Gillick v West Norfolk and Wisbech Health Authority and Department of Health and Social Security, 1985.

3. Mental Health Act. London: HMSO, 2007, www.legislation.gov.uk/ukpga/2007/12. [accessed November 2012].

4. British Medical Association. Law Society. *Assessment of Mental Capacity: guidance for doctors and lawyers*. London: BMA, 1995.

5. Department of Health. *Drug Misuse and Dependence: guidelines on clinical management*. London: HMSO, 1999.

6. Health Advisory Service. *Children and Young People: substance misuse services, the substance of young need*. London: HMSO, 1996.

7. Health Advisory Service. *The Substance of Young Needs: review 2001*. London: HMSO, 2001.

8. Home Office. *Positive Futures: impact report*. London: HMSO, 2004, http://findings.org.uk/docs/off_11_2.pdf.   [accessed May 2013].

9. McGrath J, Welham J, Scott J, *et al.* Association between cannabis use and psychosis-related outcomes using sibling pair analysis in a cohort of young adults. *Archives of General Psychiatry* 2010; **67(5)**: 440–7.

10. Fuller E (ed.). *Smoking, Drinking and Drug Use among Young People in England in 2006*. London: NatCen, 2007, www.ic.nhs.uk/pubs/sdd06fullreport   [accessed November 2012].

11. McArdle P, Wiegersma A, Gilvarry E, *et al.* European adolescent substance use: the roles of family structure, function and gender. *Addiction* 2002; **97(3)**: 329–36.

12. Kessler R C, Nelson C B, McGonagle K A, *et al.* The epidemiology of co-occurring addictive and mental disorders: implications for prevention and service utilization. *American Journal of Orthopsychiatry* 1996; **66(1)**: 17–31.

13. Rutter M. Resilience in the face of adversity: protective factors and resistance to psychiatric disorder. *British Journal of Psychiatry* 1985; **147**: 598–611.

14. Kessler D, Wilkenfeld J, Thompson L. The Food and Drug Administration's rule on tobacco: blending science and law. *Pediatrics* 1997; **99(6)**: 884–7.

15. Kandel D, Faust R. Sequence and stages in patterns of adolescent drug use. *Archives of General Psychiatry* 1975; **32(7)**: 923–32.

16. Knight J R, Sherritt L, Shrier L A, *et al.* Validity of the CRAFFT substance abuse screening test among adolescent clinic patients. *Archives of Pediatric and Adolescent Medicine* 2002; **156(6)**: 607–14.

17. Commander M J, Odell S O, Williams K J, *et al.* Pathways to care for alcohol use disorders. *Journal of Public Health Medicine* 1999; **21(10)**: 65–9.

18. Prochaska J Q, DiClemente C C. Stages and processes of self-change of smoking: toward an integrative model of change. *Journal of Consulting and Clinical Psychology* 1983; **51(3)**: 390–5.

19. Neale J. Suicidal intent in non-fatal illicit drug overdose. *Addiction* 2002; **95(1)**: 85–93.

20. Winstock A, Mitcheson L. New recreational drugs and the primary care approach to patients who use them. *British Medical Journal* 2012; **344**: 35–40.

21. Zeitlin H. Psychiatric comorbidity with substance misuse in children and teenagers. *Drug and Alcohol Dependence* 1999; **55(3)**: 225–23.

22. Conrod P J, Castellanos-Ryan N, Mackie C. Long-term effects of a personality-targeted intervention to reduce alcohol use in adolescents. *Journal of Consulting and Clinical Psychology* 2011; **79(3)**: 296–306.

23. McCambridge J, Strang J. The efficacy of single-session motivational interviewing in reducing drug consumption and perceptions of drug-related risk and harm among young people: results from a multi-site cluster randomized trial. *Addiction* 2004; **99(1)**: 39–52.

24. Miller W R, Rollnick S. *Motivational Interviewing: preparing people for change.* New York: Guilford Press, 1991.

25. Diamond G, Josephson A. Family-based treatment research: a 10-year update. *Journal of the American Academy of Child and Adolescent Psychiatry* 2005; **44(9)**: 872–87.

CHAPTER 18

Women and drug use

Sharon Dawe, Lauren Vogel and Paul H. Harnett

IN THIS CHAPTER

Introduction ‖ Gender differences in the prevalence of drug use and entry into treatment ‖ Gender-specific problems for women with substance use problems ‖ Physical health issues for women with substance misuse problems ‖ Psychological health ‖ Pregnancy and drug use ‖ Treatment for women ‖ Conclusion

Introduction

Women with substance use problems face a number of gender-specific challenges that affect key aspects of assessment and treatment. From the outset, the initial trajectory that leads a woman to develop a substance misuse problem involves higher rates of childhood maltreatment that in turn can have a profound effect on adult wellbeing. The use of illicit substances typically requires access to large sums of money and to drug dealers. Many women manage this by an association with a drug-using partner and/or involvement in sex work. This results in a complex interplay between drug supply and violence and victimisation. Added to this difficult picture are concerns around parenting in a high-risk context and the additional shame and stigma that deter women from seeking treatment.

Primary care practitioners are well positioned to help women with substance misuse problems in the course of routine clinical care. Such opportunities typically present around contraception, pregnancy and child health issues. It is possible to identify women with substance use problems by asking a series of simple questions that may provide an opportunity for engagement in either treatment with the primary care practitioner and/or liaison with specialist agencies. This chapter will provide an overview of the key gender differences with a focus on prevalence, treatment engagement, physical and psychological sequelae of substance use and, finally, the special issues around management of pregnant women and their babies in the immediate postpartum period. A focus on parenting of young infants, outcomes for children raised in families with parental substance misuse and safeguarding concerns are discussed in this chapter.

Gender differences in the prevalence of drug use and entry into treatment

Rates of drug use have shown a downward trend in recent years. Data from England and Wales for 2009/10 indicates that 8.6% of adults had used one or more illicit drugs within the last year compared with 10.1% in 2008/9. Over the longer term this shows an overall decrease from 11.1% in 1996. There are gender differences in the use of substances across Europe with men much more likely to report lifetime and current use of both alcohol and illicit drugs. For example, in 2009/10, 11.9% of men reported the use of any illicit drug in the previous year compared with 5.4% for women.[1] These gender differences were also reflected in the numbers of people who were dependent on drugs. Data from the Adult Psychiatric Morbidity in England Survey (APMS) in 2007 show that the prevalence of drug dependence in 2007 was 4.5% for men and 2.3% of women. Most dependence was on cannabis only (2.5%), rather than on other drugs (0.9%).

However, there is increasing evidence that this gender difference is closing with rates of substance use in younger women, in particular, matching rates seen in young men. Findings from the World Health Organization (WHO) World Mental Health Surveys indicated not only that younger people were more likely to use drugs, but also that gender differences in drug use were becoming less pronounced in this younger cohort (18–29 years).[2] Similar patterns were found in surveys of the European Union, that while men continue to use drugs more, women are increasingly catching up, particularly in younger cohorts (in this case school students) and in relation to cannabis and ecstasy.[3]

There has been a longstanding view that women are under-represented in treatment settings with a number of studies finding that approximately 25–30% of admissions to treatment programmes were women. While there are certainly greater rates of drug use amongst men, and thus some disparity in admissions for treatment are to be expected, it is not clear whether this is an underestimation of the ratio of women to men problem drug users. This is a complex epidemiological issue as the data upon which to base a comparison are the gender differences for dependent or problem use rather than lifetime use. In the USA it would appear that the rate of substance dependence in men and women is 2.2% and 1.5% respectively. Thus, having only 30% of women in treatment would be a clear underrepresentation of those in need of treatment.[4] Restricting the analysis to crack cocaine and heroin only, the National Treatment Agency came to a slightly different view. It argued that, as best available estimates indicate that only a quarter of problem drug users are women, the finding that approximately 25% of the treatment population in the UK are women suggests that women appear to be well represented.[5] There are, however, early indications that there has been a 25% reduction in younger women entering treatment for heroin dependence. What is clear is that many women with high-risk alcohol use fall through the treatment net and thus additional efforts to identify and then engage women in treatment is strongly recommended.

Gender-specific problems for women with substance use problems

There are many common risk factors contributing to the development of substance misuse problems in men and women; these include chaotic family environments characterised by financial difficulties, parental substance abuse and mental health problems. Early school failure and the development of behavioural problems have been widely reported and these, in turn, are associated with initial substance use and criminal activity.[6] For women, there are additional factors that contribute to their dependent and problematic use. Young women with substance abuse problems tend to be younger when they start using and have fewer years of formal education. High rates of childhood trauma, in particular childhood sexual abuse, are reported amongst women substance abusers. In addition to historical factors that differentiate men and women there are a number of gender-specific consequences associated with substance misuse, as reviewed below.

Physical health issues for women with substance misuse problems

Reproductive health

The vast majority of women with substance use problems are of reproductive age[7] and therefore need to be able to access contraceptive and reproductive health care. Access to family planning services is particularly important if unwanted pregnancies are to be avoided.

Disruption to menstrual cycles is a common problem in women with substance misuse problems and this may be either related directly to the substance used or be secondary to the effects of drug use on weight and nutritional status. For example, the misuse of opiates can suppress the production of luteinising hormone and follicle-stimulating hormone from the pituitary gland. This disturbance affects menstruation but does not necessarily prevent ovulation. Long-term use of many drugs including amphetamines and opioids can cause severe weight loss, which itself affects menstruation. Amenorrhoea is common amongst opiate users – related in part to poor health but also to low weight. It is important to be aware that when substance misuse is either reduced as in the case of amphetamine or a woman is on substitution therapy for opioids, weight gain and restoration of menstrual functioning often occurs and thus issues around contraceptive use need to be discussed from the outset of treatment. Also for women drug users there can be an increased risk of reproductive complaints secondary to increased prevalence of pelvic inflammatory disorder.

Family planning

A family planning consultation begins by taking a comprehensive history that includes current and past drug use, current alcohol use and previous (or current) history of sexually transmitted diseases, including episodes of pelvic inflammatory disease, needle sharing and infection with blood-borne viruses. Lifestyle issues, in particular the ease of taking regular medication, should also be considered. There is little point in prescribing once-a-day oral contraception if the woman has a chaotic lifestyle with many disruptions in accommodation.

The choice of contraception will depend on contraindications for the different options. A woman with high risk of sexually transmitted diseases should be discouraged from using an intrauterine device and one with liver disease or hepatitis C or B should avoid the oral combined contraceptive pill. The progesterone-only pill may not be appropriate where there are concerns about stability.

A woman who is dependent on alcohol may need specialist assessment as her choices of family planning are likely to be predicated by the state of her liver and general physical state. It may be more appropriate in women who have many physical problems to take the safest option, which is the depot progesterone injection.

Progestogene-only contraceptive implants are increasingly being used by drug-using women. The implant consists of a small plastic rod about the size of a matchstick, which is flexible and not likely to be visible, that is inserted just under the skin on the inside of the upper arm. The hormone is released slowly from the device into the bloodstream over three years. The implant is highly effective at preventing pregnancy, and in clinical trials so far no pregnancies have been reported by women using this implant. It is particularly useful for women who cannot tolerate oestrogen, which is contained in the most commonly used oral contraceptives. Women who have difficulty remembering to take daily contraception also prefer this method. However, it should not be used in women who have severe liver disease.

Vulnerability to blood-borne virus infections

The number of women living with HIV in the UK has steadily increased in the last 20 years and appears to have peaked in 2004 with some evidence of a slight decline in numbers of new infections among women.[8] Heterosexual contact is proposed to account for around 45% of all diagnosed HIV infections, with relatively lower rates in injecting drug users of approximately 5%. However, women who inject drugs are at particularly high risk for HIV infection due to unprotected sex and unsafe injecting practises.[9] Despite concerted public health campaigns focusing on the importance of safe sexual practices, women who inject drugs are typically in positions of powerlessness, which significantly impact on their capacity to negotiate safer sex. For example, prevalence rates for intimate partner violence have been found to range from 25–57% in women who are in drug treatment,[10] while it is common for women to trade sex for drugs and/or money. In both circumstances insisting upon safe sexual practices is often unrealistic and may carry an increased risk of physical and sexual violence. Women who are in relationships with another drug user are both more likely to borrow a used needle and to have been given their first injection by a male sexual partner. Indeed there are significant gender-ascribed roles with male partners typically playing a lead role in obtaining the drugs and injecting equipment, and also injecting their female partners.[11]

Clearly, ensuring that a woman does have an understanding of safe injecting and sexual practices can be checked within the context of a routine consultation. However, this may be even more effective if there is also discussion around potential barriers to the implementation of either or both. This, in turn, may help generate some solutions around the use of harm minimisation strategies.

Psychological health

There are some significant gender differences in the pathway to problematic substance misuse that play a role in the nature of the more common difficulties in women substance misusers. For example, while family history is a significant risk factor in the development of substance use problems for both men and women, there are a number of studies indicating that women are more likely than men to have family members who are also substance abusers.[12] Women are also more likely to have experienced sexual and physical abuse as children, although rates for both men and women with substance misuse problems are considerably higher than for the general population. The chaos that often accompanies parental substance misuse and childhood abuse both impact on healthy emotional development and, in particular, appears to be linked to poor affect regulation and mood disturbances in addition to substance abuse problems.[13] Thus many of the psychological difficulties experienced by women substance misusers with a history of trauma relate specifically to their ability to understand and manage emotions, leading at times to highly impulsive and reactive behaviours.

Not surprisingly, given higher rates of childhood abuse, rates of mood disorders in women substance abusers are higher than for their male counterparts although not necessarily across all studies.[12] The ongoing victimisation, high rates of sexual assault in women drug users and high rates of intimate partner violence add to a complex picture of trauma and distress. It has been proposed that this results in a range of personality or behavioural tendencies that meet diagnostic criteria for Borderline Personality Disorder.[14]

There is now a substantial body of research demonstrating improvements in psychological wellbeing and a reduction in substance misuse in women with this diagnostic presentation using Dialectical Behaviour Therapy.[15] It is not the role of the primary care team to undertake such complex psychological treatment but sensitivity and understanding may help in the management of what often appears to be self-destructive behaviours. The National Institute for Health and Clinical Excellence guidelines[15] have recommended that mental health trusts establish multidisciplinary specialist teams and/or services for people with personality disorders that, *inter alia*, provide consultation and advice to primary and secondary care services. It is worth investigating whether this is an option within a local area and what the referral pathway may be.

Finally, women drug users are more likely than their male counterparts to have parental responsibility. Often mothers who are attempting to bring up their children in chaotic environments have the same set of difficulties and problems found in their own family of origin. Added to this is a lack of understanding or knowledge about how to be a 'good enough' parent to their children. Women substance misusers often perceive themselves as failed parents and, although drug use plays a role in parenting, contextual factors such as poverty and a mother's perception of the extent of her child's difficulties influence parenting style. There is now growing evidence that an intergenerational pattern of substance misuse occurs, with many young drug users reporting high rates of parental illicit drug misuse.[6]

Pregnancy and drug use

Exact prevalence rates of illicit drug use in pregnancy are difficult to obtain, as national surveys addressing the use of drugs by pregnant women are infrequent and the figures obtained are regarded as estimates. In the UK, national estimates of pregnant women who are using drugs are lacking; however, a commonly cited figure is that one-third of drug users in treatment are female and over 90% of these are of childbearing age.[16] In Europe, it has been estimated that as many as 30,000 pregnant women use opioids each year and it is possible that the number of pregnant women using other drugs is equally as high.[17] Illicit heroin use was the primary drug of misuse, followed by cocaine, reported by women accessing a perinatal addictions service in London.[18]

In the US National Survey on Drug Use and Health, 4.4% of pregnant women aged 15 to 44 were current illicit drug users based on data averaged across 2009 and 2010. Illicit drug use during pregnancy was more common in younger cohorts: 16.2% among pregnant women aged 15 to 17, 7.4% among pregnant women aged 18 to 25, and 1.9% among pregnant women aged 26 to 44 years.[19]

Table 18.1   **Special problems of women drug users**

Area of need	Risks
Physical health	Increased risk of reproductive complaints secondary to increased prevalence of pelvic inflammatory disorder and complications in pregnancy.
	Gynaecological problems and sexually transmitted diseases common.
	Increased vulnerability to HIV infection.
	Same injection drug use-related problems as men for hepatitis and many other medical problems
Psychological and social health	Increased risk of affective disorders (depression, anxiety, attempted suicide, low self-esteem).
	High rates of childhood trauma including child sexual abuse.
	High rates of adult trauma including sexual assault.
	Poorer social networks
Economic and legal status	Poorer occupational functioning.
	Often economically dependent on men through prostitution or exchanging sex for drugs, food, shelter, etc.
	Low levels of vocational training and job skills.
	High rates of unemployment.
	Majority have at least one legal conviction

Drug misuse and dependence during pregnancy are associated with a variety of adverse maternal and child outcomes.[16] However, disentangling the direct effects of the substance from environmental factors, such as poor nutrition, stress, violence and poverty, is extremely difficult.[20] Maternal smoking, drinking, cocaine and crack cocaine use can all have a direct negative impact on pregnancy and offspring.

Management of pregnant drug-using women

Pregnancy is often seen as a window of opportunity for recruiting women with a substance misuse problem into treatment. The primary care practitioner is ideally placed to provide both antenatal treatment and assist in the stabilisation of drug use by careful prescribing practices. There is a strong consensus amongst clinicians that an encouraging and non-judgemental attitude towards the pregnant woman and her partner is important in enabling her to engage effectively with treatment services and antenatal care.[21] This does not imply that drug use should be condoned, but rather that a caring attitude is expressed with an emphasis on helping the woman achieve the best outcome for herself and her baby. Although drug use is clearly not in the best interest of the infant, the detrimental effects of such use are compounded by erratic use, a lack of antenatal care and environmental factors such as domestic violence and poverty. Providing a practice environment in which there is a strong and clear message that pregnant drug users will be fairly treated is an important first step in ensuring that women attend for care.

Women who attend treatment services usually have better antenatal care and health, even if they continue to use drugs. Management and treatment options for drug use during pregnancy vary according to the drug/s of choice and the stage of pregnancy. Harm reduction is the primary aim in the management of pregnant drug users so while abstinence is clearly desirable for many substances such as alcohol and benzodiazepines, reduction and stabilisation are preferred goals for opioid use. Safe drug administration and use should be strongly encouraged and withdrawal symptoms treated as necessary. There is a range of effective pharmacological management options available as well as psychosocial measures that can address substance use issues in the long term.

Opioids

There are two options for the treatment of opioid use: substitution therapy or detoxification. Early research suggested that detoxification in pregnant women was linked to miscarriage in the first trimester or premature labour as well as foetal death *in utero* in the third trimester.[22] Recent research has shown that detoxification in the second and third trimesters of pregnancy is not linked to an increase in adverse perinatal events.[23] However, it is important to note that detoxification is generally unsuccessful, with high rates of relapse and the attendant risks involved in subsequent drug-seeking behaviour and use.[16] For this reason detoxification is not recommended for pregnant drug-using women unless they are highly motivated and have a stable and supportive social network. The risks and benefits should be discussed fully and if detoxification is to be attempted admission to a clinic is recommended after the first trimester. Detoxification may be undertaken in small frequent reductions, for example 2–3 mg methadone every three to five days is suggested by the Department of Health,[24] as long as illicit opiate use is not continuing. Unsupervised withdrawal should be discouraged as there is the possible risk of miscarriage or pre-term delivery. Box 18.1 outlines the general principles and advantages of substitution treatment for pregnant women.

Methadone maintenance treatment is commonly used to manage illicit opioid dependence. There is a range of benefits of methadone maintenance including reduced illicit drug use,[25] physical and psychological stabilisation,[20] improved prenatal care,[22] longer gestation, higher birth weight and increased rates of infants discharged with mothers.[23] Infants born to methadone-maintained women do tend to be smaller than drug-free controls; however, they generally catch up by 12 months.[23]

354

Box 18.1   **Substitution treatment in pregnant opioid-dependent women**

> ✓ Enables stabilisation of drug use and lifestyle.
>
> ✓ Reduces need for additional illicit drug use.
>
> ✓ Facilitates access to antenatal and other health care.
>
> ✓ Reduces risks inherent in illicit drug use lifestyle.

As any regular antenatal exposure to opioids, including methadone, can result in neonatal abstinence syndrome (NAS), pregnant drug-using women should be informed about NAS (discussed below) and that their infants will be closely monitored for symptoms and signs of NAS during their hospital stay after birth.

Methadone maintenance treatment should be started (or continued) as soon as possible after confirmation of pregnancy.[22] Methadone is taken once daily and can be prescribed as a maintenance dose or as a planned reduction throughout pregnancy.[20] UK guidelines suggest maintaining a non-pregnant population on doses of methadone between 60–120 mg daily. Studies examining drug-using women who are pregnant report a range of doses from 20–160 mg. A stable dose of methadone ensures that the infant experiences minimal *in utero* withdrawal and is not exposed to drugs of unknown concentration and impurities. Thus the importance of providing adequate dosages of methadone is perhaps even more important than in the non-pregnant state.

Physiological changes in the third trimester of pregnancy such as increased blood volume, metabolic changes and drug metabolism of the foetal/placental unit may result in the need for higher dosages of methadone in order to prevent breakthrough or withdrawal symptoms.[16] It is critical that both doctor and patient are clear that this is not a consequence of the use of additional non-prescribed opioids, but rather a direct effect of the pregnancy. It may be necessary to increase the dose of methadone or split it from once-daily consumption to twice-daily consumption, or occasionally to increase both dose and consumption.[24]

Some clinicians are hesitant to increase methadone dose due to the possibility of increased risk for NAS in the newborn infant. The research regarding this link is inconclusive, with some studies suggesting no link between dose and NAS[26] and other studies indicating that increased dose results in greater risk for NAS[27] or increased length of required treatment.[28] Regardless of whether there is a link or not, most studies recommend increasing methadone dose as necessary but remaining at the lowest dose required to remain effective. NAS can be effectively treated and adequate methadone dose is effective in reducing the risk of illicit drug use during pregnancy.

Buprenorphine is an alternative opioid substitute. The benefits of buprenorphine appear to mirror those of methadone, including reduced need for illicit drugs and stabilisation of lifestyle. Some evidence indicates that an additional benefit of buprenorphine may be a reduction in the incidence and severity of NAS [23] as well as the fact that it is a partial agonist with a ceiling effect thus reducing the risk of overdose. Buprenorphine has been used for over a decade in France and naturalistic cohort studies have found it to be a favourable alternative to methadone.[16] A Cochrane review [25] found no significant difference in newborn or maternal outcomes for women maintained on methadone, buprenorphine or oral slow-release morphine. At present buprenorphine appears to be a viable alternative to methadone; however, more research is needed to reach a definite conclusion. Importantly, buprenorphine is not licensed for use in pregnant women in the UK, although increasing numbers of women who are stable on buprenorphine are becoming pregnant. In these cases, it is recommended that, if the woman is stable on buprenorphine and informed of the risks, then the prescribed dose of buprenorphine should be continued rather than transferring to methadone and risk inducing withdrawal in the foetus.[24]

Slow-release morphine is a third option; however, only small-scale studies have been conducted and it is not registered widely for treatment.[29] The Cochrane review mentioned above [25] found that oral slow morphine was equally as effective as methadone and buprenorphine, and additionally that it was superior to methadone in preventing relapse in the third trimester of pregnancy with no influence on birth weight or duration of NAS. However, given the lack of research on slow-release morphine, methadone (and increasingly buprenorphine elsewhere in the world) remains the treatment of choice.

Benzodiazepines

As a general rule, benzodiazepine exposure should be avoided during the first three months of pregnancy.[16] However, if benzodiazepines are taken for a mood disorder, then potential adverse effects of foetal exposure need to be weighed against possible consequences of an untreated mood disorder.[29] It is recommended that a risk–benefit analysis be conducted and specialist advice sought in order to decide on the most appropriate course of action in these cases.

For illicit benzodiazepine use, identifying a mutually agreeable and realistic goal with the patient is usually key to successful management.[22] This could include low-dose maintenance, gradual reduction or detoxification. Given the higher risk of teratogenicity associated with benzodiazepine use, withdrawal during the first trimester of pregnancy, with careful monitoring, is preferable.[16] Women who are dependent on benzodiazepines can also be stabilised on diazepam, and when this can be tolerated without restarting illicit use the dose can be reduced.[24] In cases where benzodiazepines are prescribed for anxiety and mood disorders, psychosocial intervention may be particularly useful, especially if benzodiazepine use is going to be reduced or eliminated. Infants whose mothers used benzodiazepines are vulnerable to NAS.[29]

Given the prevalence of polydrug use, it is not uncommon for a pregnant woman to present with benzodiazepine misuse in combination with opiate abuse. In these cases, stabilisation of opiate use with substitution therapy is the first priority.[21] After this is achieved, benzodiazepine misuse should be the second priority and phased reductions initiated.[21] If the woman is on a methadone programme, then no attempt should be made to reduce methadone dose while benzodiazepine use is reduced.[21]

Stimulants, hallucinogens and cannabis

These drugs of abuse are combined in this section as there are no effective pharmacological treatments available that are safe for pregnant women to use. Pharmacological options available for treating cocaine misuse in a non-pregnant population (e.g. antipsychotics and antidepressants) are not recommended for use during pregnancy due to adverse perinatal and foetal outcomes. Although it has been suggested that these pharmacological treatments can be administered in a hospital setting,[22] UK clinical guidelines report that there is no safe drug for substitute prescribing in cases of cocaine dependence.[24] These guidelines suggest psychological therapies as an effective treatment option. Similarly, psychosocial therapies are the treatment of choice for other psychostimulant, hallucinogen and cannabis use as there are no licensed pharmacological substitute options available.

In cases of stimulant use, a common approach is the combination of symptomatic interventions for severe agitation during the withdrawal phase with psychosocial interventions, although there has been limited research into the effectiveness of this treatment approach in pregnant drug-using women. Short-acting benzodiazepines can be used in severe cases to alleviate mood symptoms associated with stimulant withdrawal. The risk of the potential effects of non-compliance due to severe withdrawal symptoms must be weighed against the potential risk of benzodiazepine use to the foetus.

Alcohol and nicotine

Women should abstain from drinking alcohol if pregnant, or at least reduce consumption to 1–2 units of alcohol once or twice a week.[24] In some cases, simply giving women information regarding alcohol use during pregnancy and providing them with an opportunity to consider the positives and negatives of their drinking behaviour has been shown to be effective in reducing consumption.[20] In other cases, it may be appropriate to offer a referral to a psychosocial intervention where more intensive treatment is available. For a pregnant woman who is physically dependent on alcohol, pharmacological treatment and supervised withdrawal is an option. They should be advised to avoid sudden cessation of alcohol consumption as this may harm the foetus, and they should be referred to an inpatient setting where chlordiazepoxide, or occasionally diazepam, is used in a graduated withdrawal regimen.[20]

Support and advice should be offered to women who are smoking while pregnant in order to assist them to cease. In the first instance, information should be provided on local smoking cessation support services if available or any telephone support services. Nicotine Replacement Therapy (NRT) is licensed for use in pregnancy and may be a useful option for women who are unable to cease otherwise. Intermittent-dosage NRT (e.g. gum or nasal spray) may be preferable to a patch that gives a continuous dose of nicotine. If a patch is used it could be removed at night. The lowest effective dose of NRT should be used. It is recommended that counselling be continued or began while undergoing NRT as this is more effective in prolonged abstinence from smoking.[20]

Treatment of neonatal abstinence syndrome

NAS is a constellation of symptoms that can be present in infants who have been exposed to substances ingested by their mother throughout pregnancy, including opioids, benzodiazepines, alcohol and barbiturates. NAS appears after birth when exposure to substances taken by the mother ceases abruptly. Symptoms and severity of NAS are variable, both across time in the same infant and between infants. Specific symptoms of NAS can be found in Table 18.2. Although symptoms of NAS may vary according to the type of drug used by the mother, it is unclear the extent to which severity correlates with dose or duration of exposure. Furthermore, the presence of polydrug use as well as other adverse life circumstances associated with drug use makes it difficult to predict the manifestation, severity and duration of NAS in an infant.

Approximately half of infants experiencing NAS will require pharmacological treatment. Medication use is based on symptom severity and category of NAS in order to allow the infant to withdraw from the substance gradually while controlling withdrawal symptoms. This is achieved by the gradual reduction in dose so that the infant can tolerate mild withdrawal symptoms while still feeding well and sleeping for appropriate intervals.[30] Several medications are available for treatment, depending on the symptoms exhibited and the substance to which the infant has been exposed (although frequent polydrug use can make this difficult to determine). Treatments available include methadone, clonidine, chlorpromazine, tincture of opium, diazepam and phenobarbital.

Regardless of the need for pharmacological measures, all infants who have been exposed to drugs *in utero* should receive individualised non-pharmacological support.[31] Non-pharmacological treatment involves measures aimed at pro-

Table 18.2 **Symptoms of neonatal abstinence syndrome**

Central nervous system	Gastrointestinal	Vasomotor
Cry is excessive or high-pitched	Excessive sucking	Sweating
Difficulty sleeping	Poor feeding	Low-grade fever
Tremors	Vomiting	Nasal congestion
Skin breakdown	Diarrhoea	Respiratory distress
Hypertonia/hyperreflexia	Frequent sneezing	
Myoclonic jerks	Frequent yawning	
Seizures		

Source: adapted from Beauman.[32]

moting infant relaxation, although the long-term outcome of these measures in regards to NAS has not been tested robustly.[33] Recommended strategies include gentle handling but avoidance of excessive swaddling, provision of a darkened, quiet environment to reduce sleep disturbance, and provision of a pacifier.[30] Infants experiencing NAS have an increased risk of sudden infant death syndrome (SIDS) so appropriate precautions should be encouraged, such as avoidance of a soft sleeping surface.[32] Breastfeeding should also be encouraged as it fosters mother–child attachment and some research indicates that it may contribute to a shorter duration of pharmacological treatment for NAS.[34]

Box 18.2 **Suggestions to provide to mothers whose infant has had *in utero* exposure to substances**

✓ Gentle handling and quiet, calm voice.

✓ Avoidance of excessive swaddling.

✓ Calm and quiet environment to reduce sleep disturbance.

✓ Provide a pacifier.

Treatment of NAS will require a prolonged hospital stay and expectant mothers who are using drugs should be prepared for this possibility. The mother of a newborn who is suffering from NAS may experience guilt and anxiety as a result, which in turn may trigger relapse to drug use, disruption of mother–child attachment and subsequent developmental issues in the child. Thus it is important that the mother is well-informed about the possibility of her newborn experiencing NAS and that various supports are in place to assist her to deal with any issues that arise in the postnatal period and beyond.

Upon discharge, appropriate community supports should be in place to assist the mother and infant. These could include referrals to counselling and continuation of treatment to address substance use issues. In the UK, the GP and the baby's health visitor are important in maintaining continuity of care and monitoring treatment in the infant and mother, particularly in regards to ongoing non-pharmacological support for the infant who experienced NAS and any ongoing support and treatment of the mother.

Treatment for women

Women drug users have complex needs, which are not always recognised or met by some existing drug services. For example, approaches to treatment need to be sensitive to the possible sexual and physical abuse histories of women, as well as the gender-specific potential consequences associated with substance abuse. Acknowledging and supporting both men and women who are primary carers of children are also critical needs for drug services. Attending to issues that include parenting skills and housing and schooling needs are as important as determining basic medical needs and drug stabilisation (see Box 18.3).

Identification and screening

The most important first goal is to engage women in treatment. Women are more likely than men to attend their GP for general health, family planning and antenatal needs. Thus the GP and practice nurse have the opportunity to identify drug and/or alcohol users, and provide appropriate intervention. Primary care practitioners are unsystematic in their questioning about drug use, with only 20% of GPs reporting that they 'occasionally' ask pregnant women about alcohol or drug use while 60% report that they never ask.

The identification of women with a substance misuse problem can be done through the use of initial screening questions. Most screening instruments are sensitive to low-level misuse of a substance, but are less sensitive to determining a range of use and dependence (that is, they have a ceiling effect). Screening instruments have been developed to help clinicians identify women with substance misuse problems. The Alcohol Use Disorders Inventory (AUDIT) was developed by the WHO to screen for a range of drinking problems and in particular

Box 18.3 **Treatment needs of women**

> ✓ Food, clothing and shelter.
>
> ✓ Transportation.
>
> ✓ Job counselling and training.
>
> ✓ Legal assistance.
>
> ✓ Literacy training and educational opportunities.
>
> ✓ Parenting management techniques.
>
> ✓ Couples counselling.
>
> ✓ Medical care.
>
> ✓ Child care.
>
> ✓ Social services.
>
> ✓ Social support.
>
> ✓ Psychological assessment and mental health care.
>
> ✓ Family planning services.

for hazardous and harmful consumption. It is particularly suitable for primary healthcare settings and has been used in a number of different countries and with diverse cultural groups (see Chapter 12).

Conclusion

Primary care practitioners have a unique opportunity to educate women about their substance use and to identify those with problems. Early identification and intervention can significantly limit the adverse consequences of all substance misuse. Primary care practitioners are ideally placed to help women access a range of specialist treatment services as well as support and treat their primary substance misuse problem.

References

1. Health and Social Care Information Centre. *Statistics on Drug Misuse: England, 2010.* Leeds: NHS, 2011.

2. Degenhardt L, Chiu W-T, Sampson N, *et al.* Toward a global view of alcohol, tobacco, cannabis, and cocaine use: findings from the WHO World Mental Health Surveys. *PLoS Medicine* 2008; **5(7)**: e141.

3. European Monitoring Centre for Drugs and Drug Addiction. *Differences in Patterns of Drug Use between Women and Men: European drug situation technical data sheet.* Lisbon: EMCDDA, 2005.

4. Brady T M, Ashley O S (eds). *Women in Substance Abuse Treatment: results from the Alcohol and Drug Services Study (ADSS).* Rockville, MD: SAMHSA, 2005.

5. National Treatment Agency for Substance Misuse. *Women in Drug Treatment: what the latest figures reveal.* London: NTA, 2010.

6. Dawe S, Frye S, Best D, *et al. Drug Use in the Family: impacts and implications for children.* Canberra: Australian National Council on Drugs, 2007.

7. Kuczkowski K M. The effects of drug abuse on pregnancy. *Current Opinion in Obstetrics and Gynecology* 2007; **19(6)**: 578–85.

8. *AVERTing HIV and AIDS*, 2011, www.avert.org   [accessed November 2012].

9. El-Bassel N, Terlikbaeva A, Pinkham S. HIV and women who use drugs: double neglect, double risk. *Lancet* 2010; **376(9738)**: 312–14.

10. El-Bassel N, Gilbert L, Wu E, *et al.* Relationship between drug abuse and intimate partner violence: a longitudinal study among women receiving methadone. *American Journal of Public Health* 2005; **95(3)**: 465–70.

11. Bryant J, Brener L, Hull P, *et al.* Needle sharing in regular sexual relationships: an examination of serodiscordance, drug using practices, and the gendered character of injecting. *Drug and Alcohol Dependence* 2010; **107(2–3)**: 182–7.

12. Pelissier B, Jones N. A review of gender differences among substance abusers. *Crime and Delinquency* 2005; **51(3)**: 343–72.

13. Kendler K S, Bulik C M, Silberg J, *et al.* Childhood sexual abuse and adult psychiatric and substance use disorders in women: an epidemiological and cotwin control analysis. *Archives of General Psychiatry* 2000; **57(10)**: 953–9.

14. American Psychiatric Association. *Diagnostic and Statistical Manual of Mental Disorders* (4th edn). Washington, DC: APA, 2000.

15. National Collaborating Centre for Mental Health. *Borderline Personality Disorder: treatment and management.* London: NICE, 2009.

16. Madgula R M, Groshkova T, Mayet S. Illicit drug use in pregnancy: effects and management. *Expert Review of Obstetrics and Gynecology* 2011; **6(2)**: 1–14.

17. Gyarmathy V A, Giraudon I, Hedrich D, *et al.* Drug use and pregnancy: challenges for public health. *European Surveillance* 2009; **14(9)**: 33–6.

18. Mayet S, Groshkova T, Morgan L, *et al.* Drugs, alcohol and pregnant women: changing characteristics of women engaging with a specialist perinatal outreach addictions service. *Drug and Alcohol Review* 2008; **27(5)**: 490–6.

19. Substance Abuse and Mental Health Services Administration. *Results from the 2010 National Survey on Drug Use and Health: summary of national findings.* Rockville, MD: SAMHSA, 2011.

20. Prentice S. Substance misuse in pregnancy. *Obstetrics, Gynaecology and Reproductive Medicine* 2010; **20**: 278–83.

21. Moran P, Madgula R M, Gilvarry E, *et al*. Substance misuse during pregnancy: its effects and treatment. *Fetal and Maternal Medicine Review* 2009; **20(1)**: 1–16.

22. Day E, George S. Management of drug misuse in pregnancy. *Advances in Psychiatric Treatment* 2005; **11**: 253–61.

23. Wong S, Ordean A, Kahan M. SOGC clinical practice guidelines: substance use in pregnancy. *International Journal of Gynecology and Obstetrics* 2011; **114(2)**: 190–202.

24. Department of Health (England) and the devolved administrations. *Drug Misuse and Dependence: UK guidelines on clinical management.* London: Department of Health (England), the Scottish Government, Welsh Assembly Government and Northern Ireland Executive, 2007.

25. Minozzi S, Amato L, Vecchi S, *et al*. Maintenance agonist treatments for opiate dependent pregnant women. In: *The Cochrane Database of Systematic Reviews.* Issue 2. Chichester: Wiley, 2008.

26. Pizarro D, Habli M, Grier M, *et al*. Higher maternal doses of methadone does not increase neonatal abstinence syndrome. *Journal of Substance Abuse Treatment* 2011; **40(3)**: 295–8.

27. Cleary B J, Donnelly J, Strawbridge J, *et al*. Methadone dose and neonatal abstinence syndrome: systematic review and meta-analysis. *Addiction* 2010; **105(12)**: 2071–84.

28. Lim S, Prasad M R, Samuels P, *et al*. High-dose methadone in pregnant women and its effect on duration of neonatal abstinence syndrome. *American Journal of Obstetrics and Gynecology* 2009; **200(1)**: 70.e1–5.

29. Winklbaur B, Kopf N, Ebner N, *et al*. Treating pregnant women dependent on opioids is not the same as treating pregnancy and opioid dependence: a knowledge synthesis for better treatment for women and neonates. *Addiction* 2008; **103**: 1429–40.

30. Burgos A E, Burke B L. Neonatal abstinence syndrome. *Neoreviews* 2009; **10(5)**: e222–9.

31. Jansson L M, Velez M. Neonatal abstinence syndrome. *Current Opinion in Pediatrics* 2012; **24(2)**: 252–8.

32. Beauman S S. Identification and management of neonatal abstinence syndrome. *Journal of Infusion Nursing* 2005; **28(3)**: 159–67.

33. Kassim Z, Greenough A. Neonatal abstinence syndrome: identification and management. *Current Paediatrics* 2006; **16(3)**: 172–5.

34. Isemann B, Meinzen-Derr J, Akinbi H. Maternal and neonatal factors impacting response to methadone therapy in infants treated for neonatal abstinence syndrome. *Journal of Perinatology* 2011; **31(1)**: 25–9.

CHAPTER 19

Parenting and drug use

Paul H. Harnett and Sharon Dawe

IN THIS CHAPTER

Introduction ‖ Developmental impact of prenatal exposure to substances ‖ Specific drug effects ‖ Outcomes for children raised in families with parental substance abuse ‖ The determinants of poor child developmental outcomes ‖ Treatment programmes that improve outcome for children in substance-misusing families ‖ Safeguarding responsibilities

Introduction

Helping parents who misuse substances meet the developmental needs of their children is a complex issue. In addition to the challenge of parenting a child that may have special developmental needs as a result of *in utero* exposure to substances, the parent may face the adverse influences associated with a drug-using lifestyle. The case of Jane presented in Box 19.1 (overleaf) highlights many of the issues facing women who misuse drugs and/or alcohol. Clearly, any intervention aimed at improving her parenting will need to be comprehensive, and raises the question of whether programmes targeting substance-misusing parents can be effective. The case study also raises issues concerning the safeguarding of her children. What are the responsibilities of GPs concerning this mother's capacity to parent her 5-year-old son and the prevention of potential risks to her unborn child?

Developmental impact of prenatal exposure to substances

Disentangling the effects of substance use and lifestyle factors on developmental outcomes in children prenatally exposed to most substances has many challenges. Many women with a primary problem with one class of substances also use a range of other substances, with the majority at least smoking cigarettes. Added to this are the difficulties associated with poor nutrition, stress, violence and other lifestyle factors including higher rates of infections such as hepatitis B and C, up to 29% in some studies.[1] However, the combination of preclinical animal laboratory studies and a number of longitudinal cohort studies has added considerably to our understanding of the mechanisms that influence early brain development. Notably, both preclinical studies and carefully controlled cohort studies have also

Box 19.1 **The case of Jane**

Jane, aged 28 years, is a well-known patient of the practice. She was a rather chaotic heroin user in the past, injecting at least 1 g/day for a number of years. For the past two years she has been receiving a maintenance buprenorphine prescription from her GP and has been very stable. However, four months ago she met up with an ex-boyfriend who had led her to start using substances in her late teens. He has recently been released from prison for a range of drug-related offences.

Jane has slowly increased her involvement with a drug-using culture due to his ongoing visits. She initially used crack cocaine a couple of times but has been using almost daily for the last month. She has not picked up her prescription for over a week and this has resulted in use of illicit heroin.

Jane has a son, Billy, aged five years. He was subject to a child protection plan at two and a half years of age. This was deregistered after two years as a result of Jane's stable lifestyle. Jane and Billy are well known in the practice. He has been seen a number of times for minor illnesses such as earache and flu. He had mild asthma as a toddler but appears to be growing out of this. Billy attends a local nursery school and presents as a cheerful and compliant little boy, with behaviour that is manageable and age appropriate. Jane's accommodation is currently stable but she has not paid rent for over a month and has outstanding electricity bills.

She presents to her GP as 13 weeks pregnant, desperate to try to 'make a go at getting back on track'. Her drug use at this time is around half a gram of heroin a day, crack cocaine 3–4 times a week, and cannabis several times a week. She also smokes 20 cigarettes a day and reports that she is not currently drinking alcohol.

found that environmental enrichment appears to be a key factor ameliorating some of the negative effects of prenatal exposure.[2] Thus, while many substances have both a direct and indirect effect on brain development, the importance of providing an environment that can foster a child's emotional, social and cognitive development cannot be understated. In the following section a brief review is provided of recent developmental studies investigating the consequences of prenatal exposure to substances on child outcome (see Table 19.1 on p. 373 for summary).

Specific drug effects

Opioids

The use of opioids during pregnancy is associated with low birth weight, premature delivery and small head circumference. Babies exposed to opiates in pregnancy are likely to experience neonatal addiction and withdrawal symptoms. The syndrome, characterised by irritability, hyperactivity, abnormal sleep, poor sucking and high-pitched cry, can persist for two to three weeks after birth (see Chapter 18 for a further discussion of management of neonatal abstinence syndrome). There have been relatively few longitudinal studies investigating the developmental outcomes associated with prenatal exposure to opioids and findings are somewhat mixed. Studies that have investigated developmental outcomes in early infancy typically report delays. For example, Hunt *et al.* found delays at three years across a number of domains of cognitive development and adaptive behaviour in opiate-exposed infants compared with control mothers.[3] Notably, the control group was not matched on sociodemographic status and was reported as drug free (which also implies a non-smoking status). Thus, it is possible that these data reflect in part the specific effects of prenatal exposure compounded by the often impoverished early environment associated with low socioeconomic status, both during and following birth (see, for example, Minnes *et al.*).[4] It is notable that one of the few longer-term studies looking at developmental outcome at 5–6 years found that children born to heroin-dependent mothers and adopted at a young age had a similar outcome to matched controls, while those who had not been adopted had poorer outcomes.[5] This again highlights the importance of providing an enriched early environment for young children who begin life with many disadvantages, so that they can have the opportunity to develop to their full potential.

Cocaine and amphetamines

Prenatal exposure to cocaine, with or without other drug exposure, is associated with significant increases in neonatal mortality from intrauterine growth retardation and prematurity.[6] The powerful vasoconstrictor effect of cocaine may be the factor in foetal growth retardation. Spontaneous abortion and premature birth are more frequent in women who use cocaine, with one study finding that the increased risk of spontaneous abortion was unrelated to cocaine dose.[7] The increased risk of *abruptio placentae* occurs only when cocaine is used close to delivery.[8] There is a link between sudden infant death syndrome and *in utero* cocaine exposure, and there have been reports of respiratory pattern abnormalities in cocaine-exposed infants as compared with methadone-exposed infants.[9]

Preclinical data based on studies in laboratory animals have consistently identified a relationship between prenatal cocaine exposure and the development of brain systems associated with executive function, memory, inhibitory control and reversal learning.[10] These findings are reflected in studies of infants and children exposed prenatally to cocaine. In an extensive review of the literature, Ackerman and colleagues emphasised the complexity of disentangling environmental risk from prenatal exposure in school-aged children.[11] Thus, an association between indices of growth, cognitive and academic functioning, and cocaine exposure were considered modest at best, particularly when compared with children living in similar low-income urban settings. However, performance on tasks that require sustained attention and behavioural regulation do appear to be consistently poorer in children prenatally exposed to cocaine. For example, in a recent special issue devoted to the topic of prenatal drug exposure, three out of four studies on prenatal exposure to cocaine reported differences in a range of measures of attention and inhibitory control, although both male gender and environmental risk status played a role in performance deficits found in one of these studies.[12] Notably, the one study with the longest follow-up to 17 years did not find attention or inhibitory control deficits.[13]

A somewhat similar pattern appears for children exposed prenatally to methamphetamine, although the extant studies cover a relatively shorter time period than those investigating prenatal exposure to cocaine. The most recent large-scale study, conducted by Smith and colleagues,[14] once again emphasised the complexity of disentangling direct effects of the methamphetamine from environmental factors. Nonetheless, at three years there were no differences in fine motor performance, measures of cognitive functioning and behavioural indices between children prenatally exposed to methamphetamine and a comparison group matched on key demographic characteristics including race, birth weight and maternal education.

Cannabis

Studies in laboratory animals have now found a relationship between prenatal exposure to delta-9-tetrahydrocannabinol (THC) and deficits in physical, cognitive, emotional, social and motor functioning of offspring in preclinical studies.[15] In particular, administration of even low doses of cannabinoid compounds during development resulted in atypical development of locomotor activity, cognitive impairments, altered emotional behaviour and enhanced drug sensitivity later in life. Translating these findings to humans is complex, but there are parallels between the preclinical and clinical studies. For example, in one of two longitudinal studies, there appeared to be an enduring difference between children with prenatal exposure to THC and comparison children. Early differences were found in babies in sleep continuity while at three years differences were found on memory and verbal reasoning tests. Measures of attention and impulsivity also showed differences at 10 years and again at age 14. As these are well-established risk factors for externalising behaviour problems, a further investigation look-ing at the relationship between prenatal exposure and delinquency was under-taken.[16] Given the pattern of attention problems documented in earlier studies it is not surprising that prenatally exposed children were twice as likely as non-exposed children to be classified as delinquent based on parent and self-report. Importantly, however, when child depression at age 10 was taken into account there was no longer a significant relationship between prenatal exposure and the delinquency scores. When attention problems at age 10 were taken into account the relationship between prenatal exposure and delinquency scores was only just significant. Again, these findings highlight the complexity of disentangling drug effects and environmental events.

Alcohol

The most current recommendations regarding alcohol consumption in pregnancy contained in the NICE guidelines advise against drinking any alcohol in the first three months and very limited drinking beyond this time period (see Box 19.2).[17]

Box 19.2   **Alcohol consumption in pregnancy**

Pregnant women and women planning a pregnancy should be advised to avoid drinking alcohol in the first three months of pregnancy if possible because it may be associated with an increased risk of miscarriage.

If women choose to drink alcohol during pregnancy they should be advised to drink no more than 1 to 2 UK units once or twice a week (1 unit equals half a pint of ordinary-strength lager or beer), or one shot (25 ml) of spirits. One small (125 ml) glass of wine is equal to 1–1.5 UK units (there is a range because wines vary in the percentage of alcohol content). Although there is uncertainty regarding a safe level of alcohol consumption in pregnancy, at this low level there is no evidence of harm to the unborn baby.

Women should be informed that getting drunk or binge drinking during pregnancy (defined as more than five standard drinks or 7.5 UK units on a single occasion) may be harmful to the unborn baby.

Source: National Collaborating Centre for Women's and Children's Health.[17]

The evidence that alcohol acts as a teratogen is extensive in both animal and human studies.[18] Heavy consumption of alcohol is associated with a range of abnormalities that are referred to as foetal alcohol syndrome (FAS) and its less severe form, foetal alcohol spectrum disorders (FASD).[19,20] The consequences of heavy alcohol use depend in part on timing of exposure, with the primary teratogenic effects occurring during the first eight weeks of embryogenesis, while exposure in later pregnancy affects behavioural and cognitive functioning and growth. While there is a consensus amongst researchers that there is a relationship between high alcohol use and foetal alcohol effects, it is not clear at what dose such effects are likely to occur.

FAS is characterised by a distinct constellation of characteristic facial anomalies, growth retardation and central nervous system (CNS) dysfunction. The characteristics associated with FASD vary in severity and clinical outcome, and are often confounded and/or exacerbated by impoverished environments.

Box 19.3   **Characteristics associated with FAS**

Facial dysmorphology – FAS is commonly associated with abnormal facial features including short palpebral fissures, a thin upper lip vermilion and a smooth philtrum.

Pre- and postnatal growth deficiency – babies born with FAS are commonly smaller than other babies and typically remain smaller throughout their lives.

CNS dysfunction – damage to the CNS results in the permanent impairment of brain function that may lead to intellectual and developmental disabilities, attention deficits, poor social understanding, hyperactivity, learning disabilities, poor coordination and planning, poor muscle tone, working memory deficits, receptive language deficits, executive functioning deficits (e.g. difficulty in organising and planning) and the inability to learn from the consequences of their behaviour.

Source: BMA Board of Science.[20]

The exact prevalence rates of FAS and FASD are difficult to ascertain, and there is considerable variability across jurisdictions, which are likely to reflect real differences in actual consumption patterns (for particularly high-risk indigenous populations for example) and variability in methodology underpinning the estimate. Worldwide estimates suggest that 0.97 per 1000 live births are affected by FAS while estimates for the UK suggest this may be closer to 0.84 per 1000 births.[21] However, it is extremely difficult to obtain estimates for children affected by FASD due to a lack of reliable data and difficulties in diagnosis.[20]

Outcomes for children raised in families with parental substance abuse

The outcomes for children brought up in families in which either or both parents use drugs is often poor. Behavioural difficulties can start to emerge in the early toddler years, and if they become established can lead to oppositional, defiant and non-compliant behaviours in the pre-school and early primary years. Poor outcomes are found across generations.[22] The children are also at a greater risk of developing a substance misuse problem themselves.[23] Children of alcohol-dependent parents are at two to ten times greater risk of developing problematic alcohol use than other children and are at increased risk of other substance misuse and dependence, including nicotine.[24]

Parental substance abuse is a significant risk factor for child maltreatment, particularly in early infancy and toddlerhood, and has been clearly implicated in poor child outcomes in many government reports including child death reviews and commission of inquiries regarding child protection issues.[25-27] The rate of child abuse and neglect in substance-misusing families is high, with the result that there is often intervention by social services. The 2003 *Hidden Harm* report found that around half (54%) of children with drug-using parents were living in other families (45% with other members of their family, and 9% in care).[28] The proportion of children living away from their biological parents had increased since a previous survey in 1996. These figures are concerning given the number of drug-using parents in England and Wales. In a more recent UK report, around 30% of children under 16 years (3.3–3.5 million children) were estimated to be living with at least one binge-drinking adult, 8% (around 978,000) with an illicit drug-using adult, 4% (500,000) with an adult defined as a problem drinker with a co-morbid mental health problem, and 72,000 children with an injecting drug user.[29]

The primary reason for removing a child from a family in which there is problematic drug use is the high risk of child abuse and neglect.[30,31] Unsurprisingly, drug-using parents who do retain the care of their children display fewer risk factors than parents whose children are removed into alternative care. These parents engage in lower-risk sexual and injecting practices, have largely refrained from illicit drug and alcohol use in the preceding six months, do not use stimulants regularly, are less likely to be sharing injecting equipment, and have more stable accommodation.[32,33] The children who are taken into care display poor developmental outcomes, including conduct problems and anxiety and depression. This places a greater demand on mental health services for treatment[34,35] and has significant financial and social costs. For example, Scott and colleagues calculated that the average cost associated with a child diagnosed with conduct disorder was £15,382 (range £5411 to as much as £40,896) over and above the normal expenditure by parents,[36] with the greatest cost falling on the families, education authorities, health services, social services and benefit agencies.[37] Follow-up studies of antisocial children into adulthood show that by the age of 28 the mean individual cost was £70,019, a figure ten times higher than asymptomatic children.

While there are occasions when removal of a child/children is necessary, it is also important to bear in mind that there is evidence that the fostering experience can contribute uniquely to negative outcomes for children.[34] This highlights the importance of both developing interventions that decrease the potential for child abuse and neglect in substance-using families and improving the foster care system to ensure that problems are not compounded.

The determinants of poor child developmental outcomes

In the literature reviewed above, it is clear that drug use *per se* is not the sole determinant of poor child developmental outcomes. Rather, the issue is the extent to which the drug use impacts on the parent's capacity to provide a safe, stable and nurturing environment for the child – the particular balance of risk and protective factors present in the family.[38] A summary of common risk and protective factors relating to child outcomes is presented in Table 19.1.

There is wide agreement that a crucial factor for the healthy development of a child is the quality of the parent–child relationship. A child needs to feel safe and loved right from early infancy. This requires a parent who is able to be emotionally available to the infant/child, who is sensitive to his or her child's cues and is able to respond to the child's needs. For example, in early infancy this may be reflected in the parent's ability to accurately differentiate between a distressed or hungry baby or a tired toddler. In the literature reviewed above, the negative impact of exposure to substances is documented. Identification of babies whose parents misuse substances and appropriate intervention during the woman's pregnancy has the potential to minimise risks before the baby is born.[39] Infants exposed prenatally to substances display sleeping, eating and social engagement difficulties.[40] There is increasing understanding of the role myelinated fibres of the vagal system play in the parasympathetic inhibition of the sympathetic nervous system – a process critical for an infant's capacity to self-regulate.[41] A developmental increase in myelinated vagal fibres is observed from 30–32 weeks gestational age to approximately six months postpartum.[41] If the vagal system of an infant is immature due to premature birth, or compromised as a result of *in utero* exposure to toxins, the infant's capacity for visceral and behavioural regulation is reduced. Such babies are hard to soothe when distressed, unsettled during feeding, and irregular in their sleep patterns. These 'difficult' behaviours are stressful for the parent and can have a detrimental impact on the quality of the parent–child relationship. When the parent is a young mother, single and trying to cope with limited social support, she is also likely to be experiencing anxiety and low mood. Under these

Table 19.1 **Common risk and protective factors of child developmental outcomes**

Risk factors	Protective factors
Child	
Premature birth, birth anomalies, low birth weight, prenatal exposure to substances. Difficult temperament	Secure attachment with primary carer. Easy temperament
Physical/cognitive disability	Above-average intelligence
Parental	
Parental psychopathology, including substance misuse	Secure attachment with child
History of child maltreatment as a child	Positive experience of childhood
Emotionally dysregulated	Ability to label and manage negative emotions
Poor knowledge of child development and parenting practices	Effective parenting skills
Unrealistic expectations of child	Realistic expectations of child
Family	
Domestic violence	Stable and cohesive family relationships
Single parent	Involvement of extended family
Social/community	
Poverty	
Social isolation, lack of support	Availability of supportive adults
Inadequate and unstable housing	Stable and suitable housing
Dangerous/violent neighbourhood	Safe neighbourhood
Poor schools	High-quality schools
Lack of accessible services – medical, social services, child care	Accessible services
Exposure to racism/discrimination	Cultural pride and positive ethnic identity

Note: see www.childwelfare.gov/can/factors for a more comprehensive list of risk and protective factors.

conditions sensitive and responsive parenting is extremely difficult and parents require a great deal of help to create the conditions in which they can better meet the needs of their children.

While a drug-using parent may have made poor life decisions in the past, it is helpful for these parents to be given the message that the multiple difficulties they are currently facing represent a significant challenge – rather than dwell on the past. It also follows that an intervention plan to help these parents must address the multiple issues in their lives. At the very least, a key role for the primary healthcare team is to support the parent by emphasising the positive steps the parent can take to help the infant. These will include ensuring a quiet and calm home environment, and an infant who is spoken to in a gentle voice and gently rocked and held after feeding. Such steps will not only enhance the mother's attachment to her infant but also may well be the first step in ameliorating the effects of *in utero* exposure.

Treatment programmes that improve outcome for children in substance-misusing families

In 2009 the National Academy of Parenting Practitioners conducted a review to identify effective programmes aimed at parents who misuse substances and their children.[42] Included in the report were a number of key messages for working with parents who misuse drugs and/or alcohol. Of particular importance is recognising that parents will be coping with numerous problems, requiring interventions that address these multiple issues in order to have any impact. For those at the front line of practice, it is important to work within the wider context of an integrated multi-agency treatment environment. While different services may be available to respond to different needs within a family, it is important that referrals and communication between the agencies are coordinated to be optimally effective. The results of a meta-analysis carried out in 2012 examining the effectiveness of programmes that integrate pregnancy or parenting, child-related and addiction services found that integrated services had a more beneficial impact on child development and the emotional and behavioural functioning of children than non-integrated programmes, although the difference was small.[43]

Therapeutically, a common target for services should be to promote a healthy parent–child relationship. This is the heart of the Every Child Matters programme – that children need to feel loved and valued, and supported by a network of reliable and affectionate relationships.[44] Unfortunately, the multiple difficulties facing drug-using parents can interfere with or lessen their ability to provide a child with a safe, loving and nurturing environment.[45]

The first step in helping a family is to carry out a comprehensive assessment. In the UK, the *Framework for the Assessment of Children in Need and Their Families* provides resources that can help identify the specific issues facing each family.[46]

As the specific problems for each family will differ, they must each be responded to in a flexible and highly individualised manner. There are a limited number of programmes that have been developed to deliver intensive parenting interventions with multi-problem families.

A programme that is receiving attention in the UK is the Parents Under Pressure (PuP) programme (www.pupprogram.net.au).[39,42,47] As part of a systematic review of programmes undertaken by Asmussen and Weizel in 2009, the PuP programme was identified as meeting the criteria for an evidence-based programme targeting substance-misusing parents as defined by the 'Evaluating the Evidence Scale'.[42] The PuP programme was specifically designed for substance-misusing parents and consists of 12 modules addressing multiple domains of family functioning. The programme integrates a number of theoretical approaches including Attachment Theory within an ecological perspective.[48–50] These theoretical influences provide a framework for working with families that emphasises the central role of the parent–child relationship. The ecological context of the family (stressors, social isolation) is seen as a source of stress that takes its toll on all relationships within the family, the parents' ability to manage their own emotional state and, in turn, their capacity to be emotionally available to their children.[51,52] A randomised controlled trial was conducted for parents on methadone with children in the 2–8-year-old age range. There was a reduction in child abuse potential, parenting stress and methadone dose for those families receiving the PuP programme, some slight improvement in families receiving a brief intervention based on behavioural parent training and a significant increase in child abuse potential in families receiving standard care.[53] Notably, this programme is currently being delivered by 11 National Society for the Prevention of Cruelty to Children (NSPCC) service centres across the UK as part of a comprehensive approach to reducing child maltreatment in infants (see Box 19.3, overleaf).[39]

Safeguarding responsibilities

The 2009 Care Quality Commission (CQC) review pointed out that NHS Trust boards have a legal duty relating to safeguarding and promoting the welfare of children and young people.[54] Their responsibilities are set out in the Children Acts 1989 and 2004, and in the government's statutory guidance. For Primary Care Trust (PCT) commissioners it is a legal requirement that clinical support and supervision be provided by 'designated' or 'named' clinicians and professionals. The CQC review found that designated doctors were typically paediatricians by profession, while 39% of named doctors in PCTs were GPs. Trusts are responsible for ensuring that all their staff are competent and confident in carrying out their responsibilities for safeguarding and promoting children's wel-

Box 19.3   **Sites providing the PuP programme as part of the NSPCC initiative**

Referral criteria

A parent of an infant under 2.5 years of age who is currently in treatment for a substance use problem (excludes self-help programmes such as AA and NA).

Exclusion criteria

Active domestic violence; child is not currently resident with primary carer; actively psychotic or suicidal.

Sites

Croydon, Nottingham, Ipswich, Liverpool, Warrington, Glasgow, Coventry, Stoke on Trent, Swindon, York, Bristol.

Note: for further information on the NSPCC initiative, see www.nspcc.org.uk/what-we-do/NSPCC-in-your-area/nspcc-in-your-area_wda84792.html.

fare, as stated in *Working Together to Safeguard Children*.[44,55] These responsibilities include being able to recognise when a child may require safeguarding, and knowing what to do in response to concerns about the welfare of a child. Appropriate and comprehensive training is therefore essential if staff are to be effective in safeguarding, and if trusts are to have confidence in the safeguarding skills of their staff. The minimum requirements for training for all staff are set out in the intercollegiate guidance *Safeguarding Children and Young People: roles and competences for health care staff*.[56] This document specifies the competencies required to safeguard, protect and promote the welfare of children and young people. Six levels of competency are defined, with each level including a combination of the skills, knowledge, attitudes and values required for safe and effective practice. GPs who have infrequent contact with children and families may be eligible to train at Level 2, while Level 3 training is the minimal requirement for all clinical staff, including GPs working with children, young people and/or their parents/carers. The 2009 CQC report[54] found that only 35% of GPs eligible for Level 2 training were up to date with the required training. The percentage of eligible GPs who had received Level 3 training was not reported, but it was noted that 27% of organisations did not keep records of staff requiring and receiving training at Level 3. This situation may change as the development and implementation of a safeguarding plan, which includes the training of eligible staff, will help meet the requirements for CQC registration.

It should be noted that at the time of writing the Department for Education was seeking views on three proposed statutory guidance documents: *Working Together to Safeguard Children; Managing Individual Cases: the framework for the assessment of children in need and their families; and Statutory Guidance on Learning and Improvement* (available at www.education.gov.uk/consultations/index.cfm?action=consultationDetails&consultationId=1839&external=no&menu=1).

This consultation process was initiated in response to Professor Eileen Munro's final report on the child protection system.[47] The report concluded that the child protection system was too centrally prescriptive with practitioners overly focused on procedures, resulting in a risk-averse culture of compliance at the expense of professional judgement and local innovation. The government proposal is to promote local frameworks to guide assessment and intervention. While the outcome is yet to be announced, it is likely that there will be an emphasis on locally developed safeguarding plans implemented by well-trained professionals, which include the coordination of multiple agencies at the local level. A well-coordinated local approach is essential in meeting the needs of multi-problem families with complex needs.

Safeguarding responsibilities of the primary care team

Given that parental substance abuse is a significant risk factor for child maltreatment, it is essential that all professionals who have contact with this population of parents are aware of their responsibilities for the safeguarding of children. The past 15 years have seen many changes in legislation, policy and practice relating to the protection of children. In 1999 the government of the time released the document *Working Together to Safeguard Children: a guide to inter-agency working to safeguard and promote the welfare of children*. The intention was to provide a national framework within which agencies and professionals could work together at the local level to ensure the welfare of children. The document *Framework for the Assessment of Children in Need and Their Families* was released at the time to provide a standardised approach to assessment of children and families.

Lord Laming's report on the inquiry into the death of Victoria Climbié in 2003 led to a government initiative known as Every Child Matters and the Children Act 2004 that provided the legislative underpinning of the Every Child Matters programme. The aim of this programme was to give all children the support they need to:

▶ be healthy

▶ stay safe

▶ enjoy and achieve

▶ make a positive contribution

▶ achieve economic wellbeing.

Working Together to Safeguard Children was revised in 2010 following Lord Laming's 2009 progress report on the protection of children in England.[44] Also, in 2009, the CQC carried out a review of child protection systems in the NHS at the request of the Secretary of State for Health following the conclusion of the legal case relating to the death of Baby P.[54] The review focused on governance arrangements, training and staffing, and arrangements for health organisations to work in partnership with others to safeguard children. Of particular note is that the CQC made clear in their report that GPs are at the heart of an effective child protection system. The Royal College of General Practitioners (RCGP) has also highlighted the important role of GPs and members of the primary practice team in the safeguarding of children. Recommendation 5 of the RCGP Child Health Strategy 2010–15 states that all members of a practice team should be responsible for safeguarding children and young people.[45] Further, within each practice there should be a nominated lead professional for child safeguarding who provides advice and promotes awareness amongst every member of a practice. Together with the NSPCC, the RCGP has produced a comprehensive guide on safeguarding children for GPs.[45] The guide aims to equip practices in the UK with the knowledge and tools to integrate the safeguarding of children and young people into practice systems and processes. The guide provides highly accessible information including a series of templates that provide structured formats for recording information. Appendix 9 of the guide provides a series of case studies headed 'Practice dilemmas' that emphasise the importance of using clinical judgement conducted within a consultative professional framework that is respectful of the families involved. Training modules published in 2011 that complement the Toolkit are available to members of the RCGP via the RCGP website.

Box 19.4 **Revisiting the case of Jane**

Jane has a 5-year-old and an unborn child. The safeguarding needs of both should be considered.

Actions to consider

1. Report the matter immediately to the Children's Social Care?

2. Refer to specialist midwife?

3. Ask the health visitor to call?

4. Talk to the nursery school teacher about the family?

5. Arrange for an appointment for Jane with the substance use service?

6. Begin Jane on opiate replacement therapy?

Notes

1. You may be correct. If you judge that Billy is likely to suffer harm (s47 Children Act 1989) as well as being a child in need (s17) then you should refer immediately. *Working Together to Safeguard Children* guidance (2006) advises speaking to a senior colleague with responsibilities in safeguarding, for example the practice safeguarding lead or the local NHS Named Nurse first to gather more information.

2. You may be correct. A referral to a midwife who specialises in substance misuse would be important in the prevention of potential risks before the baby is born. A midwife can offer individual antenatal care and, if appropriate, may organise a visit to special care baby unit.

3. You may be correct. The family is well known to the practice and the health visitor may well be able to provide support for the mother as well as gather more information about the home. If then you judge that the boy is likely to suffer harm (s47 Children Act 1989) as well as being a child in need (s17) then you should refer immediately.

4. You may be correct, although you should usually seek the mother's permission before doing this. If concerns for the child outweigh the mother's misgivings about this, latest information-sharing guidance reminds us of the primacy of the child's wellbeing (HM Government 2008 Information Sharing Guidance). You need to check with others who know the child about their observations. If then you judge that the boy is likely to suffer harm (s47 Children Act 1989) as well as being a child in need (s17) then you should refer immediately.

5. You may be correct. This would be good practice as Jane may well benefit from involvement in other services. Note, however, that she has managed her addiction extremely well in the last two years with support from the GP practice so this would need to be a discussion between the GP and Jane.

6. Correct. This is recommended practice.

References

1. Goel N, Beasley D, Rajkumar V, *et al*. Perinatal outcome of illicit substance use in pregnancy: comparative and contemporary socio-clinical profile in the UK. *European Journal of Pediatrics* 2011; **170(2)**: 199–205.

2. Singer L, Richardson G A. Introduction to 'Understanding developmental consequences of prenatal drug exposure: biological and environmental effects and their interactions'. *Neurotoxicology and Teratology* 2010; **33(1)**: 5–8.

3. Hunt R W, Tzioumi D, Collins E, *et al*. Adverse neurodevelopmental outcome of infants exposed to opiate in-utero. *Early Human Development* 2008; **84(1)**: 29–35.

4. Minnes S, Lang A, Singer L. Prenatal tobacco, marijuana, stimulant, and opiate exposure: outcomes and practice implications. *Addiction Science and Clinical Practice* 2011; **6(1)**: 57–70.

5. Ornoy A, Michailevskaya V, Lukashov I, *et al*. The developmental outcome of children born to heroin-dependent mothers, raised at home or adopted. *Child Abuse and Neglect* 1996; **20(5)**: 385–96.

6. Greene O, Varghese A, Tuamokumo F. Perinatal outcome after cocaine +/- polydrug exposure. *Annals of the New York Academy of Sciences* 1998; **846**: 396–8.

7. Ness R B, Grisso J A, Hirshinger N, *et al*. Cocaine and tobacco use and the risk of spontaneous abortion. *New England Journal of Medicine* 1999; **340(5)**: 333–9.

8. Ostrea E M, Brady M, Gause S. Drug screening of newborns by meconium analysis: a large scale, perspective, epidemiologic study. *Pediatrics* 1992; **89(1)**: 107–13.

9. Bauer C R. Perinatal effects of prenatal drug exposure. *Clinics in Perinatology* 1999; **26(1)**: 87–106.

10. Dow-Edwards D. Translational issues for prenatal cocaine studies and the role of environment. *Neurotoxicology and Teratology* 2011; **33(1)**: 9–16.

11. Ackerman J P, Riggins T, Black M. A review of the effects of prenatal cocaine exposure among school-aged children. *Pediatrics* 2010; **125(3)**: 554–65.

12. Bridgett D J, Mayes L C. Development of inhibitory control among prenatally cocaine exposed and non-cocaine exposed youths from late childhood to early adolescence: the effects of gender and risk and subsequent aggressive behavior. *Neurotoxicology and Teratology* 2011; **33(1)**: 47–60.

13. Betancourt L M, Yang W, Brodsky N L, *et al*. Adolescents with and without gestational cocaine exposure: longitudinal analysis of inhibitory control, memory and receptive language. *Neurotoxicology and Teratology* 2011; **33(1)**: 36–46.

14. Smith L M, LaGasse L, Derauf C, *et al*. Motor and cognitive outcomes through three years of age in children exposed to prenatal methamphetamine. *Neurotoxicology and Teratology* 2011; **33(1)**: 176–84.

15. Campolongo P, Trezza V, Ratano P, *et al*. Developmental consequences of perinatal cannabis exposure: behavioral and neuroendocrine effects in adult rodents. *Psychopharmacology* 2011; **214(1)**: 5–15.

16. Day N L, Leech S L, Goldschmidt L. The effects of prenatal marijuana exposure on delinquent behaviours are mediated by measures of neurocognitive functioning. *Neurotoxicology and Teratology* 2011; **33(1)**: 129–36.

17. National Collaborating Centre for Women's and Children's Health. *Clinical Guideline 62, Antenatal Care: routine care for the healthy pregnant woman*. London: NICE, 2010.

18. Clark C M, Li D, Conry J, *et al*. Structural and functional brain integrity of fetal alcohol syndrome in nonretarded cases. *Pediatrics* 2000; **105(5)**: 1196–9.

19. Mattson S N, Schoenfield A M, Riley E P. Teratogenic effects of alcohol on brain and behaviour. *Alcohol Research and Health* 2001; **25(3)**: 185–91.

20. BMA Board of Science. *Fetal Alcohol Spectrum Disorders: a guide for healthcare professionals.* London: BMA, 2007.

21. Morleo M, Woolfall K, Dedman D, *et al.* Under-reporting of foetal alcohol spectrum disorders: an analysis of hospital episode statistics. *BMC Pediatrics* 2011; **11(14)**.

22. Brook J, Whiteman M, Zheng L. Intergenerational transmission of risks for problem behaviours. *Journal of Abnormal Child Psychology* 2002; **30(1)**: 65–76.

23. Nurco D, Blathcley R, Hanlon T, *et al.* Early deviance and related risk factors in the children of narcotic addicts. *American Journal of Drug and Alcohol Abuse* 1999; **25(1)**: 25–45.

24. Sher K. Psychological characteristics of children of alcoholics. *Alcohol Health and Research World* 1997; **21(3)**: 247–54.

25. Wood J. *Report of the Special Commission of Inquiry into Child Protection Services in NSW: executive summary and recommendations.* NSW: NSW Government, 2008.

26. Munro E. *The Munro Review of Child Protection. Interim report: the child's journey.* London: DE, 2011.

27. Australian Institute of Health and Welfare. *Child Protection Australian 2007–08. Cat. no CWS 33.* Canberra: AIHW, 2009.

28. Advisory Council on the Misuse of Drugs. *Hidden Harm: responding to the needs of children of problem drug users.* London: Home Office, 2003.

29. Manning V, Best DW, Faulkner N, *et al.* New estimates of the number of children living with substance misusing parents: results from UK national household surveys. *BMC Public Health* 2009; **9**: 377.

30. Tracy E M. Maternal substance abuse: protecting the child, preserving the family. *Social Work* 1994; **39(5)**: 534–40.

31. Chaffin M, Kelleher K, Hollenberg J. Onset of physical abuse and neglect: psychiatric, substance abuse and social risk factors from prospective community data. *Child Abuse and Neglect* 1996; **20(3)**: 191–203.

32. Pilowski D, Lyles CM, Cross SI, *et al.* Characteristics of injection drug-using parents who retain their children. *Drug and Alcohol Dependence* 2001; **61**: 113–22.

33. Advisory Council on the Misuse of Drugs. Estimates of the scale of the problem. In: *Hidden Harm: responding to the needs of children of problem drug users.* London: Home Office, 2003, pp. 20–8.

34. Dozier M, Albus K, Fisher P A, *et al.* Interventions for foster parents: implications for developmental theory. *Development and Psychopathology* 2002; **14(4)**: 843–60.

35. Leslie L K, Gordon J N, Ganger W, *et al.* Developmental delay in young children in child welfare by initial placement type. *Infant Mental Health Journal* 2002; **23(5)**: 496–516.

36. Scott S. Aggressive behaviour in childhood. *British Medical Journal* 1998; **316(7126)**: 202–6.

37. Scott S, Knapp M, Henderson J, *et al.* Financial cost of social exclusion: follow up study of antisocial children into adulthood. *British Medical Journal* 2001; **323(7306)**: 1–5.

38. Dawe S, Frye S, Best D, *et al.* Drug Use in the Family: impacts and implications for children. Canberra: Australian National Council on Drugs, 2007.

39. Cuthbert C, Rayns G, Stanley K. *All Babies Count: prevention and protection for vulnerable babies.* London: NSPCC, 2011.

40. O'Brien J C, Jeffery H E. Sleep deprivation, disorganization and fragmentation during opiate withdrawal in newborns. *Journal of Paediatrics and Child Health* 2002; **38(1)**: 66–71.

41. Porges S W, Furman S A. The early development of the autonomic nervous system provides a neural platform for social behaviour: a polyvagal perspective. *Infant and Child Development* 2011; **20(1)**: 106–18.

42. Asmussen K, Weizel K. *Evaluating the Evidence: what works in supporting parents who misuse drugs and alcohol.* London: The National Academy for Parenting Practitioners, 2009.

43. Niccols A, Milligan K, Smith A, *et al.* Integrated programs for mothers with substance abuse issues and their children: a systematic review of studies reporting on child outcomes. *Child Abuse and Neglect* 2012; **36(4)**: 308–22. Epub 5 April 2012.

44. HM Government. *Working Together to Safeguard Children: a guide to inter-agency working to safeguard and promote the welfare of children.* Nottingham: HM Government, Department for Children, Schools and Families, 2010.

45. Royal College of General Practitioners, National Society for Prevention of Cruelty to Children. *Safeguarding Children and Young People: a toolkit for general practice.* London: RCGP, NSPCC, 2011.

46. Department of Health. *Framework for the Assessment of Children in Need and Their Families.* London: TSO, 2000.

47. Munro E. *The Munro Review of Child Protection: final report.* London: DE, 2011.

48. Belsky J. Etiology of child maltreatment: a developmental-ecological analysis. *Psychological Bulletin* 1993; **114(3)**: 413–34.

49. Bronfenbrenner U. *The Ecology of Human Development: experiments by nature and design.* Cambridge, MA: Harvard University Press, 1979.

50. Cicchetti D, Toth S L. Child maltreatment: past, present, and future perspectives. In: R P Weissberg, H J Walberg (eds). *Long-Term Trends in the Well-being of Children and Youth: issues in children's and families' lives.* Washington, DC: Child Welfare League of America, Inc., 2003, pp. 181–205.

51. Biringen Z. Emotional availability: conceptualization and research findings. *American Journal of Orthopsychiatry* 2000; **70(1)**: 104–14.

52. Harnett P H, Dawe S. Review: the contribution of mindfulness-based therapies for children and families and proposed conceptual integration. *Child and Adolescent Mental Health* 2012. DOI: 10.1111/j.1475-3588.2011.00643.x.

53. Dawe S, Harnett P H. Reducing potential for child abuse among methadone-maintained parents: results from a randomized controlled trial. *Journal of Substance Abuse Treatment* 2007; **32(4)**: 381–90.

54. Care Quality Commission. *Care Quality Commission Review: safeguarding children.* London: CQC, 2009.

55. HM Government. *Working Together to Safeguard Children: a guide to inter-agency working to safeguard and promote the welfare of children.* London: TSO, 2006.

56. Royal College of Paediatrics and Child Health. *Safeguarding Children and Young People: roles and competences for health care staff.* London: RCPCH, 2006.

CHAPTER 20

Black and minority ethnic groups

Robina Rowley-Conwy

Definition

The term 'black and minority ethnic' (BME) can be defined as individuals belonging to any minority group who have a shared race, nationality, or language and culture.[1-9] The definition also acknowledges that there is considerable diversity within BME communities. In this chapter ethnic minority communities can often be concealed by the use of generic terminology such as describing 'South Asian' population groups from Bangladesh, India and Pakistan. The term 'black communities' also refers to people of African (Somalia, Democratic Public of Congo, Zimbabwe, Uganda, Ethiopia, Sierra Leone, Zambia) and Caribbean (Caribbean Sea, its islands and the surrounding Central and South American coasts) heritage.

Introduction

This chapter will provide an understanding regarding differing needs and challenges associated with drug use among diverse minority communities within the UK. It will provide insights into the preferences of illicit drug use within BME communities. However, in the UK, even within groups of the same ethnic background there are differences in illicit drug preference associated with factors such as generational and wider socioeconomic differences. Therefore, patterns of drug use and the barriers and attractions to treatment can be very different for particular ethnic groups.

The focus on treating opioid dependence in the UK in recent decades has predominantly been a focus upon Caucasian populations from lower socioeconomic status, yet many individuals from BME groups use other non-opioid drugs. This chapter will discuss ways in which primary care practitioners and managers of services can ensure that BME patients are given the treatment they require and help identify gaps required for action.

Prevalence of drug use in BME communities in the UK

Evidence from both quantitative and qualitative surveys strongly indicates that prevalence of drug use within BME groups is increasing and that, even where it is shown to be less than in the Caucasian population, it is still significant.[4]

From both empirical research and a report from the Department of Health the prevalence of illicit drug is much higher amongst the Caucasian community (9.4%) than BME groups (5.1%).[10–13]

In the non-Caucasian population, a combined three-year dataset (2006/7, 2007/8 and 2008/9) from the British Crime Survey (BCS) revealed the proportion of 16–59-year-olds reported using drugs in the last year were highest amongst the black or black British population (5.8%).[5] Further analysis highlighted that use of Class A drugs was most popular amongst the black Caribbean group (1.4%) compared with the black African group (0.8%).[4,5,11–13]

Compared with the black community, the prevalence of illicit drug use amongst the Asian population was much lower. The Asian or Asian British population presented the least drug-using population (3.0%). The ethnic background in the South Asian population drug users was further divided into Pakistani (2.9%), Indian (2.7%) and Bangladeshi (2.6%) origins. Within the South Asian population, the Indian population was the highest to have used Class A drugs.[5,12] The majority of participants in the study were of Pakistani and Bangladeshi origins, and many described their religion as Islam. The mean age of the South Asian drug-using population was much younger compared with the general population, especially with the Bangladeshi sub-population.[9]

Statistically, there is a smaller proportion of South Asian and black African females than females in the general population who had used illicit drugs. However, this may be under-represented as females from this ethnic minority group are much more reluctant to disclose their illicit drug use behaviours. There is strong evidence to suggest a link between cultural and religious values and beliefs that prevents BME individuals seeking help from external agencies. However, studies have revealed that illicit drug use is perceived to be increasing amongst the South Asian population, especially females.[2,9]

Patterns of substance misuse

A detailed literature review by the National Treatment Agency for Substance Misuse gives a more in-depth guide into the use of drugs. Not surprisingly cannabis is the most widely used illicit drug among the majority of BME groups.[4,6,8,9,14] In the black African and Caribbean groups this is perceived as culturally acceptable: 'Using cannabis is seen as something that "everybody" does and not harmful.'[6] Sources have revealed that it is widely used by both genders (although significantly less in women from black African communities)[6] and various age ranges from teenagers to pensioners. In the non-black minority ethnic groups, cannabis is also the preferred choice of drug, and most adolescents have tried cannabis through experimentation with peers.[2,9,11,13] The majority of primary cannabis users are thought to be young South Asian males with ages ranging from 16–29 years' old.[9]

However, there is also some evidence that crack cocaine use is increasing in BME populations. Data from the National Drug Treatment Monitoring System (NDTMS), particularly from the London region, indicate that crack cocaine is the preferred Class A drug of choice amongst black Caribbean groups.[8,15]

In the South Asian population group, heroin is the preferred *Class A* drug of choice and after cannabis is the second most commonly illicit drug used.[1,6] There have been cases in which youths as young as 12 years' old have reported the primary drug of choice to be heroin, although this is not typical of South Asian children. For example, glue and solvent use was reported significantly higher in Bangladeshi youths compared with youths in other BME groups.[15] The factors associated with the increase in heroin use have been poverty, overcrowded housing, poor education, low employment aspirations, experimentation and adapting a 'Western' lifestyle.[1,7,9,15,16] Most of the primary drug users are thought to be young males. Other key trends are that there is little evidence to suggest a high prevalence of injecting drug behaviour across BME groups. However, there is evidence to suggest the rate of drug use in females from BME communities is increasing.[1,9]

So-called 'dance drugs' (ecstasy, LSD, amphetamines) appear to be less used amongst ethnic minority groups although some evidence suggests it is preferred by young black Caribbean populations, as it has been cited as the most commonly used drug after cannabis.[8]

Some non-black ethnic minority groups around the UK use non-illicit substances such as paan. Paan, known as betel leaves, is prepared and used as a stimulant.[17] The paan leaf with or without tobacco is chewed before spitting or swallowing. The paan has habit forming and euphoriant properties. There is evidence that lifetime paan use exists within South Asian populations, as paan is a culturally accepted substance across such populations.[2,6,16]

Some BME groups use khat, a stimulant consisting of the leaves and tender shoots of the plant. This is the most commonly used stimulant amongst Somalis and Ethiopians. Whilst use in the UK has been recognised and documented,[2,6] use of khat was not recorded in the BCS survey since use was not specifically surveyed. In the black African community this is perceived as a culturally acceptable drug. In keeping with cannabis use in this community, it is associated with low levels of stigmatism and taboo, just like cannabis.

Perception of drug use in the BME community and barriers to treatment

An important element for health professionals is to understand and address the factors that facilitate some individuals from minority communities into treatment and also barriers to care that prevent others from accessing treatment. Primary care practitioners and healthcare managers will benefit from understanding the cultural views a drug user from an ethnic minority background faces within his or her community and what barriers are created before even seeking help for issues relating to substance misuse. Unsurprisingly, there is a danger in the UK that treatment services can become too oriented towards the Caucasian population and less focused towards the demands of BME substance misusers.

BME groups are likely to be under-represented in surveys where stigma, cultural and religious values play a key role in preventing individuals within these communities from revealing their drug use to researchers, i.e. they tend to be secretive about their use. The following case studies highlight the barriers facing individuals from BME communities seeking help from GPs and treatment services for problematic drug use.

Case study 1

A young South Asian woman Nazia, aged 20, socialises with friends from different backgrounds. Most are of South Asian background. She finds herself experimenting with and trying cannabis, and is regularly smoking it with her friends. Her mother hears a rumour from her community that her daughter is trying 'drugs', also noticing a distinct smell on her. Upon hearing the rumours the mother decides to challenge her daughter and searches her bedroom and handbag. A bag of cannabis is found and the daughter confesses she uses cannabis with her friends. The mother is concerned that her daughter is 'addicted'. The mother has limited English vocabulary. They plan an appointment together to see the GP.

What advice and services would be suitable for this young woman from a minority ethnic background?

Points to consider

▸ What is her cultural background?

▸ What is the stigma associated in her community?

▸ What advice and help could be offered to her and her family?

Key learning points

The majority of South Asian families have limited knowledge of drug use and where to seek help. The initial route to access drug services is through GPs. South Asian communities hold a high degree of confidence and trust in the information and drug treatment provided by their GPs. This is often the most crucial step a family belonging to this community takes in seeking help to tackle problems relating to illicit drug use.[2,4,9]

There is a strong sense of family values in this community and usually the drug user may prefer to have the support and involvement of his or her family. An emphasis is placed on the stress it causes the drug user's family, especially that of the mother. In South Asian culture the upbringing of children and conferring cultural, religious and social values is considered predominantly the female role. The family can be heavily ostracised by the community if seen as neglecting to bring up children with traditional beliefs.[16] Therefore in the case of Nazia it is important to assess whether she is in fact dependent upon cannabis or using the drug recreationally. It is possible that family members with well-meaning intentions could be pushing for treatment to 'cure' Nazia, when in fact she is simply using the drug in a non-hazardous way. Therefore the GP can be a source of considerable reassurance to the family by emphasising that Nazia is not dependent upon cannabis. On the other hand a robust assessment may reveal that Nazia is dependent upon cannabis and therefore referral for community drug service support could be indicated. Therefore, if Nazia consents, it may be beneficial to include the family unit when community drug treatment services are involved. This may provide clear understanding and assurances to the drug user and his or her family in understanding the drug use and the treatment options available.[9]

Patient confidentiality is a key factor. This needs to be repeatedly emphasised to the drug user and his or her family. The community is a central focus, and there is stigma placed upon the drug user and his or her family. It is thought that a member of the family who is a drug user has an impact on the whole family, and there is fear of shame and loss of honour.[9,18] Additional pressures are placed where the impact of the drug user extends further to his or her family member's future:

It brings so much shame to the family within the community, people just look down on you, they think the whole family is bad. The drug user won't get a marriage proposal, and neither will the sisters if their brother is a drug user.

(Drug user's sister)[9]

There is anxiety from the family being the centre of gossip in the community and tarnishing the family's name. It is more acceptable to try to hide the problem, rather than seek external help.

In summary, case study 1 highlights that there are many barriers faced by the drug user and his or her family, including:[2,9,14,16]

▶ stigma from the local South Asian community, leading to users being secretive about their use

▶ shame and loss of honour of the drug user's family

▶ religious and cultural barriers

▶ in extreme cases, fear of being sent back to the country of origin and to be possibly married there. Some individuals in the community hold beliefs that the distraction of being moved would help in dealing with the problem of drug dependence. The drug user would not be able to easily access the drug source and is kept away from peers and drug-using lifestyles (also referred to as 'Westernisation')

▶ lack of knowledge and understanding of substance misuse

▶ lack of awareness of the availability of substance misuse treatment provision in the area

▶ absence of appropriate informal and formal support.

Case study 2

A young Muslim black African male Abdul, aged 19, socialises with his cousins and friends. He has left college and is unemployed. He spends most of his recreational time smoking cannabis and has been experimenting with heroin. He does not realise the potential for heroin dependence and soon enough he spends his job seeker's allowance on buying heroin. His allowance does not provide sufficient monies to fund his habit and he starts to steal from his mother. His mother notices changes in her son but is afraid to ask questions. He is withdrawn, agitated and has been losing his appetite. He eventually confesses to his mother that he is addicted to heroin and does not know what to do about it. They plan an appointment together to see the GP.

Points to consider

▸ What is the religious and cultural background?

▸ What are the barriers faced before accessing help from the GP?

▸ What advice and help could be offered?

Key learning points

There are many pressures that the drug user and his family face before seeking help from external agencies; it is a big step for the drug user and his or her family to seek help from the GP. The GP is the trusted health provider and a key link for this community to access drug treatment and advice services. There are many barriers faced by the individual and the family from the community including:[7]

Limited knowledge of drug services

There have been reports to suggest members of the black African community have limited knowledge of illicit drugs. It has often been perceived that the treatment for drug dependence is through counselling from a trusted member of society such as family, friends (who may themselves have been taking illicit drugs) and/or religious leaders. The majority of drug users and their families lack the knowledge of either opiate detoxification or substitute prescribing options. There is lack of awareness regarding interventions available to help with illicit drug use. It would be beneficial to explain to individuals and their families the nature of the types of drug services and treatment interventions available. An emphasis should be placed upon open discussion. There have been reports indicating that individuals from this community feel that drug service providers lack cultural understanding. It is good practice to identify drug services in the local area that are oriented towards the black minority community. In some such services there may be black African drug workers who some clients will readily indentify with, thus reducing a sense of stigma or intimidation.

Family values and social upstanding

There is a strong sense of family values in the community and usually the drug user may prefer to have the support and involvement of the family. With consent, it may be beneficial for the drug user and the family to understand the nature of the illicit substance and the options available in managing and treating substance misuse. This is a crucial stage and with clear understanding and guidance the drug user can be supported by his or her family and progress in seeking further help to tackle problems relating to drug dependence.

Religion and beliefs

Most commonly, with the pressures of religion in the black African community the drug user's family face the stigma of being associated with drug problems. The usual response to dealing with illicit drug problems in this community is denial.

In many cases religious institutions do not accept that followers of the faith are drug users and often the family are ostracised. This has been noted particularly for Muslim followers as Islam prohibits the use of drugs (narcotics), which are '*haram*' – unlawful or not permitted due to their potential to cause effects of intoxication.[6,19]

Stigma, taboo and confidentiality issues

The family of the drug user most fear being rejected and stripped of their social standing in the community. Therefore there is strong stigma associated with illicit drug use such that to even talk about drug addiction is perceived as a taboo subject. Reports of punishment and rejection have been experienced in the black African community and drug users are aware of this and are afraid of how their families will react towards them. If a family member is categorised as a drug user then the black African community would suffer as a whole. Due to stigma and consequences, it is important to emphasise confidentiality in every consultation because there is a fear of reprisals if information is leaked into the community.

Case study 3

A middle-aged black Caribbean male, Carl, admits to his girlfriend that he snorts crack cocaine. She is aware that he smokes cannabis on a regular basis but is worried that his crack cocaine addiction will impact on her life. He has been continuously fighting the addiction and promises her that he will make an appointment tomorrow morning to see the GP.

Points to consider

▸ What concerns does he face?

▸ What is the community perception of his drug use?

▸ What are the barriers in accessing drug treatment services?

Key learning points

The overall perception of illicit drugs is varied in the community.[2,7,8] The perception of cannabis is that it is a culturally acceptable drug, and it is categorised by the black Caribbean community as a 'natural herb' with medicinal properties. A report has suggested that, due to the Rastafarian movement, most black Caribbean Rastafarians have used cannabis as part of their religion and culture.[8] However, the report has also suggested that many BME drug misusers have used the Rastafarian religion as an excuse for using cannabis.

In the black Caribbean community, crack cocaine has been perceived as a drug of choice even though the use has been under-reported in the literature. Unlike cannabis use, there is stigma associated with illicit drug users taking crack/cocaine. The perception amongst members of the black Caribbean community is that users impact on their communities by committing crimes, promoting violence such as 'gang culture' and gun crimes, and therefore damaging the reputation of the community and the local area.

There has been evidence to suggest that black Caribbean drug users face barriers to drug treatment/advice services due to a lack of cultural understanding. Drug users from a black Caribbean background believe that service providers will stereotype them as a 'black person' taking drugs and react negatively towards them by passing judgement on them as drug dealers. Although drug users of black Caribbean origin did not feel that they were victims of racism *per se*, they expressed a concern that Caucasian drug workers might hold stereotypical views. This concern led to a disconnect between clients and workers, making them less likely to engage with the available drug services.

Lack of confidentiality and discrimination are the key barriers. The evidence base would suggest that drug workers of the same ethnic background could help promote trust and cultural understanding when tackling drug use in the community.[8]

Good practice and evidence of successful engagement with individuals from BME communities

Promoting communication

Most of the research has indicated that drug users and families from BME communities experience language difficulties, where English is not their first language.[6,9,20,21] The language difficulty can extend to a wide range of ethnic communities, especially the older generations.[6,7,9] A common and effective way of addressing the barriers presented by language is the provision of leaflets in different languages and dialects. This is a good way of getting key messages across to ethnic communities and reducing the widely felt impression that some drug services are primarily run by Caucasian drug workers.[22] Websites such as FRANK have proven successful in delivering information on drug services, especially for the younger generation where anonymity is guaranteed.[6,9]

Non-written information such as telephone helplines, videos, DVDs and CDs in various languages can be used by drug users and ethnic minority families in the privacy of their homes. This also helps individuals with poor reading skills who would struggle to assimilate information presented in the written leaflet format.[4,8]

A drug awareness week within the community for all members in the local area has also been suggested as a way to promote communication and drug service information.[6]

Provision of drug education

It has been widely documented that knowledge of drug information within the BME community is very limited. The sources of information that many individuals from the ethnic community use are GPs, family, friends, social networks, religious and community organisations.[4,6,9,14]

There have been suggestions to improve the approachability and therefore access to drug services for users from an ethnic background. Suggestions include the creation of meaningful engagement of professionals with religious institutes, the inclusion of BME community members in planning, delivery and organisation of drug services, and the provision of adequate training in substance misuse.[6,9]

With a strong sense of taboo and stigma in the community, most BME members find that delivery of drug information and advice in familiar surroundings such as community centres, health centres, places of worship and GP surgeries to be much more comfortable. Most BME drug users and their families have expressed that they would access help when all avenues have been exhausted and they have no alternative but to seek help from external services. GPs have been cited by the BME community as the most trustworthy and knowledgeable health professionals from whom to seek help. Therefore general practice has a crucial role to play in delivering effective drug information and treatment.[6,7,9,23] For the younger generation, the delivery of drug information has included education in schools, religious institutions, youth clubs, colleges, universities and sport centres.[6,7,9]

Cultural and religious understanding

Understanding and empathising with the diverse nature of culture within the BME population is critical for professionals seeking to work with this group.[4,6,14,22] One of the issues raised is the lack of cultural understanding, which has been cited as a barrier for many ethnic minorities in accessing drug treatment services.[2,4,6,8,9]

Some communities have felt they would be discriminated against and would be the target of racism if they were to seek help from drug services, especially those who were not able to speak English fluently.[6] Some studies have suggested that many BME members are put off by the lack of ethnic staff in the drug service, as they believe non-ethnic drug workers would not be able to understand their culture and they would be discriminated against.[6,8]

> *I used to walk past this drug service every day and everyone in there – they were all white. And they were all smiling and happy. I used to look at this service ... and I was afraid to go in there. I was afraid. Until one day there was a Black worker in there.*

(Drug service client)[8]

Many studies have indicated a lack of religious understanding by professionals, especially towards the Muslim population. Drug-related problems are a major issue for the drug user, his or her family and the community; there is taboo and a religious view of condemnation for BME individuals. There have been recommendations for religious leaders to be involved in addressing drug-related problems. This may not be the case because, due to strong beliefs, religious leaders are less likely to be involved with drug problems and often deny any substance misuse problems occurring in the community. It would be beneficial for drug services to address religious understanding with BME drug users. One of the recommendations has included drug workers completing 'cultural competence training'. This would allow drug workers to understand the social and religious diversity among the BME community and enable barriers to be broken down by encouraging religious leaders to be involved in drug treatment services.[6,8,9] There is a strong religious belief within some BME communities that many of the problems caused by drugs can be solved by religious leaders praying at the mosque or church. It is important to understand the importance of religion in many of the BME communities; many of the studies have indicated incorporating religious leaders and institutes through a drug delivery forum.[6,9]

There has been evidence and recommendations for 'Muslim-friendly' services for women. Mixed-gender services have posed a barrier, where it has been culturally unacceptable for women to mix with men. A crucial point for primary care practitioners is the finding that BME women are most likely to enter treatment later, often missing out on harm minimisation interventions. Many studies have recommended provisions for women-only services at their homes or at a chosen venue.[4,6,7,9]

Ethnic minority drug users face stigma from their communities, with issues including the fear of losing their right to live in the UK,[6] loss of family honour, and the impact on drug users' lives and their family members' future.[9] By understanding the cultural and religious beliefs an effective drug delivery service is promoted, thus allowing BME members to be effectively engaged and committed to the delivery of drug services.

Trust and confidentiality

The recurrent themes throughout this chapter are those of trust and confidentiality.

The BME drug user and his or her family face stigma by the community. Due to the close-set community, the drug user may feel that seeking help from external agencies will mean confidentiality being breached: nothing is kept private and the family is 'named and shamed'.[6,9] It is important to strongly reassure the drug user from an ethnic minority background regarding the confidential nature of drug treatment. This is particularly important in the South Asian and African populations where drug use is heavily associated with stigma. There is evidence of loss of trust when seeking help from drug treatment and advice services. It is essential that community members feel reassured that trust and confidentiality will not be breached.

Ambiguous confidentiality statements such as 'we operate a strict confidentiality policy' or 'this is a confidential service' are not sufficient. It does not reassure the BME patient that the information they provide will not 'leak out' in the community.[9]

Therefore, to reinforce a positive message regarding confidentiality, a specific statement should be provided to patients that professionals will not disclose sensitive information to either parents, any family member, the police or any other interested party. [9]

It is important to emphasise that information provided will be kept anonymous (if possible) and strictly confidential between the drug user and the health service provider. Assurances are required that the information provided will not be discussed with anyone in the community and consultation will be kept private.[8,21]

Conclusion

There is clear evidence that use of illicit drugs in BME communities is increasing and that, even where it is shown to be less than in the Caucasian population, it is still significant. A key theme is that most of the BME communities have used cannabis and many find it a culturally acceptable drug. However, there has been evidence that problematic use of the Class A drugs heroin and crack cocaine have been the main trigger for drug users from BME communities consulting external agencies for help. However, due to taboo and stigma, most drug users from BME communities keep their drug-using behaviour a secret and only as a last resort at the point of desperation are these services approached. Many drug treatment agencies are failing to recognise that these communities will often need support and encouragement before using available drug services. There has been an emphasis upon the lack of drug information and treatment knowledge in BME communities, mainly because this is a taboo subject and not openly discussed. There have been suggestions to involve religious institutes and leaders to break down barriers.[6,9] It is not an easy task, and many religions prohibit the use of illicit drugs, but with perseverance and involvement positive changes can occur in cultural perceptions of drug users.

This chapter has highlighted good-practice themes to help overcome barriers to accessing drug treatment services by BME communities such as:

▸ providing a variety of information in various media such as leaflets in different languages/dialects, CDs, DVDs, the FRANK website and helplines

▸ a mix of substance misuse workers from different ethnic backgrounds

▸ understanding of religious and cultural barriers

▸ understanding the stigma and taboo associated with drug use and the importance of assuring and maintaining confidentiality

▸ an ability to cater for the needs of females in communities where it is not culturally acceptable for females to mix with males

▸ to provide drug service provisions in comfortable surroundings such as GP surgeries and community centres

▸ to provide formal and informal support to the drug user and (with patient consent) to the wider family.

References

1. Uddin M S, Bhugra D, Johnson M R D. Perceptions of drug use within a UK Bengali community. *Indian Journal of Psychiatry* 2008; **50(2)**: 106–11.

2. Fountain J, Bashford J, Winters M. *Black and Minority Ethnic Communities in England: a review of the literature on drug use and related service provision.* London: NTA, 2003.

3. Ndegwa D. *Social Division and Difference: black and ethnic minorities.* London: NHS, 2002.

4. UK Drug Policy Commission. *Drugs and Diversity: ethnic minority groups. Learning from the evidence.* London: UKDPC, 2010.

5. Hoare J, Moon D. *Drug Misuse Declared: findings from the 2009/10 British Crime Survey. England and Wales.* London: Home Office Statistics, 2010.

6. Fountain J. *Issues Surrounding Drug Use and Drug Services among the Black African Communities in England.* Preston: UCLAN, NTA, 2009.

7. Williams S, Chana S, Eziefula U, *et al. The Mental Health Needs of Black and Minority Ethnic Communities in Chapeltown and Harehills.* Leeds: Adult Social Care, 2008.

8. Fountain J. *Issues Surrounding Drug Use and Drug Services among the Black Caribbean Communities in England.* Preston: UCLAN, NTA, 2009.

9. Fountain J. *Issues Surrounding Drug Use and Drug Services among the South Asian communities in England.* Preston: UCLAN, NTA, 2009.

10. Davies C, English L, Stewart C, *et al. United Kingdom Drug Situation: annual report to the European Monitoring Centre for Drugs and Drug Addiction (EMCDDA).* London: DH, 2011.

11. Davies C, English L, Lodwick A, *et al. United Kingdom Drug Situation: annual report to the European Monitoring Centre for Drugs and Drug Addiction (EMCDDA)*. London: DH, 2010.

12. Smith K, Flatley J. *Drug Misuse Declared: findings from the 2010/11 British Crime Survey. England and Wales*. London: Home Office Statistics, 2011.

13. UK Focal Point on Drugs. *The State of the Drugs Problem in Europe. Annual report to the European Monitoring Centre for Drugs and Drug Addiction (EMCDDA)*. Lisbon: EMCDDA, 2012.

14. National Institute for Health and Clinical Excellence. *Clinical Guideline 120, Psychosis with Coexisting Substance Misuse*. London: NICE, 2011.

15. Barn R. Parenting in a 'foreign' climate: the experiences of Bangladeshi mothers in multi-racial Britain. *Social Work in Europe* 2002; **9(3)**: 28–38.

16. Shaw A, Egan J, Gillespie M. *Drugs and Poverty: a literature review*. Glasgow: Scottish Drugs Forum. 2007.

17. Oxford dictionaries online, available at http://oxforddictionaries.com/definition/american_english/paan   [accessed November 2012].

18. Alam M Y, Husband C. *Reflections of Young British-Pakistani Men from Bradford*. York: Joseph Rowntree Foundation, 2006.

19. The divine book of Islam, *Qur'an*, Surah 5: 91–2.

20. Fountain J. *Issues Surrounding Drug Use and Drug Services among the Kurdish, Turkish Cypriot and Turkish Communities in England*. Preston: UCLAN, NTA, 2009.

21. Butt J, O'Neil A. *'Let's Move on': black and minority ethnic older people's views on research findings*. York: Joseph Rowntree Foundation, 2004.

22. Chantler K. *An Analysis of Present Drug Service Delivery to Black Communities in Greater Manchester*. Manchester: Black Drug Workers Forum North West and Greater Manchester Drug Action Partnership (SRB Initiative), 1998.

23. Weaver T, Rutter D, Hart J, *et al. National Evaluation of Crack Cocaine Treatment and Outcome Study (NECTOS): a multi-centre evaluation of dedicated crack treatment services*. London: NTA, 2007.

| # Drug use and housing issues

Nat Wright

IN THIS CHAPTER

What is homelessness? Challenging the myth of migrancy || The relationship between housing status and drug use || Where will homeless drug users access primary care? || Structured counselling to address problematic drug use || Key issues in safe prescribing for homeless drug users || Homelessness and criminal justice || Hospital care and homelessness || Developing integrated working – key principles

What is homelessness? Challenging the myth of migrancy

Having a home has been defined as 'having an adequate dwelling (or space) over which a person and his/her family can exercise exclusive possession, being able to maintain privacy and enjoy social relations, and having a legal title to occupy'.[1]

Often both professionals and homeless people can adopt a narrow definition of 'homelessness' as rough sleeping.[2] The popular stereotype of the 'tramp' or 'drifter' remains. However, at the start of the twenty-first century, such a stereotype could not be further from the reality of the lives of the UK homeless drug-using populations who access primary care services daily.

Many homeless drug users reside in their place of birth. Research in Leeds demonstrated that, regardless of age, homeless drug users were more likely than homeless people with alcohol dependence or mental ill health to access primary care in their city of birth.[3] For general practices working with homeless drug users, it will often entail working with people who have grown up in their practice area or locality; whereas the housing situation of some can change frequently, often such change is within the same local geographical area.

It is important for primary healthcare practitioners to realise that health, housing and social needs are interlinked. Provision of effective primary healthcare provision can help break the cycle of chronic homelessness. Adequate housing can provide the homeless drug user with the stability required to facilitate access to primary health care. Chronic homelessness can include movement into or between any of the following housing states:[1,4–6]

▶ 'roofless' describes rough sleepers, newly arrived immigrants, and victims of fire, flood or severe harassment or violence

▶ 'houseless' describes those living in temporary or emergency accommodation (for example night shelters, hostels or refuges) and those released from long-term institutions (for example psychiatric hospitals, prisons, detention centres or community or foster homes with nowhere to go upon release)

▶ 'living in insecure accommodation' includes individuals who are staying with friends or relatives on a temporary or involuntary basis, tenants under notice to quit, those whose security is threatened by violence or threats of violence, or squatters

▶ 'living in inadequate accommodation' includes overcrowded or substandard accommodation. Such homeless people are often 'concealed' (also described as 'hidden') as people involuntarily share accommodation on a long-term basis because they cannot secure or afford separate housing.

The relationship between housing status and drug use

The link between poor housing and ill health has been recognised for well over a century. In the Victorian era, environmental health activists were instrumental in developing housing policy that sought to address the impact of urban slums upon poor health.[7,8]

Since that time the challenge has been to marry the medical intervention centred upon the individual with wider public health interventions to provide healthy housing. This challenge remains today in the health care of homeless drug users.

There is an emerging evidence base describing the relationship between housing status and problematic drug use. Qualitative research has documented a tendency for many drug users to increase drug use when in the hostel environment. This appears to be due in part to being surrounded by drug-using peers.[9] For some, drug use is reduced when rough sleeping owing to reduced financial means. Initiation into injecting heroin instead of smoking it because of the practical difficulties of smoking outdoors in a windy environment has also been described. Some homeless drug users describe a progression to injecting alone once they have acquired stable accommodation. As injecting alone is a risk factor for drug-related death, the move to solitary accommodation as a drug career progresses could in part explain the findings of an increase in the mean age of heroin-related death despite a reduction in the average age of initiation into heroin use.[10,11] Also, homelessness is a risk factor for illicit drug overdose and there is an association whereby drug users at high risk of overdose are likely to witness more overdoses.[12]

Quantitative surveys amongst UK homeless drug users have described the drugs commonly used by homeless people. They include heroin and crack cocaine, and polydrug use is common. However, owing to either unsafe injecting practices or a lifestyle that is not conducive towards maintaining adequate personal hygiene, many drug users have multiple health morbidity. Such morbidity includes:

- ileofemoral deep vein thrombosis due to persistent injecting into the femoral vein

- pulmonary embolus

- blood-borne viruses – hepatitis B, hepatitis C or HIV

- bacterial infections – septicaemia, cerebral abscess, spinal cord abscess, endocarditis, cellulitis and skin abscesses

- also difficulty of many homeless drug users in successfully carrying out routine daily living skills causing common chronic diseases (e.g. epilepsy, diabetes, asthma), which are often more challenging to manage.

Where will homeless drug users access primary care?

Homeless drug users will access primary care in a variety of settings. In part this is a response to barriers towards homeless people accessing mainstream primary care services. Such barriers include practice opening times, appointment procedures and financial disincentives for GPs to work with this patient group.[13]

Discrimination against homeless people can also be a barrier to primary care access and includes inaccurate generalisations that they are violent, antisocial or 'undeserving' of support.[14,15]

Some homeless people face a double risk of discrimination due to age, gender, ethnic background or sexual orientation.[9,16–18] To address such stigma and aid integration of homeless drug users into primary care treatment provision, both legislation and local innovation have helped by providing a variety of effective frameworks for delivering health care to homeless populations.[1,19] Such models entail providing primary care to homeless drug users in the following settings:

- mainstream general practice

- mainstream general practice with a special interest in homelessness

- specialised general practice for homeless people

- provision of primary health care within the secondary care hospital setting.

Mainstream general practice, defined as provision of care through normal registration in a primary care practice, remains the ideal setting for primary care provision for homeless people. It normalises primary care for homeless drug users. Its wide coverage means there is ease of access for homeless drug users, particularly in rural areas.

Because it is often a difficult setting to access for many homeless drug users, particularly when presenting with acute illness, and also for roofless people with uncontrolled problematic drug use, many such drug users present to 'specialised' general practices. These have become more common with primary medical service legislation permitting trusts or independent contractor practices to appoint salaried GPs and other health staff not normally employed in the primary care setting (for example community psychiatric services or client support workers). The strength of such practices is that they can provide more focused and intensive care for large numbers of homeless drug users who have complex multiple morbidity. The centres, however, are concentrated in urban areas and therefore are not a solution to the problem of rural homelessness.

Theoretical arguments against specialised practices for homeless people are that they ghettoise primary care provision and therefore further marginalise homeless people. Current thinking would therefore encourage registration with the specialised general practice at times of health and social crisis to provide early treatment and rehabilitation. Once the acute condition has stabilised and the user is familiar with the primary care setting, registration with mainstream primary care should be encouraged. Often the drug user will require support to attend the new general practice and there is a role for patient/client support workers, or receptionists from the specialised general practice to provide such support. Many of these practices now provide services commissioned by the Primary Care Trust through enhanced services.

Planned primary care provision in the hospital setting is not a common model in the UK. It is more commonly found in Europe, and models vary from a single centralised unit to all hospital departments offering care. Key to the success of such models appears to be social worker support for the homeless person. Such primary care programmes for homeless people have led to a reduction in hospital admissions.[20]

Structured counselling to address problematic drug use

There appears to be a paucity of UK research evaluating the impact of structured counselling approaches to address problematic drug use by homeless people. US research has evaluated behavioural and empowerment drugs health promotion approaches. Common findings are that assertive community treatments retain users in services but do not yield high rates of abstinence,[21] and residential therapeutic communities for those with dual diagnoses result in greater reductions in drug use than community interventions. Both modalities reduce drug use.[22–24]

Limiting disability payments to homeless persons with a dual diagnosis of drug misuse and mental ill health in an effort to reduce drug use does not lead to a reduction in number of substance-using days per month.[25]

Compared with those receiving typical day care programmes, homeless crack cocaine abusers who were randomised to an enhanced day treatment programme, plus abstinent contingent work therapy and housing, had fewer positive cocaine toxicologies, fewer days homeless and more days employed.[26] Behavioural approaches amongst homeless drug users should therefore seek to adopt a non-coercive, harm reduction approach. Where drug users express a wish to achieve abstinence, this is best achieved in a therapeutic community/residential setting.

Key issues in safe prescribing for homeless drug users

Best-practice guidelines for professionals working with drug users, which are applicable to homeless drug-using communities, include GPs only prescribing with the support of a drugs nurse/therapist. The drugs nurse/therapist should offer an adequate assessment to inform an agreed treatment plan prior to initiating substitute opioid medication.[27]

It is important to avoid pressure to prescribe opiates for maintenance other than buprenorphine or methadone maintenance medication, as these are the only opiates that have demonstrated reduced crime and reduced drug use.[28] Prescribing of other opiates should take place only in a research setting.

Some homeless drug users move areas and present to primary care requesting immediate continuation of the prescription prior to assessment. The prescriber should agree to this only once the history has been confirmed with the previous prescriber to minimise the risk of duplicate prescribing. Homeless drug users are at increased risk of drug-related death.[29] Prescribing practice that has the potential to increase the risk of either unintentional or intentional death should be avoided. Such practice would include: concomitant prescription of methadone and benzodiazepines; prescribing without good reason for less frequently than daily pick-up from the pharmacist; not undertaking supervised dispensing of maintenance opiates for at least three months.

Homelessness and criminal justice

Many homeless drug users receiving maintenance therapy spend periods of time in prison. There is a growing evidence base for the effectiveness of prison-based opiate maintenance schemes and therefore maintenance should be continued for such users, particularly if they are on remand or a short sentence. However, mean daily amounts of heroin consumed are usually much lower in the custodial setting than in the community and users are more likely to become abstinent if their detoxification is completed in the prison setting, rather than released part way through a sentence.[30] A recently published US randomised controlled trial recruited 211 users in the prison setting who were randomised to either: counselling in prison, with passive referral to treatment upon release; counselling and transfer (counselling in prison with transfer to methadone maintenance treatment upon release); or counselling and methadone (methadone maintenance and counselling in prison, continued in a community-based methadone maintenance programme upon release). Results showed a higher engagement in treatment and lower proportion of individuals testing positive for illicit opiates at one month in the group who received prison-based methadone maintenance.[31]

The main positive outcomes of opiate replacement therapy (namely a reduction in both illicit drug use and acquisitive crime) are common occurrences in the prison custodial setting. Where maintenance medication is initiated in the prison setting, there is a need to first ensure that there is a community prescriber willing to continue prescribing the medication upon release.

Hospital care and homelessness

Drug users often spend a period of time in the inpatient hospital setting. This can present a dilemma for hospital clinicians, many of whom have limited experience of working with drug users. This dilemma is demonstrated by the case study in Box 21.1. It shows that many drug users present with unusual symptoms as a consequence of injecting. This often necessitates hospital admission. It demonstrates a training need for many hospital colleagues on aspects of drug misuse.

In this case, the patient was discharged on a cocktail of dihydrocodeine and diazepam, a combination for which there is no evidence of effectiveness as maintenance medication.

Clearly there is a need for close communication between GPs and hospital doctors. Despite having serious health problems, many homeless drug users will discharge themselves so as to access drugs to mitigate acute opiate withdrawal symptoms. One of the major positive benefits of replacement opiate maintenance therapy is retention in service provision. Ideally such users should be considered for opiate maintenance therapy. We would argue that the primary goal of such treatment should be retention on the ward until the acute medical condition is controlled.

At the time of writing, there appears to be a dearth of best-practice care pathways for transfer of care between hospital and primary care drug treatment services. It could be argued that hospital addiction clinicians should prioritise the initiation of opiate maintenance therapy for those with acute or multiple medical

Box 21.1 **Case study of care of a homeless drug user while in hospital**

A male resident in a homeless hostel, who has been homeless for 32 years, registered for a new appointment with his GP. He had an eight-year history of intravenous heroin use and was currently injecting into his groin. He presented to his GP with a one-week history of tiredness, malaise and difficulty walking. Examination revealed low-grade pyrexia and reduced power in the lower limbs, associated with paraesthesia to light touch, but no other neurological abnormality. There was evidence of groin injecting but no evidence of infection at the injection sites. The GP was unable to make a definitive diagnosis but referred the patient to the local hospital as an emergency medical admission with a diagnosis of possible Guillain-Barré syndrome. Hospital baseline investigations revealed a raised white cell count and a raised plasma viscosity. A CT scan revealed an extradural thoracic abscess. This was evacuated leaving residual weakness in the lower limbs. While on the ward, he also received a positive diagnosis for hepatitis C. He was discharged on $14 \times 30\,mg$ dihydrocodeine per day and $9 \times 5\,mg$ diazepam tablets per day. The discharge summary to the GP stated that he had been referred to physiotherapy. However, he never received an appointment and when the GP tried to re-refer the patient he was informed that the referral needed to come from the consultant. The GP phoned the consultant's secretary who agreed to raise the matter with the consultant. The secretary phoned the GP the following day and informed him that the consultant did not feel that physiotherapy was necessary. The patient still complained of residual weakness and reduced proprioception in the lower limbs so the GP persisted with a request for physiotherapy. Two weeks later the physiotherapy department accepted the referral.

morbidity. Community addiction clinicians should prioritise such referrals into their services owing to the high level of complex physical morbidity.

Developing integrated working – key principles

In whatever setting homeless drug users receive drug treatment, care will need to be integrated with partner organisations. Key stakeholders include housing, social service, hospital and prison providers. There have been historical barriers to integrated working. Although in some areas collaboration between health and social care organisations has been reasonably good, often housing agencies have been omitted from collaborative working.[32] The following have been described as common threats to collaborative working:

▶ lack of understanding of other agencies, their roles and responsibilities, boundaries between them, and the constraints that others are working under

▶ uncertainty of the services provided by, and personnel within, other agencies

▶ collaboration at strategic level not being implemented or mirrored at service delivery level

▶ difficulties in communication and sharing information between agencies, including false expectations and mistrust of other professional groups

▶ unsuccessful user involvement at strategic level.

Clearly primary care clinical staff taking on roles as board members of primary care organisations, housing, social service or prison agencies can seed significant opportunities for effective partnership working.

Within the confines of the consulting room there is much that the general practitioner or practice team member can do to aid partnership working. One key area is in providing meaningful letters of support for housing. This should take place only when first requested by the housing department. Patient-led requests for housing letters tend not to aid integrated working. Where the patient presents a request to the GP, he or she should be directed to the housing department so that the need for a GP support letter can be assessed. If such a letter is deemed appropriate, the content of the letter can significantly help the homeless drug user.

In England, under the Homeless Act 2002, drug dependence by itself does not qualify as a medical condition granting 'medical priority' for rehousing. Priority can be granted if the drug user is vulnerable as a result of: old age; mental illness or handicap; physical disability or other special reason; fleeing violence (including domestic violence); having spent time in the armed forces, prison or remanded in custody; age 16–17 (unless social services have a responsibility for accommodating); care leavers under the age of 21 who were looked after by social services when they were 16 or 17 (with some limited, uncommon exceptions). Many drug users will be experiencing one or more of these conditions; it is important to highlight this in the medical letter. It is also important to be explicit about the user's drug habit. Being explicit also entails highlighting that you would expect a diagnosis of 'drug dependence' not to be a diagnosis of 'exclusion' from adequate housing.

Many housing departments, housing associations and private landlords are now able to provide all kinds of different supported housing options. This ranges from frequent visits from a client support worker, to shared housing, to semi-independent hostel accommodation. Being explicit in the support letter regarding the drug user's level of competency in carrying out daily living skills can help housing agencies find the most appropriate accommodation to support rehousing of homeless drug users.

At a policy level such work is supported by the recent introduction of a government framework for housing-related support services. This entails local authorities taking over the funding, governance and monitoring of such support services. It is the largest wholesale change to the housing sector in recent years. The ethos is one of a constantly evolving programme, building new partnerships across probation, health and social services. Such programmes at local level will have a great potential to provide an integrated approach to meeting the full range of homeless drug users' basic needs as they seek rehousing.

Research conducted amongst female sex workers in Canada showed that gender-based violence was more common if the workers were homeless, unable to access drug treatment, serviced clients in cars or public spaces, had prior episodes of assault from the police, had drug use paraphernalia confiscated by the police without arrest, or if they moved working areas away from main streets due to policing initiatives.[33]

Further reading

Wright N. *Homelessness: a primary care response.* London: RCGP, 2002.

References

1. Edgar B, Doherty J, Meert H. *Review of Statistics on Homelessness in Europe. Brussels: European Federation of National Organisations Working with the Homeless.* Brussels: FEANTSA, 2003, www.feantsa.org.

2. Hutson S, Liddiard M. *Youth Homelessness: the construction of a social issue.* London: Macmillan, 1994.

3. Tompkins C N, Wright N M J, Sheard L, *et al.* Associations between migrancy, health and homelessness: a cross-sectional study. *Health & Social Care in the Community* 2003; **11(5)**: 446–52.

4. Bramley G, Doogan K, Leather P, *et al.* (eds). *Homelessness and the London Housing Market.* Bristol: School for Advanced Urban Studies, 1988.

5. Connelly J, Crown J. *Homelessness and Ill Health. Report of a working party of the Royal College of Physicians.* London: RCP, 1994.

6. Fitzpatrick S, Kemp P, Klinker S. *Single Homelessness: an overview of research in Britain.* Bristol: Policy Press, 2000.

7. Wright N. *Homelessness: a primary care response.* London: RCGP, 2002.

8. Hawtin M. Collaboration for meeting housing needs. In: P Gill, G de Wildt (eds). *Housing and Health: the role of primary care.* Oxford: Radcliffe Medical Press, 2003, pp. 79–98.

9. Wright N, Oldham N, Jones L. Homelessness and heroin related death: a qualitative study exploring associations. *Drug and Alcohol Review* (in press).

10. Darke S, Ross J. Heroin-related deaths in Southern Western Sydney, Australia 1992–1996. *Drug and Alcohol Review* 1999; **18**: 39–45.

11. Hall W, Darke S. Trends in opiate overdose deaths in Australia 1979–1995. *Drug and Alcohol Dependence* 1998; **52(1)**: 71–7.

12. Bohnert A S, Tracy M, Galea S. Characteristics of drug users who witness many overdoses: implications for overdose prevention. *Drug and Alcohol Dependence* 2012; **120(1–3)**: 168–73.

13. Griffiths S. *Addressing the Health Needs of Rough Sleepers. A paper to the Homelessness Directorate.* London: HMSO, 2002.

14. Riley A J, Harding G, Underwood MR, *et al.* Homelessness: a problem for primary care? *British Journal of General Practice* 2003; **53(491)**: 473–9.

15. Lester H, Bradley C. Barriers to primary healthcare for the homeless: the general practitioner's perspective. *European Journal of General Practice* 2001; **7**: 6–12.

16. Crane M. The associations between mental illness and homelessness among older people: an exploratory study. *Ageing and Mental Health* 1998; **2(3)**: 171–80.

17. Edgar B, Doherty J, Mina-Coull A. *Women and Homelessness in Europe.* Bristol: Policy Press, 2001.

18. Kruks G. Gay and lesbian homeless/street youth: special issues and concerns. *Journal of Adolescent Health* 1991; **12(7)**: 515–18.

19. Crane M, Warnes A M. Primary health care services for single homeless people: defects and opportunities. *Family Practice* 2001; **18(3)**: 272–6.

20. Doering T J, Hermes E, Konitzer M, *et al.* Health situation of homeless in a health care home in Hannover [German]. *Gesundheitswesen* 2002; **64(6)**: 375–82.

21. Meisler N, Blankertz L, Santos A B, *et al.* Impact of assertive community treatment on homeless persons with co-occurring severe psychiatric and substance use disorders. *Community Mental Health Journal* 1997; **33(2)**: 113–22.

22. Conrad K J, Hultman C I, Pope A R, *et al.* Case managed residential care for homeless addicted veterans. Results of a true experiment. *Medical Care* 1998; **36(1)**: 40–53.

23. De Leon G, Sacks S, Staines G, *et al.* Modified therapeutic community for homeless mentally ill chemical abusers: treatment outcomes. *American Journal of Drug and Alcohol Abuse* 2000; **26(3)**: 461–80.

24. Nuttbrock L A, Rahav M, Rivera J J, *et al.* Outcomes of homeless mentally ill chemical abusers in community residences and a therapeutic community. *Psychiatric Services* 1998; **49(1)**: 68–76.

25. Frisman L K, Rosenheck R. The relationship of public support payments to substance abuse among homeless veterans with mental illness. *Psychiatric Services* 1997; **48(6)**: 792–5.

26. Milby J B, Schumacher J E, Raczynski J M, *et al.* Sufficient conditions for effective treatment of substance abusing homeless persons. *Drug and Alcohol Dependence* 1996; **43(1–2)**: 39–47.

27. National Treatment Agency for Substance Misuse. *Models of Care for Treatment of Adult Drug Misusers.* London: NTA, 2002.

28. Mattick R P, Kimber J, Breen C, *et al.* Buprenorphine maintenance versus placebo or methadone maintenance for opioid dependence. In: *The Cochrane Database of Systematic Reviews.* Issue 2. Chichester: John Wiley, 2003.

29. Home Office. *Reducing Drug Related Deaths. A report by the Advisory Council on Misuse of Drugs.* London: HMSO, 2000.

30. Wright N M J, Sheard L, Adams C E, *et al.* Comparison of methadone and buprenorphine for opiate detoxification (LEEDS trial): a randomised controlled trial. *British Journal of General Practice* 2011; **61(593)**: e772–80.

31. Kinlock T W, Gordon M S, Schwartz R P, *et al.* A randomized clinical trial of methadone maintenance for prisoners: results at 1-month post-release. *Drug and Alcohol Dependence* 2007; **91(2–3)**: 220–7.

32. Arblaster L, Conway J, Foreman A, *et al. Asking the Impossible: inter-agency working to address the housing, health and social care needs of people in ordinary housing.* Bristol: Policy Press/Joseph Rowntree Foundation, 1996.

33. Shannon K, Kerr T, Strathdee SA, *et al.* Prevalence and structural correlates of gender based violence among a prospective cohort of female sex workers. *British Medical Journal* 2009; **339**: b2939.

CHAPTER 22

Drug misuse, dual diagnosis and wider co-morbid illness

Rajan Chawla, Ed Day and Clare Gerada

IN THIS CHAPTER

Definition || Relationship between addiction and mental health problems || What is the role of the primary care practitioner? || Prevalence || Patterns of drug and alcohol use || Clinical implications || Reasons for substance use || Assessment of co-morbidity || Treatment approaches || Depression with alcohol misuse or dependence || Depression with opioid dependence || Cocaine and depression || Anxiety and alcohol/drug dependence || Summary of treatment strategies || Conclusion

Definition

The term 'dual diagnosis', or co-morbidity, has risen to higher prominence in recent years. The definition tends to be applied to people with a diagnosed mental illness, usually psychotic illness, who also experience difficulties with alcohol and/or drug use, as well as to people with problematic alcohol and drug use who develop symptoms of mental illness, perhaps as a result of their substance use.

Unfortunately the term is imprecise, as these patients seldom have just two problems. The combination of psychiatric and drug/alcohol problems means that individuals are at risk from a number of problems, ranging from physical ill heath, homelessness, unemployment, social exclusion and so on. The term 'multiple morbidity', suggested by Wright and colleagues,[1] might more accurately describe the common predicament of patients who have more than one health problem. For the sake of brevity the term dual diagnosis will be used in this chapter.

Relationship between addiction and mental health problems

The relationship between those with addiction and mental health problems is complex, with possibilities for the following interrelationships:

▸ a primary psychiatric illness precipitating or leading to substance use

▸ substance use worsening or altering the course of a psychiatric illness, for example intoxication and/or substance dependence leading to psychological symptoms

▸ substance use and/or withdrawal leading to psychiatric symptoms or illnesses

▸ substances, particularly alcohol, cannabinoids, hallucinogens and stimulants (especially amphetamines and cocaine), that can produce psychotic symptoms directly without mental illness.

What is the role of the primary care practitioner?

Why should the primary care practitioner need to know anything about patients with dual diagnosis? After all, these patients have complex needs that should place their management outside the normal confines of general practice. It is the authors' belief that the more complex the patients' problems, the greater their need for highly coordinated care, and primary care services are ideally placed to direct this.

Good primary care services are vital to make sure that these patients do not slip through the net of multiple carers and services. It is the very complexity of their problems, requiring many contacts with health and social care professionals, that makes primary care such an important part of their overall management, able to provide continuity throughout their care. This does not negate the key working role undertaken by specialist mental health or dual-diagnosis services, or the importance of other services in providing valuable input, as ultimately it is through effective shared care that these patients are best served.

Box 22.1   **What primary care can offer patients with complex co-morbidities**

✓ Continuity of care.

✓ General medical services.

✓ Enhanced services for coexisting physical problems.

✓ Coordination between services.

✓ Crisis intervention.

✓ Containment.

✓ Care to the family.

✓ Advocacy.

✓ Medication review.

✓ Help with housing and benefits issues.

Prevalence

Most large-scale epidemiological work has been conducted in the USA. The US Epidemiological Catchment Area (ECA) study surveyed over 20,000 people living in both community and psychiatric settings.[2] Substance use problems were more prevalent among individuals with mental illness than among the general population, with mental illness, on average, doubling the chance of a coexistent substance use problem. The ECA study also reported the chances of lifetime substance use by diagnosis as follows:

▸ schizophrenia, 47%

▸ any bipolar disorder, 56%

▸ any affective disorder, 32%

▸ any anxiety disorder, 24%.

Other US epidemiological research suggests that both substance use and mental health disorders are more common than most clinicians believe, with dual diagnosis becoming the rule rather than the exception. The National Co-morbidity Survey highlighted that 41–66% of individuals with a lifetime substance use disorder also had at least one other mental health disorder. Likewise, of those with a lifetime mental disorder around 50% also had a lifetime history of at least one substance use disorder.[3]

However, rates of co-morbidity vary considerably between geographical areas (e.g. they are higher in cities) and between treatment settings (i.e. inpatient mental health units, community mental health teams and general population settings). It is possible that levels and pattern of illicit drug use in the USA, combined with the specific elements of the US welfare and healthcare system, may lead to different results in other parts of the world. European studies are relatively rare, but a systematic review of rates of co-morbidity of functional psychotic illness (i.e. schizophrenia or schizoaffective disorder) and drug and alcohol misuse or dependence in UK settings found broad differences in the reported rates, with most studies reporting 20–37% in mental health settings and 6–15% in addiction treatment settings.[4] These rates were therefore not as high as in US studies, although were higher in inpatient or crisis team settings (38–50%) and forensic settings. Rates were highest in inner-city samples, and some ethnic groups were over-represented.

Using the General Practice Research Database in work commissioned by the Department of Health, Frischer *et al.* looked at the prevalence of dual diagnosis in primary care in England and Wales from 1993 to 1998.[5] The database recorded 1.4 million patient contacts with 230 practices. They checked for recorded individuals with both substance misuse and a psychiatric disorder, and found that the rate for dual diagnosis increased by 62% during this period, with significant increases in schizophrenic disorder (128%), paranoia (144%) and psychotic disorder (147%). The authors also noted a regional variation, with a 300% increase in the Northern and Yorkshire district and a slow increase in London. This study identified alcohol and cannabis to be the drugs most frequently used by individuals with schizophrenia, and smaller UK studies have reported the same.

Patterns of drug and alcohol use

The European Monitoring Centre for Drugs and Drug Addiction (EMCDDA) is a European Union agency that provides Member States with a factual overview of illicit drug problems. The EMCDDA annual report in 2011 noted that prevalence levels of drug use were high in Europe by historical standards, but they are rising.[6] In the UK, there has even been some evidence of a slight decline in use of the most popular substances. The 2011 country overview for the UK[7] contains information about prevalence of illicit drugs among the adult population from household surveys such as the British Crime Survey (BCS). Data are presented in Table 22.1 and show that 36.4% of respondents had tried any illegal drug at least once in their lives. In 2009/10, last-year prevalence of cannabis use was reported to be 6.6%, showing a steady decline in cannabis use since 2003/4 (10.8%). Furthermore, despite an increase in cocaine use between 1996 and 2008/9, the most recent survey shows a decline in last-year prevalence down to levels observed between 2003/4 and 2007/8.

The European Schools Project on Alcohol and other Drugs (ESPAD) survey provides data for students aged 15–16 every four years. In England, ESPAD data showed that lifetime use of cannabis decreased from 41% in 1995 to 35% in 1999, rose again to 38% in 2003 and decreased to 29% in 2007. Last-year prevalence of cannabis use was reported by 22% of the students in 2007, compared with 31% in 2003 and 35% in 1995.[8]

Research findings concerning the substances preferred by people with mental illness are equivocal. An early study reviewed patterns of drug use among people with schizophrenia. A propensity to use stimulants as a possible mechanism for alleviating negative symptoms was reported.[9] Currently cannabis appears to be the illicit substance most commonly used by people with mental illness in the UK, mirroring the high use by those without mental health problems shown in Table 22.1. The EMCDDA highlights a rapid development in the use of synthetic drugs (such as mephadrone) and a general trend towards the use of a wider set of substances.[6] As any drug becomes more readily available it should be expected that its increasing levels of use will permeate many existing drug cultures, including those with which psychiatric patients have contact.

Table 22.1   **Epidemiology of illicit drug use in the UK**

	Year	Country data	EU range	
			Min.	**Max.**
Recent school surveys (15–16-year-olds)				
Lifetime prevalence of cannabis use	2007	29%	4%	45%
Lifetime prevalence of cocaine use	2007	5%	1%	5%
Prevalence in young adults (15–34-year-olds)				
Lifetime cannabis use	2008	38.8%	2.9%	45.5%
Last-year cannabis use	2008	12%	0.9%	21.6%
Lifetime cocaine use	2008	13.4%	0.1%	13.6%
Last-year cocaine use	2008	4.8%	0.1%	4.8%
Prevalence in all adults (15–64-year-olds)				
Lifetime cannabis use	2008	30.6%	1.5%	32.5%
Last-year cannabis use	2008	6.6%	0.4%	14.3%
Lifetime cocaine use	2008	8.8%	0.1%	10.2%
Last-year cocaine use	2008	2.5%	0%	2.7%
Problem drug use – rate per 1000 population aged 15 to 64 years old	2008	10.1	0.5	10.1
Injecting drug use – rate per 1000 population aged 15 to 64 years old	2008	3.7	0.22	15.1
Drug-related deaths	2008	2481	6	2481
Number of new clients entering treatment	2009	45,048	21	45,048
New clients entering treatment				
% opioids as primary drug	2009	41%	3.1%	92.8%
% cocaine as primary drug	2009	21.8%	0%	56%
% cannabis as primary drug	2009	28%	1.9%	80.2%
Number of all clients in substitution treatment	**2009**	**143,219**	**189**	**137,541**

Source: adapted from the EMCDDA 2011 Country Overview for the UK.[7]

It should also be noted that it is not just illicit drugs that may be used problematically. Patients with schizophrenia have a three-fold greater risk of developing alcohol dependence than individuals without a mental illness.[10]

Co-morbid mental health and substance use problems are especially prevalent in the homeless and rough sleepers, and in offenders, including prisoners. There are significant differences between men and women in their patterns of substance use and psychiatric co-morbidity.[11] For example:

▶ women who use substances are significantly more likely than other women or men to have experienced sexual, physical and/or emotional abuse as children

▶ substance use lifestyles can impact on women's sexual health and establish a pattern of 're-victimisation', e.g. women are more likely to fund their habit through prostitution and hence are more likely to place themselves at risk of violence, assault and abuse

▶ women are more likely to present at mental health or primary care services for psychological difficulties rather than for any associated substance use problem

▶ women tend to access alcohol and drug services later than men and this may explain their more severe presentation

▶ women may have children, or want children, and this can deter them from contact with statutory services for fear that their children will be removed from them, thus they are likely to present later for care at a time when their use has become more problematic.

Clinical implications

Box 22.2 **Case study**

> *Charlie is 35 years old and lives with his brother. Charlie has been diagnosed as having schizophrenia and has been started on antipsychotic medication by the community mental health team. Both he and his brother use heroin (smoking) and cannabis, recently using crack cocaine too. Both came to you requesting help. They felt that life as users was getting dangerous, with Charlie having been assaulted several times and finding that the crack was 'getting to his head'. Their housing situation is relatively stable though they often have unwelcome guests.*
>
> ✓ Where do you start?
>
> ✓ Who should be involved in the care of Charlie and his brother?
>
> ✓ What risks does Charlie face?

The implications for people with mental health problems who also misuse drugs and/or alcohol can be serious and it is important that the primary care practitioner is aware of them. Substance use by individuals with psychiatric disorders is associated with significantly poorer outcomes, including:[12–15]

▸ worsening psychiatric symptoms

▸ increased rates of suicidal behaviour

▸ increased rates of violence

▸ poor medication adherence and increased risk of HIV infection

▸ higher service use and higher rates of homelessness.

Both mental health problems and substance use are associated with higher rates of physical illness, including complications related to cigarette smoking, poor nutrition and infections, including tuberculosis. The primary care practitioner has an invaluable role in making sure that none of these problems is ignored.

Reasons for substance use

People with mental illness are more likely to be misusing drugs and/or alcohol than people without. As described above, the frequency with which substance misuse and schizophrenia present together is many times higher than would be expected by chance. There is no single explanation for this association, and several theories have been proposed to explain the high rates of substance use among people with schizophrenia.[16] The NICE guidelines on psychosis with coexisting substance misuse highlight three main theories to explain this:[17]

Substance misuse precipitates or causes psychosis

Many psychoactive substances are known to produce psychotic symptoms when taken in large enough doses, e.g. stimulants, cannabis and hallucinogens. However, these symptoms tend to only follow significant doses of the drug, to be dose related, and to resolve rapidly when the drug is removed. Psychotic symptoms induced by drugs differ in quality from those in schizophrenia, and tend to be associated with prominent agitation and confusion.[17]

There is now a significant body of epidemiological evidence that cannabis use plays a causal role in the aetiology of some psychotic illnesses. It is not an essential or sufficient risk factor as not all schizophrenic patients have used cannabis and the majority of cannabis users do not develop schizophrenia. However, a systematic review of the current literature suggests that the risk of psychosis is increased by nearly 40% in people who have used cannabis, increasing to 50–200% in heavy users.[18] The potency of cannabis used may be associated with the degree of harmful effects,[19] and high-potency varieties of cannabis such as 'skunk' have three or four times more delta-9-tetrahydrocannabinol (THC) than traditional marijuana or resin.[20] Prospective studies show that first-time use of cannabis during adolescence is associated with an increased risk of psychotic symptoms in adulthood,[21, 22] possibly because the adolescent brain is still developing. Those with an established vulnerability to psychosis are also more at risk (i.e. a strong family history).

Some commentators now believe that there is sufficient evidence to warn young people that cannabis use will increase their risk of psychosis later in life.[23] If there is a true causal relationship between cannabis use and psychosis, an increased risk of 40% would mean 14% of psychotic outcomes (i.e. nearly 800 cases per year) in the UK might not occur if cannabis was not used.[23] On the other hand, if cannabis causes schizophrenia in those who would not otherwise ever have the disease the prevalence of schizophrenia should have increased with the prevalence of cannabis used.[17] Hickman *et al.* have calculated that 1360 men and 2480 women aged 20–24 would have to be prevented from smoking cannabis in order to prevent one case of schizophrenia.[24]

Psychosis causes substance misuse

This is commonly known as the 'self-medication' hypothesis, and the idea that illicit drugs are used to cope with the distressing symptoms of psychosis is compatible with much clinical experience. Antipsychotic medication may also worsen the situation as it blocks the dopaminergic reward systems in the brain, and substance use may act to counteract this effect. However, it is also well documented that many people experience a worsening of their symptoms after substance use, and there is strong evidence that substance use provokes relapse and poorer outcomes than in those with psychosis alone.[25] Substance misuse is also rarely specific to particular symptoms, and degree of use has not been shown to be related to symptom severity.

Drugs may be used to alleviate general low mood. The experience of suffering from psychosis includes stigma, social exclusion, loss of functioning and financial problems, and substances may provide short-term relief for these chronic problems. This is a population at the margins of society and people may feel more accepted in the drug-using population. Their socioeconomic situation too may mean that they are housed in areas where drug misuse is more common

A common cause for both disorders

There has been recent interest in a proposed gene–environment interaction involving the catechol-O-methyltransferase gene, suggesting a common genetic risk factor for both psychosis and substance misuse.[26] However, current evidence

414

suggests that this relationship is too non-specific to be causal.[17] Further research has proposed that abnormalities in the hippocampus and frontal lobes may cause symptoms of schizophrenia and these areas also provide positive reinforcement of drug reward and reduce inhibition of drug-seeking behaviour.[17] People with antisocial personality disorder tend to develop both psychosis and substance misuse disorder at a younger age.

Assessment of co-morbidity

GPs are commonly the first healthcare professionals that individuals, families, carers or significant others will choose to consult, and they often have a long-term relationship with and perspective on people and families on their list. They are therefore in an ideal position to detect the gradual decline in functioning that may be the first signs of a psychotic illness. General practice and other primary care services play a key role in early identification and appropriate referral, with full assessment of psychosis and harmful substance misuse taking place in secondary care mental health or addictions services.[27]

It is important for the GP to maintain a high index of suspicion for either substance misuse in people with psychosis, or mental illness in people who misuse substances. Such is the frequency of co-morbidity of the two conditions, initial assessment for the other disorder should always take place when psychosis or substance misuse is detected. A key early task is to distinguish between substance-induced and substance-related psychiatric disorders, and it is advisable to allow three to four weeks of abstinence before making a diagnosis of mental health disorder. A complete substance history should be obtained, with urinalysis and blood tests if possible.

The assessment should elucidate the individual's pattern of substance use, its context, severity, risk and associated needs. These aspects of use can be obtained by history taking in the following areas:

▶ *patterns of use* – the amounts of each substance used, frequency of use, length of time used and by which route of administration

▶ *context of use* – personal and environmental factors that may be associated with an individual's drug use, including peer group attachments, positive and negative expectations of use, and experiences of physical and/or psychological dependence

▶ *severity of use* – patterns of use can give some indication of severity of dependence. This can be specified with instruments designed to gauge severity of alcohol use,[28] drug use [29,30] and, more appropriately, substance use among individuals with serious mental illness [31]

▶ assessment of risks – including suicidal behaviour, aggressive or antisocial behaviour,[32] blood-borne infections from sharing injecting equipment, risk of accidents, and potential harms to family and children. The safety of prescribing a particular medication must be determined with regard to drug–drug interactions and how the medication is delivered or monitored.

It will usually be helpful to make an assessment of the person's social support network of family, friends and co-workers, and the degree to which these networks are predicated around substance use activities. Families, carers or significant others may also need an assessment of their needs.

Exclusion of physical causes for presenting symptoms is a key role (including acute intoxication, withdrawal and side effects from medications), as is the management of physical co-morbidities such as liver damage, blood-borne viruses, cognitive changes and nutritional deficiencies.

Although accurate diagnosis of all co-morbid conditions is important, clinical decision making should be focused on supporting the attainment of individual goals and identification and treatment of all modifiable and non-biological factors. Cosci *et al.* advocate the use of macro- and micro-analysis, staging and evaluation of subclinical symptoms in order to enhance the diagnostic process. Without this broad, holistic background there may be a danger of concluding that two subjects satisfying the diagnostic criteria for the same substance use disorder and co-morbid psychiatric disorder may benefit from the same therapeutic approach although they have different complaints and associated 'ailments'.[33]

Treatment approaches

Practitioners need to have a realistic and long-term view of treatment and be aware of the range of approaches that may be necessary. The Cognitive-Behavioural Integrated Treatment Approach (C-BIT) was developed in the UK and provides a useful structure for planning and delivering treatment.[34] The overall objective of the approach is to negotiate and facilitate some positive change in the client's problematic drug or alcohol use. There are five phases to treatment:

▶ **assessment phase** – screening and assessment

▶ **treatment phase 1** – engagement and building motivation to change

▶ **treatment phase 2** – negotiating some behaviour change

▶ **treatment phase 3** – early relapse prevention

▶ **treatment phase 4** – relapse prevention and relapse management.

C-BIT is designed to be delivered flexibly, allowing the clinician to conduct this work in the time available to him or her and over whatever period is appropriate to the client. In addition to elements of Motivational Interviewing (MI), Cognitive Behavioural Therapy and relapse prevention, there is also the option to incorporate skills building and work with families and social network members. It is therefore a practical approach that incorporates many of the general principles of effective treatment.

Which do you treat first?

Management should involve the two problematic elements: treating the substance misuse and treating any coexisting mental health problem.

The NICE guidelines for the treatment of dual diagnosis highlight the challenge faced by clients in negotiating the varying clinical models used in different parts of the care system, particularly between substance misuse specialty services and the mainstream mental health services.[17] This has been compounded by the two services being funded and commissioned separately, and variation and confusion over which service holds clinical responsibility for people with differing relative severities of each condition.

Historically, three approaches to delivering services to patients with dual diagnosis have been described:

Sequential treatment

This addresses the more acute problem first, the other problem receiving greater attention later. This model is commonly used in acute hospitals, where, for example, little attention would be paid to substance use in a patient exhibiting florid psychosis.

Parallel treatment

This addresses both disorders simultaneously but in different settings and often by different services.

Integrated treatment

Both problems are dealt with together, in the same setting. This method of service delivery is reported to be associated with the best outcome.

A Cochrane review of different interventions found little evidence to support the effectiveness of any particular treatment, or to recommend one approach over any other.[35] The research suggests a growing agreement that integrated mental health and substance use services offer a more tolerant, non-confrontational approach for patients and are probably the best and most appropriate way forward. Different models exist that vary according to the psychiatric disorder, but the current preferred treatment model in England for treatment of psychosis with co-occurring substance misuse is 'mainstreaming', i.e. overall responsibility is taken by the mental health team, with clinical input and training from substance misuse specialists.[11] The GP with a Special Interest (GPwSI) may have an important role in determining which service is commissioned. Whatever model is used, a most important aspect of any service is the ability to be flexible and to offer services that meet the needs of that individual patient, at the time he or she presents.

Champney-Smith makes the point that, whatever the model of service provided, there are a number of steps that should be considered in order to maximise the effectiveness of treatment: [32]

▸ comprehensive assessments of both mental health and substance use problems

▸ training for mental health workers in the recognition and management of substance use problems

▸ training for substance use workers in the recognition and management of mental health problems

▸ services that are non-judgemental, flexible and take account of the principles of harm minimisation

▸ assertive outreach with appropriate case loads

▸ clear understanding of roles and responsibilities

▸ good liaison between agencies, clearly identifying who has the lead

▸ development of care pathways

▸ evaluation of new services using a range of outcome measures.

NICE Clinical Guideline 120 produced a care pathway for people with psychosis and coexisting substance misuse (see Figure 22.1). GPwSIs may have a role in supporting patients with dual diagnosis, helping them move across the many interfaces of care, but all primary care practitioners will play an important role.

Depression with alcohol misuse or dependence

Alcohol dependence and depression often coexist. The dilemma facing clinicians is which to treat first; it is not always simple or obvious. In this situation it is good practice to assist the patient to withdraw from alcohol as the first line of treatment and then to reassess the mental state. It is difficult to assess a person's mental state accurately when he or she is drinking heavily. Alcohol can both cause and mask

Figure 22.1 **Adult care pathway for substance misuse with coexisting psychosis**

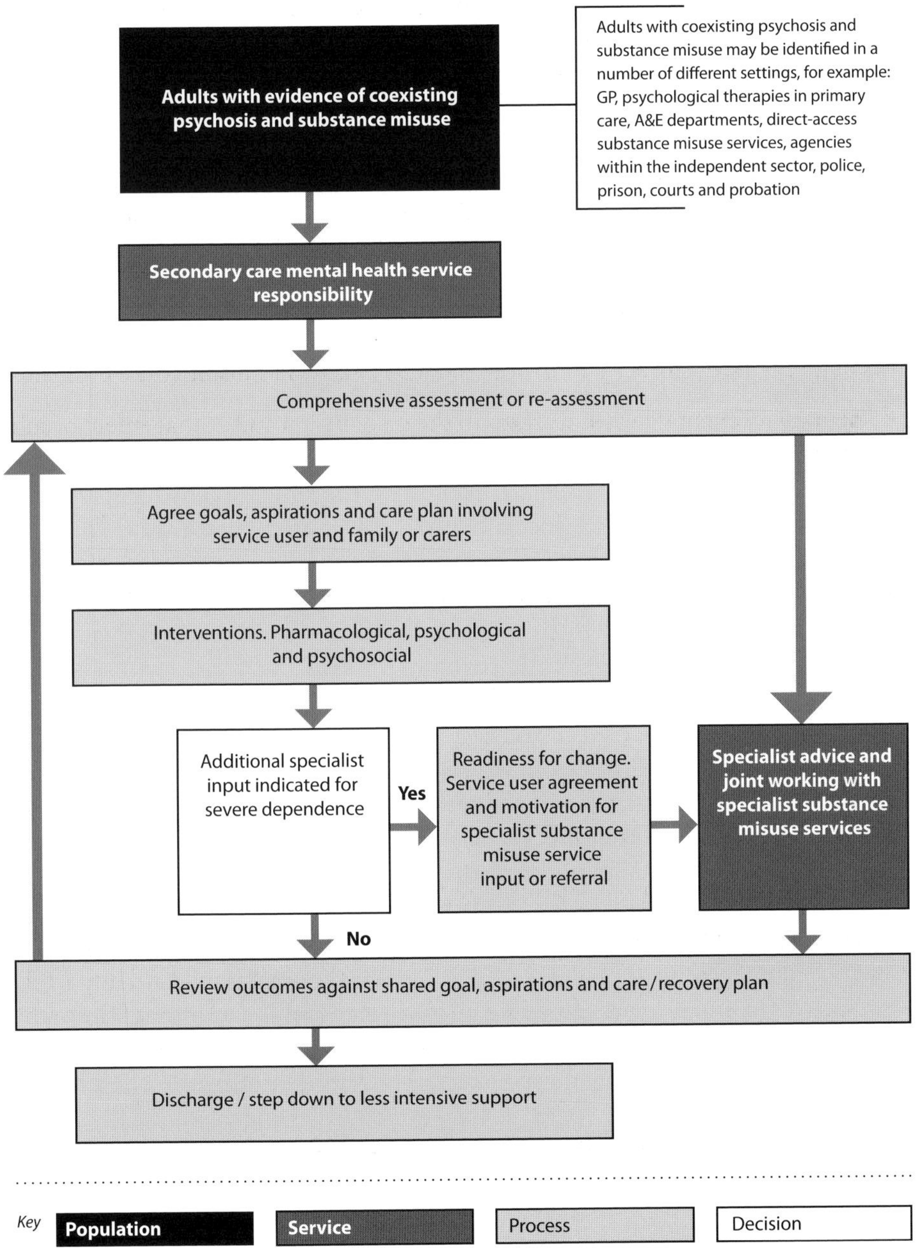

Key

| Population | Service | Process | Decision |

underlying mental health problems. It is likely that alcohol misuse has contributed to the depressive features and once abstinence has been achieved that the depressive symptoms will significantly reduce.

Antidepressant medication is effective in treating mood disorders, but has fewer clear-cut effects on drinking outcomes. Improvement in drinking outcomes is related to improvement in depression, and the best results have come from studies combing SSRI medication with psychosocial interventions, e.g. Cognitive Behavioural Therapy. The prescribing of antidepressants for patients who continue to drink needs to be done with caution. Tricyclic antidepressants (TCA) are best avoided completely owing to potentially serious interactions with alcohol, including cardiotoxicity and death in overdose.

Depression with opioid dependence

As with alcohol dependence, opioid use is a significant risk factor for the development of depression and may persist even when the patient is abstinent. Patients withdrawing from opioids, especially methadone, often report dysthymia and depressed mood, as do patients on buprenorphine.

For long-term users, the loss of not only the drug but also of the lifestyle involved in taking drugs (which can be a full-time occupation) leaves them empty and deflated. Coming off drugs also exposes the losses associated with a lifetime of drug taking: the years spent seeking and using illicit substances rather than pursuing relationships, education and employment.

There are limited studies from which to derive recommendations, and most have focused on patients on methadone maintenance. While primary treatments such as opioid substitution therapy or residential rehabilitation have been associated with improvements in depressive symptoms, there is no good evidence to support the effectiveness of antidepressants.[36] However, Nunes and Levin report that antidepressants may have an indirect effect in reducing substance use through their effects on depression.[37] Perhaps the most important impact the primary care practitioner can make is 'being there' and continuing to provide regular support, certainly for the first six months following abstinence.

Where patients continue to use opioids (prescribed or otherwise) as with concurrent alcohol misuse, TCAs are not recommended owing to potentially serious interactions including cardiotoxicity and death in overdose.

Cocaine and depression

As Chapter 11 dealing with cocaine addiction discussed, depression is a common feature of cocaine use and can be so severe as to risk deliberate self-harm. As with other drugs of abuse, achieving abstinence or minimising misuse is critical in trying to improve mood. Antidepressants may directly compensate for cocaine-related reduction in neurotransmitters such as dopamine, serotonin and noradrenaline.

In all pharmacological studies, the importance of psychosocial interventions has been emphasised and should be addressed since there is no robust evidence showing pharmacotherapy is effective. Torrens *et al.* suggest that antidepressants are mildly effective in reducing depressive symptoms but have no impact on cocaine use.[36] TCAs are not recommended owing to potentially serious interactions including cardiotoxicity and death in overdose.

Anxiety and alcohol / drug dependence

Because anxiety is a feature of alcohol withdrawal, waiting until the acute withdrawal period is over for a clearer assessment is critical. There is limited knowledge about treating this co-morbid condition. Tricyclic antidepressants have the most evidence for treatment of anxiety disorders, but as mentioned previously their high toxicity and extensive side effect profile limit their use in practice. SSRIs and venlafaxine are therefore the treatment of choice.

Prescribing benzodiazepines for anxiety in patients who currently misuse alcohol, or have done so previously, is not generally recommended. Abstinent alcohol-dependent patients may be at greater risk of benzodiazepine abuse and dependence owing to greater rewarding effects. Those patients who are severely dependent, with antisocial personality disorder or with polysubstance misuse, are most at risk of abusing benzodiazepines. There is evidence to suggest that, for those who are less severely dependent, benzodiazepine prescribing may not result in abuse.[38]

How should you treat anxiety in substance-misusing patients? Should they be denied benzodiazepines and so risk under-treatment, or be prescribed benzodiazepines for the anxiolytic effect and risk contributing to addiction? There is no definitive answer and, although most benzodiazepine prescriptions are not misused,[39] a history of alcohol and drug misuse suggests high potential for benzodiazepine misuse.

Substance misusers may ingest benzodiazepines for recreational purposes, and it is worth remembering that 30–50% of alcoholics undergoing detoxification and 44% of intravenous drug abusers may also be misusing benzodiazepines.[40] Benzodiazepines are cross-tolerant with alcohol, and alcoholics may use them with alcohol or as a substitute when alcohol is unavailable. They may also self-medicate with benzodiazepines to ease alcohol's withdrawal symptoms. Opiate, amphetamine and cocaine misusers may use benzodiazepines with their drugs of choice, as may younger abusers of MDMA ('ecstasy') and LSD.

Even patients who begin taking benzodiazepines for legitimate reasons may end up misusing them. In one study of 2600 patients prescribed diazepam, up to 60% had misused and/or become dependent.[41] Long-term users of prescribed benzodiazepines often develop tolerance and may escalate their doses to get the same desired effect. If their supply is threatened, these patients may seek benzodiazepines illicitly. Benzodiazepines may enhance or prolong the elation ('high') associated with other drugs or mitigate the depression ('crash') that follows a stimulant 'high'. Sometimes benzodiazepines are the drug of choice, as high doses of potent, short-acting agents may provide a stimulant 'high'.

Prescribing benzodiazepines to substance misusers is not absolutely contraindicated, despite an elevated relative risk of misuse or dependence. In the absence of convincing data, physicians must decide on a case-by-case basis the merits of using benzodiazepines to treat anxiety in substance abusers. However, they should not routinely be prescribed for co-morbid anxiety conditions in the primary care setting. Practical treatment algorithms for benzodiazepine misusers presenting with anxiety are available.[42]

Non-pharmacological treatments have been shown to reduce substance use and control anxiety in some studies. These include Cognitive Behavioural Therapy, motivational enhancement therapy, interpersonal therapy and brief dynamic therapy, among others. Their use requires specific training or referral to more experienced colleagues. For information on these treatments, consult the websites of the National Institute on Drug Abuse (www.drugabuse.gov/) and National Institute on Alcohol Abuse and Alcoholism (www.niaaa.nih.gov/). Group and self-help therapies such as Alcoholics Anonymous or Narcotics Anonymous have also been shown to reduce substance use.

Summary of treatment strategies

Kelly *et al.* have identified a number of key evidence-based principles for managing dual diagnosis (See Box 22.3).[43]

Conclusion

Patients with coexisting serious mental/physical problems and substance use problems place great challenges on treatment services, including primary care services. As a group they are more difficult to treat and manage because of their higher level of physical, social and psychological impairment. Gaining compliance with taking medication can also be a problem and reduce the chance of improvement. Keeping these patients engaged is perhaps the greatest impact that primary care can make, so that primary care practitioners, in partnership

Box 22.3 **Key evidence-based principles for treating substance-misusing patients with co-morbid psychiatric disorders** [43]

✓ A multifaceted approach is the most effective strategy for treating co-morbidity, i.e. a combination of psychological therapy + pharmacotherapy + behavioural treatment.

✓ Severe conditions should be matched to higher-intensity treatments to maximise psychiatric and substance-related outcomes.

✓ It is important to gain some control over substance dependence in order to assess depressive or anxiety-related symptoms. Partial or full hospitalisation can be very useful in this respect, as can behavioural strategies such as contingency management that don't rely on insight.

✓ Patients maintain improvements longer in outpatient treatment when abstinence is achieved early on, but this may be difficult to obtain. Non-substance-related pathology must not be neglected early on in treatment, e.g. improving depression and post-traumatic stress disorder precedes improvement of substance use disorder.

✓ The therapist relationship is the bedrock of effective treatment planning, and techniques such as MI can be useful in enhancing the therapeutic alliance.

✓ Combinations of therapies are most effective, e.g. MI, contingency management and 12-Step approaches

✓ Research on all substances of misuse suggests that the longer a patient spends in treatment, the better the outcome.

✓ Treatment effects decrease with time, so low-intensity treatment over a prolonged period of time may be the most cost-effective approach.

✓ Medication is useful in treating the symptoms of mental health disorders, but extrapyramidal side effects have an impact on medication compliance and treatment retention, and so should be minimised wherever possible.

---

with their specialist colleagues, can provide these patients with effective care. Too many dual-diagnosis patients fall through the net as treatment services pass responsibility to each other. A primary care practitioner is in the obvious position to prevent that.

Further reading

Department of Health. *Mental Health Policy Implementation Guide: dual diagnosis good practice.* London: DH, 2002, www.dh.gov.uk/en/Publicationsandstatistics/Publications/PublicationsPolicyAndGuidance/DH_4009058   [accessed November 2012].

Graham H. *Cognitive-Behavioural Integrated Treatment (C-BIT). A treatment manual for substance misuse in people with severe mental health problems.* Chichester: John Wiley & Sons, 2004.

National Institute for Health and Clinical Excellence. *Clinical Guideline 120, Psychosis with Coexisting Substance Misuse.* London: NICE, 2011, http://guidance.nice.org.uk/CG120 [accessed November 2012].

Rassool H. *Dual Diagnosis: substance use and psychiatric disorders.* Oxford: Blackwell, 2001.

Ziedonis D, Day E, O'Hea EL, *et al.* Treatment of co-occurring psychiatric and substance use disorders. In: P Tyrer, KR Silk (eds). *Cambridge Textbook of Effective Treatments in Psychiatry.* Cambridge: Cambridge University Press, 2008, pp. 442–58.

References

1. Wright N, Smeeth L, Heath I. Moving beyond single and dual diagnosis in general practice: many patients have multiple morbidities, and their needs have to be addressed. *British Medical Journal* 2003; **326(7388)**: 512–14.

2. Regier D, Farmer M, Rae D, *et al.* Comorbidity of mental disorders with alcohol and other drug use: results from the Epidemiologic Catchment Area (ECA) Study. *Journal of the American Medical Association* 1990; **264(19)**: 2511–18.

3. Kessler R C, Nelson C B, McGonagle K A, *et al.* The epidemiology of co-occurring addictive and mental disorders: implications for prevention and service utilization. *American Journal of Orthopsychiatry* 1996; **66(1)**: 17–31.

4. Carra G, Johnson S. Variations in rates of comorbid substance use in psychosis between mental health settings and geographical areas in the UK: a systematic review. *Social Psychiatry and Psychiatric Epidemiology* 2009; **44(6)**: 429–47.

5. Frischer M, Hickman M, Kraus L, *et al.* A comparison of different methods for estimating the prevalence of problematic drug use in Great Britain. *Addiction* 2001; **96(10)**: 1465–76.

6. European Monitoring Centre for Drugs and Drug Addiction. *Annual Report 2011: the state of the drugs problem in Europe.* Lisbon: EMCDDA, 2011.

7. European Monitoring Centre for Drugs and Drug Addiction. EMCDDA 2011 Country Overview for the UK, www.emcdda.europa.eu/publications/country-overviews/uk/data-sheet   [accessed November 2012].

8. Davies C, English L, Lodwick A, *et al. United Kingdom. New developments, trends and in-depth information on selected issues. 2010 national report (2009 data) to the EMCDDA.* Lisbon: EMCDDA, 2010.

9. Schneier F, Siris S. A review of psychoactive substance use and abuse in schizophrenia: patterns of drug choice. *Journal of Nervous and Mental Disease* 1987; **175(11)**: 641–52.

10. Crawford V. Comorbidity of substance use and psychiatric disorders. *Current Opinion in Psychiatry* 1996; **9**: 231–4.

11. Department of Health. *Mental Health Policy Implementation Guide: dual diagnosis good practice guide.* London: DH, 2002.

12. Carey M, Carey K, Meisley A. Psychiatric symptoms in mentally ill chemical abusers. *Journal of Nervous and Mental Disease* 1991; **179(3)**: 136–8.

13. Drake R, Wallach M. Substance abuse among the chronic mentally ill. *Hospital Community Psychiatry* 1989; **40(10)**: 1041–6.

14. Kelly J, Heckman T, Helfrich S, *et al*. HIV risk factors and behaviors among men in a Milwaukee homeless shelter. *American Journal of Public Health* 1995; **85(11)**: 465–8.

15. Smith J, Frazer S, Boer H. Dangerous dual diagnosis patients. *Hospital Community Psychiatry* 1994; **45**: 280–1.

16. Siegfried N. A review of comorbidity: major mental illness and problematic substance use. *Australian and New Zealand Journal of Psychiatry* 1998; **32(5)**: 707–17.

17. National Collaborating Centre for Mental Health. *Psychosis with coexisting substance misuse. The NICE guideline on assessment and management in adults and young people.* London: British Psychological Society, Royal College of Psychiatrists, 2011.

18. Moore T H M, Zammit S, Lingford-Hughes A, *et al*. Cannabis use and risk of psychotic or affective mental health outcomes: a systematic review. *Lancet* 2007; **370**: 319–28.

19. Di Forti M, Morgan C, Dazzan P, *et al*. High-potency cannabis and risk of psychosis. *British Journal of Psychiatry* 2009; **195**: 488–91.

20. Potter D J, Clark P, Brown M B. Potency of delta 9-THC and other cannabinoids in cannabis in England in 2005: implications for psychoactivity and pharmacology. *Journal of Forensic Sciences* 2008; **53**: 90–4.

21. Arseneault L, Cannon M, Witton J, *et al*. Causal association between cannabis and psychosis: examination of the evidence. *British Journal Psychiatry* 2004; **184(2)**: 110–17.

22. Fergusson D M, Horwood J L, Swain-Campbell N R. Cannabis dependence and psychotic symptoms in young people. *Psychological Medicine* 2003; **33**: 15–21.

23. Nordentoft M, Hjorthoj C. Cannabis use and risk of psychosis later in life. *Lancet* 2007; **370**: 293–4.

24. Hickman M, Vickerman P, MacLeod J, *et al*. If cannabis caused schizophrenia: how many cannabis users may need to be prevented in order to prevent one case of schizophrenia? England and Wales calculations. *Addiction* 2009; **104**: 1856–61.

25. Wade D, Harrigan S, Edwards J, *et al*. Substance misuse in first-episode psychosis: 15-month prospective follow-up study. *British Journal of Psychiatry* 2006; **189**: 229–34.

26. Caspi A, Moffitt T E, Cannon M, *et al*. Moderation of the effect of adolescent-onset cannabis use on adult psychosis by a functional polymorphism in the catechol-O-methyltransferase gene: longitudinal evidence of a gene x environment interaction. *Biological Psychiatry* 2005; **57(10)**: 1117–27.

27. National Institute for Health and Clinical Excellence. *Clinical Guideline 120, Psychosis with Coexisting Substance Misuse.* London: NICE, 2011, http://guidance.nice.org.uk/CG120 [accessed November 2012].

28. Babor T F, Higgins-Biddle J C, Saunders J B, *et al*. *AUDIT: the Alcohol Use Disorder Identification Test. Guidelines for use in primary health care.* Geneva: World Health Organization, 2001.

29. Marsden J, Gossop M, Stewart D, *et al*. The Maudsley Addiction Profile (MAP): a brief instrument for assessing treatment outcome. *Addiction* 1998; **93(12)**: 1857–68.

30. Raistrick D, Bradshaw J, Tober G, *et al*. Development of the Leeds Dependence Questionnaire (LDQ): a questionnaire to measure alcohol and opiate dependence in the context of a treatment evaluation package. *Addiction* 1994; **89(5)**: 563–72.

31. Drake R, Osher F, Noordsy D, *et al*. Diagnosis of alcohol use disorders in schizophrenia. *Schizophrenia Bulletin* 1990; **16**: 57–67.

32. Champney-Smith J. Dual diagnosis. In: T Petersen, A McBride (eds). *Working with Substance Users: a guide to theory and practice.* London: Routledge, 2002, pp. 267–74.

33. Cosci F, Fava G A. New clinical strategies of assessment of comorbidity associated with substance use disorders. *Clinical Psychology Review* 2011; **31(3)**: 418–27.

34. Graham H L, Copello A, Birchwood M J, *et al.* Cognitive-Behavioural Integrated Treatment approach for psychosis and problem substance use. In: H L Graham, A Copello, M J Birchwood, *et al.* (eds). *Substance Misuse in Psychosis: approaches to treatment and service delivery.* Chichester: John Wiley & Sons, 2003, pp. 181–206.

35. Jeffrey D P, Ley A, McLaren S, *et al.* Psychosocial treatment programmes for people with both severe mental illness and substance misuse. In: *The Cochrane Database of Systematic Reviews.* Issue 2, Chichester: John Wiley, 2000.

36. Torrens M, Fonseca F, Mateu G, *et al.* Efficacy of antidepressants in substance use disorders with and without comorbid depression. A systematic review and meta-analysis. *Drug and Alcohol Dependence* 2005; **78(1)**: 1–22.

37. Nunes E, Levin F R. Treatment of depression in patients with alcohol or other drug dependence: a meta-analysis. *Journal of the American Medical Association* 2004; **291(15)**: 1887–96.

38. Ciraulo D A, Sands B K, Shader R I. Critical review of liability for benzodiazepine abuse among alcoholics. *American Journal of Psychiatry* 1988; **145(12)**: 1501–6.

39. Woods J H, Katz J L, Winger G. Use and abuse of benzodiazepines. Issues relevant to prescribing. *Journal of the American Medical Association* 1988; **260(23)**: 3476–80.

40. Shaw M, Brabbins C, Ruben S. Misuse of benzodiazepines. Specify the formulation when prescribing. *British Medical Journal* 1994; **308(6945)**: 1709.

41. Woody G E, O'Brien C P, Greenstein R. Misuse and abuse of diazepam: an increasingly common medical problem. *International Journal of the Addictions* 1975; **10(5)**: 843–8.

42. Sattar S P, Bahatia S. Benzodiazepines for substance abusers. Do addiction worries outweigh the need for effective anxiety treatment? A sobriety-based algorithm addresses both concerns. *Journal of Family Practice* 2003; **2(5)**.

43. Kelly T M, Daley D C, Douaihy A B. Treatment of substance abusing patients with comorbid psychiatric disorders. *Addictive Behaviors* 2012; **37(1)**: 11–24.

CHAPTER 23

Drugs, doctors and the GMC

Rhona Knight

Introduction

This chapter will discuss how doctors can be affected by substance misuse, how they present and what can be done to help them. It will also look at how doctors can make errors in managing substance misuse in their own patients, and look at how these errors can be prevented. It will include some information on the RCGP Health for Healthcare Professionals programme, which aims to develop the required knowledge and skills for those caring for doctors and other health-care professional patients.

Problems with controlled drugs

The relative autonomy of doctors in prescribing controlled drugs, although with ever increasing accountability, reflects the desired principle for doctors to have the necessary freedom to treat their patients appropriately. Whereas most doctors behave honestly and with integrity in their dealings with controlled drugs there are a few who do not. The actions of the former GP Harold Shipman demonstrated one way in which doctors can abuse their privileged position of trust. Doctors also, like non-medical patients, are at risk of substance misuse, while their position of trust enables easier access to addictive medication. The evidence indicates that doctors are more at risk of the four Ds: Drugs, Drink, Depression and Death.[1] Doctors affected by substance and alcohol misuse not only impact on their own health adversely but also are at risk of compromising their fitness to practise, thereby impacting adversely on the health of their patients.

Doctors and the General Medical Council

The General Medical Council (GMC) recognises the importance of doctors' health, indicating on its website that 'Looking after your own health is just as important as looking after your patients.'[2] Unfortunately drugs and/or alcohol are often implicated when doctors appear in front of the GMC where the doctors' own addiction has caused them to run into problems, or their management of drug users has been deemed as seriously irresponsible or inappropriate (Box 23.1).

Box 23.1   **Examples where health professionals have problems with aspects of controlled drugs**

✓ Doctors addicted to drugs and/or alcohol where use interferes with their clinical practice or where they obtain their drug through self-prescribing, from 'returns' from patients, or stolen from wards or general practice stock.

✓ Doctors who self-medicate for their anxiety, depression or physical pain.

✓ Doctors who prescribe in an irresponsible or inappropriate manner, usually in the context of the management of drug-using patients.

✓ Doctors who treat family with controlled drugs.

✓ Criminal doctors who exchange prescriptions for money.

✓ Shipman, who used controlled drugs to murder.

The GMC receives about 400 new referrals each year that relate to the doctor's own health, and most of these referrals come through employers or the police. About a third of these referred doctors are found to have impaired fitness to practise. Almost all of these cases are due to mental illness or substance misuse.

The GMC has the responsibility of ensuring patient safety, but it only seeks to restrict a doctor's registration if there are significant fitness to practise concerns. The GMC may also take action if there have been significant misconduct issues, for example if a doctor has received a drink driving offence. The threshold for referral is often difficult to ascertain, and the GMC has published a document outlining thresholds for referral to the GMC.[3]

In this they indicate that:

Only a relatively small number of doctors with a health concern are referred to the GMC each year. There is no need for GMC intervention if there is no risk to patients or to public confidence because a doctor with a health issue has insight into the extent of their condition, and is seeking appropriate treatment, following the advice of their treating physicians and/or occupational health departments in relation to their work, and restricting their practice appropriately.

As a rule of thumb GMC referral is not generally needed if the doctor:

▸ has insight into his or her condition

▸ is seeking appropriate help

▸ is following medical advice of treating physicians and occupational health

▸ is restricting his or her practice appropriately.

GMC referral is recommended if:

▸ the doctor's health issues are uncontrolled

▸ the doctor is not following medical advice.

The GMC is also happy to discuss cases anonymously over the phone, and has a useful website guide for referred doctors and others involved in GMC fitness to practise investigations on the grounds of ill health.[4]

Analysis of cases of doctors referred to the GMC for health reasons often reveals that there have been tell-tale signs of ill health impacting on a doctor's fitness to practise that could have been picked up on at an earlier stage. However, the way doctors behave as patients and the problems they have in accessing appropriate care often militate against early presentation.[5] This, combined with better treatment success rates seen in doctor patients, indicates that this is an area that needs to be addressed, both for the benefit of the sick doctors themselves and for their patient care.

Addicted professionals

There is growing concern about addiction in professional groups.[6] While accurate figures are difficult to come by, it is estimated that as many as 1 doctor in 15 may be affected by drug or alcohol dependence problems at some point during their professional life.[7,8] The work of healthcare professionals places them at risk of mental health problems,[9] and they are more likely to develop problems associated with the misuse of drugs and alcohol. It is common for doctors to drink heavily at an early stage of their careers, especially during training and as medical students, yet it appears from one study in Scotland that there is significant risk of alcoholism in the over-45s.[10]

A further study found that about two-thirds of recently qualified doctors exceeded recommended safe drinking limits, and 10% were drinking at hazardous levels. A quarter of the doctors in this sample were using cannabis, and 10% were using hallucinogens.[11] The work of the Practitioner Health Programme (http://php.nhs.uk/) has affirmed that doctors who misuse alcohol are often also taking other drugs, and may switch from one substance to another over time. The three-year report from this service highlights its headlines at three years, which can be seen in Table 23.1. The report also gives a breakdown of mental health and addiction diagnoses, shown in Figures 23.1 and 23.2 respectively (see p. 432).[12]

Fowlie, in his article[13] on the misuse of alcohol and other drugs, emphasises the need for increased awareness of the identification and management of the misuse of alcohol and other substances in doctors, and for education in this area throughout the medical career, from medical school to ongoing continued professional development.

Why do health professionals become addicted?

As with non-practitioner patients, health professionals present with physical and mental health problems, often complicated by social, financial, emotional and employment issues. In many cases misuse of drugs by healthcare professionals may begin with a 'legitimate' reason such as insomnia, depression or back pain, particularly when these professionals choose to diagnose and treat themselves, usually inappropriately. However, common routes into substance use are personality predispositions and anxiety or depression. Complicating and contributing factors can include the increased pressure imposed by the changing nature of the medical profession and the requirements of increased accountability and transparency.

Doctors, pharmacists and nurses may not be an obvious high-risk group. They tend to be successful, intelligent, committed and economically stable individuals. Yet, a significant minority run into problems. For doctors, the long years of medical training are characterised by intense competition, excessive workload and fear of failure. To these stresses is added the increasing risk of litigation and complaints as well as a perception of loss of professional autonomy and the perceived threats of revalidation. All these appear to contribute to increase the occupational health risks for practitioner patients.

In doctors these increased pressures impact on a group for whom 'the very traits that make "good" doctors, such as empathy and involvement in the care of their patients, may militate against good mental health'.[14] Studies also indicate

Table 23.1 **Practitioner Health Programme three-year report on addiction diagnoses**

General
▶ 554 practitioner patients and 20 other health professionals (accepted during the prototype period) making 574 in total.
▶ 53% men, 47% women.
▶ 92% doctors, 5% dentists, 3% other.
▶ Increasing numbers of younger practitioner patients

Employment
▶ 77% of practitioner patients remained in or returned to work after contact with the service over the three-year period (an increase of almost 7% compared with Year 2).
▶ 29% involved in GMC or General Dental Council process

Practitioner patient diagnoses
Practitioner patients have often presented with co-morbidities, most commonly mental health and alcohol problems.
▶ 85% of practitioner patients have a mental health diagnosis.
▶ 28% of practitioner patients have an addiction diagnosis.
▶ 17% of practitioner patients have a physical health diagnosis.
As practitioner patients present with multiple health issues falling across these categories the percentage exceeds 100%

Mental health	Addiction	Physical health
▶ Depression, 55%. ▶ Eating disorders, 5%. ▶ Psychosis, 2%. ▶ Bipolar affective disorder, 6%. ▶ Anxiety disorders, 12%. ▶ Adjustment reaction/ stress, 10%. ▶ Various, 10%	▶ Alcohol dependence or problem drinking present in 66% of addiction diagnoses. ▶ Predominantly male case load. ▶ Substance misuse, including ketamine, heroin, cocaine, amphetamine, benzodiazepines and cannabis. ▶ 79% currently abstinent (increase of 8% from Year 2)	▶ 18% of practitioner patients present with physical health issues ranging from cancer, HIV, epilepsy, brain injury to minor health issues

Source: © Practitioner Health Programme.[12] Used with permission.

Figure 23.1   **Practitioner Health Programme mental health diagnoses**

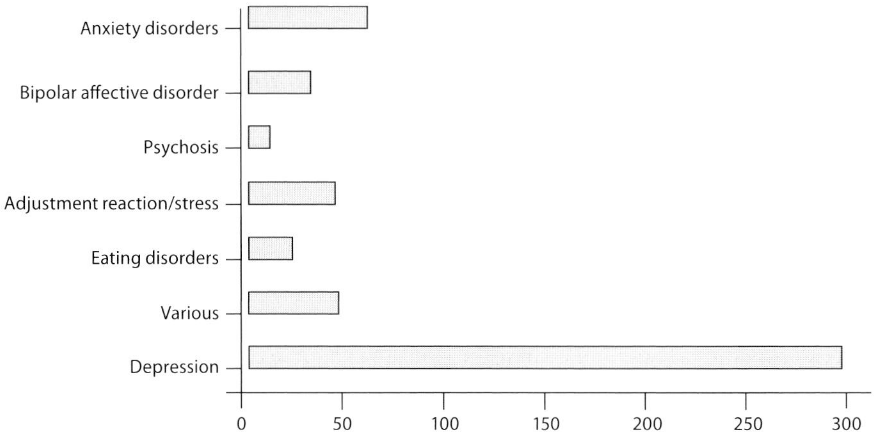

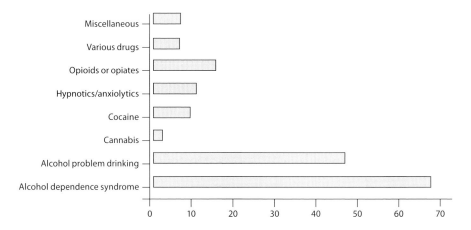

Source: © Practitioner Health Programme.[12] Used with permission.

Figure 23.2   **Practitioner Health Programme addiction diagnoses**

Source: © Practitioner Health Programme.[12] Used with permission.

that personality characteristics, including perfectionism and conscientiousness, which are very common in doctors, can increase the risk of mental health problems.[15,16] As Duggins summarises in his article:[1]

> Students who show diligence, commitment, co-operativeness, agreeableness, open-ness and extraversion, are encouraged to be doctors, and when they are doctors they do well. However, under stress these positive personality factors can become an Achilles' heel, when for example conscientious traits under stress become perfectionism, commitment becomes compulsiveness, or extraversion becomes narcissism.

Yet, despite the increased risk of illness and suicide,[17] doctors are very unlikely to seek professional help.[18] It is therefore understandable that doctors, a profession with easier access to medication, are at higher risk of drug and alcohol misuse.[19,20]

How do they present?

Doctors present with substance and alcohol misuse in a variety of ways, and at different stages of addiction. They may present in crisis. They may be in denial. They may self-present with insight and a desire for help.

It is important to be aware of the signs that a colleague may be unwell. Doctors with addiction problems can often be identified at work. While they may arrive at work smelling of alcohol, they may also be struggling with their job or be late, failing to turn up for clinics. Paperwork may be behind or they may be noted to be taking extended breaks, or to have poor concentration and performance.

Crisis presentations can include being found having passed out while on call, with evidence of needles or anaesthetic drugs, or being found wandering, or being drunk and disorderly in a public place or place of work. They may have been referred to the police.

Treating dependent health professionals

As outlined already, doctors' and other healthcare professionals' drug or alcohol problems can lead them into disciplinary procedures, often triggered by a crisis. This is partly because health professionals are reluctant to seek help. This reluctance can relate to stigma attached to psychological illness, in particular substance misuse, and the professional risks associated with acknowledgement of this. This is illustrated in the 2009 study of 2500 doctors in Birmingham, which demonstrated that only 13% would seek help if they suffered a psychological ill health or addiction problem.[18] Other barriers to accessing health care include: a fear of loss of confidentiality; the embarrassment at seeing a colleague; fear about being deemed unfit for practice. As a result, health professionals often try to avoid detection and do not seek help until late on in their problem. It is therefore important, as with other hard-to-reach patient groups, to find ways of attracting them into treatment programmes by making sure that they have access to high-quality, appropriate, confidential and sensitive treatment.

In the UK, awareness of the problems of healthcare professionals has been slow to develop and the NHS provides few specialist services for such professionals.[21] The data from the Practitioner Health Programme, however, demonstrates the benefits of such services in improving the health of the healthcare professional and enabling return or maintenance in the workplace.

Controlled drugs and professional practice

What is an unprofessional doctor? In its simplest terms, it is a doctor who fails to fulfil the criteria set out in the GMC's *Good Medical Practice*.[22] The duties of a doctor[23] as outlined by the GMC indicate that every doctor must:

▸ make the care of the patient his or her first concern

▸ protect and promote the health of patients and the public

▸ provide a good standard of practice and care

▸ treat patients as individuals and respect their dignity

▸ work in partnership with patients

▸ be honest and open, and act with integrity.

This requires doctors to be professionally competent and take action if there is unnecessary risk. Professional competency includes appropriate and responsible prescribing.

Responsible prescribing

A phrase that gets bandied about is that of *irresponsible prescribing*, but answering the question 'What is irresponsible prescribing?' is not easy. In most circumstances it represents prescribing that falls well short of established good practice. This is either in the type of drug – including combinations and formulations, the quantities prescribed on single prescriptions, or the means by which the doctor makes a decision to issue certain drugs. What constitutes good practice is therefore dynamic and changing with time as new evidence emerges, emphasising the need for prescribers to remain up to date. The changing emphasis on maintenance as opposed to abstinence is a case in point. The 1991 National Clinical Guidelines, for example, placed great emphasis on methadone detoxification, to be carried out over days or weeks. Maintenance prescribing, especially by GPs, might have been deemed irresponsible and inappropriate. Increased evidence led to recommending maintenance prescribing, and it would now be considered irresponsible to stop a methadone prescription merely because of an arbitrary time scale. Recommended doses also change. In the past experts may well have condemned doses of much more than 100 mg/day of methadone. Now doses of 60 and 120 mg are seen as part of good practice. One generation's irresponsible prescribing has become another's good practice. Professional practice, however, is more than prescribing alone, and cannot be separated from the overall care that the practitioner provides to the patient. Perhaps the best definition of irresponsible prescribing is practice that places either the public or the patient at risk, whereby the doctor fails to take necessary precautions to ensure that the right drug is being administered in the correct dose, to the right patient, for the right indication, and in a manner that reduces the risk of diversion.

Common themes

So are there any common themes that cause doctors to digress from good practice to such an extent that they are censured by the GMC? Box 23.2 outlines some key characteristics. While it is difficult without conducting a large study to pull out common themes, an examination of cases that have appeared in front of the GMC can help to shed light on some of the types of practice that can lead to unprofessional practice.

Box 23.2 **Characteristics of doctors who run into trouble with the GMC around managing drug users**

✓ Male.

✓ Single handed.

✓ Managing large numbers of drug users.

✓ Not using shared-care management.

✓ Private care settings.

✓ Doctors with addiction problems.

✓ Prescribing for self and family.

These cases can lead us to consider several types of doctor who may be found in breach of their professional duties. The descriptions below are not of individual doctors, but are intended to shed light on ways in which professional practice can be, even with the best of intentions, compromised.

The naïve doctor

These doctors feel that they have a mission to treat drug users, and they fear that, if they do not, no one else will. These doctors tend to work in an isolated manner, perhaps single handed or, if part of a group practice, as the only doctor who cares for drug users. They may start off by seeing only a few drug users, but soon become identified either as a 'soft touch' or as the kindly doctor who looks after them. Unsupported, and often not working in shared care, these doctors soon take on more and more patients, inevitably leading them to take short cuts in treatment. It is not unknown for these doctors, for example, to post prescriptions to the patient's home for many months' treatment, rarely seeing the patient and certainly not carrying out any tests of compliance. Often this doctor tries to adhere to clinical guidelines but rarely succeeds, prescribing more erratically to larger and larger numbers of patients. Unless helped and supported this doctor is likely either to become 'burnt out' or to end up before the GMC, accused of irresponsible or inappropriate prescribing. This doctor tends to have no formal training in drug misuse, learning on the job, and hence unaware of serious gaps in his or her knowledge base. With the increasing prescribing accountability and the demands of revalidation, these cases are likely to become far less frequent.

The maverick doctor

Maverick doctors believe that they are right, that they know best, and that guidelines or protocols are for others. They tend to have some training in drug misuse, and perhaps have worked in the addiction field either as a clinical assistant or associate specialist. They frequently prescribe drugs that are not licensed for use in addiction treatment, such as dihydrocodeine, methadone tablets, amphetamines, injectable preparations or naltrexone implants. They usually ignore the advice from others practising in the area and continue to provide treatment that is outside the mainstream. When challenged they can have recourse to using the media to fight their cause. These doctors rarely use urine or other tests of compliance, and if they do the results are usually ignored. Often different patients receive the same repertoire of treatment, with little adaptation for the individual needs of the patient. These doctors are likely to come to the attention of the GMC when the volume and type of medication prescribed is discovered, usually because of a patient's death or serious overdose, or through chemist inspections. Although it is perfectly acceptable to prescribe treatment outside standard practice, it must be in the context of well thought out treatment plans. The greater a doctor deviates from standard practice the more the onus is on the doctor to justify this, to his or her patients, his or her peers and, when necessary, to the GMC.

The criminal doctor

The third type of doctor likely to come to the attention of the GMC is the doctor who practises in a criminal manner. This type of doctor is fortunately rare, though a steady stream of doctors do appear in front of the criminal justice system for offences related to the misuse of drugs. Shipman is probably the most notorious of these doctors. He obtained extra diamorphine by prescribing the 30 mg rather than the standard 5 mg or 10 mg ampoules, although during the Shipman Inquiry Dame Janet Smith heard evidence of doctors who had supplied drugs for monetary gain and of doctors obtaining controlled drugs to feed their own addiction (see Box 23.3). This type of doctor frequently prescribes drugs that have a high resale value if diverted onto the illicit market. These doctors can be responsible for a thriving illicit market in drugs, and users flock to them in the knowledge that few questions will be asked.

Box 23.3   **Examples from the Shipman Inquiry**

> In 2002, Dr X was convicted of the unlawful supply of controlled drugs, including diazepam, Rohypnol and Dexedrine. He issued private prescriptions on the payment of £30, often issuing prescriptions in false names to make detection less likely. He was also prepared to sell controlled drugs from his own supply to callers on demand.
>
> In 1996, Dr Y supplemented his living by selling temazepam capsules that he obtained from writing prescriptions for patients who were exempt from NHS charges. He would instruct the patients to go to the pharmacy and to bring back the medication for him to check. He would then remove and keep the temazepam capsules and sell them for £3–£4 each.

The self-prescriber

A fourth type of doctor who falls foul of the GMC is the self-prescriber, who may be self-prescribing for pain or to feed his or her own addiction. This type may even be prescribing for members of his or her family. Though not strictly against the 1971 Misuse of Drugs Act, the GMC, the British Medical Association (BMA) and the Royal College of General Practitioners (RCGP) all agree that self-prescribing or prescribing to family or close friends constitutes poor practice. One

Box 23.4   **Unprofessional prescribing**

Dr A

In the 1980s the GMC found Dr A guilty of serious professional misconduct for 'irresponsibly treating addicts privately by providing methadone in the long term without reasonable medical care'. Some saw this as punishment by the medical establishment for her policy of maintenance prescribing and prescribing of injectables as part of private practice. It led many to regard her as a *cause célèbre*.

Dr B

In early 2000, Dr B, a London GP, was sanctioned by the GMC after more than 25 years treating hundreds of long-term users. Both in the NHS and at his busy private clinic, he prescribed patients maintenance amphetamines, methadone ampoules and other opiates, all in very high doses to patients from all over the London area. This doctor gave patients combinations of different drugs with few checks to ensure that they were not diverted onto the illicit market. Despite an appeal to the Privy Council, the decision of the GMC to erase his name from the medical register was upheld, stating that:

The Committee heard evidence that your policy of giving patients what they asked for may have been accompanied by social and health benefits and that it helped to shield some from impure street drugs ... however ... the risks to your patients and the public as a whole far outweighed any benefits.

Dr C

A psychiatrist, Dr C, prescribed a mixture of the sedatives morphine and methadone combined with Dexedrine from his private clinic in South London. This doctor was found to prescribe before drug dependence had been confirmed in the patient. The GMC heard that the drugs ended up fuelling a black market and two patients died of overdoses. Dr C was found guilty of serious professional misconduct relating to charges involving 31 patients who travelled from far and wide to get drugs. One witness stated:

Your routine practice was to prescribe a range of controlled drugs in exceptionally large quantities, which displayed a reckless disregard for the safety of your patients and your responsibility to public health. A doctor who decides to depart from established guidelines must clearly record his reasons for doing so. This you failed to do. You were apparently oblivious to and unconcerned about the inherent dangers of over-prescribing.

Dr D

Dr D, a single-handed doctor, had a number of patients whom he treated with dihydrocodeine and various benzodiazepines for drug dependence. One of his patients, new to the practice, came to see him asking for dihydrocodeine. The patient was 16 years old at the time. Dr D prescribed this patient, on the first occasion, with 84 diazepam 20 mg tablets and 100 dihydrocodeine 60 mg tablets. The patient was admitted to hospital that night with an overdose and presented again to Dr D three days later. Dr D had been made aware of the admission by the admitting doctor and a discharge letter was faxed directly to the GP. Dr D reissued the same prescription to the patient on presenting again. This was just one case amongst ten others that was considered by the GMC to be irresponsible and inappropriate care.

Dr E

Dr E was part of a large group practice. He saw drug users, though none of his other partners did. He had well over 150 patients and saw them at an annex at the back of the surgery. Drug-using patients were expected to be segregated from other 'normal' patients. This doctor felt it his duty to care for these patients, which extended to providing them with money and to taking them to appointments. He carried out few checks on the patients' compliance and would often leave three-month repeat prescriptions at reception for collection. Despite help from the local drug service he continued to feel that the only way to manage drug users was to offer them what they wanted. He began to drink heavily to deal with the stress that the job was creating and would arrive in the surgery smelling of alcohol. The doctor began to have a sexual relationship with a patient, who then blackmailed him. The case eventually was discovered and the doctor retired.

---

of Dame Janet Smith's recommendations in the fourth report of the Shipman Inquiry was to restrict this right and to make such action a GMC offence. The GMC therefore advises that doctors avoid treating themselves and those close to them.[24] 'Objectivity is essential in providing good care; independent medical care should be sought whenever you or someone with whom you have a close personal relationship requires prescription medicines.'

It should be added that in the cases of the naïve, the maverick and the criminal doctor, it is not unknown for the local illicit market to be fuelled by prescriptions generated from these doctors. Five cases are outlined in Box 23.4.

Preventing problems

There are several key ways to avoid problems:

Acknowledging limitations

Lack of training and support are common features of doctors who run into problems in the management of drug users. It is important that doctors do not feel under any pressure to practise care beyond their level of competency. Doctors often feel that they are obliged to care for drug users, especially if other doctors in the area are unwilling.

Don't be too quick to prescribe

Remember the simple rules learnt at medical school and don't reach for the prescription pad too early. It is commonplace that when given a new patient with, for example, hypertension, a doctor will assess, investigate and plan care before resorting to the prescription pad. On the other hand, the same doctor, given a complex intravenous heroin user, will carry out a cursory history, carry out no examination or investigations, and prescribe dangerous drugs in high doses before even confirming the diagnosis of dependence.

Adequate training

To prevent these cases coming before the GMC it is important that doctors have the opportunity to attend training, preferably before they start to manage drug users, are supported through clinical guidelines, shared care and a peer network, and are able to gain the confidence to say 'no' to patients who they do not feel able to manage.

Team working

Clinical governance emphasises a team approach to developing high-quality care within a service and the importance of reflective practice within the organisation. A well-organised practice, with systems in place for audit, continuing professional development, significant event analysis and learning from patients, would prevent many of the problems discussed in this chapter, and, it is hoped, would reduce the numbers of doctors facing disciplinary action by the GMC.

The RCGP Health for Healthcare Professionals programme

As we have seen earlier in this chapter, doctors become unwell. Unlike the view, even seen in children's TV programmes, which promotes a perception that doctors are superhuman and invulnerable, doctors have health problems that can be bio-psycho-socio-spiritual in nature. They can be very complicated patients.[5] They often access health care in unusual ways. They find ways around the system, and when they are unwell there are often implications for the safety of others. In the case of doctors, there are implications for patient safety and care, and for ever spiralling NHS costs.[25] It therefore makes economic as well as ethical sense to ensure that our doctors are cared for appropriately when they are unwell.

Realising the importance and need to care appropriately for doctor patients and for healthcare professionals more generally, the RCGP has developed a two-stranded programme to train doctors to be better at caring for their practitioner patients. This training is also useful for other healthcare professionals who wish to develop the knowledge and skills needed to care for their practitioner patients better, including those at risk of or affected by substance and alcohol misuse. The programme comprises the Certificates in Practitioner Health Parts One and Two – CPH Part 1 and CPH Part 2.

The CPH Part 1 completed its pilot stage in spring 2012 and has been rolled out nationally. It comprises two e-modules. The first e-module aims to cover in more detail than this chapter allows the healthcare needs of practitioner patients, and how that care may be accessed and delivered. It also, through promoting reflection on practice, hopes to enable those consulting with practitioner patients to develop the required consultation skills. The second e-module looks in more detail at substance and alcohol misuse, regulation and the role of occupational health. In addition to the e-modules the College provides a face-to-face day of training to consolidate the e-learning content and its application in practice. The e-modules and dates for the face-to-face training can be accessed on the RCGP website,[26] and make a useful addition to the RCGP Certificate in Substance Misuse.

Support organisations and assessment and treatment services

There are a small number of organisations around the country that aim to support doctors with substance and alcohol misuse problems, although many areas are now identifying ways in which this hard-to-reach patient group can be appropriately catered for. The services below should also be able to signpost you to what else is regionally available.

Practitioner Health Programme

This confidential London-based NHS specialist service is led by GPs. It is designed for doctors and dentists with mental health or addiction difficulties, or with physical health problems influencing performance. It offers a holistic approach and services including primary care, psychiatry, addiction, Cognitive Behavioural Therapy (CBT), psychotherapy, day treatment and access to inpatient treatment if required. It accepts, if funding can be agreed, referrals from outside London. The website is: http://php.nhs.uk.

BMA Counselling Service and Doctor Adviser Service

This service offers doctors and medical students counselling from a trained telephone counsellor or support from a doctor-adviser. This is open to all medical students and doctors whether they are a BMA member or not. The website is: https://bma.org.uk/practical-support-at-work/doctors-well-being/about-doctors-for-doctors.

Doctors Support Network

This is a peer support organisation for doctors suffering mental health problems. It offers confidential advice and support. There are also regional meetings. The website is: www.dsn.org.uk.

British Doctors and Dentists Group

The British Doctors and Dentists Group (BDDG) is a mutual support organisation for doctors and dentists who wish to recover, or are recovering from, alcohol or substance misuse. It also has regional meetings and has a families group. The website is: www.bddg.org/page.php?id=1.

Sick Doctors Trust

This organisation offers a 24-hour helpline providing confidential help for doctors and medical students suffering from substance and alcohol misuse problems. The website is: www.sick-doctors-trust.co.uk.

Conclusion

Prevention is better than cure, and this applies to hard-to-reach groups of patients as well as those who find it easy to access care. Doctors are a hard-to-reach group, with occupational risk factors that can compromise their health. Doctors' ill health has wide-reaching implications, and substance and alcohol misuse are two key areas that can compromise a doctor's health and fitness to practise.

Doctors who transgress the law with respect to controlled drugs are rare. Considering their position of trust, the impact they have when they do transgress can be significant – in terms of the pain caused to themselves, to their patients and to those closest to them.

It is important that doctors do not translate clinical freedom to prescribe into the right to prescribe as they wish and to ignore the basic principle of being a doctor, which is to make the care of the patient their first concern.

It is hoped that clinical governance structures, appraisal and revalidation, and better routine monitoring of use of controlled drugs, will prevent problems before they happen.

References

1. Duggins R. Health for health professionals. 2012, www.onmedica.com/viewsarticle. aspx?id=fabbf6f9-32db-42d2-ad63-dfc6a6d09a2c [accessed November 2012].

2. General Medical Council. Doctors' health. www.gmc-uk.org/doctors/information_ for_doctors/7033.asp [accessed November 2012].

3. General Medical Council. *GMC Thresholds*. London: GMC, 2012, www.gmc-uk.org/ Guidance_GMC_Thresholds.pdf_48163325.pdf [accessed November 2012].

4. General Medical Council. Your health matters. www.gmc-uk.org/concerns/11542.asp [accessed November 2012].

5. Department of Health. *Invisible Patients: summary of the report of the Working Group on the health of health professionals*. London: DH, 2010, www.dh.gov.uk/en/Publicationsandstatistics/ Publications/PublicationsPolicyAndGuidance/DH_113540 [accessed November 2012].

6. McVeigh T. Alarm at growing addiction problems among professionals. *Observer*, 13 November 2011, www.guardian.co.uk/society/2011/nov/13/doctors-lawyers-alcohol-addiction [accessed November 2012].

7. British Dental Association. The dependent professional. *British Dental Journal* 1989; **166**: 315.

8. Working Group on the Misuse of Alcohol and Other Drugs by Doctors. *The Misuse of Alcohol and Other Drugs by Doctors*. London: BMA, 1998.

9. Department of Health. *Mental Health and Ill Health in Doctors*. London: DH, 2008, www.dh.gov. uk/en/Publicationsandstatistics/Publications/PublicationsPolicyAndGuidance/DH_083066 [accessed November 2012].

10. Harrison D, Chick J. Trends in alcoholism among male doctors in Scotland. *Addiction* 1994; **89(12)**: 1613–17.

11. Birch D, Ashton H, Kamali S. Alcohol, drinking, illicit drug use, and stress in junior house officers in North East England. *Lancet* 1998; **352(9130)**: 785–6.

12. Practitioner Health Programme. *NHS Practitioner Health Programme: 2011 annual report*. London: PHP, 2012, http://php.nhs.uk/london-practitioner-health-programme-the-3-year-report [accessed November 2012].

13. Fowlie D G. The misuse of alcohol and other drugs by doctors: a UK report and one region's response. *Alcohol and Alcoholism* 1999; **34(5)**: 666–71, http://alcalc.oxfordjournals.org/content/34/5/666.full.pdf   [accessed November 2012].

14. Peters M. Doctors' health – Why are they a special case? www.bma.org.uk/.../ Doctorscanbepatientstoo_Sept2006_tcm41-173984.doc.

15. Cohen D, Rhydderch M. Measuring a doctor's performance: personality, health and well-being. *Occupational Medicine* 2006; 5**6(7)**: 438–40, http://occmed.oxfordjournals.org/content/56/7/438.full   [accessed November 2012].

16. McManus I C, Keeling A, Paice E. Stress, burnout and doctors' attitudes to work are determined by personality and learning style: a twelve year longitudinal study of UK medical graduates. *BMC Medicine* 2004; **2**: 29, www.biomedcentral.com/1741-7015/2/29 [accessed November 2012].

17. Lindeman S, Laara E, Hakko H, *et al.* A systematic review on gender-specific suicide mortality in medical doctors. *British Journal of Psychiatry* 1996; **168(3)**: 274–9.

18. Hassan T M, Ahmed S O, White A C, *et al.* A postal survey of doctors' attitudes to becoming mentally ill. *Clinical Medicine* (London) 2009; **9(4)**: 327–32.

19. Vaillant G E, Brighton J R, McArthur C. Physicians' use of mood-altering drugs: a twenty-year follow-up report. *New England Journal of Medicine* 1970; **282(7)**: 365–70.

20. Brooke D, Edwards G, Andrews T. Doctors and substance misuse: types of doctor, types of problem. *Addiction* 1993; **88(5)**: 655–63.

21. Strang J, Wilks M, Wells B, *et al.* Missed problems and missed opportunities for addicted doctors. *British Medical Journal* 1998; **316(7129)**: 405–6.

22. General Medical Council. *Good Medical Practice*. London: GMC, 2006, www.gmc-uk.org/guidance/good_medical_practice.asp   [accessed November 2012].

23. General Medical Council. Good medical practice: duties of a doctor. 2006, www.gmc-uk.org/guidance/good_medical_practice/duties_of_a_doctor.asp   [accessed November 2012].

24. General Medical Council. Prescribing controlled drugs for yourself or someone close to you. 2008, www.gmc-uk.org/guidance/ethical_guidance/prescriptions_faqs.asp#7 [accessed November 2012].

25. Boorman S. *NHS Health and Well-being: final report*. Leeds: COI, 2009, www.nhshealthandwellbeing.org/FinalReport.html   [accessed November 2012].

26. Royal College of General Practitioners. Health for Healthcare Professionals (HHP), www.rcgp.org.uk/courses-and-events/online-learning/ole/health-for-healthcare-professionals-part-1.aspx   [accessed November 2012].

CHAPTER 24

Controlled drugs, regulations, controls and diversion

Clare Gerada and Iain Brew

IN THIS CHAPTER

Introduction || Drug diversion || Brief history of legislation of controlled drugs || Prescriptions || Administration || Registers and other record keeping || Disposal || 2004 Shipman Inquiry || Conclusion

Introduction

The main aim of laws governing controlled or dangerous drugs must be to minimise the serious harms that these drugs can do, both to the individual and to society. At the same time, any law must be consistent with the UK's international obligations. For the GP and other members of the primary care team, drug laws should be understood in so far as transgressing such laws would cause serious problems to the clinician or to the patient. This chapter offers clinicians current information about laws relevant to their day-to-day practice and places the current Misuse of Drugs Act (MDA) in a historical context.

The main instrument for drugs control in the UK is the Misuse of Drugs Act 1971, which is now over four decades old. This act should be seen in the context of other acts of parliament and United Nations conventions on drugs. A review of the MDA by an independent inquiry, chaired by Viscountess Runciman, was undertaken in 1997. The task of the inquiry was to consider the changes that had taken place in society since the MDA was first enacted and to assess whether the law as it currently stands needed to be revised to make it both more effective and responsive to these changes. In all, the committee made 81 recommendations, in which the reclassification of cannabis from Class B to C is perhaps the best known.[1] In the face of concern about the increasing potency of cannabis, the Advisory Council on the Misuse of Drugs (ACMD) reviewed the classification of cannabis again. Despite concerns, the Council recommended that cannabis remain a Class C drug in 2008.[2] However, the then UK government decided in 2009 to reclassify cannabis to Class B.

Over recent years, a number of so-called 'legal highs' have come onto the market. These have increased the need for Temporary Class Drug Orders (TCDOs) being recommended by the ACMD, pending full recommendations on the need for permanent controls. Such drugs include the stimulant methcathinone ('M-cat' or ephedrone) and methoxetamine (also known as 'mexxy' and MXE), a supposedly safer ketamine equivalent.

Drug diversion

In modern times, a major problem with controlled drugs is that of drug diversion, where the drug prescribed is not used in the manner or by the patient that it was initially prescribed or dispensed for. Harold Shipman killed so many of his patients by diverting controlled drugs, using various different ruses to obtain drugs in the name of patients (alive and dead). Fortunately, cases of doctors diverting drugs in order to harm their patients are very rare. A far commoner problem is patients selling their prescribed drugs for resale on the illicit market to be used by others or drug users obtaining prescriptions by deception.

Diverted drugs generally form part of a polydrug-using repertoire of heavy drug users. There have been few UK studies dealing solely with prescription drug diversion; perhaps the best of those that have been published is a qualitative study of users in different settings by Fountain *et al*.[3] She and her colleagues found that factors influencing the risk of drugs being diverted included doctors prescribing large amounts on single prescriptions and lack of identity checks on patients requesting medication from GPs.

It is possible that these forms of diversion have been made easier since the discontinuation of the Home Office Addicts Index. Patients may now 'shop around' until they find a naïve practitioner who is willing to prescribe controlled drugs to them.

Techniques used to dupe prescribers include:

▸ exaggerating the amount of drugs used in order to obtain a larger prescription of substitute medication than needed

▸ claiming to be addicted to alcohol in order to obtain benzodiazepines

▸ professing to be trying to reduce opiate use and asking for benzodiazepines to alleviate withdrawal symptoms

▸ claiming insomnia/stress in order to obtain drugs

▸ giving false identities in order to obtain multiple prescriptions

▸ claiming to be a temporary resident

▸ exploiting prescribers who are judged to be sympathetic

▶ claiming to be an injector by displaying false injecting marks

▶ claiming drugs have been stolen/spilt/lost etc.

▶ forging prescriptions.

In some cases, the names of 'sympathetic' private doctors or pharmacists have been sold.

The two main reasons why drug users in treatment sell their prescribed drugs are to raise money to buy drugs and/or formulations preferred to those prescribed, or to pay for a private prescription.

It is generally accepted that some diversion of controlled drugs is unavoidable and is the price to pay for attracting and retaining large numbers of drug users in treatment. The right balance needs to be achieved between a prescriber's freedom to prescribe and attract and maintain patients in treatment, on the one hand, and the need to minimise the risk of diversion by instituting safe, effective practices, such as those outlined in the clinical guidelines, on the other.

Brief history of legislation of controlled drugs

Pharmacy Act 1868

The Pharmaceutical Society of Great Britain was established in 1841 and granted a Royal Charter in 1843 (it was to become the Royal Pharmaceutical Society of Great Britain in 1988). Soon after the original formation of the society, there were calls to restrict the right to practise pharmacy to those who were licensed to do so; the aim was to promote and maintain professional standards, and to establish control on the sale of drugs.

Until the second half of the nineteenth century, apothecaries, chemists and druggists, as well as medical practitioners, supplied medicinal drugs. Any general dealer, equivalent to the grocers of today, could also sell them. To prevent the unregulated sale by 'quacks' of dubious potions, tonics and remedies (some of which contained opium), restrictions were placed on who could sell medicines and hence the Pharmacy Act 1868 was introduced. The Pharmacy Act outlined a number of drugs, including opium, that could be sold only by 'pharmaceutical chemists'.

In 1916, a regulation was passed, under the Defence of the Realm Act, to curb the use of cocaine and opium by soldiers in London on leave from war service – the effect of the drug being to encourage rampant sexual activity with prostitutes. The Americans had their own legislation enacted a few years earlier with the Harrison Act 1914, which banned heroin prescriptions, whether for addicts or for more orthodox requirements. To this day heroin cannot be prescribed in the USA.

Dangerous Drugs Act 1920

This prohibited the importation and exportation of certain dangerous drugs, including opium, cocaine, morphine and diamorphine except under special licence granted by the secretary of state. It also created an offence of being an occupier of premises that permitted the smoking of prepared opium.

Dangerous Drugs Regulations 1921

This legislation laid down the formal obligations of doctors and pharmacists with regard to prescribing and dispensing dangerous drugs. Many of these obligations still exist today. The regulations stipulated that these drugs had to be dispensed only from written prescriptions when issuing publicly funded prescriptions for dangerous drugs and that doctors should use the same prescription form as for other medicines. This new 'official' form would be used for the private prescribing of dangerous drugs. It is ironic that the recommendation to reinstitute an 'official form' should be made nearly 80 years later by Dame Janet Smith in her fourth report on the Shipman Inquiry. The regulations also required a pharmacist to record relevant transactions in a register and imposed an obligation of record keeping on a doctor supplying dangerous drugs to a patient. This obligation persists to this day.

Rolleston Report 1926

A committee, chaired by the president of the Royal College of Physicians, Sir Humphrey Rolleston, was commissioned by the Ministry of Health as a result of concerns from the Home Office of doctors prescribing dangerous drugs to addicts. His task was to assess the extent of the opioid problem in the UK and to make recommendations.

At this time the Home Office opposed the treatment of addiction and the prescribing of maintenance prescribing. The committee, made up mainly of doctors, recommended that in most cases the steady prescription of the drug of addiction was appropriate. The committee set the scene for what is now called maintenance prescribing in that it recommended, for patients where it was impossible to wean them away from a longstanding addiction, the issuing of a small maintenance dose of their drug of addiction and that addiction should be regarded as an illness and not as a 'mere form of vicious indulgence'.

In the report, Rolleston identified many of the same problems seen today: some doctors were prescribing large amounts of dangerous drugs to patients on an open-ended basis with no obvious treatment plan; some doctors were seeing their patients too infrequently – in some cases the prescriptions were sent by post; and some doctors had supplied dangerous drugs or had issued prescriptions to people unknown to them and without making any attempt to contact the patients' normal medical practitioners. There were even cases where the person had obtained drugs from different medical practitioners at the same time. Finally, the committee found that in some cases supplies had been purchased or prescribed by practitioners for self-administration. The Rolleston Report set the UK apart from many other countries in that treatment (at this time heroin) could be given for medical reasons. Consequently, this treatment philosophy was termed 'the British System'.

The Single Convention on Narcotic Drugs 1961

This is an international treaty prohibiting the production and supply of (currently) 161 substances without a licence except for medicinal or research use. The Commission on Narcotic Drugs and the World Health Organization add, remove or reassign drugs between the four schedules I–IV, with IV being the most restricted class (including heroin, which to date is not prescribable in the USA and many other countries).

Brain Committees

In the years that followed the Rolleston Committee, far from containment of the addiction problem to a few 'respectable' iatrogenic addicts, the heroin problem expanded into new, young users, with a burgeoning black market of diverted prescribed heroin. Again at the instigation of the Home Office, the Brain Committee was set up. This time the remit was to review the policy of using dangerous drugs for the treatment of addiction. The stimulus for the First Brain Report was the manufacture and use of new synthetic opioids, which were being used by doctors for therapeutic reasons yet were causing addiction in large numbers of individuals.

The First Brain Report in 1961 endorsed many of the conclusions of the Rolleston Committee, in particular that there was no need to change existing British legislation governing dangerous drugs and the view that addiction should be regarded as an expression of mental disorder rather than a form of criminal behaviour and that the satisfactory treatment of addiction was possible only in 'suitable institutions'. This report was, however, criticised for failing to acknowledge the emerging and serious drugs problem in the UK and the committee was asked to reconvene in 1964 to examine the growing heroin problem in the UK (the Second Brain Committee). At this time the type of addict was changing from the 'typical', predominantly health professional, stable addict, using mainly prescribed heroin, to the younger, more chaotic person using 'diverted' illicitly obtained pharmaceutical heroin. The total number of drug addicts in 1967 was reported as 1299 and by 1967 there were 381 heroin addicts under the age of 20.

The committee concluded, in its second report, that the main new source of heroin on the illicit market was over-prescribing by a very small number of GPs. The committee heard evidence of apparent indiscriminate prescribing by GPs where large amounts of heroin were being prescribed by a small number of doctors, especially GPs working in London. The committee concluded that there were serious problems with the unrestricted practice of these doctors and recommended that the prescribing of certain drugs to addicts, in particular heroin and cocaine, should be restricted to doctors with special Home Office licences.

The committee also recommended that the treatment of addiction should take place in specialised clinics (these became the precursors of drug dependence units) and that the clinics should be run by specialists, thus taking care away from the generalist and untrained GPs.

It also recommended sanctions, in the form of referral to the GMC, for doctors who were thought to be prescribing in an irresponsible or inappropriate manner.

Finally, the committee recommended the formation of a central register for drug addicts; this was to become the Home Office Addicts Index until its demise in 1997. In reaching the conclusions, the Brain Committee considered the dilemma facing authorities responsible for the control of dangerous drugs in this country:

> if there is insufficient control it may lead to the spread of addiction – as is happening at present. If, on the other hand, the restrictions are so severe as to seriously discourage the addict from obtaining any supplies from legitimate sources it may lead to the development of an organised illicit traffic.

This dilemma persists today with the current debate of expanding the number of patients being treated with prescribed heroin.

The dangerous drug legislation of 1967 and 1968 implemented some of the recommendations of the Second Brain Committee. Under the 1968 act practitioners were prohibited from prescribing, supplying or administering heroin or cocaine to addicts, except in the treatment of organic disease or injury, unless they were specially authorised to do so by the Home Secretary. In practice these doctors were granted authorisation only if they worked in the newly created specialist drug dependence clinics.

Misuse of Drugs Act 1971

The Misuse of Drugs Act 1971 (the act) replaced the Drugs (Prevention of Misuse) Act 1964 and the Dangerous Drugs Acts of 1965 and 1967. It thus brought controlled drugs under the same statutory framework and in doing so incorporated the following:

- the relatively new system of licensing doctors to prescribe heroin and cocaine to addicts

- the requirements for all doctors to notify addicts to the Home Office

- regulations on safe custody of drugs and national stop and search powers for the police.

The act also set up the ACMD, whose main duty was (and is still) to keep under review:

the situation in the United Kingdom with respect to drugs which are being or appear to them likely to be misused and of which the misuse is having or appears to them capable of having harmful effects sufficient to constitute a social problem

and to give:

advice on measures (whether or not involving alteration of the law) which in the opinion of the Council ought to be taken for preventing the misuse of such drugs or dealing with social problems connected with their misuse, and in particular on measures which in the opinion of the Council ought to be taken.

The act's system of classification was also new. It divided drugs into the three classes A, B and C, listed in schedule 2 of the act, and penalties for offences were related to the class of drug involved in the offence. Confusingly the drugs are sometimes described as being schedule 1, 2, 3, 4 or 5 drugs; such references are not to the classes in schedule 2 to the act but to the schedules to the related Misuse of Drugs Regulations 1985.

Class of the drug relates to the different penalties for offences under the act. The class reflects the level of potential harm inherent in the drug. Class A drugs are those that are considered to be the most harmful if misused (e.g. morphine, cocaine, diamorphine) and as such offences in relation to class A drugs include the more severe penalties. Class C drugs such as anabolic steroids and benzodiazepines are considered to be less harmful and hence carry lower tariffs for offences.

Section 8 of the MDA made it an offence for the occupier or someone concerned with the management of premises knowingly to permit those premises to be used for:

- production

- supply of any controlled drugs

- preparation of opium for smoking

- smoking cannabis.

Table 25.1   **Classification of illicit drugs with penalties for possession and dealing**

	Examples	**Possession**	**Dealing**
Class A	Ecstasy, LSD, heroin, cocaine, crack, magic mushrooms, injected amphetamines, MDMA	Up to seven years in prison or an unlimited fine or both	Up to life in prison or an unlimited fine or both
Class B	Amphetamines, barbiturates, codeine, methylphenidate (Ritalin), pholcodine	Up to five years in prison or an unlimited fine or both	Up to 14 years in prison or an unlimited fine or both
Class C	Cannabis, tranquilisers, anabolic steroids, gamma hydroxybutyrate (GHB), ketamine	Up to two years in prison or an unlimited fine or both	Up to 14 years in prison or an unlimited fine or both

It is this section that the 'Cambridge Two', Ruth Wyner and John Brock, who ran a hostel for homeless people fell foul of. These two were sentenced to five years' imprisonment in 1999 for 'allowing' illicit drugs to be used at the hostel. It set in train a debate to try to clarify the legal obligations of those running institutions where drug taking may be taking place and the dilemmas of having to weigh up the needs of the individuals using these premises against the rigorous interpretation of the law.

Section 9A makes it an offence to supply or offer to supply any article (except a hypodermic syringe) that the supplier believes to be used or adapted to be used in the unlawful administration (including self-administration) of drugs. The purpose of this section of the act, which was inserted in 1986, was to outlaw the supply of cocaine kits, which contained items for facilitating drug use, such as razor blades, foil and lemon juice. An exception was made for sterile syringes and needles to permit the supply of clean injecting equipment to reduce sharing of such.

Despite this legislation many pharmacists and needle exchange schemes did provide drug users with swabs and sterile water, and hence were technically in breach of the act and theoretically risked prosecution, although the police and the Crown Prosecution Service took the view that prosecution in such cases was not in the public interest.

In August 2003, after a review by the ACMD, an amendment was made to section 9 of the MDA that now allowed medical practitioners, pharmacists and drug workers (including nurses and employees of needle exchange schemes) to supply certain items for drug injecting:[4,5] swabs, utensils for the preparation of a controlled drug, citric acid and filters. The supply of ampoules of water for injection is also allowed, but only when supplied or offered for supply in accordance with the Medicines Act 1968, which means supply to an individual 'in accordance with a prescription' or when supplied to an individual under a patient group direction. The change in the law above applies in the first instance only to England, Wales and Scotland. The Northern Ireland administration has subsequently amended its legislation to allow the same dispensations to apply in the province.

Section 10 gives powers to the secretary of state to make regulations around safe custody, documentation of transactions, record keeping, packaging and labelling, methods of destruction, and so on.

Misuse of Drugs Regulations 1973 and 2001 (the 'Main Regulations')

The regulations under the MDA specify the requirements for handling controlled drugs by certain authorised persons, including who can produce, supply, prescribe or administer controlled drugs in the practice of their work. They also apply selective controls to groups of drugs, which are defined in the five schedules of the current (2001) regulations.[4] The schedules correspond to the therapeutic usefulness and misuse potential of the drugs.

The schedules under the Misuse of Drugs Regulations (MDR) are to ensure that practitioners are appropriately exempt from offences under the act while undertaking their lawful practice and include issues around supply, recording, storage and destruction.

Misuse of Drugs (Amendment No. 2) (England, Wales and Scotland) Regulations 2012

A statutory instrument came into force in April 2012,[5] amending the Misuse of Drugs Regulations 2001 (the '2001 regulations') to permit a non-medical prescriber (nurse or pharmacist) to prescribe, carry, administer and give directions for the administration of any controlled drug specified in schedules 2 to 5 of the 2001 regulations. Cocaine, diamorphine and dipipanone are excluded in cases where patients are addicted to these drugs unless the prescription is to treat pain. The amendments also allow a nurse independent prescriber and a pharmacist independent prescriber to supply 'certain articles' (as above) for administering or preparing controlled drugs.

Summary of the Misuse of Drugs Act and its regulations

This is not comprehensive guidance; the reader is advised to consult the 'further reading' texts recommended at the end of this chapter for specific details pertaining to their requirements under the MDR.

Table 25.2   **Misuse of Drugs Regulations 2001**

Schedule 1 (controlled drug licence only)	This contains the most strictly controlled drugs of all, and includes those that have no therapeutic use in standard practice. A Home Office licence is required to possess, produce, supply or administer drugs in this schedule: cannabis in its various forms, hallucinogens such as LSD, ecstasy and other drugs such as raw opium
Schedule 2	For medical practitioners this is the most relevant schedule as it includes pharmaceutical opioid and amphetamines used in clinical practice. Over 100 drugs are in this schedule. Schedule 2 drugs are subject to safe custody requirements, dispensing, and recording and destruction requirements
Schedule 3	Includes a small number of minor stimulants and other drugs not thought so likely to be misused and not as harmful if misused. Most are exempt from safe custody requirements, except drugs such as flunitrazepam, temazepam, and buprenorphine
Schedule 4	Part 1 includes most of the benzodiazepines and eight other drugs, including zolpidem but excluding zopiclone and zaleplon. Possession of a drug in schedule 4 part 1 is an offence without the authority of a prescription. Part 2 includes anabolic steroids. There is no restriction on the possession of a part 2 schedule 4 drug when contained in a medicinal product
Schedule 5	Drugs included in this schedule are exempt from most controls, primarily those prohibiting possession, importation and exportation, which apply to drugs in schedules 2 and 3. It does not contain any preparations intended for injection. The drugs in this schedule include preparations, often in minute quantities, that contain codeine, dihydrocodeine, medicinal opium and dextropropoxyphene. The schedule contains both prescription (POM) and pharmacy (P) medicines. The latter can be sold over the counter (OTC) under the supervision of a pharmacist

Note: several amendments have been made since its original iteration in 1973.

Misuse of Drugs (Safe Custody) Regulations 1973

Retail pharmacists, private hospitals and nursing homes must store schedule 2 and some schedule 3 controlled drugs in a receptacle that complies with the requirements of these regulations.

Misuse of Drugs (Supply to Addicts) Regulations 1997

These regulations prohibit doctors prescribing or administering heroin, cocaine and dipipanone for the treatment of addiction unless the doctor has the necessary Home Office licence.

Misuse of Drugs Act Regulations 2001 purchasing (requisition)

A requisition is required before any schedule 2 (or 3) drug can be supplied to medical or dental practitioners or a person in charge of a nursing home (unless on a prescription or by way of administration). The supplier must be reasonably satisfied that the signature on the requisition is genuine and the signatory is engaged in the profession or occupation stated. There are no limits on the amount of controlled drugs that can be held in a general practice surgery and it is entirely dependent on the dictate of the practitioner/s. In an emergency, practitioners may personally obtain from a supplier a schedule 2 or 3 drug if, for some reason, they cannot immediately supply a signed requisition. However, they must provide the supplier with the necessary requisition within 24 hours.

Prescriptions

All prescriptions for schedule 2 and 3 drugs must comply with the detailed requirements of the regulations. This is the requirement that causes most problems for the dispensing pharmacist. Not infrequently controlled drug prescriptions contain minor errors, for example the date is omitted, the total quantity is added up incorrectly or the doctor has forgotten to comply fully with the requirement to write this in both words and figures. The pharmacist is then faced with an irate patient – as it is a criminal offence to dispense the medication before the prescriber rectifies these errors.

Until 2005, prescriptions for controlled drugs were required to be handwritten, signed and dated in ink by the prescriber. The amendments to the 2001 regulations, which came into force in November 2005, removed this requirement such that computer-generated printed prescriptions are acceptable and only the signature of the prescriber currently has to be handwritten.

At the time of writing, prescriptions should contain the following information, either written in indelible ink by the prescriber in his or her own handwriting or computer generated:

▶ patient's name, address, age (where appropriate)

▶ name and form of the drug even if only one form exists

▶ strength of the preparation where appropriate

▶ dose to be taken

▶ total quantity, or total number of dosage units, to be supplied in both words and figures.

From October 2003, extended nurse prescribers have been permitted to prescribe independently any of the following six controlled drugs:

- diazepam, lorazepam, midazolam (for palliative care only)
- co-phenotrope
- dihydrocodeine
- codeine.

From October 2003, the supply and administration of the following controlled drugs has been allowed under patient group directions:

- diamorphine – for the treatment of cardiac pain by nurses working in coronary care units or hospital accident and emergency departments
- all drugs, in any situations, except injectable formats, for the purpose of treatment of a person who is addicted to a drug in schedule 4 except anabolic steroids
- all drugs in schedule 5, at any time.

Prescribing in instalments

In England, an FP10 MDA (or FP10 MDA-S for computer generation) is written for interval collection of schedule 2 drugs, buprenorphine (including Suboxone) and diazepam for the treatment of addiction, allowing for advance dispensing to cover weekends and bank holidays. The prescriber needs to specify the number of instalments, intervals and the quantity to be dispensed at each time. In Wales, WP10 MDA prescriptions may be used for any controlled drug. Form SP2 is used for CD instalment prescribing in Northern Ireland and the Hospital Based Practitioner (Addiction) or HBP(A) in Scotland.

Such prescriptions cover a maximum of 14 days' dispensing, are valid for only four weeks after writing and, since 2006, must be signed for by the collecting patient or identified proxy.

Administration

Doctors may administer or direct any other person to administer these drugs to patients for whom the drug is properly prescribed. In most cases doctors delegate this task to a primary care or palliative care nurse who administers controlled drugs that have been prescribed by a GP in accordance with their directions. Community midwives can possess and administer pethidine and pentazocine.

No entry needs to be made by a doctor or dentist for any drug supplied to a patient on prescription and dispensed by a pharmacist even if it is then administered by the doctor or dentist. It is, however, considered good practice that full and robust records are kept in the patient's records of all drugs for personal administration (i.e. given by the doctor/nurse to the patient from requisitioned stock). These records should make clear the details of the date, approximate time of administration, strength, presentation and form. A record of the batch number and expiry date would also be considered good practice.

Registers and other record keeping

This is the area that is perhaps least complied with and understood by GPs. It relates to drugs kept personally by the doctor in the surgery (or bag) and not to those prescribed to the patient by way of a prescription. The MDA dictates that all registers must be kept for recording transactions in all drugs specified in schedule 2. Regulations govern the details of how entries are to be made in the record book and the form of book that can be used. For instance, the register must be in a bound book; loose-leaf formats are not permissible. Doctors working in groups or partnerships in shared premises may keep a joint register, or individual registers, but not both.

An area of confusion exists about record keeping of personally administered items from the doctor's bag. This is perhaps the most confusing and contentious area, and causes more problems to prescribing and dispensing practices than any other aspect of compliance with controlled drug regulations and legislation. The doctor's bag and the central stock must be considered to be one and the same, with one controlled drugs register. Confusion arises where different doctors use the same bag, with the inevitable failure in the audit trail where drugs are then used and not recorded. In all cases, doctors are not precluded from making informal notes about drugs supplied or administered to patients they attend away from their surgery, but this must be entered in the central register later.

Disposal

Once prescribed, controlled drugs become the property of the patient, who can destroy them if they are no longer required. If they are returned to a doctor or pharmacist, there is currently no legal requirement to make a record of their destruction. It is good practice to dispose of such returns in the presence of a witness so that proof of their fate can be documented, and ensuring that they do not fall into unauthorised hands. The witness should sign the record of destruction. Stock-controlled drugs may need to be destroyed if they are out of date. Schedule

2 drugs can be destroyed only in the presence of an authorised person. A record of their destruction must be made detailing date, strength and quantity of the drug destroyed. Returned drugs cannot be recycled for further use. Persons authorised to witness destruction are any serving police officer, Home Office inspectors, other persons authorised by the secretary of state and Royal Pharmaceutical Society inspectors.

2004 Shipman Inquiry

The activities of Harold Shipman and general issues of irresponsible prescribing are discussed in greater detail in Chapter 23. In July 2004 Dame Janet Smith published, in her fourth report, recommendations for the regulation of controlled drugs in the community.

These recommendations include:

- the formation of a controlled drugs inspectorate comprising small multidisciplinary teams

- placing restrictions on doctors prescribing to themselves or to close members of their family

- ensuring that doctors who have been convicted or cautioned in connection with a controlled drug offence should be under a professional duty to report the conviction or caution to the GMC

- introducing a special printed form for use when prescribing a controlled drug, whether within the NHS or on a private basis, and that such forms should be supplied only to doctors who need to prescribe such drugs in the course of their 'actual clinical practice'

- limiting the amount of a controlled drug that can be dispensed on a single prescription to a supply sufficient to last 28 days

- limiting the validity of a prescription for controlled drugs to 28 days.

With respect to pharmacists, the report has recommended that, where the prescriber's intentions are clear, there should be some relaxation of the strict requirement that a pharmacist is not permitted to dispense a controlled drug prescription unless there is full compliance with every technical requirement of the MDR 2001. There are many other recommendations made in the fourth report and the reader is encouraged to read these in full and to follow the debates to consider which recommendations are implemented in full, in part or not at all (available at: www. shipman-inquiry.org.uk/fourthreport.asp).

Conclusion

Controlled drugs are an important part of the armamentarium for the treatment of patients with a number of acute and chronic physical and psychological conditions. The enlarging number of prescribers and widening variety of clinical background of those prescribers is at the same time exciting in terms of improved service delivery, but there are risks as well. Nobody can say that there will never be another Shipman, but training, governance and peer review through current and future guidelines will help to reduce the risks to patients and prescribers alike.

Further reading

British Medical Association, Royal Pharmaceutical Society of Great Britain. Controlled drugs and drug dependence. In: *British National Formulary*. London: BMA and RPSGB, 2004, www.bnf.org.

Department of Health. *Drug Misuse and Dependence: guidelines on clinical management*. London: HMSO, 1999.

National Prescribing Centre. *A Guide to Good Practice in the Management of Controlled Drugs in Primary Care (England)*. London: NHS, 2004.

Police Foundation. *Drugs and the Law. Report of the independent inquiry into the Misuse of Drugs Act 1971*. London: Police Foundation, 2000.

Report of the International Opium Commission, Shanghai, China, February 1 to February 26, 1909 (1909), http://archive.org/details/cu31924032583225.

Royal Pharmaceutical Society of Great Britain. *Medicines, Ethics and Practice: a guide for pharmacists*. London: RPSGB, 2004.

The Shipman Inquiry. *Fourth Report. The regulation of controlled drugs in the community*. London: HMSO, 2004.

Department of Health (England) and the devolved administrations. *Drug Misuse and Dependence: UK guidelines on clinical management*. London: DH (England), the Scottish Government, Welsh Assembly Government and Northern Ireland Executive, 2007.

NHS Prescription Services. Guidance on instalment dispensing (regularly updated).

References

1. Police Foundation. *Drugs and the Law. Report of the Independent Inquiry into the Misuse of Drugs Act 1971*. London: Police Foundation, 2000.

2. Advisory Council on the Misuse of Drugs. *Cannabis: classification and public health*. London: ACMD, 2008.

3. Fountain J, Griffiths P, Farrell M, *et al.* Diversion tactics: how a sample of drug misusers in treatment obtained surplus drugs to sell on the illicit market. *International Journal of Drug Policy* 1997; **9(3)**: 159–67.

4. Statutory instrument 2003 No. 1653 Dangerous drugs. The Misuse of Drugs (Amendment) (No. 2) Regulations 2003, www.hmso.gov.uk.

5. Statutory Instrument 2012 No. 973 The Misuse of Drugs (Amendment No.2) (England, Wales and Scotland) Regulations 2012.

Index

Note: page numbers in *italics* refer to figures, tables and boxes.